UP AGAINST
THE CORPORATE WALL

UP AGAINST
THE CORPORATE WALL

———◆———

MODERN CORPORATIONS
AND SOCIAL ISSUES OF THE SEVENTIES

S. PRAKASH SETHI

School of Business Administration
University of California, Berkeley

63044

PRENTICE-HALL, INC., ENGLEWOOD CLIFFS, NEW JERSEY

© 1971 by Prentice-Hall, Inc., Englewood Cliffs, New Jersey

Printed in the United States of America

P—13-939025-1
C—13-939033-2

Library of Congress Catalog Card No.: 70–146497

Current Printing (last digit):

10 9 8 7 6 5 4 3

Prentice-Hall International, Inc.   *London*
Prentice-Hall of Australia, Pty. Ltd.   *Sydney*
Prentice-Hall of Canada, Ltd.   *Toronto*
Prentice-Hall of India Private Limited   *New Delhi*
Prentice-Hall of Japan, Inc.   *Tokyo*

To
those "haves" and "have-nots" among us
who still have hopes
that when men of reason get together
they will plan the survival
and not the extinction
of the human race and of humanity
this book is affectionately dedicated.

PREFACE

———◆———

As the United States enters the seventies and the decades beyond, it carries a plethora of new problems and social conflicts that have added to the nation's rhetoric. These include the protection of our environment by restricting both the amount of pollution and the amount of destruction, the concern for social justice, the search for relevance in our work and play, the protection of individual rights from abrogation by large institutions—public and private, and the reordering of national priorities.

Most of these problems have been with us for quite some time, but during the past ten years a variety of factors has brought them new importance:

1. The population mix has changed and a large segment is now composed of people born in the postdepression era, who are not haunted by the fear of scarcity, are not motivated by the specter of ever-increasing consumption, and are not willing to accept without question a system whose primary concerns are based on economic rationality.

2. A communications explosion, especially of television, has made millions of people aware of the inequities in social justice, the differences between the "haves" and "have-nots," and the frustration and anger caused by social and economic deprivation.

3. A benign neglect of the problems of pollution and the exploitation of natural resources without regard to their effect on our environment have brought about a dangerous situation which cannot be ignored. Issues become salient to the public by personal experience, and the deterioration of the environment can no longer be hidden or wished away.

4. Economic, social, and political institutions have increasingly become less responsive to the changing needs of their constituents, leading the dissatisfied members of society to conclude that their grievances cannot be redressed without a restructuring of social institutions and a reordering of national priorities.

Another remarkable change has been the emergence of large business corporations as the main culprits, in the eyes of the public, for major social ills. In this context, the large business corporation has assumed a place equal to, if not higher than, that of the big government as the villain. The corporations have been accused of creating "values" that are highly materialistic and thus undermine the normative values of the "good life." They have been accused of polluting the environment for their own financial gains, undermining the individual intellectual activity and creativity of the human mind by trivializing its work and achievement; bureaucratizing a large part of human activities and standardizing products, culture, and performance to the lowest common denominator of economic efficiency; exercising considerable authority—along with the Congress and the Pentagon—on the prosperity or decline of various communities and their inhabitants; sapping the political vitality of the middle class; and contributing to the alienation of faceless masses from the democratic processes.

The ills of the society cannot solely be attributed to large business corporations. Those who loudly accuse the corporations of prostituting the physical, social, and political environment cannot escape part of the blame for they also share in the ill-gotten gains of the corporations. However, the corporations are responsible because of their close identity with the economic goals of society. Their loud disclaimers notwithstanding, corporations have not given consumers "what they want," because the selection processes of consumers are determined by the number of alternatives available to them and by their ability to evaluate the alternatives: both these factors are considerably influenced by the corporations. The large size of individual corporations and their control, individually and collectively, of the nation's productive facilities make it difficult to believe that they are passive instrumentalities subject to the control of market mechanisms.

It is therefore understandable that segments of the population have increasingly resorted to confrontation tactics in their efforts to involve corporations in activities that are nonprofit oriented and might very well force these corporations to offer new rationales for their activities, change their manner of operation, and even increase the cost of doing business.

The corporations have to some extent recognized their partial immunity from competition, their increased economic and social power, and their responsibility for contributing to a better community life within which they must exist. However, this recognition has come hesitantly, in insufficiently small doses, invariably as partial cure rather than as preventive measure, and above all, only if it did not hurt the firm's profitability. Thus corporations have insisted on complete independence in determining products and profits, have fought measures of public control in pollution and other areas as economically prohibitive, and have demanded tax and other incentives for going into "nonprofit" activities. The emphasis has been on measuring the effect of these "nonprofit" activities on the profit potential of the corporation rather than on evaluating the effect of their "for profit" activities on the larger social goals. It is like allowing one department of a large company to exploit all the other departments to increase its own profitability.

The results have been predictable and disappointing. During the past few years business corporations have started, jointly and individually, a host of programs in community help—urban renewal, minority hiring, beautification, pollution control, communication with students—but their success, taken in the aggregate and in relation to their capacity, and barring a few isolated instances, has been either negligible or negative.

Conflicts between large corporations and other segments of society are likely to be intensified because neither the corporations nor other ruling members of the establishment seem willing to perceive these changes or willing to take bolder steps to revitalize the system. Their efforts are still directed at putting down brush fires and repairing occasional leaks to make the system work in its present form. As Neil Chamberlain pointed out in "The Life of the Mind in the Firm" (*Daedalus*, Winter 1969):

> It is still considered a high economic virtue that our major corporations behave like somewhat softened, but scrimping Scrooges or modest, but misanthropic misers—whose actions are governed only by the test of whether they are efficient in adding to a revenue stream and whose only purposes are limited dispersal to a limited stockholder clientele and reinvestment to maintain or augment the profit flow.
> . . . The argument is concerned with the standards that apply to the conduct of those organizations which give our society its special character. If our corporations were wholly government-owned, but still applied only the profit efficiency test to their operations, the result would be the same. . . . There is much to be said for leaving control over our giant corporations in private hands—diffusion of discretion and power is a value not to be given up lightly—if we can broaden the standard by which we judge their activity, if we can free them from a test of efficiency more relevant to the past than to the present.

The objective of this book is to expose the student, through a series of case studies involving business corporations, to a variety of problems that are increasingly becoming the prime concern of both business and society. It is aimed at developing in the reader a sensitivity to the issues involved, an awareness of the complexity of the motives of various parties, and a familiarity with the success and failure of their strategies and tactics. The areas covered can broadly be divided into: business and the quality of life, business and other social institutions, business and the community, business and the individual, business and government, military industrial complex, and business and foreign policy.

Case studies were selected on the basis of their timeliness and their ability to bring out as many facets of the problem as possible. I have tried to provide equal depth in every topic covered, but because of the difficulty in gathering data I might not have been uniformly successful. I have also tried to make the material as factual and objective as possible so as not to bias the reader with my own opinions and prejudices.

This book is primarily designed for executive development programs and for readers interested in business and society, business and public policy, business and government, and management policy. The issues involved are complex and of broad social import, and the case studies are somewhat long because they cover many facets of the conflicts and parties involved.

This book would not have been possible without the cooperation of many corporations and their executives, who generously contributed their time and information. However, the responsibility for material included in the cases and for errors of omission and commission is strictly my own. Thanks are especially due to Allen-Bradley Company, Bank of America, Crown Zellerbach Corporation, Dow Chemical Company, Eastman Kodak Company, Fairchild Camera and Instrument Corporation, and Motorola, Incorporated. Chandler Publishing Company graciously permitted the use of copyright material from my book, *Business Corporations and the Black Man*. A debt of gratitude is due also to Professor Ivar Berg (Columbia University), Professor Michael Conant (University of California), Professor Rick Pollay (University of British Columbia), Professor Lee E. Preston (State University of New York), and Professor Dow Votaw (University of California), for their valuable comments in the preparation of this book.

In addition to my research assistant, Michael Hawkins, other graduate students contributed in varying degrees, especially Peter Stoppello, Norbert Schaefer, and Rodney Gully. Their assistance is gratefully acknowledged. I also want to thank my editor, Mrs. Jan Seibert, who contributed greatly to the readability of the manuscript, and Patricia Murphy, who typed it in many drafts. Acknowledgments are also due to the School of Business Administration and to the Institute of Business and Economic Research, University of California, Berkeley, for typing and clerical assistance in the preparation of the manuscript.

- And finally, I am grateful to my wife, Donna, who in the months immediately preceding and following our marriage encouraged me with affection and helped me with constructive criticism by reading the various drafts of the manuscript.

S. PRAKASH SETHI
Berkeley, California

CONTENTS

———◆———

II
CORPORATE INTERESTS
AND
SOCIAL AND ECONOMIC NEEDS
OF
ETHNIC MINORITIES

A.
DISCRIMINATION

B.
SOCIAL
AND
ECONOMIC PRESSURES

III
CORPORATIONS, THEIR DEPENDENCIES, AND
OTHER SOCIAL INSTITUTIONS

A.
CORPORATIONS
AND
THE INDIVIDUAL

B.
CORPORATIONS
AND
THE STUDENTS

C.
CORPORATE DECISIONS
AND THEIR EFFECTS
ON URBAN COMMUNITIES

D.
CORPORATIONS
AND
THE NEWS MEDIA

E.
CORPORATIONS
AND
THE CHURCH

IV
THE CHANGING NATURE OF GOVERNMENT AND BUSINESS RELATIONSHIPS

A.
INDIRECT/DIRECT USE
OF THE
PRESIDENT'S EXECUTIVE AUTHORITY

B.
GOVERNMENT AND BUSINESS
AS
PARTNERS

C.
CORPORATIONS
AND UNITED STATES
FOREIGN POLICY CONFLICTS

D.
POLITICS
AND
BUSINESS

I

THE QUALITY
OF
LIFE

A.
CONSERVATION
OF THE
NATURAL ENVIRONMENT

Pacific Gas & Electric Company, San Francisco

Attempt to Construct a Nuclear Power Plant at Bodega Bay

To hell with posterity! After all, what have the unborn ever done for us? Nothing. . . .
To hell with posterity! That, too, can be arranged.

—A statement made facetiously by Lord
Ritchie-Calder, noted newspaperman and author
and long concerned with problems of ecology.

BACKGROUND

Bodega Head is a thumblike peninsula jutting out of the California coastline approximately fifty air miles north of San Francisco. The headland, until 1959, was privately owned by three families, and as a result its natural beauty and ecology remained intact. Two of these private holdings, 648 acres owned by Mrs. Rose Gaffney and the tip of the headland owned by Mr. Garry Stroh, could be traced to the original Spanish land grant.

Because the headland had been preserved, the State of California Division of Beaches and Parks became interested in acquiring the land for a recreation area and, independently, the University of California became interested in the area as a site for a Northern California marine facility.

3

The site was also chosen by the Pacific Gas and Electric Company, a private California utility, as being suitable for the location of a generating plant to provide electrical power to the rapidly growing metropolitan San Francisco Bay Area.

In 1953 an informal faculty committee was formed at the University of California (U.C.), Berkeley, to obtain a marine facility in Northern California. Dr. Cadet Hand, a marine biologist at U.C., was a member of the committee and was influential in its organization. Dr. Hand discovered the beauty and richness of the peninsula when he first visited it shortly after World War II. "I was overwhelmed with it," Hand said later. "There were the ocean, the cliffs, the tidepools, and over here those rich mudflats in the harbor. It was a biologist's paradise."[1] The committee was given formal recognition by the university administration in 1955, and in the summers of 1956 and 1957 classes were held in a rented shack at Bodega Bay. Spurred by Dr. Hand and awed by what they saw, the committee began actively pursuing plans for a permanent marine laboratory on the headland.

In this attempt the committee first learned of the state of California's interest in Bodega Head for a recreational park. The State Division of Beaches and Parks had included the headland in its 1955 master plan for park development, and $350,000 was appropriated in the 1956–57 budget for acquisition of the land. However, under California's "home rule" law, which requires local concurrence with state proposals, the Sonoma County Board of Supervisors held absolute veto power over the state's park plan. The board requested that Bodega Head be included in the master plan for the county, but County Planning Director Jack Prather refused. The board upheld this decision and approved the plan without Bodega Head.

In April 1957, the state, still seeking the inclusion of Bodega Head in its park system, agreed to meet with the university to coordinate their plans, and in May a joint committee reached a mutually acceptable plan of action. Three months later, however, in July 1957, the Division of Beaches and Parks reported cryptically that its plans for Bodega Head had "been forestalled by planned purchase of a major portion of the headland by a private utility company."

PG&E STEPS IN

The Pacific Gas and Electric Company moved quickly in the acquisition of the permits and rights necessary for a generating plant on Bodega Head.

---

[1] David Pesonen, "A Visit to Atomic Park," unpublished manuscript. San Francisco, California. Used with permission of the author.

Experience over the years had taught it that this was the best way to handle the delicate task of establishing a generating plant. The first public announcement of PG&E's plans was not made until May 1958. PG&E president M. R. Sutherland issued a brief statement to the effect that "preliminary purchasing negotiations" were underway for a site on which to build a "steam-electric" generating plant.[2]

Although no mention was made of a nuclear facility, there were rumors that the plant would be atomic. These rumors were fueled when in September 1958 Kenneth Diercks, the company's land agent in Sonoma County, told the supervisors: "No decision can be made as to when actual construction of this facility will commence or as to the type of plant to be constructed, whether conventional or nuclear, until the time of installation is much nearer at hand."[3] However, the previous month a PG&E spokesman had told a meeting of the American Institute of Electrical Engineers that PG&E was committed to a course that would lead the utility to large-scale use of economic nuclear power.[4] And only six months later President Sutherland told reporters at a press conference in San Francisco that "an atomic power plant will be built in one of the nine Bay Area counties . . . as soon as it can be done at reasonable cost" and that it was to be in operation "by 1964 or 1965."[5] Although he would not say that he was referring to Bodega Head, no other acquisitions were being made that would have been remotely feasible for an atomic power plant.[6]

PG&E continued to acquire the necessary rights and permits for a conventional generating plant. In September 1958, the county supervisors granted a delay in the improvement of a small airstrip which was in the proposed path of high-power lines from the Head as requested by PG&E, even though the company owned no property in the county at that time.[7] In October 1958, the company filed condemnation proceedings against all of Mrs. Gaffney's property and indicated that the Stroh ranch would also be acquired. It stated that it needed all this land for site access for borings and so on. No mention was made of the AEC requirement for a three-quarter mile radius around a nuclear installation (a reactor at Horseshoe Cove would necessitate owning approximately six hundred acres of headland).[8]

[2] *Santa Rosa Press Dispatch*, May 23, 1958.

[3] David Pesonen, unpublished manuscript.

[4] *San Francisco Chronicle*, August 20, 1958.

[5] *Santa Rosa Press Dispatch*, April 5, 1959.

[6] David Pesonen, unpublished manuscript.

[7] Joel W. Hedgpeth, "Bodega Head—A Partisan View," *Bulletin of the Atomic Scientists*, 3, March 1965, 3.

[8] David Pesonen, unpublished manuscript.

On October 15, 1959, the company announced that the site had been changed to the tip of the headland to get away from the San Andreas Fault zone, although the type of plant was still unannounced.[9] The suit against Mrs. Gaffney was modified to include only sixty-five acres, and plans were made to purchase the Stroh ranch. This modification of land area coincided with an AEC revision stating that only a one-half mile radius was required around a nuclear installation—the revised property line followed such a radius.[10] Although the ranch had been in Mrs. Stroh's family for over a century and the family repeatedly stated that they did not want to sell, a grant deed to PG&E was filed in the Sonoma County Courthouse less than one month following the announced site change.[11] Allegations that Stroh was intimidated into selling via a party-crashing incident causing "great violence, destruction and bloodshed"[12] were stoutly denied by PG&E, which stated in 1961, in answer to the charge, that "the transaction was concluded in terms satisfactory to Mrs. Stroh."[13]

Then in November 1959, the Sonoma County Board of Supervisors granted a use permit to PG&E for power lines over Doran Park, a sandspit running northeast from the Head. The supervisors deemed a public hearing unnecessary despite a petition carrying thirteen hundred signatures in opposition.[14]

Gene Marine, writing in *The Nation*, cited this as only one of many instances of flagrant disregard for the public interest:

> Then there's Doran Park, a sandspit which, with Bodega Head, makes Bodega Bay one of the only five safe harbors along 300 miles of tortuous, treacherous Pacific Coast. Doran Park was turned over to Sonoma County by the State of California on condition that it be preserved as a park. At its widest point, it's less than 350 feet wide. PG&E will run power lines down the center of the park; its easement is 180 feet wide. Why don't they put the wires underground? "Uneconomical."[15]

In February 1960, the Sonoma County Board of Supervisors granted the company a use permit to build a steam-electric plant on Bodega Head, again without public hearings and without the submission of plans as this would "impose a hardship on the company."[16]

[9] Hedgpeth, "Bodega Head—A Partisan View," p. 4.

[10] *Ibid.*

[11] David Pesonen, unpublished manuscript.

[12] *Ibid.*

[13] *Ibid.*

[14] *Ibid.*

[15] Gene Marine, "Outrage on Bodega Head," *The Nation*, June 22, 1963, p. 525.

[16] J. B. Neilands, "Industrial Radiation Hazard," unpublished manuscript. University of California, Berkeley, February 1963.

REACTION BY THE UNIVERSITY OF CALIFORNIA, BERKELEY

Meanwhile, neither the state nor the university faculty committee had given up on Bodega Head. The state announced in July 1958, one year after abandoning the Head, that it had been negotiating with PG&E to buy whatever portion was left for the park system.[17] The university's reaction, at the faculty level at least, was less submissive. The faculty committee wanted to fight the company and asked permission to seek the governor's intervention. The administration declined this request and told the committee to find another site for the marine facility.[18]

Since July 1958 the University of California faculty committee had investigated the possibility of acquiring alternate sites for a marine laboratory and had further investigated the impact the PG&E facility would have on the Bodega Bay marine environment. Members of the committee asked two professors from the Scripps Institute of Oceanography to meet with PG&E to assess the impact of the plant on the surrounding environment. They indicated that the discharge from the plant might not disperse as rapidly as originally thought but might displace normal tidal flows for a considerable period of time.[19] Chancellor Seaborg reported in a letter to Philip Flint of the Sierra Club:

> Horseshoe Cove might be expected to be bathed for periods of some hours in the essentially unmixed effluent at near discharge temperatures. . . . The fact that the ecological future of Bodega Head was unpredictable made it undesirable to locate a marine laboratory at Horseshoe Cove, in view of the plans for the power station.[20]

However, on November 29, 1960, the committee told Chancellor Seaborg that, despite the obvious drawbacks, Bodega Head was still the best site available for the marine laboratory.[21] The committee still felt that the university ought to oppose PG&E's proposed plant officially. The committee summed up this negative feeling by concluding:

> Weighing all relevant aspects, we agreed unanimously that there was not a single one of these sites that was equal to Bodega Head as

[17] David Pesonen, unpublished manuscript.

[18] Hedgpeth, "Bodega Head—A Partisan View," p. 3.

[19] J. D. Frautschy and D. L. Inman, Preliminary Report of Investigation of Bodega Head, made to Professor Roger Y. Stenier, Department of Bacteriology, University of California, Berkeley, June 14, 1960.

[20] Marine, "Outrage on Bodega Head," p. 526.

[21] Daily Californian (UCB), December 14, 1962, p. 3.

it now stands. Bluntly stated, a unique Class A site for a marine facility is being exploited for power production.[22]

As a result of this decision, a portion of the headlands was purchased and plans were made to share the peninsula with PG&E. No official position of opposition was taken by the university. The following comment on the report appeared in *The Nation:*

> In fact nothing was done about that report at all. It was written twenty-three days after the election of John Kennedy; a short time later the Chancellor [Seaborg] became the chairman of the AEC.[23]

The article also noted that the AEC contributed a sizable sum to the university.

PG&E ANNOUNCES PROPOSED POWER PLANT TO BE A NUCLEAR FACILITY

In July 1961, after obtaining county permits for a conventional steam-generating plant, PG&E announced its intention to build a nuclear power plant on Bodega Head.[24] Prior to this announcement the controversy centered primarily on the best use of the land—for research and recreation or for power generating—and secondarily on the manner in which the land-use issue was being decided. However, with the formal announcement of a nuclear facility, public safety became a major issue. Three problem areas were associated with establishing this nuclear facility:

1. The geological instability of the Bodega Head and the proximity of the reactor to the San Andreas Fault zone.
2. The location of a nuclear reactor near a major population center.
3. The problem of radioactive waste discharge.

GEOLOGICAL INSTABILITY OF BODEGA HEAD

PG&E apparently chose the site without much advance consideration of its geologic features.[25] To study it in detail, however, it hired a competent

[22] *Ibid.*

[23] Marine, "Outrage on Bodega Head," p. 22.

[24] William E. Bennett, "Dissenting Opinion in the Order Denying Reopening of Hearings on the Application for a Certificate of Public Convenience and Necessity for the Bodega Bay Atomic Park," Decision No. 65706.

[25] Hedgpeth, "Bodega Head—A Partisan View," p. 3.

staff of experts, which included Dr. Dan Tocher, a consulting seismologist from U.C.; Dr. William Quaide, a consulting geologist from Claremont; the firm of Dames and Moore, soil mechanics engineers; and Dr. George Housner of Cal Tech, PG&E's principal consultant on structural design.

Drs. Tocher and Quaide filed a report to the company on September 18, 1960. This study showed the reactor site to be approximately one thousand feet from the western edge of the San Andreas Fault[26] and indicated that the headland is "strongly jointed and is faulted on old minor faults. However, there have been no movements in these faults in the past few thousand years . . . [which] strongly implies, but does not guarantee, that there will be no movements throughout the life-expectancy of a power plant."[27] It also revealed that "the intensity of the faulting and jointing in the rock is so great that the formerly massive rock is now broken into a mosaic of blocks with average dimensions of approximately one foot."[28] In June 1960, Dr. Housner wrote to Mr. Worthington, PG&E's civil engineer: "As regards gross ground movement produced by faulting, I would say that if there appeared even a small likelihood of this happening, then the site should not be used. The investigation of Dr. Tocher and Dr. Quaide should be aimed at assessing the likelihood that active movement will occur in the San Andreas Fault zone near the site on Bodega Head. . . ."[29] "No evidence was found in the geologic examination to indicate the existence of a *large fault* beneath the plant or tunnel sites. Chances of disruption of the sites by breakage along a large fault are therefore small."[30]

Dames and Moore filed three reports, with the last the most definitive. From borings at the test site, they found the bedrock to be of poor quality and much deeper than originally thought.[31] As a result they concluded that the reactor pit, designed to be ninety feet deep, could be excavated without blasting, except for the "last twenty to thirty-five feet."[32] Furthermore, the generating plant and other surface installations would be based on approximately sixty-five feet of sands and clays at the point of juncture with the reactor.[33] This despite Tocher and Quaide's earlier admonition:

It is important from the standpoint of ability to withstand strong ground shaking that the buildings and any other large appurtenances be constructed on foundations resting on the hard quartz-diorite

[26] California Public Utilities Commission, Application 43808, Appendix IV.
[27] *Ibid.*, Sec. 8, p. 12.
[28] *Ibid.*, Sec. 7, p. 5.
[29] *Ibid.*
[30] *Ibid.*, Sec. 8, p. 9. (Emphasis added.)
[31] *Ibid.*, Sec. 17, log of boring shaft 16.
[32] *Ibid.*, Sec. 17, conclusions.
[33] *Ibid.*, Sec. 12.

bedrock. Should the borings reveal that bedrock will not be reached at practicable depths where it is proposed to erect structures, serious consideration should be given to alternate sites.[34]

PROXIMITY OF PLANT TO URBAN CENTERS: DANGERS OF RADIATION TO THE POPULATION

The location of the plant in an earthquake fault area compounded the ordinary problems of public safety generally associated with the location of a nuclear facility near large population concentrations. The first such problem can arise when an accident caused by seismic activity or other origins results in a major failure of the nuclear safety systems. The company based its safety system on "pressure suppression containment," a novel design used to replace the traditional dome. One of the factors leading to the adoption of this system seems to have been its significantly lower cost.[35] The AEC originally rejected this type of system when it was proposed for the Humboldt County nuclear facility; it reversed itself four months later, however,[36] and called it an improvement over traditional containment systems, even though there was no operational experience upon which to base this opinion.[37] Dr. James E. McDonald questioned the integrity of the safety system on the basis of testimony given by PG&E witnesses to the effect that if an earthquake caused movement of two feet the first two barriers could be punctured, but the critical system would be undamaged; he argued that "the *triple* barrier to escape of volatiles is admitted to be, potentially, reduced to a single barrier [the reactor vessel itself] in event of major seismic displacements. . . . [This] clearly demands that very serious consideration be given to the . . . consequences of fission-product release at Bodega. . . ."[38]

No one knows what would happen if the core melted down. In 1963 the AEC was given $19 million to build a reactor in Idaho and allow it to suffer the maximum credible accident to see what would happen. Until this is done, all assumptions will be mere speculation. However, one recognized study conducted by the AEC in 1957, known as the Brookhaven Report, gives some startling statistics. Based on a 100 to 200 megawatt

---

[34] *Ibid.*, Sec. 8, p. 11.

[35] J. B. Neilands, "Industrial Radiation Hazard," unpublished manuscript, p. 8.

[36] Marine, "Outrage on Bodega Head," p. 524.

[37] AEC Docket No. 50-205, p. 12.

[38] Dr. James E. McDonald, "Meteorological Aspects of Nuclear Reactor Hazards at Bodega Bay," published by the Northern California Association to Preserve Bodega Head and Harbor, June 1964, p. 43.

capacity reactor (much less than the 325 megawatt capacity of PG&E's reactor) located thirty miles from a major city, it theorizes the following results of a major accident: thirty-four hundred deaths, forty-three thousand injuries not including several hundred thousand cases of long-term radiation damage, and property damage of from $2 billion to $4 billion.[39] Dr. McDonald's study of meteorological conditions on the Bodega coast stated that due to the prevailing wind patterns and temperature inversion traps, radioactive gases from the site could easily be funneled into the San Francisco Bay Area without appreciable diffusion.[40] Thus, the conditions surrounding the Bodega reactor were, if anything, more extreme than the hypothetical Brookhaven case. Dr. Samuel Glasstone, in commenting on a boiling water reactor slightly smaller than the one proposed for Bodega, wrote: "Some doubt has been expressed concerning the stability of a boiling water reactor operating at such a high power, but the problem can be resolved only by experience."[41] There have been several major reactor accidents in the past, and seldom has there been a full explanation of the causes: Great Britain's Windscale in 1957; Arco, Idaho's, incident in 1955, in which three people were killed; Chalf River reactor in Canada, in which nine hundred safety devices did not prevent a meltdown which released ten thousand curies of fission products.[42] Of course, design changes have been made which make these particular types of accidents unlikely, but it is presumptuous to assume that no new imperfections will arise.[43]

PROBLEMS OF WASTE DISPOSAL

Another significant hazard of the Bodega reactor was the nuclear wastes which were to be discharged into the water and air. Dr. McDonald outlined some of the problems of radioactive wastes in the air. Included among the hazards were a plume-down wash for the stack directly into the channel traveled by the fishing boats[44] and fog- and drizzle-borne con-

[39] Adolph J. Ackerman, "Atomic Power, a Failure in Engineering Responsibility," *Journal of Professional Practice, Proceedings of the American Society of Civil Engineers,* October 1961, p. 48.

[40] McDonald, "Meteorological Aspects of Nuclear Reactor Hazards at Bodega Bay," p. 51.

[41] Samuel Glasstone, "Sourcebook on Atomic Energy," AEC, p. 471.

[42] Lindsay Mattison and Richard Daly, "A Quake at Bodega," *Nuclear Information,* VI, No. 5, April 1964, 3.

[43] David E. Lilienthal, "When the Atom Moves Next Door," *McCall's,* XCI, No. 1, October 1963, 228.

[44] McDonald, "Meteorological Aspects of Nuclear Reactor Hazards at Bodega Bay," pp. 28–29.

tamination due to shifts in prevailing winds.[45] With regard to this second point, an excerpt from an article by C. Auerbach in *Nature* disclosed that milk samples taken in the Windscale area *"before* the accident contained 44 $\mu\mu$c. of Iodine—131/1, as compared with 5.6 in the United Kingdom as a whole."[46] Dr. Neilands, professor of biochemistry at U.C., calculated that based on the discharge control system at Humboldt Bay, the exhaust valve (which closed automatically if the release rate of radioactive noble and activation gases exceeded two million microcuries per second over a ten-minute period) would not have been activated until after over seventy-eight hundred million microcuries had been discharged.[47]

The other type of waste release, that is, through the cooling system into the ocean, also presented a hazard. While the annual discharge rate was very small, comprising only one-third of the natural radiation in the sea water, the elements produced by the plant were far different from those occurring naturally. More important is the remarkable ability of shellfish, in which the area abounds, to concentrate radioactive ions which can then be ingested by people.[48]

The concern regarding nuclear hazards was also related to the issue of solid waste disposal. David Lilienthal, former chairman of the AEC, stated the problem very clearly in a *McCall's* article in 1963:

> The AEC tells us that in another fifteen years or less a substantial percentage of the electricity of the country will be produced in atomic power plants. Dr. Donald R. Chadwick, Chief of the Division of Radiological Health of the U.S. Public Health Service, estimated in April 1963, that "the accumulated volume of radioactive wastes from nuclear installations . . . will increase from about one and a half million gallons, the estimated 1965 volume, to two billion gallons in 1995." These huge quantities of radioactive wastes *must somehow be removed* from the reactors, must—without mishap—be put into containers that will never rupture; then these vast quantities of poisonous stuff must be moved either to a burial ground or to reprocessing and concentration plants, handled again and disposed of by burial or otherwise, *with a risk of human error at every step*.[49]

He further stated that to continue to project as our goal ten or twelve full-scale power plants in a dozen years, before a safe method of meeting this problem had been demonstrated, was irresponsible financially and

[45] *Ibid.*, pp. 30–31.

[46] C. Auerbach, "Effects of Atomic Radiation," *Nature*, April 27, 1963, p. 343.

[47] Neilands, "Industrial Radiation Hazard," p. 6.

[48] *Ibid.*, p. 6.

[49] Lilienthal, "When the Atom Moves Next Door," October 1963, p. 52.

revealed a questionable attitude toward public health and safety.[50] Not only did the wastes have to be disposed of, but they had to be kept out of circulation for centuries.[51] This created another problem:

> At the present time, these wastes are mainly stored in stainless steel tanks, the life of which is expected to be much less than the duration problem. It is thus possible that we are passing on to future generations a formidable commitment to guard and juggle our atomic garbage.[52]

The Role of the Atomic Energy Commission

The responsibility for insuring the public safety with regard to nuclear power has been vested in a federal agency, the Atomic Energy Commission (AEC). In 1954 the Atomic Energy Act charged the AEC to promote civilian uses of nuclear power as well as to license and regulate privately operated reactors. In 1955, the AEC announced a demonstration program in which it offered to underwrite part of the cost of certain atomic power projects. This program was expanded in 1957 to include all types of projects, as long as (1) they could make significant contributions toward the achievement of commercial atomic power and (2) construction could be completed by June 1962.[53] The requirement for early completion was motivated by the agency's desire to show concrete results in its development program as insurance for its continued funding. Government aid and subsidies to civilian commercial reactors were considered necessary to insure continued development of nuclear power which was not competitive with conventional power.

On January 31, 1961, the AEC optimistically predicted that more than one million kilowatts of nuclear power would be available by the end of 1963, compared with three hundred fifty thousand kilowatts then available. Most of the new generating capacity would be added in 1961–62 when fifteen nuclear power plants were expected to start up.[54]

The AEC's dual role of regulating and promoting civilian reactors carried an inherent conflict, which the *Wall Street Journal,* on March 20, 1961, reported that the agency recognized and was trying to alleviate:

> The AEC announced it is reorganizing in order to separate its regulatory and promotional functions.

---

50 *Ibid.,* p. 228.

51 Ackerman, "Atomic Power, a Failure in Engineering Responsibility," p. 47.

52 Neilands, "Industrial Radiation Hazard," p. 5.

53 Ackerman, "Atomic Power, a Failure in Engineering Responsibility," p. 46.

54 *The Wall Street Journal,* January 31, 1961, p. 15.

The aim is to ensure that the AEC's regulatory responsibilities, concerned with such matters as the location and licensing of atomic reactors and licensing of industrial use of radioisotopes, are not jeopardized by the commission's eagerness to promote industrial use of the atom.

. . .

The [House-Senate Atomic Energy] committee will also publish the record of a University of Michigan Law School study on A.E.C. organization conducted by two former A.E.C. attorneys, William H. Berman and Lee M. Hydeman. Their report will urge that the preferred step is total separation of the A.E.C.'s regulatory and promotional functions.[55]

The AEC did not totally separate the two functions and even under its reorganization could not eliminate the conflict in responsibilities. At the 1962 hearings pursuant to Section 202 of the Atomic Energy Act, Congressman Chet Holifield, chairman of the Joint Committee on Atomic Energy, read a letter that he had written to AEC Chairman Seaborg earlier that month, in which he expressed concern and disappointment at the pace and extent of the atomic power program. In commenting on budget requests, he said that the AEC had shown a lack of enthusiasm for "our civilian atomic power program" and recommended accelerated development of a number of projects including Bodega Bay.[56] The committee then spent the entire day chiding Seaborg for distorting press releases, emphasizing weapons and space, and delaying programs by "studying them to death." In defending himself, Seaborg mentioned several times that the Bodega Bay plant was one situation in which the Commission was moving ahead.[57]

Dr. Seaborg cited another source of pressure in a report to the president in 1962:

It should be recognized that, largely as a result of early optimism, we have, in a short space of time, developed a competitive nuclear equipment industry which is over-capitalized and under-used at the present time. . . . Fortunately, it now appears that only relatively moderate additional government help will be necessary to insure the building of a substantial number of large, *water-type* power reactors that will be economically competitive in the high-fuel-cost areas of this country and the world. This would increase public acceptance, keep the nuclear industry healthy and help to furnish the plutonium

55 "A.E.C. Reorganizing in Effort to Separate Its Regulatory, Promotional Functions," *The Wall Street Journal*, March 20, 1961, p. 7.

56 Marine, "Outrage on Bodega Head," p. 525.

57 David Pesonen, unpublished manuscript.

necessary for a breeder reactor economy as soon as it can be adequately developed.[58]

In response to pressure from Congress and the industry, the AEC granted concessions to PG&E, some of which could adversely affect the public safety:

1. In the interim between PG&E's becoming interested in Bodega Head and its filing with the AEC, regulations regarding locating a site near an active earth fault were liberalized three times.[59] Even so, the Bodega site was less than the currently required one-quarter mile distance, and nothing had been said.
2. The pressure suspension containment system used at both PG&E plants, which cost considerably less than the traditional dome, was approved after having been rejected as unsafe.
3. Shortly after PG&E announced interest in the site, the AEC reduced fuel charges by 34 percent.[60]

It also appeared likely that the AEC had tacitly agreed to license the Bodega Bay reactor before the case ever began. As noted, the commission was using the plant as evidence that it was "moving ahead" long before the application was even submitted; even more persuasive was the fact that PG&E had spent over $4 million before the hearings were even scheduled.

THE CONTROVERSY

In November 1961, PG&E overcame the final hurdle at the county level when the Sonoma County Board of Supervisors approved, again without public hearing, the company's suggested route for the access road, which followed the tidelands around the bay. When the tidelands road was proposed, the university objected.

One of the university's basic considerations in acquiring this particular facility was the variety of organisms to be found in the mudflats of the bay. Chancellor Strong wrote a letter of protest outlining the university's position to the Army Corps of Engineers, who had to approve the route since

[58] United States Atomic Energy Commission, *Civilian Nuclear Power*, a report to the president (Washington, D.C.: Government Printing Office, 1962).

[59] David Pesonen, unpublished manuscript.

[60] *Ibid.*

it might affect navigation in the bay.[61] The County Board of Supervisors was apoplectic at this opposition[62] and ordered the Harbor Commission to meet with the chancellor and "explain the facts of life to him."[63] There is no account of this meeting, but it seems to have had an effect on the chancellor's position, for in January 1962 he wrote to Ray Ruebel, secretary-manager of the Bodega Bay Chamber of Commerce, stating that the university was interested only in that portion of the road crossing the university's property and that the remainder was of less importance.[64] The faculty committee did not share this view, however (which was, in fact, contrary to Strong's position less than two months previously): At the public hearings on the road in February, Dr. Cadet Hand opposed the tidelands route in its entirety, stating that any disturbance of the mud-flats would affect the ecology of the area so vital for effective research.[65] Dr. J. B. Neilands made the following statement concerning the tidelands road to the northern section of the University Academic Senate:

> Not long after a firm decision to locate at Horseshoe Cove had been reached, it was announced that a tidelands access road would be built around the inner rim of the harbor in order to connect the southern tip of Bodega Head to the mainland. This roadway proved to be a convenient arrangement between PG&E and certain Sonoma County officials, the latter now completely dazzled by the prospect of acquiring a giant tax bonanza for the county. The tidelands in question had been leased to the county from the State with the provision that, for final transfer of title, a major improvement must be placed thereon within a certain time period. The lease was running out on the county. PG&E required an access road as well as a convenient place to dump their fill and rip-rock from the excavation. The towns-people were, and still are, much opposed to the roadway and with some difficulty they succeeded in forcing the county to apply to the Army Engineers for the necessary permit.
>
> The hearing was held on February 15; the entire proceedings have been transcribed and the transcription exists as a public document. It describes a bitterly fought contest between Sonoma County officials on one side and the fishermen of Bodega Bay plus certain expert marine biologists on the other side. On this occasion the Acting Director stated that he had the authority of the Chancellor to oppose

[61] Letter to Col. John A. Morrison, Army Corps of Engineers, from Chanc. Edward Strong, University of California, Berkeley, December 1961.

[62] *Santa Rosa Press Democrat*, December 15, 1961.

[63] *Ibid.*

[64] Letter to Mr. Ray Ruebel, Bodega Bay Chamber of Commerce, from Chanc. Edward Strong, University of California, Berkeley, January 31, 1962.

[65] Letter to Chanc. Edward Strong, University of California, Berkeley, from Dr. Cadet Hand, acting director, Bodega Marine Laboratory, February 21, 1962.

the roadway "in its entirety" and that a *previous realignment arrangement* with the county did not prevent the destruction of "some of the very values which led us to choose this headland as our site in the first place." In this stand he is strongly supported by the Western Society of Naturalists and by a number of other marine biologists.[66]

Professor Neilands suggested the possibility that a "family relationship" between the university and PG&E may have prevented the university from "fighting to preserve its biological integrity." He pointed out that:

1. PG&E Board Chairman James Black raised $2.4 million for the campus student union in 1958;
2. Walter Haas, who contributed the money to build the Walter Haas Clubhouse at Strawberry Canyon, was on the Board of Directors of PG&E;
3. The senior attorney for the company was John Sproul, son of R. Gordon Sproul, president emeritus of the university; and
4. The university could cut its $2 million annual electric bill in half if it bought power directly from the Central Valley Project, but inexplicably had not.[67]

Dr. Neilands said:

Unfortunately I can find not a shred of evidence that the University has taken advantage of this cordial relationship in order to persuade the company to place the proposed power plant where it would be less destructive to scenic, recreational and possibly scientific values.[68]

In October 1961, PG&E filed an application with the California Public Utilities Commission for a "certificate of public convenience and necessity to construct, install, operate and maintain Unit #1, a nuclear power unit, at its Bodega Bay Atomic Park."[69] Hearings were held on March 7, 8, and 9, 1962, with little opposition, and it appeared as if the company had surmounted another major hurdle without encountering any significant opposition.

At the Public Utilities Commission hearings, Richard Ramsey, Sonoma County counsel, submitted a booklet containing all twenty-six of the

[66] *Daily Californian*, October 29, 1964, p. 3.
[67] *Ibid.*
[68] *Ibid.*
[69] California Public Utilities Commission, Application 43808, Preface, p. 1.

county's resolutions involving the plant, none of which even remotely suggested that it would be atomic.

The company was obviously not eager to delve too deeply into the geology and seismology of the Bodega Bay area at these PUC hearings. When asked if the consultants' reports were to be placed in evidence, PG&E counsel John Morrissey replied:

> Well, we didn't intend to put any of them in. They are quite lengthy, they are quite voluminous. Certainly, they are available for the Commission staff to look at and to study. Indeed, if we can get extra copies, we will give you an extra copy. . . .[70]

PUC counsel Bricca then argued that, without documentation and direct testimony of the consultants, the assurances given by Mr. Worthington constituted hearsay.[71] But this line of inquiry was interrupted by a recess and not raised again until the close of the proceedings, three months later. At that time, Worthington rather reluctantly agreed to submit the reports[72] and subsequently filed the compilation known as Exhibit 48 on July 9, 1962.

At this point, however, public sentiment began to grow in opposition to PG&E's use of Bodega Head. PG&E's repeated refusals to hold public hearings made people more and more critical. Dr. Wayne Olson of Sonoma State College was quoted as saying, "The decision to build was made not by the people, but by a power elite—the AEC, the PG&E and the county supervisors."[73]

In response to an article entitled "Nature vs. the Atom,"[74] printed February 11, 1962, Karl Kortum, director of the San Francisco Maritime Museum and a native of Sonoma County, wrote a letter to the editor of the *San Francisco Chronicle*, protesting the process through which engineers were making the decisions on the establishment of social priorities. The letter, which appeared on March 14, 1962, presented the following imaginary dialogue between PG&E officials.

> Conservationists from the State Park Commission and the National Park Service came in the last decade to walk among the lupine and decide that this should be a public preserve.
> But about the same time came men of a different type. They too

---

[70] California PUC Hearings, Application 43808, transcript, pp. 37–38.

[71] *Ibid.*, p. 38.

[72] *Ibid.*, pp. 1402–13.

[73] K. S. Roe, "Bodega, Symbol of a National Crisis," *American Forests*, 69, December 1963, 25.

[74] *San Francisco Chronicle*, "This World," February 11, 1962.

walked out on the point and gave it the triumphant glance of demigods.

I am reconstructing. These men are engineers from a public utility and as a member of the public it is my privilege and duty to specu- late. The scene shifts to the home office.

"Our engineering boys think we ought to grab Bodega Head."

"They do? (low whistle) That might be a little rough."

"Why? Why more than Moss Landing or Humboldt Bay?"

"Well it's more scenic. There will be more protest. The State Park people and the National Park people are already on record for public acquisition."

"Our engineers say we need it. We'll just buy fast. Get in ahead of them. It's legal."

"Well . . ."

"What we can't buy we'll condemn."

"What about the public protest? This one could get a little noisy."

"Keep it at the county level. Or try to. Every service club in every town has got our people in it rubbing shoulders. In the country, opinion is made at the weekly luncheon . . ."

"How about the newspapers?"

"It's the local businessmen who buy the space. Oh, I don't say we haven't got some work to do. But those guys have got other things on their minds—they're scratching out a living."

"Have you got an angle? I mean apart from the fact that we want it."

"Oh sure. We'll get out some releases and speeches on how the county tax base will be improved. We might even try calling it a tourist attraction."

"And the county officials?"

"They're O.K. We'll set the tone up and they'll respond to it. Just as elected representatives should. Oh you might get some idealist . . ."

What is the matter? Why do these things come to pass?

The answer is simple. Our engineer demigods are obsolete.

The idea of shaking their pedestals to see if they will topple over has only lately come upon us. (A covey bit the dust lately when the Tiburon Bridge was cancelled.)

The engineers of this public utility may find that their callousness has crested at Bodega Head. Just as the Toll Bridge Authority engineers crested with the bridge that sags frugally from Richmond to San Rafael. Or the highway engineers with the two deck freeway that spoils the Embarcadero.

An atomic plant doesn't have to be built at Bodega Head. Without any expertise whatsoever, I can make that statement categorically. It is just a matter of whose engineers you listen to.

Engineers have amazing resources. They have been able to prove that it is mechanically impossible for a bee to fly.

"You can't lick the biggest 'city hall' of them all . . ." wrote Ed Mannion in his column in the *Petaluma Argus Courier* on February 17, pointing out that two friends, one a member of the county grand jury and the other a prominent newspaper reporter, had urged him to give up the fight.

Well, Ed, you can lick them. If everyone reading this would take five minutes to write a letter they would be licked. But a licking is not what to ask for; regulation is sufficient—regulation in the full breadth of the public interest. We have a Public Utilities Commission charged with doing just that.[75]

As a result of Mr. Kortum's letter, the Public Utilities Commission received over twenty-five hundred letters protesting the atomic plant at Bodega Head.[76] In response to this public outcry, the hearings were reopened in May and ran into June 1962.

The second set of hearings was very vocal and the "record gives the clear impression that the vast majority of the public does not want this unit at this place at this time."[77] Nevertheless, the company ultimately received a certificate of convenience from the PUC subject to AEC approval of the construction.

AFTERMATH OF HEARINGS

After PUC approval came on November 8, 1962, an *ad hoc* organization quickly entered the fray—the Northern California Association to Preserve Bodega Head and Harbor, headed by David Pesonen. On December 28, PG&E applied to the AEC for a construction permit and with it filed a "Preliminary Hazard Report." This report had the same basic documenta-

---

[75] *San Francisco Chronicle*, March 14, 1962.

[76] Hedgpeth, "Bodega Head—A Partisan View," p. 4.

[77] Bennett, "Dissenting Opinion in the Order Denying Reopening of Hearings," p. 3.

tion as Exhibit 48, filed with the PUC. Noting some fundamental differences between the two and some major discrepancies in Mr. Worthington's testimony, the Northern California Association to Preserve Bodega Head and Harbor filed a request to reopen the hearings before the PUC. The association pointed out that Mr. Worthington had testified that (1) the San Andreas Fault was "approximately a mile" from the reactor vessel; (2) the foundation would be located "in solid granodiorite";[78] and later, responding to a question concerning his reasons for believing that the Bodega site would be better than the company's site in Humboldt Bay, "Why it's on solid rock."[79] Both statements contradicted the Dames and Moore report, which was omitted from the Preliminary Hazard Report analysis. Some of Tocher and Quaide's conclusions had been significantly changed.[80] The report was finally forwarded to the AEC more than a year after the original analysis had been filed.

In July 1963, the *ad hoc* group's application for a rehearing was denied by a four-to-one vote. William M. Bennett, president of the commission, stated in his dissenting opinion:

> We are here dealing so far as seismic activity is concerned with a voluntary exposure to risk. It is obvious that few ventures are entirely risk free, but this is not to say that risk should be courted unnecessarily . . . only blind compulsion would insist upon placing this plant in the heart of one of nature's choice areas and in frightening proximity to an active fault line.[81]

Following the rehearing denial, the association brought suit in the Supreme Court of the State of California to force a rehearing. It also sued in Superior Court to have the county permits rescinded on the grounds that no public hearings were held.

As indicated at the second PUC hearings, public opposition to the Bodega Head atomic power plant was widespread. The fact that no local, state, or federal agency or organization had opposed the plant—either in its own interest or in the public interest—created an atmosphere of doubt and suspicion about the degree to which the public safety and interest were being served. The Association to Preserve Bodega Head served as a focal point for the widespread but unorganized opposition to the atomic plant. The association began to document the case for preserving Bodega Head and the dangers involved in establishing a nuclear facility there. It also

[78] California PUC Hearings, Application 43805, transcript, p. 42.

[79] *Ibid.*, p. 1004.

[80] California Public Utilities Commission, Memorandum of Action Concerning Late Filed Exhibit 48 and Related Evidence, May 6, 1963, pp. 39–41.

[81] Bennett, "Dissenting Opinion in the Order Denying Reopening of Hearings," p. 7.

began to prepare and distribute literature presenting this documentation to the press and the public.

To counter the complex technical reports provided by PG&E on the stability of the Bodega Head area, the association requested further studies. Dr. Pierre Saint-Amand, a consultant seismologist from the Naval Ordinance Test Station, China Lake, and expert analyst of Chile's 1960 quake, was asked to investigate the site. His conclusion was that "Bodega Head is a very poor location for a reactor. . . ."[82] "Each time the San Andreas Fault has moved, it has jumped a distance of four to eight meters. Strain is estimated to be accumulating at a rate of about six to seven meters per century across the Fault. Hence one could expect at least one great earthquake per century."[83] He stated that as the reactor site was on the "zone of fling" it would undergo a horizontal movement of some three to four meters[84] and "a worse foundation situation would be difficult to imagine."[85] He concluded:

> It is surprising, in view of the expert advice given by Tocher and Quaide, and by Housner, that another site was not chosen and that construction has gone ahead.[86]

At this time another study was undertaken, this one sponsored by the United States Geological Survey. The investigators, Julius Schlocker and Manuel Borilla, first inspected the site in the summer of 1963. Their work was completed in September and they found no evidence of active faulting through the reactor site.[87] However, the company continued its excavation and the AEC reported in October that a fault through the site itself had been discovered. Schlocker and Borilla returned and conducted a three-month investigation. They reported in January that the fault was comparable to that on Point Reyes, which had had considerable movement in 1906.[88]

PG&E responded to these findings with reports of its "own consultants" who advised them that the plant could still be built safely.[89] It is signifi-

[82] Pierre Saint-Amand, "Geologic and Seismologic Study of Bodega Head," published by the Northern California Association to Preserve Bodega Head and Harbor, 1963, p. 20.

[83] Ibid., p. 14.

[84] Ibid., p. 17.

[85] Ibid., p. 19.

[86] Ibid., p. 20.

[87] USGS TE-884, December 1963. As cited in David Pesonen, unpublished manuscript.

[88] Ibid., p. 14.

[89] San Francisco Chronicle, January 28, 1964.

cant to note that two of the four reports predated the discovery of the new fault and that Dr. Quaide had developed severe doubts as to the advisability of the project:

There is a chance that the fault could break beneath the plant's site in case of an earthquake. I still think the probability is low . . . but it is necessary to face the moral issue: "If there is even a slight chance of danger should we go ahead and build the plant?"[90]

On the other hand, Dr. Tocher stated:

We are firmly of the opinion that movements of this nature ["minor vibrations" associated with an earthquake along such "auxiliary faults"] will in no way constitute a hazard to the plant.[91]

As a direct result of the discovery of the shaft fault in January 1964, and possibly because of the full array of geologic and seismologic reports, the company revised its proposed structure in March 1964. To compensate for horizontal movements of from one to two feet, the pit would be packed with a compressible material of a then undetermined type.[92] This decision was a complete reversal of Mr. Worthington's earlier statement: ". . . the one thing that will not change is the fact that we are founding the reactor structure on solid rock and surrounding it with very heavy concrete structures."[93] The approach was novel and could well have been very effective according to the staffs of the AEC Division of Reactor Licensing[94] and the AEC Advisory Committee on Reactor Safeguards.[95] However, the former felt that as "experimental verification and experience background" were lacking, "we do not believe that a large nuclear power reactor should be the subject of a pioneering construction effort based on unverified engineering principles, however sound they may appear to be."[96]

At the same time, the Association to Preserve Bodega Head had published a number of booklets and pamphlets recounting the events and actions that had occurred in PG&E's attempt to establish the plant. This literature was bad publicity for the company, and the public increasingly

[90] *Ibid.*

[91] *Ibid.*

[92] U.S. Atomic Energy Commission Application Docket, No. 50-205 by Pacific Gas and Electric Company, Amendment.

[93] California PUC Hearings, Application 43808, transcript, p. 383.

[94] AEC Docket, No. 50-205.

[95] Advisory Committee on Reactor Safeguards, "Report on Bodega Bay Atomic Park, Unit No. 1," October 20, 1964, p. 2.

[96] AEC Docket No. 50-205, p. 13.

began to view PG&E and the various public agencies and organizations as irresponsible. The mounting pressure of negative public opinion as mobilized by the association began to influence the AEC.

On October 27, 1964, the AEC issued two reports regarding the Bodega Bay reactor. One, from the commission's Advisory Committee on Reactor Safeguards, stated that, in its opinion, the company's plant could be operated with reasonable assurance that it would not constitute an undue hazard to the health and safety of the public. The other, from the commission's Division of Reactor Licensing, stated that, in its opinion, "Bodega Head is not a suitable location for the proposed nuclear power plant at the present state of our knowledge." Its reason for this conclusion was the feeling that there was not enough experimental and actual operating data on the proposed design[97] to ensure that it would withstand an earthquake of potential intensity. Immediately following the AEC reports, PG&E announced that it was abandoning the project in which the company had invested several million dollars and which had caused controversy for nearly seven years. PG&E's decision was surprising since under AEC licensing procedures a final decision on the company's $61 million project would not be made until a public hearing had been held by an Atomic Safety and Licensing Board, appointed by the AEC. The initial decision of the three-member board could be protested by the company, the public, or other interested parties before final action was taken.[98]

On November 2, 1964, the following explanation for the company's decision was reported in the *Wall Street Journal*:

Robert Gerdes, PG&E president, said the doubt raised by the AEC staff "although a minority view, is sufficient to cause us to withdraw our application: We would be the last to desire to build a plant with any substantial doubt existing as to the public safety."

Mr. Gerdes stated that PG&E has made provisions "for adequate electrical generating capacity elsewhere to take care of our customers' needs for the several years immediately ahead."

The company said it has spent $4 million at the site for grading, excavating and road building.[99]

[97] *Ibid.*
[98] *The Wall Street Journal*, October 28, 1964, p. 30.
[99] *Ibid.*, November 2, 1964, p. 7.

B.
ECONOMIC INTERESTS
AND
PUBLIC HEALTH

———◆———

Warning: Smoking May Be
Hazardous to Your Health

Clash Between Economic Interests and Public Safety:
Consumer Freedom and Government Regulation

The further a man is removed from physical need the more open he is to persuasion—or management—as to what he buys. This is, perhaps, the most important consequence for economics of increasing affluence.

—JOHN KENNETH GALBRAITH
in *The New Industrial State*

In a widely televised January 11, 1964, broadcast, U.S. Surgeon General Luther Terry reported to the nation the conclusions of his advisory committee on smoking and health—smokers have a 70 percent higher fatality rate from lung cancer than nonsmokers! The report warned that "cigarette smoking is a health hazard of sufficient importance in the United States to warrant appropriate remedial action."

The report brought to a head the long dispute between health authorities and the tobacco industry. Hitherto the dispute, confined to professional journals and academic conferences, had been neutralized by the tobacco industry through advertising and promotion. Little of the adverse publicity had filtered through those journals to the public at large. The national interest generated by the surgeon general's report had, for once, stumped the tobacco industry. The American Cancer Society *and* the

Tobacco Institute had approved the members of the committee who performed the study. (The institute is composed of the nine major tobacco companies—American Brands, Brown & Williamson, Larus & Brother, Liggett & Myers, P. Lorillard, Philip Morris, R. J. Reynolds, Stephano Brothers, and United States Tobacco.)

HISTORY AND BACKGROUND

The antecedents linking smoking to cancer go back to 1900 when vital statisticians noted an increase in cancer of the lung. Their data are usually taken as the starting point for studies on the possible relationship of smoking to lung cancer, to diseases of the heart and blood vessels, and to noncancerous diseases of the lower respiratory tract.[1] The next important date for comparisons is 1930, when definite trends in mortality and disease incidence became apparent. Since 1939 there have been twenty-nine retrospective studies of lung cancer and cigarette smoking.[2] In 1950, as research and statistical analysis became more competent, more evidence pointed to a definite relationship. Two American doctors, Graham and Wydner, concluded from their research that "excessive use of tobacco, especially cigarettes, seems to be an important factor in the induction of lung cancer."[3]

In 1954 Doctors Hammond and Horn, working for the American Cancer Society, issued their now famous study which found that male cigarette smokers, smoking a pack a day, were sixteen times more likely to die of lung cancer than nonsmokers.[4] This study caused a general health scare. The cigarette manufacturers' response was unanimous. The tobacco industry established the Tobacco Industry Research Committee, set up grants for research, and manufacturers introduced filter cigarettes.

In June 1956, at the request of the surgeon general, a scientific study group established jointly by the National Cancer Institute, the National Heart Institute, the American Cancer Society, and the American Heart Association, reviewed sixteen independent studies made in five countries over an eighteen-year period. The group's conclusion that there was a causal relationship between excessive cigarette smoking and lung cancer

[1] Advisory Committee to the Surgeon General of the Public Health Service, *Smoking and Health* (Washington, D.C.: Government Printing Office, 1964), p. 33.

[2] *Ibid.*

[3] "Cigarettes and Society: A Growing Dilemma," *Time*, April 25, 1969, pp. 98–103.

[4] *Ibid.*

was officially supported by Surgeon General Leroy E. Burney in 1956 and 1959.[5] At the group's urging, President Kennedy established a commission to study the tobacco problem, and in January 1962, Surgeon General Terry and the commission were encouraged by a report issued by the Royal College of Physicians in Great Britain on "Smoking and Health," which stated that there did exist a definite causal relationship between cigarette smoking, lung cancer, and other diseases. Sufficiently motivated, the commission agreed to conduct a two-phase study consisting of (1) a review and evaluation of available data and (2) recommendations for action.

In 1963 legal considerations emerged when the question of cigarette manufacturers' liability was raised in the case of *Green* v. *The American Tobacco Company*. A district court in Miami held that, although smoking was a cause of cancer, the company was not liable since it could not have foreseen the consequences. As a result, however, the industry began to give serious consideration to a warning on cigarette packages in order to limit their liability.

In December 1963, the American Cancer Society issued results of a survey of more than one million Americans. With the most complete statistics and analysis up to that time, the society reported its conclusion that "the evidence continues to pile up, and the burden of proof that there is not a causal relationship could soon shift over to the cigarette companies."

THE SURGEON GENERAL'S REPORT OF 1964

The president's commission analyzed and evaluated three kinds of data: animal experiments, clinical and autopsy studies, and population studies. As a result of its investigation, the commission reached the conclusion that "cigarette smoking is causally related to lung cancer in men; the magnitude of the effect of cigarette smoking far outweighs all other factors." The commission also found that the risk of developing lung cancer increased with the duration of smoking and the number of cigarettes smoked per day and diminished by discontinuing smoking. According to the report, "the risk of developing cancer of the lung for the combined groups of pipe smokers, cigar smokers, and pipe and cigar smokers, is greater than for non-smokers, but much less than for cigarette smokers." In addition the report stated that cigarette smoking was the greatest cause of chronic bronchitis in the United States and greatly increased the risk of death from that

---

[5] *Congressional Quarterly 1964 Almanac* (Washington, D.C.: Congressional Quarterly Inc., 1965, p. 246).

disease and from emphysema. The report stated that for most of the United States population cigarette smoking was a much greater cause of chronic bronchopulmonary disease than atmospheric pollution or occupational exposure. The report also concluded that cigarette smoking was related to cardiovascular diseases:

> It is established that male cigarette smokers have a higher death rate from coronary artery disease than non-smoking males. Although the causative role of cigarette smoking in deaths from coronary disease is not proven, the Committee considers it more prudent from the public health viewpoint to assume that the established association has causative meaning, than to suspend judgment until no uncertainty remains.

REACTION TO THE REPORT

The tobacco industry, although somewhat defensive, was undeterred by the report. Through the Tobacco Institute it reiterated time-honored arguments: no causal relationship had been established between smoking and cancer; any ban against smoking would cause serious economic injury to a vital industry and unemployment to countless workers and farmers; a reduction in smoking would result in a significant decrease in federal, state, and local taxes; and it would be an infringement of individuals' personal freedom.

The American Medical Association (AMA) came out with a feeble statement that more research was needed and that there was a need to "find how tobacco smoke affected health, and if possible, to eliminate whatever element in smoke may induce disease."[6]

The tobacco industry then moved to back up its assertions that more research was needed. In February 1964, Dr. Raymond McKeon, AMA president, announced that six tobacco companies had given the AMA $10 million for research, without any restrictions whatsoever. In addition, all the companies began or intensified their own filter research.

On April 27, 1964, the major tobacco companies announced the formulation of a voluntary advertising code. The code was to become effective in January 1965. It outlawed any advertising that would appeal to those under twenty-one, thus barring cigarette commercials before and after television programs designed for minors. It forbade any advertising that portrayed smoking as being essential to social prominence, distinction, success, or

[6] *Congressional Quarterly 1968 Almanac* (Washington, D.C.: Congressional Quarterly Inc., Vol. XXIII, 1968).

sexual attraction.[7] The broadcasting industry also established codes to regulate cigarette advertising. The National Association of Broadcasters' television code board stated that cigarette advertising should not contain false claims and that neither programming nor advertising was to depict smoking as promoting health or as being necessary or desirable to young people. The industry agreed to subject itself to self-regulation to be enforced by an independent administrator capable of leveling fines of $100,000 for infractions.[8]

The first official government reaction came from the Federal Trade Commission (FTC), when it announced on January 18, 1964, that it was scheduling hearings for March 16 on the following proposed forms of regulation:

1. Cigarette packs and ads shall carry the warning "caution—cigarette smoking is dangerous to health and may cause death. . . ."
2. Ads and labels must not suggest that cigarettes promote health or well-being, are not dangerous, or that one brand is less harmful than another.
3. The "tar derby" or competitive safety claims will be resumed only when a manufacturer can support his claims with scientific evidence; tar and nicotine contents must be verified by testing procedures.[9]

The FTC subsequently announced proposed trade regulation rules to require a warning on cigarette packages and advertisements, the actual wording to be left to the manufacturers. FTC Chairman Paul Rand Dixon notified the House of the commission's decision and said that the labeling requirement would become effective January 1, 1965. The FTC dropped its regulation on the two other ad directives regarding claims of good health and statements that one brand may be less harmful than another. This loosening of control was the FTC's reaction to the creation of the industry's self-policing codes. There was so much opposition from the tobacco industry, however, that Chairman Dixon postponed the labeling requirement to July 1, 1965, so that the Eighty-ninth Congress convening January 4, 1965, would have time to examine the proposal.

Congressional reaction to the report and the FTC decision was mixed. Southern representatives from tobacco states fought to delay FTC requirements. They also introduced bills to provide funds for research studies on

[7] "Smoking Scare: What's Happened to It," *U.S. News and World Report*, January 11, 1965, pp. 38–41.

[8] *Ibid.*

[9] *1967 Almanac.*

the effects of tobacco on health. Congress lost little time in scheduling hearings on the matter of cigarette labeling and advertising regulation and health problems associated with smoking. The first hearings were held before the full House Committee on Interstate and Foreign Commerce in late June and early July 1964. Chairman Oren Harris introduced the hearings by pointing out the importance of the issues raised and the potential impact of regulation:

> Our responsibilities, therefore, make it important that we look into the questions raised as a result of all of these events, not only because of the jurisdiction of this committee, but also because it is contended that this problem vitally affects the public health of the country. Tobacco is grown in 21 States. There are over 500 industries, some rather substantial, in which nearly a hundred thousand people are employed in 30 States, engaged in the manufacture of tobacco products. There are about a million and a half businesses in this country that share in the tobacco trade. Over 28 percent of the tobacco leaf sold in the free world markets in 1963 was exported from the United States. I am told that some 505 million pounds of tobacco was exported with a value of over $400 million.
> In 1963 there were 70 million Americans who bought tobacco products, at a cost of approximately $8 billion. I think it is generally known that over $2 billion of this sum went to the Federal Government in taxes, over a billion dollars went to the State governments, and millions of dollars went to municipal governments. I mention this to show the far-reaching implications of this subject.[10]

These first congressional hearings provided the staging ground for the formulation and articulation of the positions and strategies adopted by the various parties involved in and concerned about the cigarette controversy.

CONGRESSIONAL HEARINGS, JUNE–JULY 1964

Three basic positions, all documented in the various hearings reports, were offered to the committee—those of the FTC, the tobacco industry, and the Department of Health, Education and Welfare (HEW).

THE FTC's POSITION. Chairman Paul Dixon contended that the commission had authority to regulate cigarette advertising under Section 5 of the Federal Trade Commission Act which authorizes the commission "to proceed against any actual or potential deception in sale, or offering for

[10] U.S., Congress, House Committee on Interstate and Foreign Commerce, Hearings, *Cigarette Labeling and Advertising*, 88th Cong., 2d session, 1964.

sale, of any product in commerce. . . . Such deception may result either from a direct statement concerning a product or a failure to disclose any material fact relating to such a product."

Dixon assured the committee that the FTC would exercise its broad responsibility discreetly. Notwithstanding, he stated that "the Commission had completed its consideration of the record in this proceeding and has determined that the public interest requires the promulgation of a trade regulation rule for the prevention of unfair or deceptive advertising or labeling of cigarettes in relation to the health hazards of smoking."

Dixon, however, was more anxious that Congress rather than the FTC take initiative and action in such a politically sensitive and explosive area. He took the position that unless instructed otherwise by Congress, the agency would consider the regulation of cigarette labeling and advertising to be within its jurisdiction and would therefore be compelled to act. Chairman Dixon testified:

I make it perfectly plain to you, we are a creature of the Congress. But until the Congress changes our basic responsibility I think we are dutybound to act. If the Congress passes a law removing this from our jurisdiction and vesting it somewhere else then we are relieved of that responsibility. If the Congress of the United States would pass a joint resolution saying you wanted us to not do anything I assure you we will not do it. But until that happens I am sworn and dutybound to enforce this law as it presently is on the statute books.

TOBACCO'S POSITION. Early in 1964 the Tobacco Institute set up a lobbying campaign utilizing the strong influence of Senator Earle C. Clements, former representative and democratic whip under Lyndon B. Johnson. At the hearings the industry's position was presented by Bowman Gray, chairman of the board of directors of R. J. Reynolds Tobacco Company, Winston-Salem, North Carolina. The industry opposed the FTC regulations regarding labeling and advertising for three reasons: (1) the FTC did not have the authority to issue such a trade regulation and the commission therefore acted unlawfully; (2) the matter was of such importance that it should be resolved by Congress and not by an agency; "the Commission's rule would not have preemptive effect, and the industry would be exposed to the possibility of diverse State and municipal laws"; and (3) "we oppose it because we believe the Commission's warning requirement is unwise, unwarranted and is not a fair factual statement of the present state of scientific knowledge."

The industry, while fully aware of the "gravity of questions concerning smoking and health," felt that there was lack of knowledge and a great deal of uncertainty on the subject and that more research was essential. To this end it had given $7 million in research grants to the Tobacco Industry Research Committee, and six cigarette manufacturers had pledged $10 million to the American Medical Association for research. Under these circumstances, the industry felt that no governmental action was necessary at that time.

If, however, some action was deemed necessary, Mr. Gray stated:

> We certainly do not think that any action should be taken by an administrative agency such as was taken yesterday by the Federal Trade Commission, and if any such action is to be taken, we believe it should be taken by the Congress and by no one else. The problem is national in scope; it is clearly not local. . . .
>
> Great care should be exercised before any action is taken which could seriously disrupt this important industry. Unwise legislation or regulation, like the trade regulation rule announced by the Federal Trade Commission, has repercussions which will be felt throughout the country's economy.
>
> We do not think that a caution notice is necessary on labels or in advertising. I assume that the principal purpose of a caution notice is to alert the consumer to possible hazards associated with the use of a product. With respect to cigarettes, however, the public has been inundated for more than a decade with charges that smoking may be injurious to health. The report of the Advisory Committee to the Surgeon General was intensively publicized in all media. The smoking and health issue receives continuing publicity. I doubt that any person who can read or listen has not been made aware of the contention that smoking may be injurious to the health of some persons. In these circumstances a caution notice would appear to be pointless.

Should the Congress consider that a warning label was absolutely necessary, Mr. Gray emphasized the following points:

1. Any such legislation should make it absolutely clear that the congressional statute preempted the field. If there was to be a caution notice, it should be uniform and again nationwide in scope.
2. The required caution notice should be fair and factual. It should be phrased in a way that reflected the lack of scientific clinical and laboratory evidence of the relationship between smoking and health.
3. If a warning was to be required on the package, it certainly should not be required in cigarette advertising.

Mr. Gray was quite emphatic about the tobacco industry's opposition to warning notices in advertising but realized that some sort of public warning was inevitable in package labeling. His arguments against warning statements in cigarette advertising were as follows:

> Advertising is basic to the successful distribution and sale of any consumer item on a national basis. The right to advertise is an essential commercial right and is virtually destroyed if one is required in every advertisement to caution against the use of the product.
>
> If cigarette advertising is required to contain statements warning or cautioning against use, a most dangerous precedent is set. Would automobile advertising be required to contain statements indicating the possible dangers of driving on the public highways? Would aviation companies be obliged to warn their prospective passengers in advertising of the possibility of plane crashes? Would the vendors of dairy products be required to warn against possible ill effects of cholesterol?
>
> The requirement for a warning in advertising, in addition to a warning on labels, is punitive in nature. It could result, as a practical matter, in an end to all cigarette advertising.

On April 27, the cigarette companies announced the Cigarette Advertising Code, thus supporting Mr. Gray's contention that the industry itself had taken action to meet voiced criticisms. The tobacco companies were using the mechanism of a membership corporation, with each cigarette company as a member, and had asked for a clearance from the Antitrust Division of the Department of Justice. In a July 1, 1964, letter to the House committee, Mr. Gray stated that the industry interpreted the Justice Department's reply as clearance to implement the voluntary code.

Another inquiry following Mr. Gray's statement raised the question of the impact of the surgeon general's report on cigarette sales. The information subsequently provided showed that sales had declined immediately but had returned to previous levels (see Table I).

HEW's POSITION. Surgeon General Luther Terry, testifying before the House Committee, presented the position of the Department of Health, Education and Welfare:

> In summary, I would like to say that the Department of Health, Education, and Welfare recognized the major public health hazard caused by cigarette smoking. The Department believes that additional regulatory and nonregulatory action is required. . . . To fulfill our major nonregulatory responsibilities in the field of public health, we do not have adequate basic legislative authority, although certain appropriation ceilings may require adjustment and additional funds and staff are needed if we are to meet fully this most challenging public health problem. . . . We must not use the need for further research as an excuse for lack of action. . . . With the overwhelming

TABLE I

MONTHLY COMPARISON OF CIGARETTES TAXED BY STATES, 1964 VERSUS 1963
[IN THOUSANDS OF PACKAGES]

| | 1963 | 1964 | Percentage Change | |
			Actual	Adjusted for Trading Days
January	1,882,458	1,749,410	—7.1	—7.1
February	1,705,653	1,456,766	—14.6	—14.6
March	1,730,826	1,735,778	—0.3	—4.3
April	1,910,037	1,851,870	—3.0	—3.0
May	2,075,503	1,825,112	—12.1	—3.7

Source: U.S., Congress, House Committee on Interstate and Foreign Commerce, Hearings, *Cigarette Labeling and Advertising*, 88th Cong., 2d Session, 1964, p. 148.

scientific evidence we now possess, I predict that the years ahead will constitute an era of action in which we will make significant progress in reducing the burden of disease, disability, and untimely death imposed upon millions of our people by cigarette smoking.

The House Commerce Committee heard further testimony from a number of senators and representatives from tobacco-producing states. The committee felt that the action taken by the Congress was highly dependent upon the question of whether the surgeon general's report "can be absolutely depended upon as a matter of fact and not necessarily taken as the judgment of experts." The committee therefore heard a good deal of professional testimony. Dr. Thomas Burford, professor of thoracic surgery at Washington University, St. Louis, testified that there was "a large volume of good scientific evidence which tends to refute the rather hastily accepted premise that cigarette smoking is causally related to lung cancer." Dr. William B. Ober pointed out that saying that a large proportion of lung cancer patients "have been heavy cigarette smokers for 20 or 30 years or longer is quite a different matter [from saying] that a large proportion of those people who smoke heavily will develop cancer of the lung." He added that the "only really scientific statement one can make at the present time is that no one really knows what causes lung cancer."

Dr. Harold S. Diehl, vice-chairman of the National Interagency Council on Smoking and Health, and Dr. Thomas Carlisle, spokesman for the American Cancer Society, said that the committee "apparently faces a basic issue as to whether in a democratic capitalistic society, human health can be given precedence over financial gain. . . ." Strongly in favor of FTC power was Dr. Carlisle who urged labeling to warn the public of the danger of cigarette smoking.

Further hearings were held before both the House and Senate Commerce Committees during the first session of the Eighty-ninth Congress, March 22 to April 1, 1965. The position of the parties remained the same. The testimony of these hearings, however, emphasized cigarette advertising regulation. It was argued, on the basis of the proper role of government and the proper relationship between government and business, that it should not be the government's role to attempt to change the behavior of individual citizens. When an industry demonstrated a willingness to regulate itself, as the cigarette industry had through its voluntary code, government regulation represented undue interference with business and free enterprise. The government, furthermore, had no right to prohibit the advertising of a product that could be legally manufactured and sold. If action was considered necessary, however, a warning on the label and not in advertising would be the proper form. The label was the traditional and expected and most effective place for hazard warnings. Testimony was also given on the nature and purposes of advertising in the cigarette industry. Advertising, it was argued, was a basic means of competition and prohibiting it would restrict competition in the industry. The intent of cigarette advertising was not to encourage people to smoke, since half the people in the country were already smoking, but to encourage smokers to change brands, that is, to increase a company's market share. The industry was mature and had a mature market place. The aim, therefore, was selective demand and not primary demand.

RESULTS OF THE HEARINGS

Congress ultimately passed S. 559, a bill introduced by Senate Commerce Committee Chairman Warren G. Magnuson, which required that all cigarette packages bear the label "Caution: Cigarette Smoking May Be Hazardous to Your Health." The bill provided for a uniform and overriding federal labeling requirement which was not expected to affect sales seriously. All action on control of advertising was suspended until July 1969. In its final form the bill called for a fine of ten thousand dollars for violations and required periodic reports from the FTC and HEW. The bill was strongly opposed by Republican John E. Moss who stated that the warning was not sufficiently forceful to curb the smoking habit. Moss charged that effective warnings were needed to alert the thousands who start smoking every day. Shortly before President Johnson signed the bill into law on July 27, 1965, eight senators, among them Robert F. Kennedy, urged a veto. They argued that S. 559 was more beneficial to the cigarette companies than to the nation's health, especially as the companies themselves had admitted that the labeling requirement would have little or no effect on consumption. Despite opposition, however, the bill was passed, and the FTC reluctantly canceled its regulations requiring a health warning in advertising. The agency did say, however, that it would continue to keep watch on cigarette advertising to make sure that S. 559 was being obeyed and that fraudulent and misleading advertising was not being used.

The controversy and the law that was finally passed had little effect on the tobacco industry's sales. For the fiscal year ending in June 1965, consumption was at a record level of more than 5.33 billion cigarettes. The U.S. Public Health Service also noted that although one million Americans were giving up smoking each year, they were replaced by 1.5 million new smokers, mostly youngsters.[11]

During 1966, the federal agencies had little regulatory power because of S. 559's restrictive provision. They concentrated on research and on determining the effect of the 1965 law on smokers. Various bills and resolutions to set new requirements for cigarette labeling and advertising were introduced in Congress. During the year the Senate Commerce Committee held three days of hearings on the development of a safer cigarette, but no further action was taken.

The March 1966 cigarette price rise may have caused some smokers to consider quitting, but the government stepped in on grounds of inflation. President Johnson persuaded the cigarette companies to roll back the price increase, thereby posing the question: Which is the greater threat, inflation or the smoking peril?

The FTC also ruled in March that companies could mention the tar and nicotine content of their cigarettes. The FTC said that the content of cigarette smoke "may be material and desired by the consuming public."[12] The next month, in response to the FTC ruling, P. Lorillard quit the industry ad council and rushed to market a new cigarette, TRUE, asserting that it would "deliver less tar and nicotine." This conflicted with the industry code which required proof of health significance and started a new "tar derby" of tar and nicotine claims. The conflicting claims were subject to much controversy, and in August the FTC decided to hold hearings on ways of uniformly measuring tar and nicotine content.

In November 1966, the Public Health Service issued a new report dealing exclusively with death-rate statistics which showed that mortality rates went up with cigarette consumption. Starting in early 1967 various executive agencies released new findings, including data gathered by the surgeon general and a report that the 1965 law was having little effect on smokers. In January 1967, after the FTC hearings concluded, HEW Secretary Gardner endorsed a Senate Commerce Committee bill that would make

[11] "Cigarettes and Society: A Growing Dilemma," *Time*, April 25, 1969, pp. 98–103.
[12] *1967 Almanac.*

cigarette firms disclose tar and nicotine content. The Tobacco Institute's position at this time was that "there is no valid scientific evidence demonstrating that either tar or nicotine is responsible for human illness."[13]

The FTC wanted the Senate bill to set up uniform testing methods. The bill requiring cigarette firms to print the tar and nicotine content of their cigarettes failed to pass Congress; however, money was appropriated for the FTC to set up its own testing procedure and to report its findings.

On February 28, 1967, President Johnson directed HEW to organize a committee to study lung cancer and cigarette smoking. The following summer, Kennedy M. Endicott, director of the Public Health Services National Cancer Institute, announced the organization of a ten-member commission to study lung cancer and smoking and the development of a safer cigarette.

That summer the new U.S. surgeon general, William H. Stewart, released a report summarizing the development of tobacco-related research since Surgeon General Terry's controversial report of 1964. Stewart said that over two thousand research programs completed since 1964 had given no evidence that conflicted with the 1964 conclusions.[14] He confirmed the relationship between smoking and health by describing four major population studies, which contained extensive data on smokers, increased data on men smokers in specific age groups, and a large amount of information on women smokers. The 1967 report concluded that the danger to males from all smoke-related illnesses increased with age, especially during the years from forty-five to fifty-four. In the thirty-five to fifty-nine age group, the deaths of one of every three men and one of every fourteen women were attributed to smoking. Women who smoked regularly had significantly higher death rates than those who had never smoked, according to the report. The difference in the mortality rates between men and women were attributed to the fact that women were less exposed to cigarette smoking than men. Other information provided by the report showed that there was a downward trend in risk from disease and death for those who had stopped smoking.[15] Younger smokers showed undesirable respiratory symptoms and shortwindedness. Death rates were higher for those who started smoking early in life. As for diseases other than lung cancer, the report indicated that smoking was the most important cause of chronic bronchopulmonary disease in the United States and that it was significantly related to peptic ulcer.

The report was sent to Congress with a letter from HEW Secretary John

[13] "Tobacco," *Time*, August 1, 1969.

[14] *1967 Almanac*, p. 737.

[15] *Federal Register*, Vol. XXXIV, No. 28 (Washington, D.C.: Government Printing Office, 1969).

Gardner outlining the department's recommendations for congressional action. He recommended that (1) action be taken to strengthen the warning label on cigarette packages by stating more specifically that smoking was hazardous to health, (2) legislation be passed to require warning on advertisements, and (3) both labels and advertising identify the tar and nicotine levels in cigarettes.[16] The conclusions reached in the surgeon general's report were also supported by the national survey conducted by the Public Health Service National Center for Health Statistics.

Another study was made by the FTC on the effect of the first eighteen months of the Act of 1965 on the smoking habits of Americans and on the advertising practices of the industry. The FTC Report concluded that 82 percent of the respondents felt that the current warning label (Caution: Cigarette Smoking May Be Hazardous to Your Health) was having no appreciable effect. In addition, the report stated that despite the voluntary advertising code, the tobacco industry continued to represent smoking as an enjoyable and even healthful activity. Also, much of the advertising was done during prime broadcasting hours and consequently was reaching young people. Since industry regulation was proving ineffectual, the report recommended that cigarette advertising be banned from radio and television. In addition, it urged a stronger warning on cigarette packages: "Caution: Cigarette Smoking Is Dangerous to Your Health and May Cause Death from Cancer and Other Diseases." Funds were requested by the National Institute of Health for the development of a safer cigarette.

THE FEDERAL COMMUNICATIONS COMMISSION STEPS IN

On June 2, 1967, the FCC ordered radio and television stations to allow time for antismoking advertisements. The seven commissioners of the FCC said that their decision was based on the *Fairness Doctrine* which states that the public should have access to conflicting viewpoints on controversial issues of public importance. This fairness doctrine, a basic principle of the broadcasting field, was made a part of the Communications Act of 1959, although it was not applied to product advertising until 1967.[17]

Thus, stations running cigarette ads had to turn over a significant amount of free time to antismoking commercials: one antismoking for every three smoking commercials. Antismoking groups such as the Ameri-

---

16 *1967 Almanac*, p. 738.

17 Federal Communication Commission Reports, "Television Station WCBS-TV," 2d series, vol. 8, May 19–August 4, 1967, pp. 381–87.

can Cancer Society filled the air with their effective anti-ads. After the ruling, the American Cancer Society distributed some eighty-nine hundred antismoking commercials in sixteen months. The anti-ads were in effect the reverse of the cigarette ads. Instead of looking happy and vigorous, smokers were presented as miserable and unhealthy. A number of celebrities were used to advocate quitting smoking, and others refused to perform on programs sponsored by cigarettes.

The person largely responsible for the FCC's application of the fairness doctrine to cigarette advertising was John F. Banzhaf III, a twenty-eight-year-old New York attorney known as "the Ralph Nader of the cigarette industry."[18] In January 1967, Banzhaf had filed a formal complaint with the FCC against WCBS-TV. The complaint maintained that the fairness doctrine required the station to give equal time to "responsible groups" to present the case against cigarette smoking. Although the FCC rejected the equal time contention, its June 3 ruling responded to Banzhaf's complaint. Banzhaf, after attaining this initial victory, formed two organizations. The first, ASH (Action on Smoking and Health), sponsored by noted physicians, raised more than one hundred thousand dollars to conduct the litigation of the fairness doctrine[19] and to enforce its application by monitoring TV stations and filing complaints against those failing to comply. The other organization, LASH (Legislative Action on Smoking and Health), raised funds and enlisted support for the congressional battles.

As the antismoking forces speeded up their efforts in 1967, the tobacco industry—through its major Washington lobby, the Tobacco Institute—continued to oppose them. In addition to carrying on its own research, the Tobacco Institute challenged the validity of almost every government study on smoking and health, and the industry introduced the 100-mm cigarette—up to half an inch longer than the regular. In his speeches and writing lobbyist Clements emphasized the industry's belief that the causes of lung cancer and heart disease were unknown and hence were not automatically related to cigarette smoking.

In May 1967, bills were introduced in Congress by various senators, including Robert Kennedy, Warren G. Magnuson, and Frank E. Moss, to strengthen the Cigarette Labeling and Advertising Act of 1965. However, no new legislation resulted. On November 27, 1967, the Consumer Subcommittee of the Senate Commerce Committee made public the FTC tests giving tar and nicotine contents of fifty-nine varieties of cigarettes. Senator Magnuson, chairman of the subcommittee, said, "This information will enable a smoker who is unable or unwilling to give up smoking

18 *The New York Times*, June 3, 1967.

19 See *Banzhaf* vs. *FCC*, U.S. Court of Appeals, D.C. Circuit, Case #21285, November 21, 1968.

to select the least hazardous cigarettes on the market." Individual companies had no comment.

Developments during 1968 also took the form of recommendations and warnings rather than legislation. On July 1, 1968, HEW Secretary Wilbur J. Cohen brought to Congress the surgeon general's 1968 Supplemental Report on the Health Consequences of Smoking and urged more strongly worded warnings of the hazards involved in cigarette smoking. He also asked Congress to require warnings on advertisements.

THE FTC PRESSURES CONGRESS INTO ACTION

The FTC, although always in favor of regulating cigarette advertising, had consistently argued that the significant political and economic implications of such a regulation made Congress the proper initiating body. However, for the same reasons, Congress was reluctant. In 1965, in a pressure play, the FTC announced that it would require a stiffer warning on cigarette packages unless Congress took action. This precipitated the 1965 Act, which would expire on June 30, 1969. The FTC used the same tactic again when in June 1968, in a three-to-two decision, it voted to ban all cigarette advertising from radio and television and strongly suggested to the Senate committee that Congress legislate on the matter. Later in the summer the surgeon general's Task Force for Smoking and Health charged that the tobacco industry was encouraging death and disease with its advertising practices and that it was unwilling to face up to the health hazards of smoking.

In reply, the Tobacco Institute stated that the report "is a shockingly intemperate defamation of an industry which has led the way in medical research to seek answers in the cigarette controversy."[20]

On February 5, 1969, the Federal Communications Commission, in a six to one decision, moved to ban cigarette advertising from radio and television. Chairman Hyde indicated that the commission would be satisfied only with a complete ban and not with the Voluntary Code restrictions. In defense of its legal power the commission said that "in the case of such a threat to public health, the authority to act is really a duty to act,"[21] and that it would appear "wholly at odds with the public interest for broadcasters to present advertising promoting the consumption of a product imposing this unique danger."[22]

The cigarette industry considered the decision arbitrary and the National Association of Broadcasters charged that the FCC was outside its normal

[20] *1968 Almanac*, p. 707.

[21] "Move to Ban Cigarette TV Ads," *San Francisco Chronicle*, February 6, 1969.

[22] "A Move to Limit Cigarette Ads," *U.S. News and World Report*, February 17, 1969.

jurisdiction. Despite the heated reaction to the FCC ban proposal, however, there could be no actual ban without extensive hearings, and there remained the possibility of contrary legislation. Thus the FTC and FCC made it clear that Congress would have to act.

Interstate Commerce Committee Hearings

The hearings began in April 1969, and it seemed that nothing had changed since 1965—the positions of the various parties were immutable and their monotonously repetitious utterances were distinguished only by their vehemence. The broadcasting industry, impelled by economic considerations, unwillingly found itself an ally of the defensive cigarette industry. In a public-support ploy, the tobacco industry circulated an article— "How Much Is Known about Smoking and Health?" by Dr. Clarence Cook Little—through paid advertising space in leading national magazines and newspapers. Dr. Cook, a retired biologist, a member of the National Academy of Sciences, a former managing director of the American Society for the Control of Cancer (now the American Cancer Society), and a founder and former director of Jackson Laboratory for Cancer Research, supported the industry's point of view:

1. The genetic makeup of the individual largely determines his susceptibility to cancer, cardiovascular disease, or chronic respiratory disease which may appear after exposure to various environmental challenges.

2. Many factors other than smoking are significantly associated with these diseases.

3. Statistical associations between smoking and lung cancer, based on study of those two factors alone, are not proof of causal relationship in the opinion of most epidemiologists.

4. Major evaluations of health and smoking have been based on painting mouse skins with artificially prepared smoke condensates. But the relative degrees of cancer-forming response observed in these experiments neither parallel nor coincide with statistical data on the association of tobacco smoking and diseases in man.

5. Interpretation of certain lung tissue changes following smoking as being unique or "precancerous" is in dispute among pathologists.

6. Rapid progress is being made in the development of improved methods for experimentation in the exposure of animals to whole smoke for the sake of better control and more accurate evaluation.[23]

[23] Clarence Cook Little, "How Much Is Known about Smoking and Health," New York Council for Tobacco Research, February 3, 1969.

The Council for Tobacco Research also argued that the cause of cancer had not yet been proved. In its booklet, "The Cigarette Controversy: Eight Questions and Answers," the council raised some questions to strengthen its position:

1. If smoking does cause disease, why has it not been proven after 15 years of intensive research how this occurs?
2. Why, if smoking causes disease, has no ingredient found in smoke been identified as the causative factor?
3. The type of malignance for which smoking is most often blamed is "epidermoid" lung cancer. Have researchers ever produced this in animals with cigarette smoke? No.
4. Why do so many more men than women get lung cancer? If cigarette smoking is indeed the hazard it is said to be, the roughly six-to-one difference is most perplexing.
5. Why is it that lung cancer often does not occur in those parts of the lung which are exposed to the most smoke?
6. Do statistics prove that cigarette smoking is a cause of lung cancer, heart disease, emphysema, bronchitis, and other diseases? It is a cardinal principle that statistics alone cannot prove the cause of any disease.[24]

In addition to criticizing the antismoking forces, the council made an interesting point about smokers. It indicated that smokers as a group could be considered a different type of people—more communicative, creative, energetic, and volatile than nonsmokers. According to the council, they drank more black coffee and liquor, married more often, preferred spicy or salty foods to blander diets, and changed jobs more often. They were more outgoing and had more drive than nonsmokers. The council concluded that people who smoked tended to differ quite significantly from those who did not and therefore it was reasonable to raise the question that smokers might have higher illness rates than nonsmokers because of the kind of people they happened to be. The council also stated that emotional, psychological, and other factors might contribute to the illnesses for which smoking was unmercifully blamed.[25]

The industry spokesman, Joseph F. Cullman, chairman of the executive committee of the Tobacco Institute, testified at the hearings and repeated the industry's arguments of no proven link between smoking and cancer.

[24] *The Cigarette Controversy: Eight Questions and Answers* (Washington, D.C.: The Tobacco Institute, 1969).

[25] *Ibid.*

He contended that the 1965 Labeling Act had achieved its objective of informing the public concerning smoking and health, and he also took strong exception to the FCC's decision of June 2, 1967, regarding the application of the fairness doctrine, which gave a significant amount of free time to antismoking commercials on TV.

In presenting its position, the tobacco industry reiterated its usual defenses.

1. Advertising restrictions would impose economic hardship on the tobacco industry and thousands of small tobacco farmers.

2. Federal agencies did not have and should not be allowed to assume the regulatory powers that they had attempted to use.

3. Medical evidence was still not sufficient to establish a causal relationship between smoking and cancer.

4. Neither Congress nor any regulatory agency had the right to discriminate against one product.

According to the tobacco industry, the warning "Caution: Cigarette Smoking May Be Hazardous to Your Health" reflected the extent of available scientific evidence, and the stricter warning proposed was unwarranted by the facts and punitive in spirit. The industry also voiced opposition to the bills that would require that a statement of tar and nicotine contents of cigarettes be placed on all packages and in advertising.

The tobacco industry was again supported by testimony of the senators and representatives from major tobacco-producing states.[26] Congressman David N. Henderson of North Carolina expounded his views:

If we should permit the FCC to take this action in regard to cigarette smoking, what is there to prevent them from deciding next year that candy is detrimental to the public health in that it causes obesity, tooth decay, and other health problems? What about milk and eggs? Milk and eggs are high in saturated animal fat and no doubt increase the cholesterol in the bloodstream, believed by many heart specialists to be a contributing factor in heart disease [p. 40].

The industry agreed that the FCC should be allowed to prohibit an advertiser from making false, fraudulent, or misleading claims, but it objected to the singling out of cigarettes for regulation. Congressman Walter Jones

[26] U.S., Congress, House Committee on Interstate and Foreign Commerce, Hearings, *Cigarette Labeling and Advertising—1969*, 91st Cong. 1st sess., Part I of three parts, statements made by various congressmen.

from North Carolina said that "there were 18,000 alcoholics in the Veterans Hospitals of this nation, or one-fourth of the patient population. Where is the censorship of the beer and wine advertisements—is it to be next?" (p. 41). "Zeroing in from the other direction," said Congressman John J. Duncan from Tennessee, "the FCC could ban all commercials of cigarettes on radio and television, leaving the industry hopeless and helpless in reaching a multitude of potential customers. One does not have to stretch his imagination very far to see how crippled the industry might become" (p. 78). Other testifiers for the industry charged that the anti-smoking forces were being guided more by their own personal beliefs and emotions than by objectivity. As stated by Congressman Carl D. Perkins from Kentucky, "Tobacco has been impeached in passion but it has not been convicted in fact. Facts, cold, hard facts, are the basis upon which Congress should legislate" (p. 16).

Again in the 1969 congressional hearings the industry stressed the need for more research and not more regulation. Congressman Nick Galifianakis of North Carolina suggested that "research is the only way that cancer will be eliminated. What would be more appropriate than for the cigarette manufacturers and the Federal Government jointly to underwrite a crash cancer program" (p. 42).

The economic arguments against regulation were also presented before congressional hearings. Representatives from the Southern tobacco-producing states argued that the small farmer who depended on tobacco as a main cash crop would be seriously affected if the industry were restricted. Not only the three million men, women, and children connected with tobacco farms but numerous others would also be affected adversely, as Congressman Duncan pointed out in his testimony:

> Involved in this industry too are the people who transport the tobacco, the dealers and warehousemen, manufacturers of tobacco products, people who work in the tobacco plants, those who are involved in making the paper wrappers and boxes, the distributors of finished products, and the retailers. The U.S. tobacco manufacturing companies themselves employ over 100,000 people who receive aggregate wages exceeding $500 million a year [p. 78].

As Congressman Mizell from North Carolina pointed out, the involvement of other industries in cigarette manufacture was significant:

> The tobacco industry also uses over 40,000 pounds of moisture proof cellophane, more than 70,000 pounds of aluminum foil, nearly 27 billion printed packs and 2.7 billion cartons. Altogether about 1,500,000 businesses share in the tobacco trade, supplying equipment,

materials, transportation, advertising, distributing, and merchandising services in every part of the country [p. 43].

As industry spokesmen indicated, severe restrictions on cigarette advertising and subsequent harm to industry would create a labor problem involving the many displaced workers, not to mention the thousands of farmers who would be left jobless.

Congressman Perkins from Kentucky pointed out that in the event of an industry slowdown, many of the nation's 625,000 tobacco farmers would be driven off their land into the city slums. To him it seemed ironic that a member of Congress who had proposed anticigarette advertising was also very much interested in urban ghetto problems (p. 17). On the economic question the industry was quick to delineate the great amount of government revenue obtained from cigarette sales. In fiscal year 1967–1968, tobacco taxes reached an all-time high. On cigarettes alone the federal tax was $2,066,159,000, state taxes $1,969,674,000, and municipal taxes $61,696,000—a total of $4,097,529,000 (p. 43). Of the $8.5 billion annual cigarette sales, each pack contributed an average of sixteen cents in combined taxes, and proposals to increase tobacco taxes continued. The industry considered cigarette taxes to be a peril to the market and unjust because no users secured any special benefit by paying the tax.[27]

Congressman John E. Moss of California, who favored stricter antismoking legislation, introduced a bill calling for a stronger warning label on packages and for a statement of tar and nicotine content to accompany every package and advertisement. Moss's bill was supported by the American Cancer Society which strongly opposed extending indefinitely the prohibition against federal or state action on cigarette advertising. Dr. Baker of the American Cancer Society indicated that organization's appreciation to the radio and television industries for free time allotted to antismoking ads and to the FCC for making possible these free ads. Baker expressed the antismoking forces' view in criticizing the effect cigarette advertising was having on young potential smokers and those smokers who were trying to quit. He stated: "One of the worst things about cigarette advertising—particularly on television and radio—is the impact it seems to have on those who are making the effort to give up smoking. It is extremely tough for nervous, struggling, irritable men or women, trying to do what they know is best for them and their children, to be constantly invited by witty, expensive, alluring television commercials to return to their dangerous habit" (pp. 309–311).

Speaking also in behalf of the American Cancer Society was Dr. Ashbel

[27] Frank Snodgrass, "Tobacco: A Very Big Industry with Very Few Defenders," *United States Tobacco Journal*, December 26, 1968.

C. Williams, a surgeon from Jacksonville, Florida, a diplomate of the American Board of Surgery and a member of the Cancer Commission of the American College of Surgeons. Like Baker he pointed to his own experiences as a doctor treating lung cancer patients and indicated a strong relationship between smoking and disease: "Every regular cigarette smoker damages himself, though not in the same degree. Smoke enough cigarettes long enough, and you will almost certainly disable or destroy yourself prematurely by cancer, emphysema, or heart and vascular disease, or perhaps ulcers of the stomach or duodenum." Further testimony by Charles D. Sherman, Jr., emphasized the antismoking medical arguments. He stated that in addition to the two hundred and sixty thousand deaths each year from smoking, "untold additional numbers are ill and hospitalized with chronic lung diseases and nonfatal cardiovascular diseases caused from smoking" (p. 373).

Concern for the young potential smoker prevailed in California Congressman Jerry L. Pettis's testimony. His bill, HR 3817, was more concerned with the young than with the confirmed adult smokers who would probably not stop smoking even with the cessation of cigarette advertising on radio and television. It would prohibit cigarette advertising between such hours as the FCC determined would be most likely to influence children of school age. According to Pettis: "This alone would be the most important single factor in reducing cigarette addiction among our youth" (pp. 79–81). Pettis's bill would also give the FCC authority to regulate the total amount of cigarette advertising to protect the general health and welfare of the public. Pettis stressed the fact that the economic considerations involved in the cigarette industry should not justify the acute medical problem at hand. Even if a decline in cigarette sales did cause a major dislocation in the economy, "the restricting of cigarette advertising is more than justified by the terrible death toll extracted by cigarettes," said Pettis.

One of the most important speakers in favor of regulation was Surgeon General Stewart who represented the Department of Health, Education and Welfare and the Public Health Service. He testified that the 1965 Cigarette Labeling and Advertising Act did not adequately inform the American public of the health dangers involved in smoking. The surgeon general maintained that the present warning was not enough. "In this nation and throughout the world, scientific evidence has continued to accumulate to strengthen and confirm the 1964 conclusion that cigarette smoking is, in fact, a proved and present danger to public health" (p. 84).

At the conclusion of the hearings the House of Representatives passed a bill which was a good deal weaker than the regulations to be imposed by the FTC and FCC. The bill reflected the strength of the Southern members of the House and was referred to by Congressman Moss as a "disgraceful performance which served the tobacco industry rather than the public interest."[28] The bill, HR 6543, was favorable to the industry because it extended until June 30, 1975, the preemptive clause of the 1965 Cigarette Labeling and Advertising Act which prohibited local, state, or federal agencies from requiring any health warning in cigarette advertising. The warning label required by HR 6543 was: "Warning: The Surgeon General Has Determined That Cigarette Smoking Is Dangerous to Your Health and May Cause Lung Cancer or Other Diseases." This label, although stricter than the one currently in use, was not as harsh as the one proposed earlier by the FCC: "Warning: Cigarette Smoking Is Dangerous to Health and May Cause Death from Cancer and Other Diseases." Another provision in the bill was that nothing in the act apart from the preemption clause limited or restricted FTC authority in regulating unfair practices in the advertising of cigarettes. It also required a report from the HEW secretary within eighteen months of the enactment of the bill and annually thereafter on the health consequences of smoking. In addition it required a report from the FTC within eighteen months of enactment and annually thereafter on the effectiveness of cigarette labeling and on current practices of cigarette advertising. In the Senate, hearings before the Senate Commerce Subcommittee on Consumers were scheduled to begin on HR 6543 on July 21. Subcommittee Chairman Frank E. Moss, who threatened to filibuster the bill out of existence, predicted that discussion in the Senate would extend past the congressional August recess.

POTENTIAL IMPACT OF REGULATION

The effect of a ban on cigarette advertising would apparently have been greater on the broadcasting industry than on the tobacco industry. The tobacco companies spent about $245 million a year on radio and TV advertising. Cigarettes, the largest single product advertised on television, accounted for up to 11 percent of television advertising time.[29] The ban on advertising would result in a large cash saving by the tobacco companies and a correspondingly large loss to the broadcasting industry, both networks and independent stations. Some contended, however, that the "loss of cigarette commercials would hardly bring economic disaster to an industry already fat with profits."[30] They suggested that potential sponsors such as department stores that had never used television in a big way could

28 "Ban on Warning in Smoking Ads," *The New York Times*, June 19, 1969.

29 "Tobacco: Trouble from an Old Friend," *Time*, July 18, 1969.

30 "Cigarettes and Society: A Growing Dilemma," *Time*, April 25, 1969.

possibly fill the gap, at least in the larger agencies. In addition, the advertising business could perhaps sell the $50 million worth of free time given to antismoking commercials, a procedure that would also certainly be welcomed by the tobacco industry. However, at this point, it was not entirely certain that these anti-ads would be discontinued. Although the larger agencies could probably withstand the blow created by the ban, the smaller ones, whose cigarette clients amounted to 40 percent of their total business, would lose much more.[31] Both large and small agencies looked rather dimly on the prospect of regulation, despite helpful suggestions from supporters of the ban.

The ban would have both bad and good effects on the tobacco industry. It would be another step in the antismoking campaign which had already hurt the industry.[32] Although the effect of the antismoking campaign seemed small, it was disturbing to an industry that had no doubt counted on steadily increased growth before the surgeon general's report in 1964.

Perhaps because of this, industry members amplified their acquisition activities.[33] One company merged with a hotel and motel theater chain; another—with two recent food acquisitions—acquired a large transportation company. Still another, which owned a safety razor company, a shaving cream company, and a chewing gum company, became a distributor for an English candy firm.[34] Other industries into which the cigarette companies branched included liquor, clothing, soft drinks, and pet food. Reflecting the trend, R. J. Reynolds and American decided to drop the word "tobacco" from their corporate names.[35]

The standfast Tobacco Institute declared that "tobacco is not going to go the way of the horse and buggy in our time."[36]

Diversification, it declared, was to improve the growth potential of the industry rather than to admit that cigarettes were as hazardous as depicted. For the big companies, at least, the diversification drive was started with the long run in mind. In the short run, a ban on radio and television advertising would freeze the market rather than cut down perceptibly on cigarette sales. Many new brands would be forced out of the market and the minor brands would become smaller and smaller. But the big brands would probably get bigger.[38] Although cigarette ad bans were in effect in

[31] *Ibid.*

[32] *Ibid.*

[33] "The Bill to Ban Cigarette Ads," *San Francisco Chronicle*, July 13, 1969.

[34] "Bad News Can Mean Good Growth," *Forbes*, November 15, 1969, pp. 50–51; see also "Caution: This Meaning Is Hazardous," *Newsweek*, April 28, 1969, pp. 82–86.

[35] "Cigarettes and Society: A Growing Dilemma," *Time*, April 25, 1969.

[36] "Tobacco Plows New Fields," *Business Week*, May 17, 1969.

[37] "No Smoking on the Air," *Business Week*, February 8, 1969, p. 36.

Czechoslovakia, Denmark, France, Italy, Norway, Sweden, and Switzerland, people continued to smoke.[38] In Britain, despite the Labor government's broadcasting ban in 1966 and its magazine and newspaper ad ban in 1967, Britons continued to smoke cigarettes in record numbers. The cigarette companies would try to cut down on the harmful long-range effects by putting money into other advertising media such as print, which was protected by the First Amendment, and into games and coupons. Also, the more than $40 million not spent on television advertising could be used to alter the profit picture of the cigarette companies.

Another path that the cigarette companies would probably take if the market at home were substantially reduced would be to look to foreign markets to offset decreased domestic sales. Exports already accounted for some 26 billion cigarettes in 1968—an enterprise ironically supported by subsidies of the selfsame federal government that restricted the industry at home.[39] However, the bigger opportunities come through establishing plants overseas, arranging for foreign licensing agreements, and obtaining foreign affiliates and subsidiaries. Philip Morris already had plants in India, New Zealand, and Venezuela. Lorillard was established in Puerto Rico and was making progress in Luxemburg, Hong Kong, and South Africa.[40] It was probable that these companies and some of the others would expand their foreign operations.

If the cigarette companies were thinking of profitable substitutes as the cigarette controversy worsened, the advertising business was becoming more and more worried. During the April hearings the National Association of Broadcasters—composed of the three television networks, 400 independent television stations, and 6,272 radio stations—became apprehensive as federal action seemed to grow nearer.[41] They thought about applying their airwave code (which bans liquor ads) to cigarettes but did not want to eliminate cigarette ads altogether. One code revision would have banned physical smoking in ads, would have prohibited ads in or adjacent to children's programs, and would have eliminated all cigarette advertising between 4:00 P.M. and 9:00 P.M. with the exception of that in newscasts. However, it became doubtful that the NAB Code would actually do a good job of regulation. On June 10, the day before the House was scheduled to vote on HR 6543, Warren H. Braren, a former employee of the NAB's television and radio code authority office in New York, charged that the broadcasting industry's self-regulation had become "nothing more than

38 "Showdown in Cigarette Advertising," *The New York Times*, Sec. 6, May 4, 1969, pp. 36ff.

39 "Cigarettes and Society: A Growing Dilemma," *Time*, April 25, 1969.

40 *Ibid.*

41 "Tobacco: Trouble from an Old Friend," *Time*, July 18, 1969.

an industry defense mechanism designed to cover up selfish interests."[42] Braren said that NAB President Vincent T. Wasilewski had misled the House Interstate and Foreign Commerce Committee during hearings on HR 6543 by giving the committee the impression that the code authority was exercising vigilance over cigarette commercials when in fact it had virtually stopped reviewing them in April 1968.[43] In reply Wasilewski did not specifically rebut the NAB's failure, thereby perhaps giving some weight to Braren's charge.

Because of these events, the NAB's move less than a month later was surprising. On July 8 the Television Code Review Board of the NAB recommended that all cigarette advertising be eliminated from television by September 1, 1973.[44] The NAB's Radio Code Board followed suit.[45] The NAB plan represented hope for orderly liquidation of what was conceded to be the inevitable loss of more than $250 million a year, or 10 percent of its total advertising revenue.[46] The broadcasting industry action thus anticipated that the FCC would fix an arbitrary date for advertising cessation without regard to the tobacco and broadcasting industries' economic inconvenience.

On July 11, 1969, the broadcasting industry's fears were realized when the FTC voted to recommend that Congress ban all cigarette advertising on radio and television. The FTC had called for strong health warnings in all smoking ads on radio and television, but the report to Congress was the first time it had agreed with the FCC that the ads should be banned. The FTC reported that "in general, current cigarette advertising leaves the impression that cigarette smoking is a healthy activity and one whose risk, to the extent that it exists, can be reduced through the presence of a filter."[47] As it had previously, the commission also recommended that the stronger health warning be used.[48] The continued FTC and FCC warnings pressured both the tobacco and the broadcasting industries into action, but the NAB's plan became virtually meaningless when on July 22, 1969, the cigarette makers agreed to stop advertising on radio and television by September 1970 if granted immunity from violation of the antitrust laws.[49] They also agreed to halt broadcasting advertising any time

[42] "Go Ahead for Bill Giving Cigarette Ads a Free Hand," San Francisco Chronicle, June 11, 1969.

[43] Ibid.

[44] "New Move on TV Ads for Cigarettes," San Francisco Chronicle, July 9, 1969, p. 1.

[45] "Cigarette Ad Ban on Radio Urged," San Francisco Chronicle, July 10, 1969, p. 2.

[46] "FTC Blast at Smoking Ads," San Francisco Chronicle, July 11, 1969.

[47] "Radio–TV Cigarette Ad Ban Proposed by FTC," Los Angeles Times, July 12, 1969.

[48] Ibid.

[49] "Cigarette Makers Agree to Ban TV Ads in '70," Los Angeles Times, July 23, 1969.

after December 31, 1969, if broadcasters would cancel the current advertising contracts. In return for its concession the tobacco industry received assurance that the government would delay for two years the requirement for a stricter warning on cigarette packages. In addition, an FTC statement assured industry that if its broadcast advertising ended, the FTC would suspend, until July 1971, a plan to seek health warnings in other ads. The move by the tobacco industry seemed to reinforce the viewpoint that industry would not really be hurt by a ban on broadcasting advertising. As NAB's Wasilewski put it: "This is no great sacrifice on their part." He went on to say that cigarette companies wanted to continue advertising in every other medium, "be it newspapers, magazines, or skywriting,"[50] and he indicated that he did not know what position individual networks and broadcasters would take on current advertising contracts.

On August 9 the American Broadcasting Company rejected a proposal to let cigarette makers out of their contracts for cigarette commercials at the end of the year. ABC President Leonard H. Goldenson contended that it would discriminate against broadcasting if it had to ban smoking commercials while cigarette advertising was allowed to continue in the printed media. Following one of the earlier arguments of the tobacco industry, Goldenson stated: "If Congress is convinced that cigarette smoking represents a clear and present danger to the health of the American public, then the only direct approach to the problem is to declare cigarettes an illegal product and to bar their advertising and sale in interstate commerce."[51]

EPILOGUE

In February 1970, Dr. E. Cuyler Hammond, vice-president in charge of epidemiology and statistical research for the American Cancer Society, and Dr. Oscar Auerbach, pathologist of the Veterans Administration Hospital, East Orange, New Jersey, and New York Medical College, reported to the Cancer Society the results of their experiments on dogs taught to inhale cigarette smoke. The study found that healthy beagles inhaling unfiltered cigarette smoke twice a day for 2½ years developed lung cancer. Healthy beagles inhaling filtered cigarette smoke over the same period developed tumors in their lungs but no cancer. Beagles exposed to no cigarette smoke at all had no cancer and a lower death rate. The society pointed out that the experiment was the *first in which lung cancer had been produced in a laboratory animal that inhaled smoke as people do* and that the study "effectively refutes" the contention that smoking and lung cancer are not

---

[50] *Ibid.*

[51] "A Setback for Smoke Ad Ban," *San Francisco Chronicle*, August 9, 1969.

linked. The society cautioned that filter cigarettes are not safe and "at best only less damaging to lung tissue" than unfiltered cigarettes.[52]

A spokesman for the Tobacco Institute challenged the results of the study, contending that no parallel could be drawn "between human smoking and dogs subjected to these most stressful laboratory conditions."[53] Indeed, in May 1970 the Institute announced that it would launch a major attack against the validity of the experiments.

After the broadcasting industry's offer to phase out cigarette advertising and the cigarette manufacturers's subsequent decision to voluntarily go off the air, the legislating of cigarette advertising lost its controversial nature. In March 1970, a House–Senate conference committee agreed to a cigarette bill which was signed by the president (who had not taken sides in the earlier controversy) and which became law April 1st.

The law banned cigarette advertising on radio and television on or after January 2, 1971 (instead of January 1st—to allow the cigarette companies to take advantage of New Years' Day football game broadcasts).[54] Effective November 1, 1970 cigarette packages would have to carry the message, "Warning: The Surgeon General Has Determined that Cigaret Smoking Is Dangerous to Your Health."[55] In addition, the law gave the FTC the authority to require, after July 1971, this or other health warnings in all cigarette advertisements after giving the Congress six months notice of its intentions.

[52] "Smoking Dogs Show Cancer Link," *San Francisco Chronicle*, February 6, 1970, p. 1.

[53] *Ibid.*

[54] "House, Senate Conferees Agree to Abolish Broadcast Cigaret Ads, as of Jan. 2, 1971," *The Wall Street Journal*, March 4, 1970, p. 4.

[55] "FTC Wants Tar, Nicotine Levels Disclosed in Cigaret Ads; Makers Doubt Authority," *The Wall Street Journal*, August 10, 1970, p. 9.

II

CORPORATE INTERESTS
AND
SOCIAL AND ECONOMIC
NEEDS
OF
ETHNIC MINORITIES

A.
DISCRIMINATION

———◆———

Crown Zellerbach Corporation, San Francisco

Conflict with the Equal Employment Opportunity Clause
of the Civil Rights Act, 1964

> *I dreamed that I had died and gone to my reward,*
> *A job in heaven's textile plant on a golden boulevard,*
> *The mill was made of marble, the machines were made of gold,*
> *Nobody ever got tired, and nobody ever grew old.*

> —JOE GLAZER,
> "Song for the Workers"

INTRODUCTION

On January 30, 1968, the United States filed action against Crown Zellerbach Corporation (C-Z) and against both the International and Local 189 of the United Papermakers and Paperworkers, AFL-CIO, CLC. The suit alleged that the defendants had, both jointly and independently, engaged in employment practices that discriminated against Negroes at C-Z's Bogalusa, Louisiana, paper mill. This violated Title VII of the Civil Rights Act of 1964 and contractual obligations that C-Z had undertaken pursuant to Executive Order 11246 which ensures nondiscrimination in employment by government contractors.[1]

---

[1] Brief for the United States on appeal from the United States District Court for the Eastern District of Louisiana in the case *United States* v. *Local 189*, United Papermakers and Paperworkers, AFL-CIO, CLC; and Crown Zellerbach Corporation; No. 25956, p. 13.

In the complaint, the United States asked the district court to enjoin the local and international unions from striking. The strike was threatened to prevent C-Z from effecting certain changes in its seniority system. C-Z had agreed with the Office of Federal Contract Compliance to implement these changes in partial fulfillment of its contractual obligations to afford black employees equal employment opportunities, as required of government contractors by Executive Order 11246. The complaint also sought an order requiring that C-Z and the unions implement a seniority and recall system which would eliminate the present effects of past discrimination.[2]

The suit against C-Z came at the end of a civil rights turmoil which had been shaking the small Louisiana town of Bogalusa since early in 1965. According to *Business Week*, "Probably no major corporation, not even U.S. Steel, with its Birmingham (Ala.) problems, has had civil rights issues more forcefully thrust into its executive offices."[3] The company had always had a very favorable civil rights reputation. Former Secretary of Labor James Mitchell, when a C-Z vice-president, had even helped to organize San Francisco's Human Relations Commission.[4] Nondiscrimination had always been the traditional policy of the company, The company, therefore, was very proud of its record.

HISTORY

Bogalusa, a town in eastern Louisiana, was founded by the Great Southern Lumber Company in 1906 and grew up around one of the largest lumber mills in the world. It originated as a company town—the company owned the houses and operated the general store, the hospital, and the utility system. In time, the lumber operation shifted to pulp and paper. The lumber mill itself closed in 1938, and the properties of Great Southern were taken over by Gaylord Container Corporation of St. Louis. C-Z became a corporate resident of Bogalusa in late 1955 when it merged with Gaylord. As a result of this merger, Gaylord's large pulp and paper mill in Bogalusa and some half million acres of pine timberlands became part of the C-Z organization.[5]

The mill and its three converting plants sit literally in the middle of Bogalusa. Partly because of the summer heat and humidity, but also because of the mill, stepping into Bogalusa has been described as stepping

2 *Ibid.*, p. 14.

3 "Caught in the Civil Rights Crossfire," *Business Week*, August 7, 1965, p. 102.

4 *Ibid.*

5 "Equal Employment Opportunity in Bogalusa, Louisiana," statement delivered by Reed E. Hunt, chairman of the board of Crown-Zellerbach Corp., April 22, 1965.

into "a hot, musty cellar, where old papers, boxes and charred lumber have steeped in stagnant pools for months and years."[6] As the largest employer and industry in this community of 23,000, employing 2,900 people (including 390 blacks out of a 30 to 40 percent black population), Crown Zellerbach has been prominently identified with Bogalusa.[7]

"The racial bias was very typical of a small southern city—separate schools for the 9,000 Negroes and 14,000 whites; Negroes in the balconies of the two movie houses; separate cemeteries; separate hospitals; white restaurants off limits to Negroes; limited job opportunities to the colored."[8] In other words, "the air in Bogalusa is almost the only thing in Bogalusa that's spread around without regard to race, creed or color."[9] Violence was part of this town long before the civil rights struggle erupted. Yet, that streak of violence and meanness could also be interpreted as a streak of stubbornness. Once sides were chosen, the game was played for keeps.[10]

RACIAL BIAS IN THE PLANT—JOB ASSIGNMENT AND PROMOTION

The racial segregation practiced in the town was also practiced at the C-Z plant—separate jobs for blacks and whites, separate unions, separate facilities. Each job was absolutely restricted to either white or black employees. All jobs in several departments in the plant were restricted to white employees only. In other departments, some jobs were restricted to white employees and others to blacks. With a single exception, all the white jobs in the mixed racial departments were more highly paid and involved greater responsibility than the best job allotted to blacks.[11]

The permanent jobs in the Bogalusa mill were organized into groups known as progression lines, with the lowest paying jobs at the bottom and the highest at the top (the usual method of mill organization practiced by the paper mill industry in the United States). Generally, an employee entered a progression line at the lowest job and was promoted to the next higher job in the line. When a vacancy occurred in a line job, the incumbents immediately below competed for it. According to job seniority, the contestant who held the lower job for the longest time usually obtained the promotion. Demotions were also based on job seniority. If demotions

6 "The Smoke Hangs Heavy over Bogalusa," Jude Wanniski, *The National Observer*, July 1965.

7 Hunt, "Equal Employment Opportunity in Bogalusa, Louisiana."

8 "The Smoke Hangs Heavy over Bogalusa," *The National Observer*.

9 *Ibid.*

10 *Ibid.*

11 Brief for Local 189a, United Papermakers and Paperworkers, AFL-CIO, CLC; *U.S.* v. *Local 189*, No. 25956, p. 2.

resulted in the demotion of an employee out of the line of progression, he had the first right to return to the progression line when a vacancy occurred. The right to return was called the "recall right."[12]

In addition to the progression lines there was a labor pool, known as the extra board of permanent employees, who were available to fill temporary vacancies in the permanent jobs. A new employee was usually assigned to the extra board until a vacancy occurred in the existing jobs of the progression line, at which time the members of the extra board and employees in other progression lines would bid for the permanent assignment. The position was awarded to the qualified employee with *the greatest seniority* in the mill. Any individual previously demoted out of that particular progression line had the recall right over any other employee.[13]

The job seniority system at Bogalusa had long been in effect in paper mills throughout the country. The system, according to C-Z, particularly reflected the needs of the paper industry by ensuring the greatest amount of on-the-job training for employees before they were promoted to higher positions. Extensive training was particularly important in the paper industry where mistakes in the operation of expensive machinery could cause tremendous financial losses. In addition to the economic considerations, there were safety factors which dictated the necessity of a seniority system that maximized on-the-job training.[14]

Due to the segregation practice at the mill before the merger, there were two unions—one for whites and the other for blacks, Locals 189 and 189a respectively, with separate extra boards and separate progression lines. A new white employee, under the jurisdiction of Local 189, would be assigned to the white extra board from which he could then reach the white progression line. A black employee would fall under the jurisdiction of Local 189a which could assign him only to the black extra board from which in turn only the black progression lines could be reached. Thus, a black person could never reach a white position, regardless of how long he had worked in the plant.[15] The company had not faced such a civil rights problem before as it was relatively new to the south.

TROUBLE AT THE PLANT

The first problem C-Z encountered at the mill was not racial but a conflict with the union. When C-Z took over, the mill studies undertaken

---

[12] Brief for Crown Zellerbach Corporation, U.S. v. Local 189, No. 25956, pp. 3–4.

[13] *Ibid.*, p. 4.

[14] *Ibid.*, p. 4.

[15] *Ibid.*, p. 5.

showed that to make the mill fully competitive in the industry, it had to be extensively modernized. It was also clear that the mill was greatly over-staffed and that the work force would have to be reduced. According to the former owner of the Bogalusa radio station:

> The paperworkers had little knowledge of a real, working day. At one time or another, practically all of the men had established the habit of punching the time clock in the morning, then, either going back out and going fishing or finding a place in the building to go to sleep, and then punching out at night. This had been going for years. C-Z, therefore, not only had to modernize the mill, but the workers as well.[16]

Although the company made every effort to explain the competitive situation to the union, tensions developed when the company started its $45 million modernization program and discharged employees because of increased plant efficiency. In August 1961, the union struck the mill. It was a costly strike to the company, the employees, and the community because it lasted for seven months.

Once the strike was settled, the company moved toward a solution of the segregation problem at the plant. Not only was discrimination against company policy but, as contract supplier to the federal government, Crown Zellerbach was subject to Executive Order 11246. The order at that time required not overnight compliance but progress toward a solution. Coming off the long labor dispute, the company moved slowly to introduce to the unions the first measure to alter the accepted pattern of race relations in the community, as the matter had always been part of a union contract.[17]

On May 17, 1964, the two extra boards were merged and, under the terms of that merger, any black employee then on the extra board and any newly hired black employee was eligible to move into any progression line in the mill, including those formerly restricted to white employees.[18] Also following the strike, Bogalusa had in consecutive years its first flood, first drought, and first freeze. In May 1964, with the conflict solved at the plant, the community began to relax because it appeared that Bogalusa had finally weathered the last of its pains.[19] In fact, this summer was only the quiet before the storm, during which the city through nationwide publicity became notorious as the Ku Klux Klan center of America, and Crown

---

[16] "A Broadcaster's Nightmare," speech by Ralph Blumberg at the Deadline Club, Sigma Delta Chi Professional Chapter, New York, January 28, 1966, reproduced in *Quill*, April 1966, pp. 12–16.

[17] Hunt, "Equal Employment Opportunity in Bogalusa, Louisiana."

[18] Brief for Crown Zellerbach Corporation, p. 5.

[19] Blumberg, "A Broadcaster's Nightmare," p. 12.

Zellerbach Corporation, identified with Bogalusa, became embroiled in the civil rights struggle.

THE EXPLOSION

The civil rights movement had gathered steam in Bogalusa. To avoid trouble, the city had kept its lines of communication open to both black and Klan leaders. As the makeshift biracial committee was making no apparent progress, the blacks began to get restless and started to plead with Washington to send CORE or the NAACP into Bogalusa.[20]

The first sign of trouble was the show of strength exhibited by the Klan. As described by Ralph Blumberg, former owner of the Bogalusa radio station:

> On May 30th, 1964, the Ku Klux Klan held a huge open meeting within the city limits of Bogalusa which actually is against the law in Louisiana. They were in full regalia . . . the multi-colored hoods and white sheets, 20-foot flaming crosses, guards on horseback armed with shotguns, and about 3,000 Klansmen. The traffic that night was so heavy that the city police were out there directing traffic. Everyone in Bogalusa and the surrounding area had come to get a look at the Ku Klux Klan in action and they weren't disappointed. . . . it was quite a show. This was the Klan's way of displaying a real show of strength.[21]

The evening was not publicized by the national media and thus received only local coverage. To avoid the racial pitfalls that had torn other communities apart, six leading citizens of Bogalusa—three clergymen, the leading attorney, the editor of the newspaper, and Ralph Blumberg—invited Brooks Hays to Bogalusa to speak to the business and professional community. Mr. Hays, a former congressman and prominent Baptist layman, had seen many racial problems firsthand in the South. As he was now working for the federal government and was thus required to speak to integrated audiences, the group decided to invite eight black leaders. The mayor and the city officials refused to be associated with the plan.[22]

The Klan received knowledge of the planned meeting—the city attorney was a Klansman—and opposed the meeting, labeling Hays a communist. Through pamphlets and direct threats, the six members of the group and

[20] *Ibid.*, p. 12.
[21] *Ibid.*
[22] *Ibid.*, p. 13.

owners of facilities suitable for such a meeting were pressured to call off the meeting. Leaflets such as the following were being distributed:

> The Ku Klux Klan is strongly organized in Bogalusa and . . . being a secret organization, we have Klan members in every conceivable business in this area. We will know the names of all who are invited to the Brooks Hays meeting and we will know who did and did not attend this meeting. Accordingly, we take this means to urge all of you to refrain from attending this meeting. Those who do attend this meeting will be tagged as integrationists and will be dealt with accordingly by the Knights of the Ku Klux Klan.[23]

The Klan in this community was able to exert so much pressure and to intimidate so many people that the meeting had to be canceled. Mr. Blumberg's station broadcast an editorial critical not of the Klan or its goals but of its methods. An organized campaign of terror followed, which included threats to Blumberg's life and family. Patrol cars watched his house every night. The Klan was so effective in intimidating other businessmen in the community that all but one boycotted his station. His automobile's windows were smashed and seven bullets were fired into his radio equipment. The transmitter door was sprayed with shotgun blasts. Although he received outside contributions, he was finally forced to sell his station. The three ministers who were part of the group had already left Bogalusa. Mr. Blumberg said that the only reason he survived was because of the FBI.[24] He was later an important witness against the Klan in the 1966 hearings of the House Committee on Un-American Activities and his story received nationwide publicity.[25]

The cancellation of Hays's speech brought national publicity. *The Nation*, a liberal magazine, "exposed" Bogalusa as "Klantown" U.S.A., pinpointing it as the heart of the KKK. According to Mr. Cutrer, then mayor of Bogalusa, it was *The Nation* article that had started all the trouble.[26] The speech had been planned for January 7, 1966. In late January the local black group, the Bogalusa Civic and Voters League (advised by outside members of the Congress of Racial Equality), carried out a test of public accommodations. Although, due to the careful planning of Mayor Cutrer, the test was carried out peacefully, ten days later two CORE workers stated that they had been attacked by a mob of white men. The attack received nationwide newspaper coverage and CORE officially

---

[23] *Ibid.*

[24] *Ibid.*, p. 14.

[25] "Klan Said to Retain Its Control of Bogalusa Despite Court Order," *The New York Times*, January 6, 1966, p. 13.

[26] "The Smoke Hangs Heavy over Bogalusa," *The National Observer*.

entered the struggle.[27] In April, A. Z. Young, for fifteen years a forklift operator at the box plant of the paper mill, a former president of the black union, Local 624 of the International Brotherhood of Pulp, Sulphide and Paper Mill Workers (IBPS), and considered a militant by many people, took over as president of the Voters League.[28]

The race problems that had smoldered below the surface in Bogalusa now burst into the open. Since the first incident that brought national coverage, a week seldom went by that Bogalusa did not make headlines. Marchers participating in civil rights demonstrations were openly attacked and severely injured while the police watched.[29] The first two black deputies ever hired in the area were ambushed by night riders while on patrol; one was killed and the other critically injured.[30] A white man bent on further assault attempted to force his way into a car that was carrying an injured demonstrator and was shot by a black man. The Bogalusa park had to be closed when attempts to integrate it resulted in violence.[31]

The moderate elements and local businessmen were conspicuous by either their silence or lack of enthusiasm in helping to solve the city's racial problems and to cool the tensions between the black and white communities. Mayor Cutrer, who had claimed that a sizable number of Bogalusa's citizens were indeed moderate, nevertheless conceded privately that he was dismayed that so few ever came out to support his moderate position. Early in June 1965, a group of moderates tried to gather signatures for a statement affirming the city's belief in law and order. The project had to be abandoned for want of enough endorsers.[32] However, some eight months later, on February 24, 1966, a full-page ad appeared in the local newspaper. The ad, sponsored by 225 business firms, strongly advocated the cause of racial cooperation.

The city's moderate white businessmen had been keeping silent for fear of revenge from the Ku Klux Klan. Similarly, the black moderates failed to counsel patience for fear of being labeled "Uncle Toms," while "teachers, lawyers, physicians, and other professional people have largely kept silent because they say they would prefer not to get involved."[33] On the other

[27] "Caught in the Civil Rights Crossfire," *Business Week.*

[28] "The Smoke Hangs Heavy over Bogalusa," *The National Observer.*

[29] "U.S. Sues to Halt Bogalusa Strife," *The New York Times,* July 20, 1965, p. 16.

[30] "Moderates Fail to Aid Bogalusa," *The New York Times,* July 11, 1965, p. 1. After a lapse of over eight months, the city hired another black policeman, and the two black deputies began patrolling their area on April 1, 1966. "Negroes Put Back on Duty at Bogalusa," *Baton Rouge Morning Advocate,* April 2, 1966.

[31] "Bogalusa Mayor Very Troubled," *The New York Times,* May 24, 1965, p. 1.

[32] "Moderates Fail to Aid Bogalusa," *The New York Times,* July 11, 1965.

[33] Allan Katz, "Race Ordeal Teaches City Vital Lesson," *New Orleans States-Item,* August 11, 1965.

hand, Saxon Farmer, a Bogalusa distributor for a major oil company and a known KKK leader, said that a majority of the city's businessmen believed "whites should resort to violence if necessary to prevent desegregation."[34] What about the executives in the large plants owned by big United States corporations? According to an article by Allan Katz, a staff writer for the *New Orleans States-Item,* "A number of executives of a large plant in the area have said they have not become involved because the company does not encourage it, and besides they are transients who may be transferred at any time."[35]

As the Crown Zellerbach Corporation was prominently identified with Bogalusa, its name was constantly in the news. The Bogalusa Civic and Voters League and CORE representatives picketed the plant. They charged C-Z with discriminatory practices and specifically demanded that more black women be hired. Many black women worked as maids for three dollars a day for white women who were working in the plant for fifteen dollars a day. Because of the modernization process in the plant, women had been and were still being laid off. As per union contract and general custom in industry, the people laid off had first recall to any new opening.

Although C-Z was seldom attacked editorially, its identification with Bogalusa, the picketing outside the plant reported in the newspapers and shown on television, and the attacks on the company by representatives of civil rights groups created a mental association of C-Z with the acts of the KKK and other racist extremists.

COMMUNITY PRESSURES AT CROWN ZELLERBACH'S HOME OFFICE IN SAN FRANCISCO

The unfavorable publicity associated with the events in Bogalusa, as reported in both national and local media, brought pressure on C-Z's San Francisco headquarters. A committee of fifty-three San Francisco civil rights and religious leaders publicly urged C-Z to use its economic strength to bring racial harmony to troubled Bogalusa. However, in a stroke of reverse segregation, it was demanded that C-Z release all employees who were members of the KKK or had participated in antiracial activities such as cross burnings or beatings. The demand was made through a press conference held by the group. W. T. Ussery, a San Francisco vice-president of CORE, had earlier sent a telegram asking C-Z officials to contact President Johnson, Attorney General Katzenbach, and other state and Bogalusa

---

[34] Jack Nelson, "Some Bogalusa Whites Said to Favor Violence," *Los Angeles Times,* July 13, 1965.

[35] Katz, "Race Ordeal Teaches City Vital Lesson."

officials to press for the rights and safety of Bogalusa citizens and to appeal publicly for the end of "mob rule and control" by the Klan. It also asked for an immediate meeting with CORE officials to discuss the exact action undertaken by C-Z to ease and correct the situation.[36]

When the company did not respond to the appeals, pressure was increased by picketing C-Z's head office and by news releases from the committee, now headed by Mr. Ussery. Other civil rights groups joined in the activities. In June 1965, the Midpeninsula Catholic Interracial Council demanded that Reed E. Hunt, chairman of the board of Crown Zellerbach, be removed from the University of San Francisco Board of Regents.[37] The events received wide coverage in the Bay Area. The message in all the interviews with civil rights leaders, as reported by television, radio, and the newspapers, was always the same: Crown Zellerbach should use its economic strength in Bogalusa by taking a firm stand on civil rights and thus help to resolve many of the problems.

Besides protests, the civil rights groups also attempted to use economic boycott to pressure the company into taking a tougher stand in Bogalusa. Leaders asked Philco's Western Development Laboratories in Palo Alto to cease purchasing paper products from C-Z.[38] The NAACP, at their convention in Denver, adopted a resolution urging its members to boycott all Crown Zellerbach Corporation products because of discrimination at the company's plant at Bogalusa.[39]

CROWN ZELLERBACH'S RESPONSE

When the racial strife erupted in Bogalusa, the company was caught in a situation unfamiliar to its executives. There was no precedent that could be used as an example for action. The company to some extent had to improvise.[40]

R. R. Ferguson, a Canadian with a background in production who was sent to the mill in 1964 as resident manager, believed that the company did not have the right to run the town or the right to tell the people what their community and social policies should be and how they should conduct themselves. He believed that the company should comply with civil rights legislation but that management should take part in community affairs as

[36] "Caught in the Civil Rights Crossfire," *Business Week*.

[37] "Ouster of USF Regent," *Palo Alto Times*, June 22, 1965.

[38] *Ibid*.

[39] "NAACP Urges Zellerbach Corporation Boycott," *San Francisco Chronicle*, July 4, 1965, p. 1A.

[40] "Caught in the Civil Rights Crossfire," *Business Week*.

individuals.[41] Since the start of the strife in January 1965, he had spent half his time on civil rights problems inside and outside the mill.[42]

Much of his activity consisted of meeting with all kinds of groups, with these meetings usually being open. He explained his policy to the white union group as follows:

> We offer jobs in the mill on a nondiscriminatory basis. This is a national policy. This is a company policy. It is a fair policy. . . . There are those who want us to tell you what to do . . . to dictate a program of social reform here, to lay down the law at Bogalusa. . . . We will not do this.[43]

Ferguson felt that such appearances were effective because C-Z was the largest employer and C-Z's explanation of the requirements of the law would have an effect.[44]

Ferguson also helped to organize a broadly based Community Affairs Committee, which eventually included six C-Z officials, to advise the mayor and city council. It was difficult to form the group in Bogalusa because few wanted to become publicly involved. The committee succeeded in getting the other members and the mayor, Cutrer, a white moderate, to accept a few proposals. It also attempted to persuade restaurants to serve blacks but failed to obtain unanimity.[45]

At the same time, a process was underway to integrate the facilities at the plant, such as locker rooms, rest rooms, pay lines, and so forth, to meet the civil rights deadline of July 2, 1965, set by the federal government under the Civil Rights Act of 1964.[46] The old traditions of segregation were hard to change. When the company ordered a concessionaire operating on the plant's property to integrate, whites stopped eating there, and within a few days the operator went out of business.[47]

At the company's national headquarters in San Francisco, management had to decide how to balance Ferguson's position at the plant against the posture of Crown Zellerbach as an internationally known company. At times the possibility of taking strong action to protect the good civil rights reputation of the company was considered. One of the possibilities discussed was "to send a task force to Bogalusa and take a firm pro-civil rights

[41] Ibid.
[42] Ibid.
[43] Ibid.
[44] Ibid.
[45] Ibid.
[46] Hunt, "Equal Employment Opportunity in Bogalusa, Louisiana."
[47] "Caught in the Civil Rights Crossfire," Business Week.

stand with the local people." The company decided, however, that it had
to back its manager "wholeheartedly," and he, in turn, was strongly supporting Mayor Cutrer, whose moderate stand drew fire from both sides.
The decision meant that the company would not use its economic weight
to force desirable social objectives. According to Hunt, "the surest way to
get into trouble in a community is to set yourself up as a political leader.
. . . This office is not going to dictate to a community 2,000 miles away."[48]

Because of this policy of noninterference by the home office in local
community affairs and the "peremptory tone" of the wire sent by Mr.
Ussery, C-Z's management in San Francisco had decided to ignore it, along
with other messages and phone calls sent from CORE. When the company received a letter from the Committee for Concern for Bogalusa (the
San Francisco civil rights group), of which Mr. Ussery was now chairman,
Crown Zellerbach president Peter T. Sinclair wrote to Ussery stating the
company's support of the civil rights act and pointing out that C-Z officials
in Bogalusa had signed a statement the previous day calling for "restraint"
and expressing support for the mayor.

Sinclair's letter drew more demands for meetings and discussions on
points outlined by CORE and the committee. The company continued to
refuse to meet with the San Francisco groups, which they held to be acting
in bad faith, having used the meeting with C-Z only as a tool to strengthen
the hands of the Bogalusa blacks in dealing with the mayor.[49]

To answer attacks on the company made by the civil rights groups, Hunt
appeared on a news program and stated company policy regarding Bogalusa:

> The committee wants us to dictate a program of social reform. We
> do not think that this is the proper function of a private corporation
> and we do not propose to dictate to any community, San Francisco or
> Bogalusa. . . . So far as civil rights issues are concerned, we feel that
> a private company should deal with them in ways which are appropri-
> ate to its role as a private employer in the community.[50]

The declaration of company policy received wide coverage. To clear the
situation further, a statement delivered at the company's Annual Share
Owner's Meeting in San Francisco, April 22, 1965, was mailed to company
stockholders. In the statement, the company's basic position was again
outlined as well as the company's emphasis on equal employment opportunity, with the following addition:

[48] Ibid.
[49] Ibid.
[50] "Company's 'Hands Off' Policy in Racial Strife," San Francisco Examiner, March
6, 1965, p. 8.

But we recognize that we have wider responsibilities and obligations in Bogalusa. These take the form of support for community institutions, support of law and order, living up to the requirements of good corporate citizenship. We are members of the Community Affairs Committee. We have expressed our point of view. We will continue to voice our opinions within this democratic forum. We listen to the opinions of others and we hope we will be listened to.

The company will do its part. We will cooperate to the utmost, in ways which are appropriate to a private corporation. We have every confidence in the integrity of the people of Bogalusa and that, given the facts, they will so conduct themselves as to reflect credit on the community.[51]

Crown Zellerbach also rejected the request that the company fire Klan members or those participating in violent acts against blacks. Ferguson, the plant manager, had rejected such steps, stating: "An employee's private life is his own. . . . If he comes into conflict with civil authorities, they take over." Mr. Hunt, as the chairman of the board, agreed with Mr. Ferguson and pointed out that the president and the vice-president of the Bogalusa Civic and Voters League, A. Z. Young and R. Hicks, had continued to work at the plant.[52] The company had also stated that "discharging an employee for membership in outside organizations, especially employees covered by labor contracts, is another question. Dismissal of the employee under such circumstances has been construed as unfair and discriminatory."[53]

The company's response was not satisfactory to the civil rights groups, which increased their pressure through the sit-ins and threatened boycotts. The demonstrations and civil rights activities in front of the C-Z headquarters received wide newspaper coverage in the Bay Area while the violence of the civil rights struggle in the South was being broadcast via national media. On July 6, 1965, C-Z agreed to meet in Bogalusa with the Civic and Voters League of Bogalusa to discuss company policy.[54] With the agreement to meet with the Bogalusa civil rights groups, tension in San Francisco subsided.

The meeting took place on July 15. Before the meeting, the two major international unions representing the production employees in the Bogalusa plant issued public statements calling attention to "their exclusive rights to bargain with the company under the provisions of the National Labor Relations Act." They further emphasized the responsibilities and

[51] Hunt, "Equal Employment Opportunity in Bogalusa, Louisiana."

[52] "Caught in the Civil Rights Crossfire," Business Week.

[53] "Coast Unit Fights Louisiana Racism," The New York Times, March 6, 1965, p. 9.

[54] "C-Z Will Meet with Rights Unit," San Francisco Examiner, July 8, 1965, p. 4.

obligations of organized labor under Title VII of the Civil Rights Act, which applied equally to employers and unions.[55] In a joint statement released after the meeting, both sides expressed the feeling that the discussion had been a "useful exchange of views."[56]

On July 30, 1965, the company released another statement which was a sequel to the one of April 22, 1965. The company again stressed adherence to the civil rights legislation and pointed out that because of the integration of the extra board both blacks and whites had worked on temporary assignment in every progression line in the mill. The pamphlet also pointed out that:

> Equal opportunity as it applies to new hires can be an empty phrase if jobs themselves are not available. . . . During the past years only white women have been hired for hourly production jobs in the bag and box plants. The continuing reduction in the work force has decreased the number of women employed in these operations. Women production employees who were laid off have the contractual right to be recalled to work before any additional new workers can be hired.
>
> We can conclude, therefore, that the principle of equal employment opportunity alone will not be sufficient to solve the long-range employment situation in Bogalusa. In the absence of new industry the community faces the prospect of a declining rate of employment.[57]

To show the company's good faith in its intent to deal with segregation at the plant, two clerical openings had been filled by black women.[58]

While the company was struggling at its headquarters with the racial problem, the intensity of the strife in Bogalusa was increasing. CORE, at its twenty-first annual convention, voted to make a major assault against segregation in Bogalusa. The delegates unanimously passed a resolution urging its members "to go to Bogalusa and stay as long as necessary." The resolution also authorized "full legal assistance" for civil rights workers in Bogalusa. The chief aim of the demonstrations was to end police brutality, obtain jobs for blacks in Bogalusa stores, and win broader employment opportunities for women.[59] A further complaint was that although the new nondiscriminatory policies dealt fairly with new employees, they did

[55] Reed E. Hunt, "Crown Zellerbach, Bogalusa and Civil Rights," sequel to the statement of April 22, 1965 (Annual Share Owner's meeting).

[56] Ibid.

[57] Ibid.

[58] Ibid.

[59] "CORE Will Seek Jobs in Bogalusa," The New York Times, July 4, 1965, Sec. 7, p. 4.

nothing for older black employees who were held back by the company's former policies.[60]

The civil rights organizations were not the only ones preparing for new pressures. Representatives of the National States Rights party, a front of the KKK, held rallies at the edge of town. The meetings attracted crowds up to two thousand out of the town population of twenty-three thousand, of which 30 to 40 percent were black. One representative made the following statement to the crowd:

> The nigger is not a human being. He is somewhere between the white man and the ape. We don't believe in tolerance. We don't believe in getting along with our enemy. Every time a nigger gets a job, that's one more job that you can't have.[61]

The ensuing marches, demonstrations, and counterdemonstrations grew in violence and intensity. On July 10, Federal Court Judge Herbert W. Christenberry enjoined the Bogalusa police from using violence or threats of violence to prevent blacks from exercising their civil rights. He further ordered the police "to protect Negroes and other civil rights advocates from harassment by white townspeople."[62] Fuming about the federal court injunction, one officer of the Bogalusa police department tore up one of the law-and-order stickers, stamped on it, and declared: "A nigger is a nigger and that's what he's gonna be till I die."[63]

By mid-July, the violence had increased to such an extent that both the city council and the civil rights leaders in Bogalusa appealed directly to President Johnson for assistance. Although the president declared that the Bogalusa problem was a local community matter, he sent the chief of the civil rights division of the U.S. Justice Department, John Doar, to represent the federal government in working out a solution.[64]

John Doar arrived in Bogalusa on July 15 at the height of the struggle. The civil rights advocates had just rejected a proposed thirty-day cooling-off period, explaining on the Huntley-Brinkley NBC network news:

> Let them quit shooting and killing and knocking and beating and refusing us for thirty days. Let them cool off for thirty days. If they want to bring peace to town, tell them to open the parks for thirty days, feed us for thirty days, integrate the schools for thirty days. Let

[60] "Negroes Resume Bogalusa Drive," *The New York Times*, July 8, 1965, p. 19.

[61] "Moderates Fail to Aid Bogalusa," *The New York Times*, July 11, 1965, p. 1.

[62] "U.S. Court Enjoins Bogalusa Police," *The New York Times*, July 11, 1965, p. 1.

[63] "Some Bogalusa Whites Said to Favor Violence," *Los Angeles Times*, July 13, 1965, p. 5.

[64] R. E. Hunt, "Crown Zellerbach, Bogalusa and Civil Rights."

them do something for a change. The black man in America has been giving and giving and giving for five hundred years. And, baby, we've given all we've got. There ain't no more left.[65]

The confrontation of the two opposing forces was again receiving national coverage—television, newspapers, and radio. The White House also named Lee White, a presidential counsel, to serve as special adviser to Mr. Johnson on developments in Bogalusa.[66]

On July 19, the attorney general initiated in the Federal District Court in New Orleans a program of broad legal action against three local law enforcement officials, the Original Knights of the Ku Klux Klan, and thirty-five white extremists to halt the racial violence. The three law enforcement officers were the Public Safety Commissioner, Police Chief Claxton Knight of Bogalusa, and a deputy sheriff of the county.[67] The two Bogalusa officials were later found to be in criminal contempt of court for not obeying the injunction of July 10 ordering them to protect civil rights demonstrators. The action against the Klan and the other group was to restrain them from threatening or assaulting civil rights workers or intimidating public officials and businessmen.[68]

Following the injunctions against the Klan and other white extremists and the contempt trial of the city officials and other law enforcement officers, the intensity of the struggle decreased. Marches for integration of schools, boycotts, and picketing of Bogalusa businesses—including Crown Zellerbach—to obtain more jobs continued. By the fall of 1965, the civil rights groups had made some progress in such areas as housing, street lighting, and integration of restaurants and other facilities, but they had failed to make serious headway in the area of employment.[69]

Bogalusa, as part of the civil rights struggle, continued to get attention from the national media. Drew Pearson, on his program from Newark, New Jersey, which was carried over a number of stations, commented:

> After all the civil rights demonstrations in Bogalusa lasting all summer, here is the net result. Two Negroes have been hired on the police force, seven children are in the schools, and one extra woman is working at the Crown Zellerbach Paper Company. Crown Zellerback could have improved the situation, but it didn't.[70]

[65] "Federal Government Intervenes," Huntley-Brinkley Report, NBC, July 15, 1965, Radio TV Reports, Inc.

[66] "Bogalusa Plans Parley on Crisis," *The New York Times*, July 10, 1965, p. 9.

[67] "U.S. Sues to Halt Bogalusa Strife," *The New York Times*, July 20, 1965, p. 1.

[68] "Two Bogalusa Aids Held in Contempt," *The New York Times*, July 30, 1965, p. 1.

[69] "Mix Strife Leaves Scars on City," *New Orleans States–Item*, August 9, 1965, p. 1.

[70] "Drew Pearson," WVNJ and other stations; September 12, 1965, Radio TV Reports, Inc.

Walter Cronkite on CBS Evening News also discussed Bogalusa; correspondent Bert Quint reported:

> They are picketing in Bogalusa, picketing for what civil rights leaders here say is the best Christmas gift of them all, a decent job that anyone, black man or white, can be proud of.
> They have been boycotting the downtown stores for months without notable progress in their drive to get them to hire Negro clerks.[71]

In the latter part of 1965 an agreement was reached at the plant which provided an additional method by which black employees could obtain entry jobs in white lines of progression. Under the agreement, employees in black lines could compete on the basis of mill seniority for white entry jobs without first returning to the extra board and sacrificing accrued seniority against reductions in the work force. However, regardless of the length of time the successful black bidder had spent in a black job or in the plant (according to the job seniority system in force), when transferring into the white line, he was no better off for purposes of future promotions or demotions in that line than the newest white employee in the line. Although the agreement provided a new opportunity for the black employees, in practice the potential transfer was associated with considerable risk.[72]

CROWN ZELLERBACH AND U.S. GOVERNMENT AGENCIES

In late 1965 a newly organized federal agency, the Equal Employment Opportunity Commission (EEOC), created under Title VII of the Civil Rights Act, entered the civil rights struggle. The agency charged that the system of promotion and demotion was still discriminatory.[73] On December 18, 1965, the company and the unions agreed on a new proposal which was enacted on January 16, 1966, and provided for the merger of some of the white progression lines with functionally related black progression lines. In theory, the merger was to provide access by promotion to higher-paying white jobs that bore a functional relationship to lower-paying black jobs. Once the merger was effected, the job seniority system would continue to operate.[74]

[71] "Walter Cronkite, CBS Evening News," December 7, 1965, Radio TV Reports, Inc.

[72] Brief for the U.S., p. 9.

[73] "F.D.R. Jr., Blasts Race Question on Promotion," *New Orleans States–Item*, December 18, 1965, p. 1.

[74] Brief for the U.S., p. 10.

The union's resistance to change was seen by many as a principal barrier to harmony in Bogalusa. On C-Z's initiative, the unions met in New Orleans with the EEOC and the above agreement was reached. Franklin D. Roosevelt, Jr., son of the late president and chairman of the commission, came himself to work toward an agreement. The unions' agreement came despite the presence of Ku Klux Klansmen on the executive board of the plant's main local.[75] Given the obstacles, the agreement has hailed as a major step forward and a breakthrough in Deep South racial employment patterns, and Roosevelt congratulated Crown Zellerbach and the union leadership for making a major contribution to the Welfare of the country.[76]

Although the agreement worked out under the auspices of the EEOC was hailed as a major breakthrough, the black workers at the plant rejected the new plan of dovetailing the progression lines by a vote of 162–0, declaring that the company had merged only two of the eleven lines of job progression.[77] Furthermore, the order in which jobs were placed in the merged progression lines was based on rates. This resulted in all but two of the newly merged lines having the highest-paying black jobs placed below the lowest-paying, entry-level white jobs. The lowest-paid, most junior position held by a white employee was placed for the purpose of promotion and demotion above the highest-paid, most senior position held by a black employee.[78]

Access to the newly opened white lines of progression was further inhibited by the contract recall right. Because of the reduction in force, many white employees who had formerly worked for some time in the white progression lines had been demoted but continued to hold recall rights to those jobs that were formerly entry jobs to the white progression lines. The presence of these recall rights meant that a vacancy in a former white entry job that now fell in the *middle* of the merged line would not be filled by the most senior black employee in the job below the vacant job as long as there was a white employee with a recall right to that job. The white employee could exercise that recall right regardless of whether the black employee had more mill seniority. Despite the structural changes in the lines of progression, the incumbent black employee therefore had little chance to compete for the better-paying and more desirable white positions.[79]

The local black civil rights organizations continued to demonstrate in

[75] "EEOC Considers Bogalusa Efforts as Step Forward," *Morning Advocate*, Baton Rouge, January 29, 1966, p. 2A.

[76] "Hiring Violation Is Charged at Bogalusa Mills," *The Washington Post*, January 29, 1966, p. 2.

[77] *Ibid*.

[78] Brief for the U.S., p. 10.

[79] *Ibid*., pp. 10–11.

Bogalusa for their goals, which included more employment at the C-Z mill, and CORE and other groups continued to support the local efforts to focus attention on the civil rights movement. Although the civil rights marches continued and the Klan continued to hold its meetings and marches, the frequency of confrontations and the intensity of the struggle had somewhat diminished, partially because of the protection afforded civil rights personnel and black marchers by the local and state police. The marches, did, however, continue to focus public attention on Bogalusa, Crown Zellerbach, and the civil rights struggle.

CROWN ZELLERBACH AND THE OFCC

The Office of Federal Contract Compliance (OFCC), placed under the secretary of labor by Executive Order 11246, was responsible for achieving nondiscrimination in employment by government contractors. On February 8, 1967, the director of the OFCC wrote to C-Z alleging, among other things, that C-Z was "operating racially segregated but functionally related progression lines" and "permitting discriminatory use of recall and seniority rights,"[80] although C-Z had implemented all requirements and suggestions made by the EEOC. The OFCC demanded that C-Z implement a newly conceived and hitherto untried combination seniority system under which promotions within the lines of progression would be based on a combination of an employee's job and plant seniority.[81] The OFCC threatened to terminate C-Z's contract with the government and debar the company from further contracts.[82]

Meetings were held regarding the seniority procedure during March 1967, which representatives of other government departments attended, including the Justice Department and EEOC. Although the subject discussed was part of the collective bargaining agreement between C-Z and the unions and was usually recognized by the courts to be a matter commonly restricted to collective bargaining, the unions were not allowed to participate because the OFCC "did not recognize the right of the union to participate."[83] However, at the insistence of the company, which brought eleven local union leaders—black and white—to Washington, D.C., at its own expense, the union representatives were allowed to sit in, but not participate in, one of the meetings. On March 19, 1967, C-Z agreed to

---

[80] Brief on Behalf of Local 189, United Papermakers and Paperworkers, AFL-CIO, CLC; and its International v. U.S.; No. 25956, p. 7.

[81] Brief on Behalf of Crown Zellerbach, p. 7.

[82] Ibid.

[83] Brief on Behalf of Local 189, p. 8.

"bargain in good faith with the unions to secure their acceptance of the OFCC mill-plus-job seniority proposal." The unions were not permitted to be a party to the agreement under the OFCC's rule.[84]

During March 1967, C-Z made an alternative proposal under which blacks would be given seniority credit dating back to July 2, 1965, the effective date of the Civil Rights Act. Under the proposal, according to a six-year projection, 235 advances in the line would be made by black employees against 204 advances under strict seniority as against 278 advances under the new and untried combination system devised by OFCC. The OFCC rejected the C-Z proposal.[85]

When no progress had been made on the negotiation during April, after C-Z and the OFCC had signed the agreement on March 19, 1967, "the OFCC by letter alleged that Crown was in violation of the March 19 agreement and a memorandum was circulated to the heads of all government agencies, directing their contracting officers to consult with OFCC before awarding any government contract to Crown."[86] This memo was withdrawn the following month.

On June 16, 1967, a new contract was signed, again without union participation, between C-Z and the OFCC.[87]

The system proposed by the OFCC constituted a radical departure from the system of progression prevailing in the industry throughout the United States and Canada. According to C-Z:

> The mill-plus-job seniority proposal was developed by the OFCC staff without the benefit of sufficient information as to how it would operate at the Bogalusa mill and without consultation with experts in industrial relations. Under the OFCC formulation, the system would not only govern the promotion of Negro employees who had suffered discrimination, but it would also operate in progression lines in which there were no Negro employees thereby governing the promotion of white employees who were competing only against other white employees.[88]

Concurrent with the OFCC–C-Z negotiations, black employees of the Bogalusa plant were filing suit in the federal district court, charging Crown Zellerbach Corporation with racial discrimination in employment practices. At the same time marches in the Bogalusa area again drew the attention of the national media.[89]

---

[84] *Ibid.*, p. 8.
[85] *Ibid.*, p. 9.
[86] Brief on Behalf of Local 189, p. 9.
[87] *Ibid.*, p. 10.
[88] Brief on Behalf of Crown Zellerbach, p. 6.
[89] "Suit Charges Bias in Bogalusa Mills," *The New York Times*, July 30, 1967, p. 45.

C-Z intended to put the OFCC proposal of the combination seniority into the negotiations for a new union contract (the current contract was to expire August 1, 1967). About July 1, 1967, C-Z and the union began bargaining for a replacement collective agreement. As expected, part of C-Z's proposal to the union, in accordance with its agreement with the OFCC, was the combination seniority system for promotion and demotion in the plant. Despite intensive bargaining extending into the latter part of August, C-Z was unable to secure union acceptance on the changes in the seniority system, although the parties had agreed upon some 150 items, including many of those contained in the agreement between C-Z and OFCC. Thereafter, the membership of Local 189 voted 777–14 to strike and Local 189a voted 82–51 to strike. On September 7, 1967, the unions notified C-Z that the strike would begin on September 19.[90]

On September 9, 1967, seven sticks of dynamite taped together in what appeared to be a home-made bomb, hidden in a brown paper bag, were discovered in a locker room of the mill. The fuse had been lit but had gone out. Although the plant had generally been integrated, the locker and the shower room had continued to be segregated. The rooms had been de-segregated in April upon OFCC demand, but white employees had turned in their keys, thus creating a black washroom. White employees no longer showered at the plant. The FBI was called in to investigate.[91]

The strike was avoided when the two parties with the aid of a representative of the Federal Mediation and Conciliation Service reached an agreement on a new contract September 18. The new contract, however, did not include an agreement by the union to accept the combination seniority system proposed by the OFCC. Instead, C-Z and the union agreed to leave the issue open to further collective bargaining. Because of the mill's economic importance in the community—and having experienced a long strike in the early sixties—the agreement was received with much relief in Bogalusa.[92] The members of Local 189a, the black union, abstained from voting on the acceptance of the contract proposal until the seniority provisions were negotiated.[93]

Negotiations on the combination seniority issue resumed in early November with the parties reaching an alternative proposal suggested by the union. As before, the OFCC found the new proposal unacceptable. "Despite Crown's persistent effort to secure union acceptance of the mill-plus-job seniority proposal,"[94] the OFCC still threatened to debar C-Z

90 *Ibid.*, p. 11.

91 "Dynamite Is Discovered in Bogalusa Mill," *Sunday Advocate*, Baton Rouge, September 10, 1967.

92 Brief on Behalf of Crown Zellerbach, p. 6.

93 "C-Z, Union to Sign Pact," *Bogalusa Daily News*, September 17, 1967.

94 Brief on Behalf of Crown Zellerbach, p. 8.

from government contracts if the company was unable to secure an agreement from the unions by December 9, 1967. C-Z was thus caught between a union-threatened strike and an OFCC debarment.[95] The uppermost concern in the minds of the C-Z officials at that time was the possibility of another "prior consultation" memo such as the one the OFCC had issued in May, which the company felt was an attempt to deprive it of government business without due process.

To extricate itself, C-Z and the union filed actions in the United States District Court for the District of Columbia against the secretary of labor, W. Willard Wirtz, and Edward C. Sylvester of the OFCC. The court issued a temporary restraining order on December 12, 1967, and a preliminary injunction on January 2, 1968, restraining the defendants from imposing sanctions on C-Z without first granting it a hearing.[96]

On January 3, 1968, C-Z entered into an agreement with OFCC by which it committed itself to install unilaterally the mill-plus-job seniority system. (C-Z reserved the right to contest the legality of the OFCC's action.) Under the provisions of the new labor contract, C-Z notified the unions on January 16, 1968, that it would institute the system requested by the OFCC on February 1, 1968. The unions in turn voted to strike on that same date to prevent the institution of the new system and thus prevent any change of the "job seniority system" in force prior to the OFCC action.[97]

On January 30, 1968, the United States filed action against Crown Zellerbach Corporation and Local 189, alleging that "the defendants had both jointly and independently engaged in employment practices which discriminated against Negroes on account of their race at the paper mill in Bogalusa." The complaint also asked the court to "enjoin the Local and International unions from engaging in a threatened strike in order to prevent the implementation by Crown of certain changes in the seniority system." An order restraining a strike was issued on January 31, 1968, and the mill job seniority system was placed into effect on February 1, 1968.[98]

ARGUMENTS IN COURT

During the hearings starting on March 20, 1968, the following issues were to be decided:

[95] *Ibid.*
[96] *Ibid.*
[97] *Ibid.*
[98] *Ibid.*, p. 9.

(a) Whether, under the facts and circumstances of this case, the job seniority system which was in effect at the Bogalusa paper mill prior to February 1, 1968 was unlawful.

(b) If the answer to the above question is in the affirmative, what is the necessary or appropriate standard or guideline for identifying the seniority of employees for purposes of promotion and demotion?[99]

THE GOVERNMENT'S ARGUMENT

As expected, the government argued that the seniority system then in effect was discriminatory, but instead of requesting the implementation of the job-plus-mill seniority system, the government demanded that promotions and demotions should be made strictly on the basis of yet another new and untried seniority system—mill seniority. During the six weeks after February 1, the job-plus-mill seniority system had proved itself useless, "causing whites to jump whites and Negroes to jump Negroes without significant advancement of Negroes to higher paying jobs."[100] Therefore the Justice Department, through its representative, demanded mill seniority (that is, length of in-plant service) as a criterion for promotion and demotion. To prove the job seniority in force at the plant unlawful, it argued as follows:

Because, in the past, Negro employees were assigned to the lower-paying, less desirable jobs and white employees were assigned to higher-paying, more desirable jobs, a system of "job seniority" deprives Negro employees of the opportunity to compete with their white contemporaries for the higher-paying, more desirable, previously white jobs; for the white employee receives credit for the period of time he served in the white lines of progression and white jobs, at a time when Negro employees were denied access to these jobs. Indeed, as we have shown more fully in the Statement above, the result of the merger of the lines of progression in January, 1966, was to make virtually all the Negro employees in the plant, including those with 20 or 30 years of service, junior for the purposes of promotion, transfer and demotion, to the most junior white employees. The main issue for decision here is whether such a seniority system which, although racially neutral on its face, perpetuates the results in present and future discrimination, is lawful under the equal opportunity requirements of Title VII of the Civil Rights Act of 1964 and the

[99] Brief on Behalf of U.S., p. 15.
[100] Brief on Behalf of Local 189, p. 12.

contractual obligations imposed by and pursuant to Executive Order 11246.

. . . The fundamental proposition underlying . . . the government's position in this and similar cases is that Title VII of the Civil Rights Act and Executive Order 11246 cast upon those subject to their provisions not merely the duty to follow racially neutral employment policies in the future, but also an obligation to correct and revise any practices which would perpetuate into the period of time subsequent to their effective dates the racially discriminatory policy pursued prior thereto. In our view, the discrimination prohibited includes not merely conduct which directly or expressly distinguishes among employees on the basis of race, but also practices which appear to be even-handed on their face, but which in actual effect, perpetuate past racially discriminatory practices . . .

. . . While past discriminatory conduct is not *eo ipso* a violation, its deliberate absorption as an integral part of a policy implemented or continued after the effective date of the Act warrants judicial relief. . . .[101]

In conclusion, the government's argument can be stated briefly in one sentence:

The "Job Seniority" system in effect at the Defendant Crown Zellerbach's Bogalusa paper mill prior to February 1, 1968, was unlawful because it perpetuated the effects of prior racially discriminatory practices and resulted in present and future discrimination.[102]

As can be seen, the government in its argument does not deal with the advantages of the present job seniority system or with the potential dangers of changing an industry-wide system but only with discriminatory policies and discriminatory effects of the current system.

CROWN ZELLERBACH'S ARGUMENT

Crown Zellerbach's argument can be divided into three parts:

1. Because while the action was pending the government demanded mill seniority rather than the mill-plus-job seniority system which had been agreed upon by C-Z and OFCC, it had repudiated the

---

[101] Brief on Behalf of U.S., pp. 17–19, 21.
[102] *Ibid.*, p. 17.

contract with C-Z. The court therefore should return the parties to the time when the job seniority system was in effect prior to the filing of the complaint by OFCC.[103]

2. The government case has never implied "that the job seniority system in effect . . . prior to February 1, 1968 was adopted for discriminatory practices."[104]

The system was adopted at a time when the progression lines were either under the exclusive jurisdiction of Local 189 or Local 189a. As there was at that time no competition between white and black employees within the progression lines, "it is obvious that the job seniority system was adopted for legitimate business purposes rather than for racial consideration."[105] The job seniority system was therefore not illegal at that time, and therefore the continuation of the system cannot be illegal.

3. The job seniority system was not chosen at random or for any reason but valid business purposes. Dr. Northrup, an expert witness called by C-Z, "testified that the job seniority system was the seniority system generally found throughout the country in the paper industry."[106] He further testified that the job seniority system "maximizes the training of employees given in one job before promotion to a higher job, and in most instances maximizes the training of employees in the higher jobs to which they will be promoted."[107] He continued by stating that "there are particular characteristics of the paper mill which make this [job] seniority system most appropriate in the paper industry: a paper mill contains very expensive and highly sophisticated machinery which when operated improperly can cause tremendous financial losses."[108] The testimony of Dr. Northrup was not contradicted at the trial.[109]

LOCAL 189's ARGUMENT

The union of white employees, Local 189, argued somewhat the same as C-Z had previously, stressing the importance of retaining the job seniority system:

[103] Brief on Behalf of Crown Zellerbach, p. 19.
[104] *Ibid.*, p. 23.
[105] *Ibid.*
[106] *Ibid.*, p. 21.
[107] *Ibid.*
[108] *Ibid.*, p. 22.
[109] *Ibid.*

1. It pointed out that the job seniority system was not inherently discriminatory and its use was not to continue discrimination but to continue accepted labor practices.

2. To change the seniority system to grant preferential employment rights to Negroes would be to contravene the intent of Congress by applying the statute retroactively.[110]

3. The job seniority system was developed in part on considerations of safety, as testified by Mr. Vrataric, an expert witness called by the defendant union.[111]

The union's argument was best reflected in the emotional appeal made, part of which was as follows:

In its zeal to eliminate one type of injustice Congress clearly did not intend to establish a right of racial preference or to create another and all-pervasive injustice for other employees. . . .

Selective compassion for one group at the expense of another group by inept and amateur tinkering with a seniority system concededly not inherently discriminatory and standard in the paper industry, not only fails in this instance to guarantee the legitimate aspirations of the Negro employees; it also tends to reduce wholesome efficiency of plant operations and to alienate further other employees whose reasonable expectations of job progression are destroyed.

Through the collective bargaining efforts of this Union the lowest rate of pay at Bogalusa for a newly hired unskilled common laborer is now $2.69 an hour, substantially higher than the average rates of pay in most other industries in the South.

Governmental imposition of a seniority system which ignores the factors of efficiency, safety and the reasonable expectations of other employees in order to give preferential treatment to Negroes will in the long run only exaggerate the feeling of frustration and inadequacy which a culturally disadvantaged group may experience as its members struggle to qualify for jobs for which their previous job training and literacy have not qualified them. It is of dubious value to colored and white men alike in the Bogalusa area if misguided manipulations of the seniority system ultimately force the employer into a personnel policy which excludes all but the better educated from opportunities for employment. . . .

. . . Equal employment opportunity has existed at Bogalusa since May of 1964; equal employment in any society cannot be mandated

---

[110] Brief on Behalf of Local 189, p. 22.
[111] Brief on Behalf of Crown Zellerbach, p. 21.

for any one group at the expense of another and Congress did not so intend.[112]

LOCAL 189A'S ARGUMENT

As the hearing affected the members of the union of black employees, and as cases against C-Z and Local 189 on charges of discrimination were pending, the Judge also decided to hear the arguments from the representatives of Local 189a. Their arguments were similar to those of the Justice Department with special emphasis on the following three points:

1. They conceded that Congress did not require reverse discrimination for wrongs committed prior to the act. But in their opinion, neither did Congress intend "to freeze an entire generation of Negro employees into discriminatory patterns that existed before the act."[113] The continuation of the present job seniority system, in their opinion, would result in such a freezing through no fault of their own, but because of their color.

2. They further conceded "that if job seniority was necessary to the proper operation of the plant, Title VII would provide no obstacle to its continued use, regardless of the effect on Negro employees."[114] If the role of the job seniority system was to ensure that the senior man was sufficiently prepared for the promotion, then the seniority system could be replaced by a requirement that "a man must spend a given amount of time in a job before he is eligible to compete for promotion."[115] The length of time would be determined by the difficulty of learning each job. Given the implementation of such a "residence requirement" the job seniority would no longer be required for the efficient running of the plant and the mill seniority system could be introduced.

3. Irrespective of what system was used for promotion "the collective bargaining agreement between the parties reserves to C-Z the paramount right to deny a promotion to any employee, if he is not 'equally capable and efficient' as any other employee eligible for promotion, regardless of his seniority."[116] The company was therefore, never obligated to advance any employee until it was convinced that the employee was qualified for the promotion and

---

[112] Brief on Behalf of Local 189, pp. 35–37.

[113] Brief for Local 189a, United Papermakers and Paperworkers, AFL-CIO, CLC; David Johnson, Sr., and Anthony Hill; 189a v. 189 and C-Z, p. 24.

[114] Ibid., p. 29.

[115] Ibid., p. 30.

[116] Ibid., p. 32.

thus would not endanger the efficiency of the plant operation or the safety of fellow employees.

CONCLUSION

To summarize the arguments:

The thrust of the government's argument was the acceptance of a seniority system to provide the greatest chance of advancement of black employees to better and higher-paying jobs, regardless of the desires of the parties to the collective bargaining agreement. The mill seniority system provided the desired results.[117]

Local 189 and Crown Zellerbach argued that the mill seniority system or the mill-plus-job seniority system decreased the efficiency of the plant and the safety of the employees, upset existing plant relations and employee expectations, and only incidentally accelerated black promotion. The job seniority system, on the other hand, fit the needs of the industry.[118]

Local 189a argued that job seniority was not required for the efficient running of the plant or for the safety of the employees because the promotion of capable employees was ensured by other means. The use of the mill seniority system, however, would eliminate present and future discrimination by providing each employee, regardless of race or color, the same chance of promotion.

On March 26, 1968, the court ruled that "in view of the racially motivated practices of denying to Negroes access to better-paying jobs in which Crown had engaged with the cooperation of Local 189, the job seniority system in effect prior to February 1, 1968, was unlawful. The court ordered defendants to replace that system with one which incorporated mill seniority as the sole determinant of promotion eligibility for qualified Negro employees who had previously been discriminatorily assigned."[119]

The court had determined that "only Negro employees hired prior to January 16, 1966, had been discriminated against."[120] Accordingly, mill seniority would only apply in situations "wherein this class of Negro employees were in competition in regard to training, promotion and demotions."[121]

Crown Zellerbach and Local 189 appealed the decision. The fifth circuit court of the United States Court of Appeals rendered its opinion on July

---

[117] Brief on Behalf of Local 189, p. 13.

[118] *Ibid.*, p. 19.

[119] Brief on Behalf of U.S., p. 16.

[120] *Ibid.*, p. 27.

[121] *Ibid.*, p. 27.

28, 1969. The court stated that the major issue in the case was "how to reconcile equal employment opportunity *today* with seniority expectations based on *yesterday's* built-in racial discrimination." The court affirmed the decision of the district court, holding that C-Z's job seniority system in effect at its Bogalusa paper mill prior to February 1, 1968, was unlawful and stated that the act required that "Negro seniority be equated with white seniority."[122]

---

[122] Opinion of the U.S. Court of Appeals for the Fifth Circuit in the case of Local 189 United Papermakers and Paperworkers AFL-CIO; United Papermakers and Paperworkers, AFL-CIO, CLC; and Crown Zellerbach Corporation v. U.S. "Appeal from the United States District Court for the Eastern District of Louisiana," July 28, 1969, pp. 2–3.

Allen-Bradley Company, Milwaukee

"Discriminatory" Hiring Practices

Now that public expectations are exploding in all directions, we can no longer regard profit and service to society as separate and competing goals, even in the short run. The company that sacrifices more and more short-run profit to keep up with constantly rising public expectations will soon find itself with no long-run to worry about. On the other hand, the company that seeks to conserve its profit by minimizing its response to changing expectations will soon find itself in conflict with all the publics on which its profits depend.

—HENRY FORD, II
Chairman of Ford Motor Co.

On May 23, 1968, the director of the Office of Federal Contract Compliance (OFCC) in the U.S. Department of Labor notified the Allen-Bradley Company of Milwaukee that he intended to institute proceedings against the company. He sought to terminate A-B's current government contracts and subcontracts and to bar it from obtaining contracts in the future. His grounds were that the company had not complied with the equal opportunity obligations required of government contractors and subcontractors under Executive Order 11246, Sections 202 and 209.[1] Allen-Bradley disagreed with the OFCC's contention and requested a hearing. On August 15, 1968, the secretary of labor established a three-man panel to

[1] See Appendix.

84

hear arguments from both sides. Hearings were conducted on August 20–21 and 28, 1968, in Milwaukee, Wisconsin.[2]

FACTUAL BACKGROUND OF THE CASE

The Allen-Bradley Company, founded in 1909, manufactures motor controls, electronic components, ferrite products, and ceramics. In 1952, forty-three years after its founding, the company hired its first black. At that time the work force numbered approximately 3,000 persons. The second black was hired ten years later. In January 1964, the company had only 4 blacks out of 6,800 employees. From April 1967 to March 1968 the company's total force grew to 7,000, of which only 32 were blacks. In that same period the company hired 822 persons.[3] Approximately, only one-half of one percent of Allen-Bradley's work force was black. As of December 31, 1967, 5,000 of Allen-Bradley's 7,000 employees had been with the company for at least five years, and 3,400 had ten years or more of service.

Allen-Bradley's labor force comes primarily from the metropolitan Milwaukee population of approximately 1,300,000. Milwaukee proper has roughly 776,000 people, of whom about 87,000—or 11 percent—are black.[4] A-B's plant is approximately two miles from the primary black residential area.

Each year approximately 18,000 persons applied to the company for an average of 1,500 jobs. Only about 1 or 2 percent of applicants and new hires each year were blacks. In 1966, for example, of 19,000 applicants, 521 were black. Of the 2,335 new hires that year, 30 were black.[5] Between January 10, 1964, and April 30, 1968, more than 73,000 persons applied for jobs, of whom 2.5 percent were black.[6] The company rarely advertised for employees nor did it use the facilities of any employment service or agency.[7]

A-B's HIRING STANDARDS AND PRACTICES. A-B's employees were selected on the basis of qualifications and without regard to race, creed, color, or na-

---

[2] Allen-Bradley Company, *In the Matter of Allen-Bradley Company Respondent,* Allen-Bradley Brief, Index and Summary of Argument, Milwaukee, October 1968, pp. 2–3; also U.S. Department of Labor, *In the Matter of Allen-Bradley Company Respondent,* Brief in Support of Proposed Findings and Conclusions, the Solicitor of Labor, Office of Federal Contract Compliance, Docket No. 101–68, Washington, D.C., October 25, 1968, pp. 2–3.

[3] Department of Labor Brief, pp. 3–4.

[4] Allen-Bradley Brief, p. 5.

[5] *Ibid.*

[6] Department of Labor Brief, p. 6.

[7] Allen-Bradley Brief, p. 5.

tional origin. Applicants had to be high school graduates, could not have
worked for more than two employers in the preceding year, and must have
been residents of the state for at least two years. A good appearance and
satisfactory past employment experience (if any) were required. The company also gave preference among applicants otherwise equally qualified to
those who had friends or relatives already employed by the company.[8]
The company stressed high qualifications in its employees. According to
A-B, the structure of the company was such that employees did not stay in
entry jobs but progressed to more difficult work. Entry qualifications were
therefore higher than they might otherwise have had to be. The company
also expected employees to be able to shift from one type of work to another as requirements changed on a day-to-day basis and to be able to work
with a minimum of supervision under a low ratio of supervisors to employees.[9]

However, as a government contractor and subcontractor, A-B filed reports with the government in which it characterized a majority of its jobs
as being unskilled or semiskilled. Table 1 shows the composition of A-B's
labor force from 1962 to 1968.

EVENTS LEADING TO THE OFCC's COMPLAINT. In April 1964, following a
complaint by four Milwaukee organizations, a contract "compliance review" was conducted by the OFCC at Allen-Bradley. The complainants
were the Milwaukee Youth Council of the National Association for the
Advancement of Colored People, the Congress of Racial Equality, the
Negro American Labor Council, and the Milwaukee Inner-City Development Project.

The investigation revealed that A-B did not use newspapers or employment agencies to recruit workers but relied primarily on its "applicant
pool" made up of "walk-in" applicants and referrals of friends and relatives
of company employees. Consequently, the company attracted relatively
few black applicants.[10] The investigator concluded that A-B was not
taking any "affirmative action to attract minority group applicants" and
suggested that A-B establish referral relationships with the predominantly
black high schools and with the Urban League. The company declined to
take action to increase the number of black applicants on the grounds that
its present number of applicants was sufficient and the company was therefore not prepared to pursue "this kind of specialized hiring."[11] Two follow-

---

[8] *Ibid.*, p. 6. This practice was later discontinued by the company. However, the
actual date of its discontinuance and its effect were the subject of disagreement between
A-B and the Department of Labor.

[9] *Ibid.*, p. 7.

[10] Department of Labor Brief, p. 15. For example, in April 1964, 1,728 whites but
only 52 blacks applied for jobs at A-B.

[11] *Ibid.*, pp. 15–16.

TABLE 1

Negro Employment in "Office & Clerical," "Operatives," "Laborers" and "Service" Job Categories

	Office & Clerical		Operatives (Semiskilled)		Laborers (Unskilled)		Service	
	Total Workers	Total Negro Workers	Total Workers	Total Negro Workers	Total Workers	Total Negro Workers	Total Workers	Total Negro Workers
1962	553	0	3,761	5	53	0	217	0
1963	553	0	3,341	2	53	0	217	0
1964	599	0	3,301	4	52	1	218	0
1965			NO DATA SUPPLIED					
1966			NO DATA SUPPLIED					
1967	940	2	947	1	2,060	30	277	0
1968	913	4	781	5	1,415	12	271	1

Source: Allen-Bradley Brief, p. 6.

up investigations took place to see if A-B had implemented OFCC's recommendation. The findings were negative.

In June 1967, the Department of Defense investigated A-B's hiring and employment practices. The investigator recommended that A-B advertise job openings in predominantly black newspapers and initiate a recruitment program to include those agencies and organizations "who can provide a continuous flow of minority group applicants." The company was also asked to submit a progress report by August 1, 1967, and thereafter by the tenth of each month until January 1968.[12]

The company responded by stating that it had "eliminated [all] reference to place of birth on its application form" and had recirculated to top management its policy statement on nondiscrimination. However, the company refused to accede to the main recommendations of the investigator. Consequently, the Department of Defense entered a noncompliance recommendation in its records against A-B. Another meeting took place on September 27, but A-B again refused to make special recruiting efforts among the minority groups, contending that it was "discrimination in reverse." At this meeting, questions were also raised regarding A-B's policy of giving preference to relatives and friends of its employees, as stated in the company's document entitled "Allen-Bradley Employment Policy."

On November 20, 1967, in a letter to the Department of Defense, the company indicated that it would "omit any reference to the company policy of hiring friends and relatives of A-B employees" when transmitting the policy to outside sources.[13] However, the company did not show any inclination to change its recruiting policies. Additional meetings took place between the representatives of the Department of Defense and A-B on February 28, 1968, and between OFCC and A-B on April 5, 1968; and the Department of Labor investigated A-B's Milwaukee facility on April 29–30 and May 1, 1968. None of the meetings changed A-B's position. Consequently, on May 23, 1968, the director of the OFCC informed A-B that he would impose sanctions on the company for its failure to comply with equal opportunity obligations under the government contracts awarded to the company.

ARGUMENTS BEFORE THE PANEL: OFCC

The OFCC's complaint was based on two arguments:

1. A-B's practices of nepotism and reliance on employee referrals and walk-in applicants discriminated against Negro persons and

[12] *Ibid.*, pp. 16–17.
[13] *Ibid.*, p. 19.

violated equal opportunity obligations under government contracts and subcontracts, and

2. A-B's failure and refusal to take positive steps to remedy the
   effects of the discriminatory practices constituted a violation of its
   duty to take "affirmative action" under equal opportunity obligations.

HIRING AND RECRUITMENT PRACTICES. The OFCC contended that contrary
to the assurances given by A-B to the Defense Department on November
27, 1967, the employee referral system was still being practiced, as disclosed
by the Department of Labor investigation. A-B further admitted that, although the policy was officially discontinued in April 1968, the notification
of this policy of discontinuance was not communicated to the receptionist
in the personnel department until June 1968, after A-B had received notice
of panel hearings. In view of the apparent inconsistencies between A-B's
pronouncements and practices in relation to nepotism, the Department of
Labor contended that A-B's mere word was no longer sufficient.

It was further contended that mere intention not to discriminate was
irrelevant. Actual discrimination was shown to be operating, since over 99
percent of A-B's employees were white. There have been numerous court
decisions in which it was held that such "grandfather clauses" violated
either the Fifteenth Amendment of the Constitution or Title VII of the
Civil Rights Act, 1964.[14] As stated by the Supreme Court in a union
membership context, proof of intent is unnecessary: the end result—in the
A-B case the percentage of Negro hires—will reflect company policy.[15]

The OFCC also contended that A-B's reliance on the pool of applicants
and walk-ins as the exclusive source of new hires "constitutes a method of
recruitment which, under the facts of this case, discriminates against
Negroes."[16] Furthermore, in terms of its collective bargaining agreement
with Local 1111, United Electrical Radio and Machine Workers of
America (UE), any information about vacancies must be disseminated
first in the departments where these vacancies occur and then to the rest of
the plant. All these practices coupled with the company's "refusal to distribute information to sources of minority applicants, and the over 99
percent configuration of its work force, combine to operate as a discriminatory referral system."[17]

[14] See, for example, *Guinn* v. *United States,* 238 U.S. 347 (1915); *Volger* v. *Mc-
Carty,* 65 LRRM 2554, 2556 (E.D. La., 1967); *Cypress* v. *Newport News Hospital,*
375 F. 2d 248 (C.A. 4, 1967); *Hawkins* v. *North Carolina Dental Society,* 355 F. 2d
696 (C.A. 5, 1962).

[15] *Radio Officers* v. *Labor Board,* 347 U.S. 17, 45(1945).

[16] Department of Labor Brief, p. 31.

[17] *Ibid.*

ALLEN-BRADLEY'S REPUTATION IN THE BLACK COMMUNITY

Testimony introduced at the OFCC hearings by representatives from ICDP, CORE, Urban League, and NAACP Youth Council stated that

> In monthly meetings held by ICDP with resident councils on the north side, the name of Allen-Bradley is greeted with laughter; the belief of these people is that A-B does not hire black Americans. The experience of the CORE director resulted in his belief that efforts to improve minority hiring at A-B are and will be fruitless. The experience of the Urban League job specialists is that Negro persons do not apply to A-B because they believe that the company does not hire Negroes.[18]

This negative image was further amplified by the publicity given to the company's 99 percent white work force and to the policy of giving preference to a relative of an employee when two applicants were equally qualified.

The OFCC argued that A-B had taken no affirmative action to dispel the image held by the minority community and by the organizations serving it. Nor had the company taken any action to communicate changes in its policy concerning preference to relatives. Such action, the government contended, would increase the number of minority applicants at A-B and would eliminate a discriminatory hiring system:

> Because A-B has a reputation in the Negro community as an employer which does not hire non-whites, non-whites are not referred by employment agencies in the business of finding them jobs and do not apply for jobs at A-B on their own. These practices, largely uncontroverted, are discriminatory, not because of any specific refusal to hire one identifiable Negro, but because the inherent effect is discrimination.
>
> However, A-B has also breached its duty to engage in affirmative action to ensure that persons are recruited and hired without regard to race.[19]

The federal government had moved against a number of companies for noncompliance under the new equal opportunity clause. It had won voluntary compliance from fifty companies, but five companies, including A-B,

---

[18] *Ibid.*, p. 14.
[19] *Ibid.*, pp. 21–22.

held out.[20] Of these five, three eventually gave in to the government's compliance program. A-B was the first of these to have hearings scheduled. The three-man panel therefore also heard arguments on the "nature of the obligation imposed by the affirmative action provision of the equal opportunity clause contained in government contracts."[21]

The OFCC argued:

> With respect to the nature of the affirmative action obligation, it is basically remedial, i.e., it is the duty to act to correct employment and recruitment practices which discriminate or have the effect of discriminating against persons because of race, color, or national origin. Where, upon correcting the particular discriminatory practice, the active consequences of discrimination remain operative, the obligation includes the use of such remedial devices as are appropriate to modify those consequences. Thus, the concept includes a recognition that equal opportunity requires positive action where a passive policy or minimal action perpetuates a continuity of discrimination and its consequences.[22]

The government's argument also implied that the affirmative action obligation imposed a *duty* upon A-B to "broaden its recruitment base to include sources of minority job applicants" even in the absence of "discrimination."

ARGUMENTS BEFORE THE PANEL: ALLEN-BRADLEY

Allen-Bradley contended in its arguments that:

1. The equal employment opportunity clause required effective nondiscrimination in those employment practices in which the contractor engaged.

2. The company had met its obligations by adopting and enforcing nondiscriminatory employment practices, as shown by the absence of any charge or evidence of discrimination by the company on the basis of race or color.

3. The government's construction of the equal opportunity clause imposed upon the company an obligation not intended by the Executive Order and one that contravened the intent of Title VII of the Civil Rights Act of 1964 and the Fifth Amendment of the

[20] "Not Discriminating Becomes Not Enough," *Business Week*, January 11, 1969, p. 90.

[21] Department of Labor Brief, p. 22.

[22] *Ibid.*, p. 44.

Constitution and represented an unconstitutional aggrandize-
ment of the powers of the presidency.

A-B's interpretation of the equal opportunity language was that it required "effective nondiscrimination," not conscious selection by color.
Allen-Bradley argued that it understood its contractual obligation under
the equal employment opportunity clause to be twofold: "first, nondiscrimination—color blindness in the employment policies in which it
engages; and second, the taking of positive steps to insure that those policies are as color blind in fact as they are supposed to be in theory."[23] In
reviewing the background and origin of the equal opportunity clause, A-B
noted that the clause was originally adopted to insure effective nondiscrimination in the employment practices of government contractors. The
intent of the provision was to effectuate public policy *against* distinctions
based on race or color.[24] The company contended that not only was this
the intent of the original Executive Orders[25] but it was also the interpretation of Executive Order 10925 given in a formal opinion prepared by
Attorney General Robert F. Kennedy. The adoption of new language
was—in the words of the company's argument:

> . . . calculated to put contractors on notice that the lax and
> ineffectual practices of the past were at an end. Lip service to the
> boilerplate nondiscrimination language of past administrations had
> been the rule. The new affirmative action language was a conspicuous
> warning: contractors would not only promise not to discriminate,
> they would do it. The burden had been shifted to the contractor to
> insure that his pledge of nondiscrimination was kept, on pain of
> invocation of the severest sort of sanctions.[26]

The new language constituted

> no new or qualitatively different obligation . . . to be imposed by
> the equal employment opportunity clause. The policy of the past,
> and that which President Kennedy intended to continue, albeit in
> more effective fashion, was one of nondiscrimination: color blindness
> in employment practices.[27]

A-B further argued, on the basis of its interpretation of the affirmative
action obligation, that

[23] Allen-Bradley Brief, p. 16.

[24] *Ibid.*, p. 24.

[25] The company cited the following cases in support of this interpretation: C. J. Stone
in *Hirabishi* v. *United States*, 320 U.S. 81, 100 (1943); *Oyama* v. *California*, 332 U.S.
633, 646 (1948); *Hernandez* v. *Texas*, 347 U.S. 475, 477–78 (1954).

[26] Allen-Bradley Brief, p. 23.

[27] *Ibid.*

if an employer engages in any of the enumerated practices, or in others, then he must take steps to insure that he does so without regard to race or color.

On this reading of the affirmative action language, the company has no obligation to create out of whole cloth a recruitment program, much less an obligation to create one utilizing minority group employment agencies for the ultimate purpose of enabling the company to increase its number of Negro employees.[28]

A-B cited the interpretation of President Roosevelt's Committee on Fair Employment Practices which held that the affirmative action obligation applied only to those practices in which an employer engaged. The company argued that since it did not engage in recruitment but relied on walk-ins and referrals, the affirmative action obligation to recruit minorities did not apply nor did it require a pledge to increase the employment status of Negroes as the government contended.[29] The affirmative action language was not remedial, the company argued.

A-B, declaring its obligation fulfilled, cited as evidence that no charge or complaint had ever been made against it nor had it ever made race or color distinctions of any kind between applicants or employees.[30] A-B also presented evidence that its practice of using employee referrals—which the government called discriminatory—had been effectively discontinued before the hearing notice was received, not because it was discriminatory but because it was no longer needed. Regarding A-B's image in the minority community, the company argued that no evidence was presented to indicate that this image was the result of discrimination against any Negroes or other minority groups. The only basis for the belief that the company did not hire minorities was presented by a member of the Latin American community who stated that "the company would not hire Latin Americans because of high requirements which Latin Americans did not have."[31] A-B had earned a reputation of being a good place to work. It therefore received enough applicants to permit selection of highly qualified personnel. This reputation as a good employer was in large part responsible for the company's success over the years. An A-B spokesman had said on many occasions that the company's practices "were in the finest traditions of Milwaukee craftsmanship."[32]

The government's proposals for compliance, the company contended, required a "color-conscious" recruiting and hiring program and effectively

[28] *Ibid.*, pp. 20–21.

[29] *Ibid.*, pp. 17, 22.

[30] *Ibid.*, p. 34.

[31] *Ibid.*, p. 16.

[32] Allen-Bradley Company, statement released to metropolitan Milwaukee area news media, August 15, 1968.

imposed quotas on the company. Such "color-consciousness" and use of quotas would, in Allen-Bradley's view, "run afoul of the letter and spirit of Title VII of the Civil Rights Act of 1964 and of the Constitution itself." The president was powerless without congressional or constitutional authority "to impose greater obligations on contractors by Executive Order than Congress has seen fit to impose by statute."[33]

The intent of Congress was clearly not to impose quotas on employers. A-B cited a statement from the House Judiciary Committee, the sense of which was ultimately incorporated in later civil rights legislation.

> It must also be stressed that the Commission must confine its activities to correcting abuse, not promoting equality with mathematical certainty. . . . Of greater importance, the Commission will only jeopardize its continued existence if it seeks to impose forced racial balance upon employers or labor unions. Similarly, management prerogatives, and union freedoms are to be left undisturbed to the greatest extent possible. Internal affairs of employers and labor organizations must not be interfered with except to the limited extent that correction is required in discrimination practices.[34]

A-B contended that the scope and aspirations of the affirmative action obligation that the government sought of A-B were much closer to the program adopted by Lockheed Aircraft Corporation under pressure from President Kennedy. Under this program Lockheed agreed to:

> . . . advise its management of the company's nondiscrimination policy . . . [and] to aggressively seek out more qualified minority group candidates in order to increase the number of employees in many job categories . . . [and to] make known its nondiscrimination policy to college placement officials and state employment offices. . . .[35]

With regard to the validity of their interpretation, A-B argued that the company's view was the only one appropriate since it imposed a definite and ascertainable obligation on contractors. The government's construction of the clause would impose an uncertain burden on the contractor, which might require that he adopt a program that would substantially increase his cost of performance. The company maintained, "The inappropriateness of such a vague, amorphous standard in a contract is in itself reason for rejecting the government's interpretation of the affirmative action language."[36]

---

[33] Allen-Bradley Brief, pp. 19, 45.
[34] Ibid., p. 27.
[35] Ibid., p. 28.
[36] Ibid., p. 29.

THE HEARINGS' ENVIRONMENT

Milwaukee, like many other urban areas with growing minority group populations and disproportionately high rates of minority unemployment, had developed an increasingly bitter minority community with increasingly militant representatives. Beginning in the summer of 1967 and extending into early 1968, the NAACP Youth Council—led by their advisor, Father James E. Groppi of Saint Boniface Catholic Church in the inner city— held more than two hundred demonstrations and marches, sometimes violent, to win an open-housing ordinance in Milwaukee.[37] The government's compliance efforts at A-B spotlighted the company's low proportion of minority employees. The Youth Council announced on August 5, 1968, that its next campaign would be in the field of employment and would begin with picketing Allen-Bradley. Father Groppi invited all those interested in "direct action" and "constructive tension" to participate. "Groppi later told reporters that Allen-Bradley would be the target of demonstrations because it was 'the guiltiest of all plants' in not hiring Negroes." In his sermon Father Groppi said, "We are beginning a phase of economic justice. The fact that we have a fair housing law means very little. Unless we knock down the walls of discrimination and open the doors of opportunity, the viewpoint of young black people is going to be 'What's the use?' "[38]

The Youth Council met with representatives of Local 1111 of UE, which represented about forty-four hundred A-B employees, to seek union support for its campaign against A-B. After the meeting the civil rights group said it would delay action against Allen-Bradley so that the union could negotiate for a nondiscriminatory hiring clause in its contract. The president of Local 1111 said that the union had been trying since at least 1954 to get A-B to include such a clause in each contract. He stated that the union's executive board needed the approval of the membership to reopen the contract to negotiate for the clause. "Father Groppi said that the union's cooperation with the Youth Council was a matter of self interest for the union because of federal government threats to remove contracts from the company."[39] Local 1111 representatives agreed, estimating that approximately 25 percent of total production was government work and that substantial layoffs would result if A-B did not comply.

---

[37] "A Model Employer Fights Back on Bias," *Business Week*, October 12, 1968.

[38] Bernice Buresh, "Youth Unit to Picket at Plant," *Milwaukee Sentinel*, August 6, 1968, p. 5.

[39] "Youth Council Gives Allen-Bradley Time," *Milwaukee Journal*, August 7, 1968, Sec. 2, p. 1.

On August 7, 1968, the Youth Council held a demonstration and march to rally support for the campaign against A-B and to bring attention to the council's negotiation with Local 1111. Leaflets were distributed which stated that less than one percent of A-B's employees were black and that because the company received federal contracts, "black tax money supports a company that refuses to hire black people."[40] At a meeting with union representatives, the Youth Council demanded that the company engage in preferential hiring practices until blacks constituted 10 percent of the company's work force. "We're looking for a victory. We don't care what tactic we have to use to attain that victory," Groppi said. "But I assured the union leaders that we won't use anything the unions haven't used in their history."[41]

At the plant gates, the union handed out leaflets announcing a special membership meeting to discuss the local's cooperative campaign with the Youth Council. The leaflet stated in part:

> If a mass campaign develops at the plant gates, government action will become even more likely—namely, the removal of the work in the plant. Since Cutler-Hammer, Square D, General Electric, Westinghouse and other electrical equipment makers aren't in trouble with the government on hiring policies, these companies will be ready, willing and able to snatch up the work that Allen-Bradley loses.
>
> Perhaps the Allen-Bradley top brass enjoys fighting with the government, but about 1,000 Allen-Bradley workers who will be laid off will have a different view.[42]

Local 1111's membership voted to open the contract and negotiate a nondiscriminatory clause and to authorize the executive committee to propose a solution to the Youth Council's demand that A-B hire more blacks until the proportion of nonwhites on A-B's payroll was the same as that in the city's population. The membership had been assured that their seniority rights would not be diluted by the increase in black employees, since it would affect only new hires. The committee also pointed out that a nondiscriminatory clause would be more effective then than at any other time, since only ninety-seven employees on layoff were eligible for recall and their recall rights would expire by the end of September, at which time the company could hire new employees.

[40] "Youth Council in First March Since Spring," *Milwaukee Sentinel*, August 8, 1968, p. 5.

[41] "Youth Council March Pushes Job Demand," *Milwaukee Journal*, August 8, 1968, Sec. 2, p. 1.

[42] *Ibid.*

On August 11, 1968, a group of Spanish-speaking Americans formed a coalition with the NAACP Youth Council. They demanded that Allen-Bradley hire enough Spanish-speaking Americans to comprise 5 percent of the work force, start a training program for minority group members, and halt its expansion, "which is destroying the neighborhood."[43]

Leaders of the two largest unions in Milwaukee sent letters to Local 1111 offering the support of the United Auto Workers and of the State, County and Municipal Employees (AFL-CIO) on August 12, 1968.

After several meetings between Local 1111 and A-B, the company agreed only to drop its policy of preferential hiring, a practice that had already been discontinued. The union held A-B's proposed changes to be insufficient, its answers unsatisfactory, and charged that the company was misleading when it offered to add a nondiscrimination clause to its labor contract. Local 1111 said the company was willing to agree to a nondiscriminatory clause for present employees but was "not yet willing to agree to a nondiscrimination hiring clause covering applicants for jobs."[44]

Support for the Youth Council campaign against A-B continued to grow. On August 16, 1968, "about 75 clergymen pledged their support and participation . . . in efforts to eliminate alleged discrimination in hiring practices at the Allen-Bradley Company."[45]

The degree of support the Youth Council was receiving was surprising. The *Milwaukee Sentinel* made the following comments on the council's campaign:

In its new "economic campaign" the Milwaukee Youth Council . . . is experiencing something relatively rare for it—cooperation.

The council has had more success in just three weeks of its new campaign than it had in eight months of trying to get a city open housing law.

The Milwaukee Common Council passed a housing law stronger than the federal government's in May. But that was after months of turmoil, more than 200 marches by the Youth Council, stiff opposition and physical assaults by whites on the south side.

But, in its attempt to increase and upgrade black employment, the Youth Council finds itself with such friends as the United States government, a large labor union, a limited number of enthusiastic Latin Americans and apparently a growing number of Negroes for

[43] "Latins Join Blacks in A-B Complaint," *Milwaukee Journal*, August 12, 1968, Sec. 2, p. 1.

[44] "Union Calls A-B Stand Misleading," *Milwaukee Journal*, August 19, 1968, Sec. 2, p. 2.

[45] "75 Clerics Join Drive to Alter A-B Job Policy," *Milwaukee Sentinel*, August 17, 1968, p. 5.

whom a paycheck has more real meaning than a law saying that they can live wherever they wish.

The difference between the two campaigns was that on housing "we had a bigoted Common Council," said Father James E. Groppi, advisor to the Youth Council.

On employment, "we have a greater concentration of power," he said.

"Either our demands are met or we close down the shop," Groppi said. "It's a beautiful constructive use of power."

It's also similar to the way labor unions have used power, something the Youth Council is fully aware of.

Twice in three weeks, the Youth Council in effect gave labor unions the option of co-operating with it or winding up in the untenable position of seeming to support management.

This week, after word of the council's new campaign got around, Negro laundry workers, although unionized, went to the council for help in settling a wage and working conditions dispute.

Within one day there was a picket line, walkout, negotiation and settlement of the dispute.

The Youth Council, a third party, joined in on the negotiations between the management and Local 3008 of the AFL-CIO Laundry and Dry Cleaning International.

Thursday night the Youth Council announced that it would help another group of workers belonging to the same union who asked for assistance.[46]

DECISION AND RECOMMENDATIONS OF THE PANEL

The three-man panel hearing OFCC and Allen-Bradley arguments found that A-B did not discriminate against any individual applicant or employee, but the company's "failure to take some affirmative action to broaden its recruitment base and increase the flow of minority applicants was, given the circumstances involved herein, a violation of the 'equal opportunity' clause."[47]

The panel based this finding on the following:

1. A-B's contention that it had no recruiting system "manifestly cannot be accepted."

[46] "Youth Council Not Alone in Job Drive," *Milwaukee Sentinel*, August 23, 1968, p. 5.

[47] U.S., Department of Labor, *Recommended Findings and Conclusions*, December 17, 1968, p. 4.

2. While the type of recruiting system used by the company has a tendency to perpetuate the racial composition of a given work force, there are conflicting opinions as to whether such a system constitutes discrimination. In any event, the question of whether or not A-B's practices constituted discrimination need not be resolved for two reasons:

   a) The government's charge of discrimination represents a shift in its position, since its compliance efforts were directed at the company's obligations under the affirmative action provision, not toward eliminating discriminatory practices.

   b) The affirmative action provision can be invoked even in the absence of an effort to remedy the effects of discrimination. Action taken by the company to fulfill the affirmative action obligation would eliminate any discriminatory practices.

3. The affirmative action obligation requires A-B to take some action to broaden its recruitment base. The clause requires a contractor to do more with respect to applicants than to see to it that a Negro who actually applies for employment is not rejected because of race. This interpretation is based on the history of the Executive Orders, the recommendations leading to the inclusion of the affirmative action clause, and the procurement regulations issued by the General Services Administration.

4. With regard to the company's contention that positive action would be in juxtaposition to the Civil Rights Act of 1964 and the Constitution, the panel reasoned as follows:

   We have, however, concluded that even if [A-B's] contentions raised substantial constitutional issues, or substantial issues under the Civil Rights Act of 1964, there would be no warrant for an interpretation of the equal opportunity clause that, in the circumstances of this case, would bar the government from requiring [A-B] to take some action to broaden its recruitment base. . . . there is nothing in the Civil Rights Act of 1964 that supports [A-B's] far-reaching contention that any action designed to add members of minority groups to its predominantly white pool of applicants would violate that statute. On the contrary, the acceptance of that contention would frustrate the underlying statutory purpose of promoting equal employment opportunity.

The panel further pointed out that despite the company's contention that it could not utilize strictly minority employment organizations, the company made no effort to utilize employment organizations that served both white and minority communities. The use of minority organizations in the company's circumstance would serve to neutralize the racially one-sided consequences of its walk-in system.

5. The company's contention that an interpretation of the affirmative action obligation requiring A-B to broaden its recruitment base would import such great uncertainty into that obligation as to make such an interpretation wholly incompatible with the idea of agreement, was in the panel's opinion not in accord with the circumstances of this case. "The affirmative action here involved is of an entirely different character. It requires only a modest supplementing of a racially one-sided recruitment system. Its cost promises to be relatively small. Its general nature and its justification were clearly set out in procurement regulations."[48]

The panel recommended that the secretary of labor direct the OFCC and A-B to agree on an appropriate program of affirmative action. If they could not reach an agreement, another panel was to be constituted to hold a hearing for the purpose of recommending an appropriate program and the sanctions to be imposed if A-B failed to take the affirmative action required. The panel also recommended the following objectives, which the program should attempt to achieve: (1) to increase the flow of minority applicants for employment with the Respondent (A-B); (2) to advise members of minority groups, among other groups, of the Respondent's hiring practices, so that their applications could receive timely consideration; (3) to remedy the Respondent's image as an employer that discriminated against Negroes; (4) to avoid excessive expenditures by the Respondent; (5) to avoid possible exacerbation of racial tensions by action that would imply job openings when none existed; and (6) to avoid any implication of quota or preferential hiring based on race.[49]

ACTIONS FOLLOWING THE DECISION AND RECOMMENDATIONS OF THE PANEL

Secretary of Labor Willard Wirtz accepted the panel's recommendations, and the OFCC and A-B prepared programs to implement them. The Milwaukee civil rights groups had mixed reactions. Father Groppi made the following comment:

The federal report says that Allen-Bradley is guilty of a violation of contract but not of overt acts of discrimination. I would question this finding. Negroes make up less than 1 percent of A-B work force.
We're waiting to see what the government will do now. We're not

[48] *Ibid.*, pp. 25–26.
[49] *Ibid.*, pp. 27–28.

pleased with the situation at Allen-Bradley, and we're not going to put up with it.[50]

Allen-Bradley proposed a six-point program designed to broaden its recruitment base. It would advise private and public employment agencies, school counselors, and college and university placement officers that A-B was an Equal Opportunity Employer making no distinctions based on race, creed, color, sex, or national origin. It would also advertise job openings both in general public and in minority group newspapers, again emphasizing the absence of these distinctions. In a press release on August 15, 1968, A-B announced that it no longer gave preference to relatives and friends of employees.[51] In addition, it would make available to OFCC at its request any of the company's recruitment and employment statistics as provided in pertinent regulations implementing Executive Order 11246.[52]

The OFCC's program provided more detailed and generally more aggressive steps to reach out into the minority community and more explicit reporting by A-B. The OFCC also proposed a "pending file" in which all minority applications not immediately accepted or rejected would be held. These "pending" applications would then be referred to when a job opening occurred for which there were no current qualified minority group applicants.[53] A-B strongly objected to this "pending file," stating that it was clearly discrimination based on race.

The OFCC and A-B failed to agree, and the OFCC reported to the new secretary of labor, George Schultz, "that its efforts to negotiate an 'affirmative action' employment program with the company had failed."[54]

The Labor Department announced that it would reconvene the three-man panel on April 17, 1969, for ten days to try another round of negotiations with A-B.[55] On May 6, 1969, the panel announced that it had reached a tentative "agreement in principle" with the company, subject to the approval of Secretary Shultz.[56] On August 11, 1969, Secretary Shultz

50 "Not Discriminating Becomes Not Enough," Business Week, January 11, 1969, p. 92.

51 U.S., Department of Labor, In the Matter of Allen-Bradley Company, Respondent, Proposed Allen-Bradley Program, Office of Federal Contract Compliance, Docket No. 101–68, Washington, D.C., October 25, 1968, pp. 3–4.

52 Ibid., pp. 4–5.

53 U.S., Department of Labor, In the Matter of Allen-Bradley Company, Respondent, Proposed OFCC Program, Office of Federal Contract Compliance, Docket No. 101–68, Washington, D.C., October 25, 1968, p. 8.

54 "Labor Secretary Studies Job-Bias Dispute Involving Hiring Policies of Allen-Bradley," The Wall Street Journal, February 11, 1969, p. 8.

55 "Allen-Bradley Called Again by U.S. Over Hiring Policy," The Wall Street Journal, April 4, 1969, p. 16.

56 "Allen-Bradley Reaches Agreement with Panel in Alleged Bias Case," The Wall Street Journal, May 6, 1969, p. 5.

accepted "with 'reservations' a previously proposed company plan to improve equal employment opportunities."

Because of his reservation about the company's proposal, however, the secretary ordered the Office of Contract Compliance to review the company's recruiting procedures in six months.

In its proposal, Allen-Bradley specifically promised to advise state employment offices and various private and college placement offices "with regard to its interest in and willingness to consider all qualified applicants, regardless of race, color, creed or sex." The company is to "utilize advertising to publicize available jobs which appeal to minority groups" and "take steps to acquaint" community minority group agencies and high schools in ghetto areas "with regard to the company's fair employment practices."

The plan further requires the company to maintain a file showing the names, addresses and race of all job applicants. A list of "minimum qualification requirements for entry-level jobs" also must be maintained and furnished to the Office of Contract Compliance along with a regular quarterly report on the company's compliance with equal employment regulations.

Secretary Schultz said he would "prefer that the commitments specify additional procedures to correct the company's violations with regard to its recruiting practices, its recruitment sources and its image as an employer which discriminates." But, saying that the company has made "substantial progress" in rectifying violations of Federal regulations, he added he had decided to accept the special panel's recommendation.[57]

Other sources speculated that Secretary Shultz's acceptance of A-B's proposal was an attempt to get rid of a troublesome legacy from a previous administration rather than to prosecute vigorously a "landmark case."

Faced with a controversy that has dragged on for five years, Shultz may have decided to settle for half a loaf—or perhaps less—simply to get the case off his desk. Accepting the company's "offer," which mainly described recent improvements in its hiring policies, the Labor Secretary remarked that Allen-Bradley apparently has made "substantial progress" in ending recruitment violations.[58]

In this and other matters, however, George P. Shultz, then Secretary of Labor, preferred voluntary solutions to those imposed by threat of sanc-

[57] "Equal Employment Opportunity Is Pushed by Flurry of Nixon Administration Moves," The Wall Street Journal, August 11, 1969, p. 8.

[58] Demonstrating Again at Allen-Bradley," Business Week, August 16, 1969, p. 44.

tions. He believed them more likely to be effective, and they required less government enforcement.

Although the dispute was officially resolved, Milwaukee's activist civil rights groups were unhappy with the outcome and would not let the matter drop. In response to Secretary Shultz's acceptance of A-B's proposal, Father Groppi and eleven pickets appeared outside A-B's plant on August 11, 1969.

> Groppi linked arms with two Negro men and all three were arrested, charged with blocking an employee entrance. The demonstrators promised to return in greater numbers.
>
> Groppi said protest picketing would continue until "definite answers" were received about "progress in giving jobs to Negroes and Mexican-Americans."
>
> "They're taking only 10 percent of their new hires from minority groups," he said. "We hardly feel this is the way to catch up when they have decades of discrimination behind them."[59]

However, the Youth Council lost some support now that government contract cancellation was no longer a threat. Local 1111 said:

> Minority workers in its plant have slowly but steadily increased in numbers: the union reports a gain in Negro employees from 35 a year ago to 185, and says the minority group total stands at about 225 now. To the union this is "fair progress" though only a start. But the union warns that "minority only" hiring would be no solution; it says it would produce an "impossible situation" for all.[60]

[59] *Ibid.*
[60] *Ibid.*

APPENDIX
EXECUTIVE ORDER 11246[1]

ALLEN-BRADLEY COMPANY, MILWAUKEE
"DISCRIMINATORY" HIRING PRACTICES

The Office of Federal Contract Compliance (OFCC) in the United States Department of Labor is responsible for implementing Executive Order 11246 (Tr. 38).[2] Since 1941, each President has issued at least one executive order prohibiting the federal government from doing business with companies which, contrary to the national policy, discriminate against and do not afford equal employment opportunity to members of minority groups.[3] Executive Order 11246 was signed by President Johnson on September 25, 1965. Parts II and III of this order require that all companies doing business with the federal government must agree that they will not discriminate against any employee or applicant for employment because of race, creed, color, or national origin, that they will take "affirmative action" to ensure that employees and applicants are treated equally,[4] and that they will comply with all the provisions of the executive order and the implementing regulations. The executive order provides for various sanctions against employers who break this agreement, including action by the United States to cancel existing contracts and to decree the employer ineligible for further contracts (E.O. 11246, Section 209). The secretary of labor is responsible for the overall implementation of the provisions of Parts II and III of the executive order, and he has delegated his responsibility to the Director of OFCC [31 F.R. 6921 (1966)].

In 1961 President Kennedy issued Executive Order 10925, which, in the words of the Third Circuit "greatly expanded the nondiscrimination pro-

---

[1] The material in this Appendix has been adapted from U.S., Department of Labor, *In the Matter of Allen-Bradley Company, Respondent*, Brief in Support of Proposed Findings and Conclusions, the Solicitor of Labor, Office of Federal Contract Compliance, Docket No. 101–68, December 17, 1968.

[2] "Tr." followed by a number refers to the page in the official transcript of the proceedings.

[3] For a history of the executive orders in this area see *Farmer* v. *Philadelphia Electric Company*, 329 F. 2d 3, 5–7 (C.A. 3, 1964) and *infra*, pp. 37–39.

[4] This "affirmative action" language first appeared in equal employment executive orders in Executive Order 10925, issued by President Kennedy in 1961 [26 Fed. Reg. 1977 (1961)]. See Price, "The Affirmative Action Concept of Equal Employment Opportunity," 16 *Labor Law Journal* 603.

visions which are to be included in most government contracts. . . ."[5]
That order added the requirement of "affirmative action" and spelled out
the obligation in the same terms as exist in the present Executive Order
11246, under which the subject proceeding was brought. The preamble to
that order stated that "review and analysis of . . . existing nondiscrimination provisions reveal an urgent need for expansion and strengthening of
efforts to promote equality of opportunity. . . ."[6] The affirmative action
obligation was added because experience under previous executive orders
calling for nondiscrimination showed that compliance with the negative
injunction against discrimination did not achieve the objective of equality
of opportunity. The President's Committee on Government Contracts,
which administered E.O. 10557, the predecessor of E.O. 10925, reported
that it was not so much "overt discrimination" as "the indifference of
employers to take action establishing a positive policy that hindered applicants and employees from being hired and promoted on the basis of
equality."[7]

In a 1961 report on employment, the United States Commission on
Civil Rights commented on the reasons for and effect of requiring
"affirmative action" thus:

> The need for affirmative action to overcome past discriminatory
> practices was well recognized by the former Committee on Govern-
> ment Contracts. . . . The Committee often urged Government
> contractors to take affirmative steps to hire Negroes, but sometimes
> met the objection that this policy gave preference to Negroes and
> therefore violated the nondiscrimination clause as much as preferen-
> tial hiring of whites. The express requirement of "affirmative action"
> in Executive Order 10925 should overcome such objections.[8]

It is clear from this history that something more than the same passive
nondiscrimination was intended to be added with the "affirmative action"
language. Those whose administrative responsibility has included the
enforcement of the executive order consistently so interpreted it.

Although not specifically concerned with the affirmative action requirement, both the Fifth and Third Circuits have held that E.O. 10925 has the

---

[5] *Farmer* v. *Philadelphia Electric Company*, 327 F. 2d 3, 6[C.A. 3, (1964)]. Government officials for agencies enforcing E.O. 10925 also similarly commented. Speck,
"Enforcement of Nondiscrimination Requirements for Government Contract Work,"
63 *Columbia L. Rev.* 243, 259; Price, "The Affirmative Action Concept of Equal
Employment Opportunity," 16 *Lab. Law Journal* 603; Powers, "Federal Procurement
and Equal Employment Opportunity," 29 *Law and Contemp. Prob.* 468, 479–80.

[6] See E.O. 10925, F.R. 1977 (Preamble).

[7] *Pattern for Progress*, Final Report to President Eisenhower from the Committee on
Government Contracts, 14 (1960).

[8] 1961 United States Commission on Civil Rights, *Employment*, Vol. 3, 76.

"force and effect of a statute enacted by Congress."[9] E.O. 11246 has also received court approval.[10] As said by the Fifth Circuit, the President has the power to require the antidiscrimination provision within the broad authority accorded to him by Congress for the establishment of "an economical and efficient system for . . . the procurement and supply" of property and services.[11] Indeed, there is also significant authority for the proposition that the Constitution requires the government to require nondiscrimination and equal opportunity in government procurement contracts.[12] To permit the use of government moneys in the production of supplies for a government project, in a manner which discriminates on the basis of race, creed, or color against persons in the United States would appear to violate the "due process" clause of the Fifth Amendment.[13] As stated by the District Court in *Ethridge* v. *Rhodes*:

> When a state has become a joint participant in a pattern of racially discriminatory conduct by placing itself in a position of interdependence with private individuals acting in such a manner—that is, the proposed contractors acting under contract with unions that bar Negroes—this constitutes a type of "state action" proscribed by the Fourteenth Amendment.[14]

These contracts contain an "equal opportunity clause" which provides that:

> The Contractor will not discriminate against any employee or applicant for employment because of race, creed, color, or national origin. The Contractor will take affirmative action to ensure that applicants are employed, and that employees are treated during employment without regard to race, creed, color, or national origin. Such action shall include, but not be limited to the following: employment, upgrading, demotion, or transfer; recruitment or recruitment advertising; layoff or termination; rates of pay or other forms of compensation and selection for training, including apprenticeship.[15]

---

[9] *Farkas* v. *Texas Instrument*, 375 F. 2d 629, 632 (C.A. 5, 1967); *Farmer* v. *Philadelphia Electric Company*, 329 F. 2d 3 (C.A. 3, 1964). See also *Todd* v. *Joint Apprenticeship Council*, 223 F. Supp. 12 (N.D., Ill., 1963) dismissed as moot without passing on issue, 332 F. 2d 243 (C.A. 7, 1964).

[10] *Ethridge* v. *Rhodes*, 268 F. Supp. 83 (S.D. Ohio, 1967); *U.S.* v. *Local 189, U.P.P.*, 292 F. Supp. 39 (E.D. La., 1968).

[11] *Farkas* v. *Texas Instrument*, 375 F. 2d 629, 632 (C.A. 5, 1967).

[12] *Ethridge* v. *Rhodes*, 268 F. Supp. 83, 87, 88 (S.D., Ohio, 1967); *Todd* v. *Joint Apprenticeship Council*, 223 F. Supp. 12, 15 (N.D. Ill., 1963). Cf., *Burton* v. *Moses Cone Memorial Hospital*, 323 F. 2d 959, cert. den. 376 U.S. 938 (C.A. 4, 1963).

[13] *Ibid*.

[14] *Ethridge* v. *Rhodes*.

[15] Department of Labor Brief, p. 1.

B.
SOCIAL
AND
ECONOMIC PRESSURES

◆

Eastman Kodak Company (A), Rochester, New York

Conflict with a Minority Group—FIGHT

It is beneficial for businessmen to indulge in introspection and in the words of Robert Burns, "see ourselves as others see us." It seems ironically fitting that the line should be from Burns' poem "To a Louse," because that is precisely how some people do see businessmen . . .

—GEORGE R. VILA,
Chairman and President, Uniroyal Inc.

Eastman Kodak is the largest producer of photographic equipment and supplies in the world. In *Fortune's* list of five hundred corporations Kodak ranks twenty-seventh, with yearly sales in excess of $2.7 billion. It has over 110,000 employees in all its plants and offices.

Kodak, headquartered in Rochester, New York, is that city's largest employer, its more than 44,000 employees being about 13 percent of the entire work force in the area. Kodak's influence on the Rochester community is such that merchants schedule sales to coincide with Kodak bonus checks.[1]

In 1918, founder George Eastman started the Rochester Community

---

[1] Jules Loh, Associated Press for Sunday A.M. papers, April 23, 1967.

Service (later the Community Chest).[2] He also founded the Eastman School of Music and made large grants to medicine and to the community theater.[3] The company enjoys a close relationship with Rochester University and other local organizations,[4] donates employee time to work in civic causes, and is considered both a good place to work and a good corporate citizen. "Evidence of the company's philanthropy is visible everywhere." In the decade of the sixties Kodak pumped nearly $22 million into the city's hospitals, schools, and Community Chest. The company sponsors a fellowship program for black teachers, and in 1964 alone it gave $1.5 million for aid to education.

Because it is nonunionized, Kodak is unusual. More than half the companies in Rochester (including General Motors, General Dynamics, and Xerox) are unionized. One Kodak executive says, ". . . the only explanation is that . . . the laws being what they are . . . people don't feel the need to be represented." The company says that "Kodak continually reviews its employment policies to assure that they do not present any barriers to the employment of anyone because of race, creed, color, sex, or age. Pre-employment testing is limited to a few jobs which require specific skills or aptitudes."[5]

The company has long had a skilled trades apprentice program which, according to one Kodak brochure, consists of up to four years of "combined classroom and on-the-job training leading to a skilled craftsman career as an electrician, instrument mechanic, machinist, pipe fitter, sheet metal worker, or tool or instrument maker. A high school diploma or equivalent and demonstrated mechanical ability are required."[6]

Kodak was one of the first one hundred companies to join President Kennedy's Committee of Equal Employment Opportunity "Plans for Progress Program," in June 1962.[7] Its brochure "How Kodak People Are Selected" says, "For any particular job, the person is chosen who appears best fitted to do that job. . . . Such things as race, creed, color or national origin neither help nor hinder in getting a job at Kodak."

Kodak has been making efforts to ensure that blacks are aware of opportunities at Kodak. In recruiting nonprofessionals, the company uses a number of community agencies, such as the Human Relations Commis-

[2] "There's a FIGHT in Kodak's Future," *Factory*, June 1967, p. 69.

[3] "Meeting of Minds," *Forbes*, 96, No. 7, October 1, 1965, 37–38.

[4] *Ibid.*, also see *Yearbook of American Churches* (New York: National Council of Churches of Christ in the U.S.A., 1965).

[5] "Equal Employment Opportunity. Eastman Kodak Company's Positive Program" (Rochester, New York: Public Relations Department, Eastman Kodak Company, 1967).

[6] *Ibid.*

[7] *Ibid.*

sion, the New York State Employment Service, the Urban League, Rochester's five settlement houses, high school counselors (with emphasis on inner-city schools), and adult education program administrators. In 1966 Kodak, which contributes to the Negro College Fund, expanded the range of its recruitment of professionals to include thirteen predominantly black colleges. During that year the company was involved with career centers in a program to help place college-trained Negroes.

A former Eastman Kodak board chairman stated in a letter of April 25, 1966:

> You will recognize that our efforts to provide equal employment opportunities are increasingly more positive and far-reaching than in past years. Previously our policy had been simply to try to employ the person best fitted to do the work available without regard for his or her background. We have moved actively beyond that position. We now seek to help the individual who lacks the necessary qualifications *to become qualified.* In other words, we are contributing to the training of the individual so that he or she can qualify for employment.

However, Kodak's sense of social responsibility, though contributing to the betterment of community life, resembles that of the benevolent Puritan father who, while making sure of his children's welfare, does not hesitate to discipline them should they fail to measure up to his standards and values. By keeping its employees happy with generous bonuses, good working conditions, and other benefits, the company has remained free of unions and has carefully guarded the established prerogatives of management.

The benevolent father image is very strong in Rochester and has been fostered so assiduously and for such a long time that to some extent both the community and the company have become its captives. As William C. Martin puts it: "It is inaccurate to think of Rochester as a company town, but he who underestimates the devotion Rochesterians feel toward Eastman Kodak does so at his own peril. . . ."[8]

ROCHESTER

According to the 1960 United States census, Rochester is the thirty-eighth largest city in the country. *The World Almanac* says that New York's third largest city is a "world leader in the manufacture of precision

[8] William C. Martin, "Shepherds vs. Flocks, Ministers vs. Negro Militancy," *The Atlantic,* December 1967, pp. 53–59.

goods and a major eastern U.S. cultural center. Located on Lake Ontario, it leads the world in the manufacture of photographic film and cameras, optical goods, dental equipment, and thermometers."[9] Rochester's largest employers are Eastman Kodak (47,000), Xerox Corporation (12,000), and Bausch and Lomb (5,300).

In a public relations ad in the *New York Times* Rochester said of itself that it was "a community of [metropolitan area] more than 700,000 people with the highest percentage of skilled, technical and professional employees of any major U.S. metropolitan area: more engineers than any one of 23 states: the highest median family income of any city in the state, sixth highest in the nation . . . 67 percent of the residents owning their own houses. For the Negro, it would seem that things never looked better. Employment of whites in the county had increased by 11 percent since 1960 but employment of nonwhites had gone up 43 percent—more than four times the national average."[10] The city housed some of the most enlightened corporations in the nation, with enviable records in labor relations and social welfare policies.

Rochester, in 1966, was suffering from all the malaise of a city in the doldrums. The vigor of its industry, high income, and employment for the majority of its work force were matched by the recurrent and persistent problems of its poor, whose lives were not being improved by the city's antipoverty and civil rights programs. Significantly, public housing units numbered 450, with only 1,400 more in the planning stage. One school board member stated that school segregation was "more severe than ever."[11] A few organizations, such as the NAACP and the Urban League, spoke for the poor and underemployed, but according to a *New Republic* article "the other civil rights organizations don't amount to much. An NAACP rally last year [1966] drew eight people."[12]

Reporting for the *New York Times* on June 20, 1966, John Kifner quoted the Reverend Herbert D. White, a young clergyman who headed the Rochester Area Council of Churches Board of Urban Ministry, on the state of the city:

> This is a city with five settlement houses, whose Community Chest Drive always goes over the top, and which prides itself on having every available service. And it's a city which has gone on line—against a lot of opposition—to have an open enrollment plan in the school

[9] *The World Almanac, 1970* (Cleveland, Ohio: Newspaper Enterprise Association, Inc., 1970).

[10] Barbara Carter, "The Fight against Kodak," *The Reporter*, January 21, 1967, pp. 28–31.

[11] *Ibid.*

[12] James Ridgeway, "Attack on Kodak," *New Republic*, January 21, 1967, pp. 11–13.

and a police review board. But one thing that is crucial here is the high degree of affluence in this community. If you are poor in this town, you really know you are poor.[13]

Affluence was everywhere—for the whites. For blacks it was a mirage, unreal, unattainable. In April 1965, there were no blacks on the city council, none on the board of education or the planning commission. In the fire department 2 of 604 were blacks and on the police force 25 of 515.[14]

BIRTH AND GROWTH OF FIGHT

Rochester's race riots (July 23–26, 1964) had made it evident that something must be done to avoid a recurrence. Most citizens of Rochester were embarrassed and shocked that this could happen in "their" city. They believed that Rochester had adequate welfare programs, far superior to those of most other cities. Most leaders were against any radically different or innovative measures, believing that the 1964 riots could not happen again.

The majority of the local clergy felt differently. They felt it necessary to inspire in the black a feeling that he had some control over his own destiny, and they believed that this could best be achieved through a viable local organization.

The Rochester Ministers' Conference (RMC), an association of black church leaders, sought assistance from Dr. Martin Luther King's Southern Christian Leadership Conference.

As the standard "King" approach did not spark much fervor among the black community, the SCL team suggested that Saul Alinsky might be able to help.

The RMC obtained help from the interdenominational Board for Urban Ministry, which was affiliated with the Rochester Area Council of Churches. The board believed that the crux of the black problems was the "lack of a potent organization to raise his hopes and needs."[15] They felt that Alinsky could channel black hatred toward whites into constructive action through an organization similar to those he had started in other cities. The Board for Urban Ministry, with help from the Council of

[13] John Kifner, "Negro Federation Points to Advances in Its First Year in Rochester," *The New York Times,* June 20, 1966, p. 26.

[14] James Ridgeway, "Saul Alinsky in Smugtown," *New Republic,* June 26, 1965, pp. 15–17.

[15] Loh, Associated Press for Sunday A.M. papers, April 23, 1967.

Churches, raised $100,000 for a two-year contract ($90,000 for expenses and $10,000 for salaries). The necessary funds flowed in from local and national church bodies and from many white liberals.

Alinsky's fame was based on his Woodlawn Organization which began in the Chicago slums in 1960. Alinsky later expanded his activities to Detroit and Kansas City. Alinsky's *modus operandi* was to seek out "natural leaders" and aid them in forming a "people's organization" whose goal was "self-determination." Alinsky's methods might polarize a community, nevertheless they were defended as being the only hope for ethnic minority poor. Alinsky believed that "people do not get opportunity or freedom or equality or dignity as a gift. . . . They only get these things in the act of taking them through their own efforts. . . . The haves never do anything unless forced."

In April 1965, FIGHT (Freedom-Integration-God-Honor-Today) was formed, allying 134 black organizations. The press warned that Alinsky's methods would result in future riots. Alinsky made an analogy between Rochester and a Southern plantation in his reply.

On June 11, 1965, the first FIGHT convention was held. The 1,000 delegates adopted a constitution, set policy goals, and elected a minister, Franklin Delano Roosevelt Florence, as temporary chairman.

Shortly after Alinsky arrived, local businessmen raised $40,000 to open an office of the moderate Urban League. In the past, funds for such an office had been unavailable. The manager of the Community Chest, threatening to withhold previously committed funds from a settlement house that had tried to join FIGHT, stated: "Chest funds could not be used to support FIGHT . . . in fulfillment of promises made to contributors." Florence accused the Community Chest of discrimination.

The *New Republic* quoted Florence as saying: "The establishment feels it can plan for us and not with us. . . . The only thing the white paternalists want to know about Negroes is whether they will riot again this year. And that all depends," he added, "on how soon the whites learn black men are human beings. They are not their simple children."[16]

In the beginning, Florence's leadership and indeed FIGHT's very survival were in jeopardy. Opposition was not only from the "white establishment" but from the "black community" as well, largely from middle-class blacks who felt that FIGHT's leadership was too militant. During its first eighteen months, FIGHT concentrated on federal antipoverty programs and urban renewal. It succeeded in getting the city to increase the number of planned low-cost housing units and also gained control of the urban renewal Citizens Committee. FIGHT obtained a $65,746 federal antipoverty grant for an adult education program and three seats on Roches-

[16] James Ridgeway, "Saul Alinsky in Smugtown."

ter's antipoverty board. FIGHT's picketing of landlords was successful in getting slum apartment buildings fixed up.

FIGHT organized a recruitment and training program with Xerox, starting with sixteen trainees and expanding to thirty the number of jobs for hard-core unemployed workers in 1967.

FIGHT claimed to represent three-quarters of Rochester's black community through its component Negro organizations—churches, settlement houses, and Black Panther clubs. Many disputed this claim. FIGHT accepted few whites, but a "Friends of FIGHT" was formed to give whites a chance to lend support. Before December 20, 1966, FIGHT's active membership was small, but it eventually increased to about three hundred. According to an Associated Press feature story, directors of a settlement house that belonged to FIGHT said that the organization represented less than one percent of the black community. Florence denied this but offered no hard membership statistics.

In its June 1966 convention, FIGHT resolved that "Eastman Kodak be singled out for special investigation this year." According to Alinsky, "Rochester . . . is under the thumb of Eastman Kodak, which also controls the banks, local university, hospitals, etc. The effect of its rule is to shut Negroes away from the rest of the community."

THE CONFRONTATION

Florence's first meeting with Kodak Board Chairman Albert Chapman, President William Vaughn, and Executive Vice-President Louis Eilers, which took place on September 2, 1966, was deceptively harmonious. Florence talked about the problems of the ghetto blacks. He demanded that Kodak implement a new training program to recruit and train blacks who could not meet regular recruitment standards. Vaughn stated that Kodak had such a program and suggested that they talk further on the proposal.

In preparation for the second meeting on September 14, 1966, Alinsky put FIGHT's proposal in writing. At the meeting, Florence read from a written statement that was distributed to everyone present. He admitted that Kodak's special preemployment training programs were a start but that the number of persons had to be increased to between five hundred and six hundred over an eighteen-month period so that they could qualify for entry level positions across the board. Florence further stated that FIGHT, as the only true representative of the unemployed in the Rochester area, should be solely responsible for recruiting and counseling the trainees. Vaughn's reply, also in writing, neither accepted nor rejected

FIGHT's demands. Vaughn described the existing programs for the unqualified and spoke of plans to expand them:

> The company hopes to benefit from suggestions which FIGHT may offer, as it has in the past been helped by the advice of a number of organizations on these matters. FIGHT and other interested organizations are invited to refer possible applicants for all these programs.

Vaughn noted that the FIGHT proposal and Kodak plans had much in common and that the company would be interested in meeting again to discuss ways in which "FIGHT might cooperate in the implementation of Kodak's plans."

Kodak seemed in no way to want to end the talks. It was obvious that Kodak had stiffened its resistance to the FIGHT proposal by repeatedly stating "its intention to retain control of all hiring. At the same time, it urged FIGHT to refer people to existing programs designed for the under-skilled."[17] FIGHT rejected Vaughn's proposal to work within the existing Kodak framework for assisting hard-core unemployed. Vaughn refused to bind the company to hiring a specific number of people, pointing out that "jobs aren't something you turn out on a machine."[18] Among the reasons given by Kodak for not accepting FIGHT's demands were:

1. Kodak could not enter into an exclusive arrangement with any organization to recruit candidates for employment and still be fair to the more than sixty thousand people who apply each year.

2. Kodak could not agree to a program that would commit it to hire and train a specific and substantial number of people in a period that would extend so far into the future.[19]

Florence and Vaughn agreed to meet the following day, but further talk was doomed. The unreconcilable difference was whether FIGHT could *demand* anything by right and whether Kodak could concede FIGHT's demands without abrogating its own rights and obligations. At future meetings, Kodak's leading representative was a second-echelon executive, Kenneth Howard of the Industrial Relations Department.

At one of the meetings, while Howard was explaining Kodak's training program, Florence repeatedly interrupted, asking, "Are we talking about FIGHT's proposal?"[20] Howard unequivocally expressed Kodak's view that

---

[17] Martin, "Shepherds vs. Flocks, Ministers vs. Negro Militancy."

[18] "The Fight That Swirls around Eastman Kodak," *Business Week*, April 29, 1967, pp. 38–41.

[19] "And Kodak Will Ask, 'How High?' " *Fortune*, June 1, 1967, p. 78.

[20] "The Fight That Swirls around Eastman Kodak," *Business Week*, April 29, 1967.

the subject was the ways in which FIGHT might cooperate in Kodak's expanded recruitment and training plans. Florence made it clear that he was "not interested in Kodak's plans." He insisted that the discussion be limited to the FIGHT proposal. Howard restated Vaughn's reasons; nothing was accomplished.

The fourth meeting was held September 19. Howard called upon Florence in FIGHT's headquarters. Florence declared that he would deal with no one lower in rank than President Vaughn. Howard then presented a letter from Vaughn to Florence restating Kodak's position and informing him that if FIGHT were willing to cooperate, further discussion could be held, otherwise Kodak would proceed without FIGHT.

Between September 22 and October 22 two letters were exchanged. In one letter Florence stated:

> Use of terms like "exclusively," "monopolistic," "arbitrary demands," etc. in reference to the FIGHT proposal does an injustice to the careful thought and consideration that has gone into our suggestions. We have not even had opportunity to discuss the details of our approach with Eastman Kodak.[21]

Vaughn replied that:

> Meanwhile, you and other members of FIGHT might be interested in knowing that while these discussions and subsequent correspondence have been going on the Kodak company has continued to employ a substantial number of people in this community, including many Negroes.[22]

Negotiations broke down completely.

On October 22, Kodak announced that it had made arrangements with the Board of Fundamental Education (BFE), a professional adult education concern, for help in expanding Kodak's training programs. One hundred people would be enrolled. FIGHT was enraged and declared the "deal" to be a fraud perpetrated on the poor. Florence then led a forty-five-man group to Kodak's office to seek "clarifications" of the program. On his arrival, he found that all the trainees had already been selected.[23] "It's a fraud—It's a trick," Florence immediately declared. And he went on the radio to say: "We can't understand, for our lives, how a company with

[21] Letter to William L. Vaughn, president of Eastman Kodak, from Minister Franklin D. R. Florence, president of FIGHT, October 7, 1966.

[22] Letter to Mr. Florence from William L. Vaughn, October 21, 1966.

[23] Carter, "The Fight against Kodak."

their creative ability can . . . take pictures of the hidden side of the moon . . . but can't create Instamatic jobs." Saul Alinsky, who was with Florence on the program said: "I can tell you this. Eastman Kodak has plenty to be concerned about, because this kind of an issue . . . if it ever develops . . . and it may well develop . . . will become a nationwide issue across the board to every Negro ghetto in America."[24]

FIGHT retaliated with an intensive campaign in the news media abusing Kodak and threatening dire consequences for the peace of the city and other ghettos all over America.[25] Alinsky bitterly accused Kodak of playing "an out-and-out public relations con game with FIGHT" and considered the hiring of BFE (rather than the acceptance of FIGHT's programs) a "backdoor deal."[26]

To the management of Kodak, it was inconceivable that their organization, with its enviable record of good corporate citizenship and assistance to minority groups, should be accused by a militant group backed by local churches and other community organizations of not helping the cause of the Negro. Kodak's incredulity was reinforced by growing evidence that the company was not holding its own in the contest. In the public forum, FIGHT repeatedly outmaneuvered and outclassed Kodak.

The human element played its role, too. Florence—described in an AP story[27] as stocky, bullnecked, with a dry voice and unpolished manners—used communications media with dramatic effect on every possible occasion. He held press conferences after every meeting with company officials, sometimes in the lobby of Kodak's headquarters building. Vaughn, on the other hand, a quiet and somewhat aloof man who found Florence's manner "intimidating—a lot of finger-pointing and all that,"[28] maintained a cool, dignified posture. Some Kodak employees attempted to help break the impasse between Kodak and FIGHT. In early December, for example, John Mulder, a Kodak assistant vice-president, met for lunch with his friend the Reverend Marvin Chandler, a member of FIGHT, and considered ways in which discussions might be resumed. Mulder had been active in civil rights causes, and his wife was a member of the Friends of FIGHT.[29] He felt that men directly responsible for hiring and training might be the most appropriate company representatives in future discussions with FIGHT.[30] He submitted this idea to Vaughn, who agreed, and on December 16, 1966, he appointed Mulder to head a new Kodak team.

24 *Ibid.*

25 *Ibid.*

26 *Rochester Times-Union*, October 24, 1966.

27 Loh, Associated Press for Sunday A.M. papers, April 23, 1967.

28 "The Fight That Swirls around Eastman Kodak," *Business Week*, April 29, 1967.

29 Loh, Associated Press for Sunday A.M. papers, April 23, 1967.

30 James Ridgeway, "Attack on Kodak," *New Republic*, January 21, 1967, pp. 11–13.

KODAK'S ABORTIVE AGREEMENT AND ITS REPERCUSSIONS

On December 19 and 20, Mulder and other Kodak representatives met secretly with FIGHT spokesmen. Mulder had expected to meet with Chandler to pursue further their earlier luncheon discussion. Instead, although Chandler was present, Florence took charge.

At 2:00 P.M., December 20, the two parties signed the following agreement:

A special committee appointed by Eastman Kodak president, William Vaughn, has been meeting Monday and Tuesday with officers of the FIGHT organization.

Kodak representatives stated that they have not employed traditional standards of hiring for the last two years. FIGHT hailed this as a step in the right direction as well as Kodak officers' statement that they will deal with the problem of hard-core unemployed.

Job openings, specifications, and hourly rates were discussed and agreed upon by the joint group.

January 15th was agreed upon as the date for a beginning of the referral of 600 employees, the bulk of which would be hard-core unemployed (unattached, uninvolved with traditional institutions).

Under the agreement, the FIGHT organization and Kodak agreed to an objective of the recruitment and referral (to include screening and selection) of 600 unemployed people over a 24-month period, barring unforeseen economic changes affecting the Rochester community. FIGHT, at its own expense, would provide counseling for the employees selected by Kodak.

Kodak agrees to the following: join with FIGHT in a firm agreement to

A. Continue semi-monthly meetings between Kodak and FIGHT to increase the effectiveness of the program.

B. Kodak will familiarize FIGHT counselors with the foremen and work skills required, and in turn FIGHT will familiarize Kodak foremen with the life and environment of poor people.

C. Kodak and FIGHT will share information on the referrals.

D. Kodak and FIGHT will issue a 60-day community progress report.

JOHN MULDER
Asst. Vice President,
Eastman Kodak
Asst. General Manager,
Kodak Park Works
FRANKLIN D. R. FLORENCE
President of FIGHT

Florence was extremely pleased and repeatedly asked Mulder if he was authorized to sign for Kodak. Upon Mulder's confirmation, FIGHT made a radio announcement of the agreement.

The nature of the content and timing of the agreement were most unusual and were indicative of Kodak's inexperienced negotiating personnel and their general handling of the situation. As Barbara Carter pointed out:

> It was a strange agreement at best. One of the six paragraphs mentioned the "referral of six hundred unemployed people," another the referral of "six hundred employees," a distinction of some importance. For a non-union company, the briefest paragraph was by far the oddest. It said simply, "Job openings, specifications, and hourly rates were discussed and agreed upon by the joint group." Moreover, semimonthly meetings on the program's "effectiveness" were also agreed on.

On December 21, 1966, Kodak's Executive Committee met and voted unanimously to repudiate the agreement. The following day the Board of Directors met and concurred with the Executive Committee's decision. In a statement issued by the company the Executive Committee stated that "for all its ambiguities [the December 20 document] violated antidiscrimination laws."[31] The committee stated that Mulder had not had the authority to bind the company. The company apologized profusely for the mix-up but flatly repudiated the whole arrangement.[32] There was no record of any written instructions from Vaughn to Mulder about the extent of the latter's authority in conducting the negotiations. Mulder, after the incident, did not talk to the press or anyone else and his side of the story remained a mystery.

William S. Vaughn, newly elected chairman of the board, said that Kodak had

> . . . two fundamental and critical objections to the FIGHT proposal: (1) We could not enter into an arrangement exclusively with any organization to recruit candidates for employment and still be fair to the more than 60,000 people who apply each year. . . . (2) We could not agree to a program which would commit Kodak to hire and train a specific and substantial number of people in a period which would extend so far into the future. Obviously, our employment needs depend on the kinds of jobs available at a particular time, and on the demand for our products.[33]

---

[31] Loh, Associated Press for Sunday A.M. papers, April 23, 1967.

[32] "Fight at Kodak," Newsweek, May 8, 1967, pp. 81, 83.

[33] "And Kodak Will Ask 'How High?,' " Fortune, June 1, 1967.

According to an Associated Press release describing the events directly following December 20, 1966, "another aspect of the agreement plainly horrified at least one high Kodak executive, who detected the faint odor of a 'labor contract.' "[34]

The community reaction ranged from incredulity to anger. The involvement of a large corporation and the controversial Alinsky resulted in national attention to what Kodak believed was a local issue.

Kodak took double-page advertisements in both morning and afternoon papers and said that it "sincerely regrets any misunderstanding." The ads repeated the company's earlier position that it could not have "an exclusive recruitment" with any group nor could it commit itself to any specific number of jobs "owing to the uncertainties of economic conditions." Furthermore, the ads gave the company's oft-stated position on social responsibility—Kodak was "deeply concerned to do all that we reasonably can to meet a pressing social need in this community, namely, to try and develop employment opportunities" and "many positive steps" had already been taken by the management.[35]

Although neither FIGHT nor Kodak made it public at that time, it seems that immediately following the repudiation of the agreement by Kodak, and after Kenneth Howard was back in control as Kodak's chief negotiator, FIGHT desperately tried to patch things up and salvage the agreement almost on *any terms acceptable to Kodak but was rebuffed by company officials.* Earl C. Gottschalk, Jr., writing in the *Wall Street Journal* on June 30, 1967, gave the following account of Kodak's attitude:

On December 23, a delegation headed by Mr. Chandler met with the executive committee. According to Mr. Chandler's account of the meeting—which Kodak agrees is accurate—FIGHT asked Louis D. Eilers, president of Kodak to sign the agreement. He declined, saying the company simply could not give a second party any voice in determining its labor relations and employment practices. Then, says Mr. Chandler, "We asked them to put into the agreement anything they wanted to, or to change it in any way they desired. Again, Mr. Eilers said no."

"At that point," says Mr. Chandler, "Mr. Florence even suggested that the entire document could be dispensed with if he and either Mr. Eilers or Mr. Vaughn could go on television and make a joint statement saying simply that FIGHT and Kodak would work together to get more jobs for ghetto Negroes. This idea met with no enthusiasm either."[36]

---

[34] Loh, Associated Press for Sunday A.M. papers, April 23, 1967.

[35] "Sheen Appoints a Vicar for Poor," *The New York Times,* January 4, 1967, p. 4.

[36] Earl C. Gottschalk, Jr., "Kodak's Ordeal," *The Wall Street Journal,* June 30, 1967, pp. 1, 14.

The issue of whether Kodak should accept FIGHT demands merged, in some people's minds, with the personality of Ken Howard. Howard said that he didn't know how widespread this feeling was. "I am aware of some of it, but most of the people who are mad at me do not talk to me about it. It has been the same here since I got this assignment. People who do not agree with you do not talk with you about it because essentially you are following the management policy and position in this area."

It would be erroneous to assume that Howard had something to do with the repudiation or that he was a better negotiator than Mulder. It would be more accurate to say that Howard's views of the situation and what Kodak ought to do were more congruent with those of the top management than Mulder's. Howard may have been wrong for the situation but he was right for the management. Being a second-echelon official he was simply presenting the management's views as well as he could. The fact that he happened to agree with the position only made him more suitable for the job.

Kodak did not visualize the effect of its repudiation on the nation. For a company of its size and resources it is hard to see how it could have been so wide of the mark in taking the pulse of the social system. While the company was handling the problem as a local issue, the controversy received national attention largely because of the efforts of FIGHT and its supporters, the National Council of Churches, the Catholic Church, and the very fact that it involved a large United States corporation. To an outsider it seemed like a fight between David and Goliath. According to Edward L. Bernays, a well-known public relations counsel and author:

> [It] fell like a bombshell into the pro-civil rights milieu of contemporary America. A company dependent on good will went against all the current social mores and folkways. It was a colossal public relations blunder that will go down in history.[37]

Alinsky caustically suggested, "Maybe their executives ought to enroll in the Head Start Program and learn to read." He charged Kodak with "playing into the hands of those who say you can't trust the white man. I don't know how much [strife] Kodak will be responsible for this summer."

Both Kodak and FIGHT held news conferences in which angry words were exchanged. In his news conference on January 6, 1967, Kodak's new president, Dr. Louis D. Eilers, charged that FIGHT's "talk about employment" was "being used as a screen" for "making a power drive in this community."[38] As reported by the *New York Times*, Dr. Eilers stated that

---

[37] *Ibid.*, p. 14.

[38] John Kifner, "Critics Assailed by Head of Kodak: He Accuses Negro Group of Power Drive Upstate," *The New York Times*, January 7, 1967, p. 25.

"since the Alinsky forces were brought to Rochester, FIGHT has run a continuing war against numerous institutions that help build Rochester— the school system, the Community Chest, the city government, and even organizations especially set up to help solve minority group problems." Dr. Eilers's statement characterized FIGHT's demands as "arbitrary and unreasonable," and he asked if the group's "goal was really to get jobs for those who need them. . . . To the best of our knowledge, FIGHT has not sent anyone to us to apply for work." Concerning Mr. Mulder, Dr. Eilers said, "We all expressed the greatest of displeasure at the signing," but added that he "didn't envision any change in Mr. Mulder's job."

In a news conference held later in his storefront office, Minister Florence (he insists on being addressed as "Minister," rather than "Reverend") said that Dr. Eilers's statement was that "of an hysterical and insecure man." He said that his group was trying to get Negroes into the "[melting] pot at Kodak." As to Eilers's statement that no one had applied for jobs through FIGHT, Florence flourished what he said were duplicates of the applications of forty-five people.

Eilers and Florence met twice, but on the third meeting Eilers was not present and Kodak's representatives were members of the Industrial Relations Department. Florence left in a huff saying, "We thought we were going to meet with Dr. Eilers, and they sent in a group of janitors."[39]

In January, Saul Alinsky began a campaign to round up national support for FIGHT. On January 3, representatives of the National Council of Churches Commission on Religion and Race, the Board of National Missions of the United Presbyterian Church, and the Board for Homeland Ministries of the Church of Christ visited Rochester and expressed their support of FIGHT in the Kodak dispute.[40] On January 10, the Citizens Crusade Against Poverty, a private group working with funds of the United Auto Workers Union, convened a closed meeting where it was decided to support FIGHT. At the meeting were delegates from the National Association for the Advancement of Colored People, the National Council of Churches, the Protestant Episcopal Diocese of New York, and the United Presbyterian Church.[41]

Hoping to make peace, the Area Council of Churches took a full-page ad urging FIGHT to endorse Kodak's training programs and Kodak to endorse FIGHT's proposal. A few days later the president of the council, a Kodak employee, and two directors, one also a Kodak employee, resigned from the council in protest against the ad, which they felt favored FIGHT. FIGHT became more "hardnosed":

39 "Kodak Job Plan Rejected," *The New York Times*, January 11, 1967, p. 19.
40 "Sheen Appoints a Vicar for Poor," *The New York Times*, January 4, 1967.
41 "Kodak Job Plan Rejected," *The New York Times*, January 11, 1967.

"We're not interested in white hope," Florence told a FIGHT meeting. "FIGHT asks Kodak where is the black hope for the underprivileged and unemployed in Rochester."

"Tell it, Brother," yelled the crowd. "Sock it to 'em."

"They talk about America being a melting pot," said Florence, "but the question right now is not whether black can melt, but whether they can even get into the pot. That's what FIGHT has been trying to do—get some of them into the pot at Kodak."[42]

As a result of its abrogation of the December 20 agreement, Kodak's corporate image was extremely tarnished. As a letter to the editor illustrates: "It is inconceivable that a man in Mr. Mulder's position could so misunderstand what he was or was not authorized to do."[43] Despite Kodak's insistence that it had not intended Mulder to initiate a new policy, *Business Week* quoted Vaughn as saying that Chandler and Mulder's decision to resume talks between FIGHT and Kodak "gave us some hope that there was a new deal here."[44]

On January 19, television reporters followed Black Power leader Stokely Carmichael into town. That night the leader of the Student Nonviolent Coordinating Committee told a FIGHT rally (approximate attendance, two hundred) of plans for a national boycott of Eastman Kodak products, vowing to "bring them to their knees."[45] Carmichael said, "We have been looking for a fight against a big company, and you've got everything we want. . . . When we're through, Florence will say 'Jump,' and Kodak will ask 'How high?' "[46] Carmichael's national boycott turned out to be picketing in four cities and involved only several dozen citizens of Detroit, Chicago, San Francisco, and Atlanta.[47]

During the first week of February Kodak announced openings for 137 to 158 unskilled persons in training programs leading to regular jobs. Kodak requested referrals from eleven agencies including settlement houses, the State Employment Service, the Urban League, and FIGHT.[48]

Four days later, Florence brought 87 people to the Kodak employment office. Kodak interviewers were ready with application forms. Describing the meeting, a Kodak official said the FIGHT People engaged

---

[42] James Ridgeway, "Attack on Kodak."

[43] Paul A. Mallon, "But and Rebut," Letters to the Editors of *America*, May 6, 1967, p. 37.

[44] "The Fight that Swirls around Eastman Kodak," *Business Week*, April 29, 1967.

[45] Loh, Associated Press for Sunday A.M. papers, April 23, 1967.

[46] Carter, "The Fight against Kodak."

[47] *Ibid.*

[48] *Ibid.*, also see Loh, Associated Press for Sunday A.M. papers, April 23, 1967.

. . . in an hour long demonstration, constantly interrupting our attempt to describe these programs to the group, they demanded that we provide jobs on the spot for those present. Our industrial relations people offered to accept applications and interview that day any members of the group who were seeking employment. Several stepped forward to volunteer only to be warned by Minister Florence, President of FIGHT, that they should not accept the offer.

The Associated Press reported that "after an hour and a half in a closed conference room, Minister Florence said his group had been offered neither jobs nor interviews, and if Kodak claimed the opposite, which Kodak did, it was 'an out and out lie.' " (The Associated Press learned that a Kodak spokesman had in fact told Minister Florence that applicants must first be interviewed and offered the chance. Minister Florence had replied, "We didn't come here to talk about interviews, we came for work.")[49] Florence also said that agencies who cooperated with Kodak in referring people for jobs were joining in a "conspiracy" (FIGHT had such an arrangement with Xerox at the time)[50] and that Kodak's training programs were "a sham and a disgrace."[51] Referrals were made and the program moved along.

Kodak decided to break off the meetings. Florence warned Kodak that it might be to blame for a "long, hot summer" in 1967.

Eilers regarded such threats as irresponsible and stated,

To tell the truth, I don't know what they want. Certainly not jobs—they could have had those, and still can. Every one of the ten referring agencies in Rochester has placed people in jobs at Kodak and none has asked for an exclusive deal. This year we'll have about 300 more in our training program. It's too bad FIGHT doesn't want to participate.

"We don't want any of Kodak's paternalism," said Florence. "The training program we've proposed is something we can do ourselves. We know ourselves better than anybody from Kodak does, and better than any Black Man who goes home to the suburbs every night and pretends he's white. We have to help ourselves by ourselves. That's what self-determination is."[52]

The *New York Times* described FIGHT's next move:

[49] Loh, Associated Press for Sunday A.M. papers, April 23, 1967.

[50] Carter, "The Fight against Kodak."

[51] "Equal Employment Opportunity. Eastman Kodak Company's Positive Program" (Rochester, New York: Public Relations Department, Eastman Kodak Company, 1967).

[52] Loh, Associated Press for Sunday A.M. papers, April 23, 1967.

In March, FIGHT bought ten shares of Kodak stock, at a cost of $1,442.65 to gain a voice at the stockholders' meeting. The organization sent out 700 letters to clergymen and civil rights groups urging them to contact fellow stockholders to protest the company's action at the annual meeting.[53]

In response to FIGHT's call, various church organizations announced that they would withhold from the management their proxies for more than 34,000 shares. In addition, twenty-one private investors accounting for 5,060 shares announced that they would withhold proxies from the management. John Kifner, writing in the *New York Times*, pointed out that "those proxy withholdings (about 40,000 shares in all) are largely symbolic since the company's latest annual report lists 80,772,718 shares of stock."[54]

A group of influential ministers developed a compromise program that they believed would bring an end to the Kodak-FIGHT controversy. Representatives from many local industries joined the ministers and agreed to hire and train fifteen hundred hard-core unemployed over an eighteen-month period. Kodak also agreed to join Rochester Jobs, Inc., as this program was known.

FIGHT complained that this was another example of the white establishment's doing something for the poor without giving them an adequate voice in the process but finally joined the program. Florence was elected a vice-president and named to key committees. Clearly, FIGHT had gained an impressive victory and was undeniably, if indirectly, responsible for a precedent-setting partnership between private industry and the poor. Though no hiring quotas were announced, Kodak's share was approximately six hundred. The poor—not six hundred, but fifteen hundred—had the promise of jobs; FIGHT had its victory; and Kodak was apparently doing all FIGHT had ever asked of it. Florence announced that the new program would not affect FIGHT's dispute with Kodak and that the protest at the stockholders' meeting at Flemington would occur as scheduled. *FIGHT wanted some kind of direct concession from Kodak.*[55]

As far as Florence was concerned the issue was no longer jobs but dignity. He maintained that Kodak had arrogantly broken a moral agreement. He said that FIGHT was only trying to solve local problems in partnership with business, instead of by resorting to the federal government. He recalled that in a previous crisis situation, during World War II,

[53] John Kifner, "21 Churches Withhold Proxies to Fight Kodak Rights Policies," *The New York Times*, April 7, 1967.

[54] John Kifner, "21 Kodak Investors Withhold Proxies," *The New York Times*, April 17, 1967, p. 25.

[55] Martin, "Shepherds vs. Flocks, Ministers vs. Negro Militancy."

industry had turned farmers into tradesmen overnight because the national good demanded it. A similar crisis situation, he said, exists today.[56]

On April 25, Kodak's annual stockholders' meeting was held in Flemington, New Jersey. Buses and carloads of white and black demonstrators from Rochester and other cities and from Cornell, Princeton, Yale, and Dartmouth arrived in Flemington during the morning, and were met by a force of state troopers, local police, and Kodak guards. There were no incidents.

Also in attendance were the ten FIGHT members who had each purchased one share of stock plus the stockholders who had withheld their proxies in support of FIGHT. William S. Vaughn, chairman of the board, opened the meeting at one o'clock.

Florence was on his feet immediately. "Point of order," Florence shouted. "I'll be heard as long as I'm on the floor." To cries of "Throw him out," Florence shouted, "We will give you until two o'clock to honor that agreement," and then walked out of the building. Outside, Florence told his followers, "This is war."

Precisely at 2:00 P.M. Florence returned to the meeting, crying "point of order" until he had Vaughn's attention.[57] Florence pointed a finger at the chairman and asked, "Are you going to recognize the December 20 agreement?" Vaughn's reply was firm: "No sir, no we are not."[58] With this Florence and some of his followers walked out. FIGHT's attempts to disrupt the meeting were not successful. The meeting was not halted nor was the management challenged.

Vaughn's defense of Kodak's record as well as its reasons for repudiation drew cheers from most stockholders present.[59] Nor did the withholding of proxies present any serious difficulties for management. Of Kodak's 80.8 million shares, 84 percent were voted for management. All Kodak officers were reelected. A month later the company took away from John Mulder his assistant vice-president title, although he retained his job as assistant general manager of Kodak's Park Plant.

Outside the meeting Florence's and Alinsky's statements received national coverage from television, radio, and the press. Kodak's corporate image suffered considerably.

Following the annual meeting Kodak tried to upgrade its public image by hiring Uptown Associates, a Manhattan-based black public relations

[56] Raymond A. Schroth, "Self-Doubt and Black Pride," *America*, April 1, 1967, p. 502.

[57] "The Fight That Swirls around Eastman Kodak," *Business Week*, April 29, 1967.

[58] "Fight at Kodak," *Newsweek*, May 8, 1967.

[59] *Ibid.*

and advertising concern specializing in "ethnic marketing." According to a
story in the *New York Times:*

> "A Kodak official in Rochester said the company contract with
> Uptown Associates was not related to its current conflict with
> FIGHT."
>
> Reuben J. Patton, head of Uptown Associates said "the company
> did not seek me out" because of the FIGHT controversy. He stated
> that he had first offered his services to Kodak in June 1964 when they
> were turned down by the company advertising director who wrote to
> Patton saying:
>
> As you know we are very much interested in the Negro market.
> . . . At the moment we do not require extra services. . . . and if the
> occasion arises where we feel you can be of additional service to us,
> please be assured that you will hear directly from us.
>
> Florence said he was "glad to hear that Kodak can sign contracts
> with Negro firms specializing in face-saving. This is proof that Kodak
> was never in good faith with the poor, but only wanted to hire
> 'instamatic' Negroes."[60]

Kodak eventually realized the ineffectiveness of its public relations
strategy and consequently tried to amend it by hiring outside agencies such
as Carl Byoir and Associates for help in dealing with ethnic groups. Kodak
also approached other professional experts in urban and ghetto problems to
help it specifically in dealing with FIGHT. Consequently, in May 1967,
Kodak invited Daniel P. Moynihan, former assistant secretary of labor and
then the chairman of the President's Council on Urban Affairs, for consultation. Mr. Moynihan talked with both Kodak officials and FIGHT
members to seek out ways of possible compromise. A week of secret meetings followed between the two parties, which resulted in an agreement.

On June 23, President Eilers sent a telegram to Minister Florence in
which Kodak recognized:

> . . . that FIGHT, as a broad-based community organization,
> speaks on behalf of the basic needs and aspirations of the Negro poor
> in the Rochester area . . . that both FIGHT and Kodak support
> RJI which promised to be an effective way of providing job oppor-
> tunities for the hard-core unemployed . . . that FIGHT and Kodak
> establish a relationship under which Kodak would send employment
> interviewers into selected places in inner-city neighborhoods in coop-
> eration with FIGHT . . . that it may be helpful to the people re-
> ferred by FIGHT and employed by Kodak to have special guidance

[60] John Kifner, "Negro Ad Agency Hired by Kodak," *The New York Times,* April
28, 1967, p. 46.

and advice from your organization [and that there be a] continuing dialogue between FIGHT and Kodak [to] cover various areas bearing on the economic needs and aspirations of the Negro community.[61]

At FIGHT's third annual convention, held that same evening, Kodak's telegram was endorsed.

In the fall of 1967 talks were renewed on Kodak's promotion of inner-city small business. FIGHT suggested that Kodak build a plant in a ghetto area and allow FIGHT to operate it. Kodak refused to do this but suggested something in the scope of small business. FIGHT was interested, so Kodak prepared a forty-page booklet entitled "A Plan for Establishing Independently Owned and Operated Business in Inner-City Areas."[62] The plan stated that Kodak would take the initiative in organizing a Community Development Corporation (CDC) and would assist in its financing along with other organizations that would be encouraged to join it. The objective of the CDC would be to support small businesses, and the plan suggested three types: wood products, vacuum-formed plastic items, and equipment service. In addition, Kodak suggested forming a microfilming service, which the company considered particularly desirable since it was labor-intensive, equipment could be rented, and required training took only a few weeks. The jobs involved would not be menial. Kodak foresaw a good-sized market in microfilming government documents.

FIGHT showed interest in the microfilming service, was disappointed that under 150 jobs were involved, and suggested an operation that would employ 500 people. Kodak estimated that it would need between $2 million and $3 million in sales to employ 500 people and emphasized that it considered such an operation unrealistic as there was no possibility of finding such a large market.

On November 4, the New York Times, giving FIGHT as its source, stated that Kodak would build a finishing plant for photographic facilities employing 100 to 150 people and that the factory would be "black-operated." A November 18 article quoted the new FIGHT president, DeLeon McEwen, as saying, "Kodak will join FIGHT in developing a microfilming factory that will hire and train 400 to 500 unskilled Negroes."

The two stories put Kodak in an awkward position: to continue talks with FIGHT would be by "deeds reinforcing their exaggerated claims"; to break off talks would contradict Kodak's desire to help FIGHT. Kodak asked FIGHT to announce the misunderstanding, but it refused—even

[61] From copy of telegram dated June 23, 1967, sent by Dr. Louis K. Eilers, president of Eastman Kodak to the Reverend Franklin D. R. Florence, president of FIGHT.

[62] "A Plan for Establishing Independently Owned and Operated Business in Inner-City Areas" (Rochester, New York: Eastman Kodak Company, November 1967).

after Kodak said it wouldn't be able to continue talks if this were not done. FIGHT, in preserving this "barrier" to talks, kept the issue alive.

On December 5, Kodak announced the "details of a plan to combat poverty in Rochester." The plans called for starting small businesses in the city's predominantly black slums, with each business employing nine to fifteen workers. Although these businesses would be started with Kodak's help, they "would eventually be independently owned and operated by employees."[63]

On April 1, 1968, Kodak announced that its program to train jobless persons from Rochester's inner city would continue in 1968. Mr. Monroe V. Dill, Kodak director of industrial relations, said that the company expected to hire two hundred persons for the program during the coming year, the same number as the preceding year. He also said that since the inception of the on-the-job program in 1964, five hundred men and women, many lacking industrial skills or adequate education, had been trained in special classes. FIGHT's president, DeLeon McEwen, responding to Kodak's announcement, said that the results of the education program were "known only to Kodak" and "they have not been enlarged to the black hard-core unemployed."[64]

This program was not connected with Rochester Jobs, Inc. (RJI). Earlier, in January, Rochester Business Opportunity Corporation (RBOC) had been formed "to promote and encourage independent business in and for the inner-city." Kodak joined with sixty of the city's largest companies to provide collateral to guarantee bank loans to finance business among the inner-city residents. RBOC's twenty-eight-member board also included several blacks and a Puerto Rican.

On April 17, Kodak announced a gift of $150,000 to the Community Chest's Martin Luther King Memorial Fund. RBOC's largest venture has been a $600,000 joint venture by FIGHT, the U.S. Department of Labor, and Xerox to start a FIGHT-managed metal stamping and electrical transformer manufacturing factory expected to employ one hundred people.

[63] "Handicraft Plan Offered by Kodak," *The New York Times*, December 16, 1967, p. 37.

[64] "Kodak to Continue Training Program," *The New York Times*, April 2, 1968.

The Bank of America

CORE Dispute on Equal Employment Opportunity

America seems to be without adequate machinery for the redress of grievances and for social change: It is a measure of this failure that little more is available to those dissatisfied with inequities of the system than ineffective demonstrations against the government, threatening rhetoric, disruptive gestures, and self-conscious life-styles.

—ROBERT BRUSTEIN
Dean of Yale University Drama School

In January 1964, three civil rights groups announced to the press their intention to launch a three-pronged attack on hiring practices of selected corporations in San Francisco. The groups—the Ad Hoc Committee to End Discrimination, the National Association for the Advancement of Colored People, and the Congress of Racial Equality—were respectively to confront hotels, auto dealerships, and banks, the latter specifically being the Bank of America, National Trust and Savings Association (B of A).

In pursuance of this policy, the Ad Hoc Committee launched a program of direct action against the Sheraton–Palace Hotel of San Francisco, alleging discrimination in the hotel's hiring policies. Following a weekend of large and often unruly demonstrations, the Sheraton–Palace, as well as other local hotels, yielded to the demands of the Ad Hoc Committee by signing an agreement which set forth hiring quotas and provided for the Ad Hoc Committee to oversee hotels' compliance with the agreement.

Although there was no direct communication from the Ad Hoc Committee, the Bank of America anticipated that it might be the committee's next target. Its fear was confirmed by press reports and indications from city officials and community leaders. In the January press conference, Norman Hill, national program director of CORE, had accused the bank of employing only "1.9 Negroes out of every 100 employees." Bill Bradley, local chairman of CORE, stated that the organization would first attempt to open communication with the bank through negotiations.[1]

The B of A did not want to be caught up in the demonstrations and backed into a corner as the Sheraton–Palace Hotel had been. It decided that it would "refuse to sign any agreement giving a private group authority to police our personnel policies." Nor would it "accede to arbitrary quota systems which disregard qualification."[2]

In terms of strategy to implement this policy, the B of A decided to engage in a massive campaign "to make our case known to the public . . . in order to win public sentiment to our cause in the face of a barrage of untrue and misleading statements being issued by various leaders of the minority groups."[3] The bank's plan of action included the following:

1. On March 12, 1964, R. A. Peterson, president of the Bank of America, addressed an open letter to Mrs. Carmen H. Warschaw, chairman of the California State Fair Employment Practices Commission (FEPC), with the intent of clarifying the bank's willingness "to discuss my alleged discriminatory practices with responsible minority groups."[4] The letter affirmed the equal opportunity employment policies of the bank, outlined practices of the bank intended to assure minority group members such opportunities, and offered to report periodically to the FEPC on the racial and ethnic composition of bank personnel (Appendix A).

2. At the same time, the bank decided to keep the press and public informed by taking the following steps:
   a. Calling press conferences—the first one took place on March 12, 1964, and was followed by two more—May 19, 1964, and June 1, 1964;

[1] San Francisco Examiner, January 18, 1964, p. 1.

[2] Bank of America, March 1964 Press Conference, Press Background Memo, pp. 4–5.

[3] "General Statement," Bank of America and the Congress of Racial Equality, A Report on the Public Relations Activities of Bank of America during Its Dispute with CORE, December 1964, p. 1.

[4] Ibid.

   b. Providing reporters with elaborate press kits delineating the bank's policies regarding hiring practices;

   c. Calling editors of major dailies and requesting them to review the materials and to write editorials on the materials if they viewed them favorably;

   d. Following the press conferences with full-page ads in major dailies documenting the bank's case; and

   e. Maintaining a steady stream of prepared speeches and press statements to branches throughout the state to use in contact with the local press and other groups.

In its letter to the FEPC, President R. A. Peterson stated that the bank would sign no agreement nor furnish any reports on the racial composition of its employees to a nongovernment agency. However, he continued, the bank was preparing to analyze its staff and would report on a three-month basis to the FEPC on the aggregate number of its employees and the proportions from Negro, Oriental, Latin American and "other" minority groups in Los Angeles, the metropolitan Bay Area, and the state as a whole. Because of the bank's policy of hiring only those applicants (without regard to race) who were qualified to assume the bank's responsibility as a "public trust," Peterson contended that the establishment of a definitive percentage of hiring from minority groups could not be agreed upon. However, in recognition of its "civic responsibility" to improve the economic opportunities of minority groups through its recruitment policy, the bank would continue to seek help actively from the California State Employment Service and from minority group organizations and would advertise in Negro and other papers by exhibiting the statement "An Equal Opportunity Employer." The president affirmed the bank's willingness to cooperate by taking part in discussions and by accepting suggestions on increasing minority employment from responsible minority-group organizations.

At their first press conference on March 12, 1964, bank officials acknowledged the bank's responsibility, along with that of other business and noneconomic institutions, to "work for equality of opportunity . . . to help the Negro in his attempt to break the bonds of prejudice," and outlined their policies, actions, and programs designed to achieve this end. However, the officials also stated that they would:

   . . . not hire people who are not qualified, nor can we lower standards. The public trust nature of our business prohibits such action. We will not sign agreements under threat or duress. We will not disclose statistical material to any nongovernmental agency.

Finally, while recognizing the right to picket and demonstrate in an orderly and lawful manner, we will not hesitate to seek injunctions and/or sign complaints of arrest if any demonstrations violate the law . . . nor will we fail to take full recourse to law in the case of malicious mischief.[5]

In opposition to CORE accusations, B of A statements to the press asserted that Negroes currently held management positions with the bank. Although it was agreed that Negro employment was about 2 percent, the bank attested that 11 percent of total employees were from minority groups, rather than CORE's figure of 2.4 percent.

The B of A's efforts to seek favorable press publicity seem to have been quite successful. The two San Francisco newspapers, the morning *Chronicle* and the afternoon *Examiner*, both owned by the Hearst newspaper chain, gave the press conference extensive coverage under such headlines as "B of A's Stand on Picketing: Will Not Take Demonstrations"[6] and "B of A Warns Pickets It Won't Be Pressured,"[7] leaving no doubt as to where the newspapers' sympathies lay. In a March 15, 1964, editorial, "Civil Rights and Lawlessness," the *San Francisco Examiner* said:

> . . . Mayor Shelley's declaration that he will not tolerate further lawlessness, and the Bank of America's warning that it will not submit to lawless pressures, have established the position for which all law-abiding citizens have been waiting.
>
> That position should now be supported by San Franciscans of all colors, and all shades of opinion on civil rights. Only thus can the rule of law survive as the community's guide in resolving minority conflicts.
>
> · · ·
>
> The enormously dangerous aspect of the lawlessness by young black and white zealots has been its success. First came the restaurant sit-ins, then the supermarket shop-ins, then the hotel sit-ins—each offense producing a victory with immunity, each success feeding the appetites of the demonstrators for bigger targets.
>
> · · ·
>
> No doubt the cause of justice for minorities has also suffered . . . but that work cannot resume on its proper scale until the rule of law is clearly restored. John Brown of Harpers Ferry has been dead for 104 years. His kind of fanatic contempt for orderly process was wrong then, as Lincoln patiently pointed out. It is intolerably wrong today.[8]

[5] Bank of America, March 1964 Press Conference, Press Background Memo, pp. 4–5.

[6] *San Francisco Examiner*, March 13, 1964.

[7] *San Francisco Chronicle*, March 13, 1964.

[8] *San Francisco Examiner*, March 15, 1964.

The views and the headlines of the other prominent northern California newspapers were no less similar.[9] The press conference also received wide coverage on local television programs in prime evening news time and included interviews with the president of B of A.[10]

Four days later, as CORE and the Bank of America were meeting for the first time, the FEPC made public its response to B of A's open letter, affirming the bank's equal employment opportunity policy and concurring in its opposition to hiring quotas. On the other hand, the FEPC called for "additional data on matters such as the distribution of minority group employees by job levels and communities," and defended "the right of peaceful and lawful petition, representation, negotiation, or demonstration by any group of citizens."[11]

Just as B of A came to the negotiating table with a press conference and with letters to and from the FEPC, CORE came with a list of demands that had apparently been prepared before the first meeting. (These demands were not presented until the third meeting when B of A requested concrete suggestions for increasing the number of qualified applicants.) The nature of the demands was clarified by a statement of CORE's strategy on employment at the time of the confrontation:

CORE works under the assumption that there cannot be fair employment unless there is relatively full employment. However, we also know that even in a full-employment economy, there need not be fair employment. Negroes could and probably would be the last hired and first fired, confined to the menial and the dead-end jobs. So CORE continues to work to end discrimination by employers and unions. Our major concern has been among consumer-oriented industries where we can be most effective and to secure unskilled and semi-skilled jobs where the largest reservoir of unemployed and underemployed manpower is available. There have been some notable examples of success.[12] [First National Bank, Boston, and A & P in New York.]

[9] See "B of A Denies Racism, Would Defy SF Sit-In," *Sacramento Bee*, March 13, 1964; "Sense versus Sentiment," editorial, *Daily Commercial News* (San Francisco), March 16, 1964; "Employers Agree with Peterson," editorial, *Palo Alto Times*, March 17, 1964; "A Forthright Stand by Bank," editorial, *Alameda Times Star*, March 18, 1964.

[10] "Bank of America News Conference," *Radio, TV Reports, Inc.*, New York, March 12, 1964; Transcripts of TV news on San Francisco television stations, namely, KRON-TV (NBC network station), 6:30–7:00 P.M., KGO-TV (ABC network station), 7:00–7:15 P.M., KTVU-TV (independent station), 10:00–10:15 P.M., on March 13, 1964.

[11] California State Fair Employment Practice Commission, *Bank of America Employment Practices, First Report*, letter from Mrs. Carmen H. Warschaw, chairman, FEPC, to R. A. Peterson, president, Bank of America, March 14, 1964.

[12] Marvin Rich, "The CORE and Its Strategy," *Annals of the American Academy of Political and Social Science*, 357, January 1965, 113–18.

The CORE demands to the Bank of America were as follows:

1. Reaffirmation to branch managers and other department heads of "equal opportunity employer" policy in all phases of hiring and promotion.[13]
2. "Equal opportunity" notices shall be posted conspicuously in various banks and office headquarters in the state of California.
3. Reaffirmation of the bank's "equal opportunity" policy to all private and state employment agencies, business and technical schools, colleges, and all other recruitment sources that supply personnel.
4. Special effort to recruit Negroes and other minority persons for training programs for executive, clerical, office machine operator, and other job categories.
    a. The bank will cosponsor with local boards of education a Distributive Education Program in local high schools with large Negro and other minority group populations.
    b. Other sources in Negro and minority group communities, such as the Urban League, ads in Negro newspapers, and so on, will be used for recruitment purposes.
    c. On-the-job training for persons who could qualify for employment with the bank but who may not meet specific formal education and experience requirements.
    d. Minority group persons with minimum required education or experience will be considered qualified for employment.
5. Minority group personnel will be distributed throughout all branches and not concentrated in ghetto areas.
6. Creation of the position of Human Relations Coordinator in the personnel department to be responsible for all phases of the equal opportunity employment policy.
7. Submission to CORE of figures of statewide turnover for the last two years during the months of March and April to be broken down by job category and race of all employees.
8. In order to insure the above, bank officials and CORE will meet one month after final negotiations are completed and the following information will be furnished:
    a. A statistical breakdown of employees by official job categories, by race, and by bank or office locality.
    b. The names and addresses of minority group persons hired and promoted, and general information concerning their termination.

[13] Bank of America, May 1964 Press Conference, "Demands—Bank of America."

 c. A statistical tally of applicants for positions by race, job category, and location assigned, and the number of individuals tested, interviewed, hired, and not hired.

 d. Regular meetings between the bank and CORE to review progress made under hiring and promotional policies. Updated statistics will be presented.

9. Press and publicity releases concerning agreements between B of A and CORE should be agreed upon before being released and should be issued jointly.

10. Any breach of agreement by a local community branch of the bank will be considered by CORE as a violation of the total agreement.

Most of CORE's "demands" were reiterations of the Bank of America's statements of policy in the open letter to the FEPC. The CORE "demands" and the bank's subsequent reply on April 10 diverged primarily on two points. In answer to the demand for on-the-job training for Negroes who could qualify for employment but who might not meet "specific formal educational and experiential requirements," the bank responded that on-the-job training as a regular feature of bank employment would be provided to minority group persons or others with "minimum required education and the ability to pass simple tests which measure their 'trainability.'" On the major point of contention, the provision of statistical information to CORE on employees, applicants, and turnover rates, the bank was adamantly opposed. The Bank of America maintained that such information was confidential, was unjustifiably expensive to compile, and would inappropriately be issued to a nongovernment agency. The provision of names and addresses of minority group employees was considered a breach of trust in the employer-employee relationship. The request for information on all applicants for jobs was considered a direct violation of the FEPC.

During the three months following the March 12 press conference, five meetings took place between B of A and CORE.[14] Ideas were exchanged and their usefulness recognized. However, the two parties made virtually no progress on the main points of disagreement—hiring a specific number of employees and providing CORE with statistical information on employees. CORE's insistence on seeking meaningful information may be somewhat explained by its distrust in the good faith of large organizations to implement agreements once signed. Following an agreement on employment levels of minority groups in Lucky Stores, CORE accused Lucky of

[14] The 1964 meeting dates were: first, March 16; second, March 23; third, March 30; fourth, April 19; fifth, May 17.

"statistical deception" because the store declared that 28 percent of new clerks were Negroes when there had only been seven beginning clerks in the previous three-month period. Of a total of sixteen hundred employees, this meant that two Negroes had been hired.[15] In the same dispute, CORE had also observed a failure on the part of Lucky Stores to utilize minority group and other employment agencies or to advertise an equal opportunity policy as the store's formally confirmed employment policy.

Further light is shed on CORE's strategy toward the newly established Fair Employment Practices Commission by former Director James Farmer's statement that "laws . . . provide a tool. . . . You can work to secure enforcement and implementation of the law."[16] The mere existence of the law does not necessarily guarantee its intent.

At the time of the fourth meeting (April 19, 1964) between the bank and CORE, the newspapers reported that the principal issue was the bank's reluctance to allow a racial headcount of current employees. The newspapers also implied that perhaps something could be worked out on the pattern of a recently signed NAACP auto dealers' agreement.

Before the evening meeting, Samuel Stewart, B of A chief legal counsel, said, "I read the text of the agreement between the NAACP and the auto dealers this morning, and, frankly, I couldn't see that they were offering anything that we weren't."[17] This fourth meeting between the bank and CORE lasted one and one-half hours.[18]

CORE ended the meeting with the statement, "there will be no further meetings until CORE hears from the FEPC." This was in reference to a letter sent to the FEPC by CORE on April 14. The objective of this letter was to present the FEPC with nine questions which, when answered, would allow CORE to determine the FEPC's ability to evaluate the bank's statistics. CORE also wanted to know if the figures furnished by the bank would be made available to the public and went on to ask if the FEPC had the power to demand all the necessary data on recruitment, hiring, promotion, turnover, and so forth, and to verify such statistics independently.[19]

The FEPC's power to act on employment malpractices was made clear in its reply to CORE. The FEPC had previously stated that, limited as the new commission was by its small staff, spot-checking of firm employment patterns would have to suffice. In the letter to CORE on April 28, the

[15] "Discrimination on the CORE Action Against Lucky Stores" (Mimeo), March 11, 1964.

[16] "Negro Leaders Tell Their Plans for '64" (interviews with Negro leaders), U.S. News and World Report, 56: February 24, 1964, 56–62.

[17] San Francisco Examiner, April 20, 1964, p. 1.

[18] Ibid., April 21, p. 1.

[19] Ibid., April 22, p. 10.

chairman said that she was "unable at this time to make a positive statement as to our capacity to carry out periodic review and analysis of the Bank of America's practices."[20] Furthermore, she continued, "FEPC has the legal power to require such information only when engaged in investigation of a formal complaint or in a commission-initiated investigation of apparent unlawful discrimination."[21] But, when an employer voluntarily cooperates in providing a review of its practices, "there is normally no occasion to fall back on legal powers to secure meaningful information."[22]

In reply to CORE's inquiry whether the FEPC had the power to take action against the Bank of America if the minority group employment situation warranted it, the FEPC responded that personnel pattern information in itself did not constitute conclusive evidence of unlawful discrimination and that enforcement power could only be exerted "in connection with formal complaints filed either by an aggrieved individual or by the Attorney General."[23]

The chairman declared that the FEPC would not remain active in "affirmative action" or voluntary cooperation with an employer providing personnel information if there was not substantial promise of an equal opportunity program. Finally, in regard to providing the public with employment data, although the commission as yet had no policy on this matter, it was likely that essential information "would be made available to interested parties, and perhaps to the general public as well."[24]

After receiving the letter from the FEPC, CORE asserted that the FEPC was incapable of authenticating Bank of America reports to the FEPC and that the Bank of America was "unreasonable" in not providing statistical information to a nongovernment agency; however, meetings with the bank would be resumed.

On May 6, the FEPC stated to the press that the commission was capable of checking alleged discrimination, even if the limited size of its staff would permit only spot-checking. If a more thorough study should become necessary, the agency would concentrate its efforts in one area on a temporary basis.

On May 2, CORE wrote to the bank, essentially reiterating its demands in order to define "those points which we have previously discussed and still require further clarification," that is, (1) a program of distributive education, (2) participation of minority group organizations in personnel

[20] California State Fair Employment Practice Commission, letter from Mrs. Warschaw to CORE, April 28, 1964. (See Appendix B.)

[21] *Ibid.*

[22] *Ibid.*

[23] *Ibid.*

[24] *Ibid.*

recruitment, (3) setting aside formal job requirements in the consideration of minority group persons, (4) distribution of minority group persons throughout all branches of the bank, (5) centralized administration of the bank's equal opportunity policy and appointment of a human relations coordinator, (6) periodic meetings every three months between CORE and the Bank of America, (7) equitable representation of Negroes in all Bank of America advertising, and (8) the provision of statistical information to CORE on the hiring of minority groups, since any distinction between government and nongovernment agencies was arbitrary.

On May 12, 1964, the B of A submitted a preliminary report to the FEPC stating that 12.85 percent of all bank employees were from minority groups, according to a statewide survey of its offices (Table 1). The following day, Bradley declared that CORE's impatience with Bank of America had been "strained to the breaking point" and that the bank's method of statistical accounting of minority groups was "inadequate" and "inaccurate." The bank replied that its employment figures would still not be given to CORE and that it was meeting, not "negotiating," with CORE.

The newspapers again centered the dispute around the bank's reluctance to give CORE the statistical information requested.

After the fifth and final meeting of CORE and the Bank of America on May 18, CORE announced that discussions had reached an impasse. The next day the Bank of America held a press conference, presenting a lengthy press kit, an accumulation of pertinent letters, and so on, and a thirteen-page statement to the press.

Included in the press kit were (1) the press statement, (2) an event chronology beginning in January, (3) a comparison of the auto dealership agreements with what the bank had stated it would do, (4) the text of the CORE demands submitted at the third CORE–Bank of America meeting, (5) the bank's reply to those demands on April 10, (6) the bank's open letter to the FEPC on March 12, 1964, and (7) a CORE memorandum of May 2 restating its demands.

The press statement was interesting not only as the bank's interpretation of the preceding two months' events but also as an example of the bank's public relations strategy with the press and the public through description of its policies and actions in comparison with CORE's.

The statement opened with a reassertion that the bank was open to constructive suggestions regarding its employment policy but would not provide statistical data to a nongovernment agency. In addition, it reaffirmed that, despite CORE statements to the contrary, the bank had continually maintained that it was not meeting to negotiate a formal agreement.

The statement went on to say that in order not to prejudice the meetings while they were in progress, the bank had remained silent "in the face

TABLE 1

Bank Staff: Statewide Totals by Principal Racial and Ethnic Groups[1]
April 30, 1964

	Total Staff	Negro	Oriental	Latin Americans	Other Groups	Total Minority Groups
State	28,553	635	694	1,942	399	3,670
% to Total Staff		2.22	2.43	6.80	1.39	12.85
S. F. Bay Area	6,599	220	254	332	122	928
% to Total Staff		3.35	3.87	5.06	1.86	14.14
City of Los Angeles	5,693	295	277	1,002	152	1,726
% to Total Staff		5.18	4.86	17.60	2.67	30.31

[1] Bank of America letter to the FEPC dated May 12, 1964.

of a continuing CORE publicity campaign of half truths and innuendos [which] has been a trial of patience."[25] Finally able to communicate with the press, a summary followed of what was included in the press kit (an organized, ready-made digest of events for reporters meeting deadlines).

Furthermore, it was emphasized that the central issue was not the bank's status as an equal opportunity employer but "whether this bank or any other corporation should give detailed statistical information about its operations to a pressure group in order that that pressure group may set itself up as a policing agency."

A history of the relations between CORE and Bank of America was then described. After becoming acquainted at the first meetings, the bank recommended at its third meeting with CORE that the best way for minority employment to be improved would be for CORE to offer concrete suggestions as to how the bank could increase the number of qualified applicants. CORE responded that it could not help find qualified applicants without detailed turnover statistics. Denying that the statistics were to establish quotas, the CORE delegation "was unable to offer any other purpose which these turnover statistics would serve."

At the same time, CORE presented a list of demands, which the bank's management "thoughtfully and carefully" considered before issuing a reply, which was reiterated in the press statement. First, it maintained that eight of CORE's demands had been met or had been accepted as worthwhile suggestions, as indicated in an earlier communication to the FEPC and CORE. Second, the demands that the bank refused were presented. The demand for statewide turnover statistics for two monthly periods in 1963 and 1964 was refused as a violation of the confidentiality of business personnel records and as an enormous undertaking serving "no useful purpose unless we are prepared to recognize CORE as a policing authority to enforce a 'quota' or 'goal.'" The demand for names and addresses of minority group personnel was refused as a "breach of trust in the employer-employee relationship." Finally, the demand for a statistical accounting of job applicants by race, job classification, and location was declined as a "direct violation" of the Fair Employment Practices Act and useful only as a "form of pressure tactics." Third, a positive response to the CORE demand for meetings with the bank at regular intervals was recorded. It is interesting to note that the bank did not reply to the CORE demands on a point-by-point basis but regrouped them according to some other criteria.

After the third meeting, the report observed, stories of undetermined origin appeared in the press declaring "that a snag had been hit in the CORE discussions with the bank." At the fourth meeting, CORE denied

[25] Bank of America, May 1964 Press Conference, Text of Bank of America Statement to the Press: Re CORE, May 19, 1964.

responsibility for the stories, at the same time announcing an expected reply to a CORE letter to the FEPC. CORE, having stated that it would specifically comment to the bank on the FEPC reply, failed to do so, and immediately released its reply to the press. In describing CORE's response to the FEPC letter (that FEPC was incapable of handling Bank of America reports), the press statement said, "It seems that the Congress of Racial Equality claims to know more about the FEPC than does that agency itself!" The report then described the FEPC's rebuttal to the press, in effect supporting the capabilities of this fledgling government organization.

Following in the statement was an item-by-item reply to CORE's May 2 letter to the Bank of America. It was maintained that most of the items had already been answered. In specific response to CORE's demand for a dismissal of "formal requirements" in the consideration of job applicants, the report declared that the hiring of "minority group members who have not completed high school is a lowering of standards which we cannot accept because of the public trust nature of our business."

In stating a need for a centralized administration of the bank's equal opportunity policy, CORE had recommended that the bank's senior personnel officer have sole and exclusive responsibility for the implementation of the policy. He would depend on the advice of a human relations director or coordinator whose office was advisory in nature and directly responsible to the president. An authority on minority problems, he would be appointed by the bank subject to the approval of the Interim Committee on Human Relations in San Francisco and the FEPC "to provide the greatest guarantee that this person will be qualified and acceptable to the concerned communities in California." In its statement to the press, the bank stated that "CORE add[ed] . . . specific directions as to how our bank should organize itself, and indicate[d] that our appointment of a Human Relations Coordinator must be approved by outside agencies. No self-respecting corporation is going to abdicate its right to draw organization lines as it sees fit, nor is it going to surrender personnel promotion power to an outside organization."

Finally, in response to the point that the bank should maintain equitable representation of the Negro in its advertising, the Bank of America demonstrated to the press its willingness to cooperate by accepting the "sound suggestion."

After a positive rundown of Negro employment in the Bank of America, the statement avers that the bank will do what it can to alleviate a severe social problem consistent with its "primary duty to provide competent service to the public" by seeking and hiring "qualified" Negro applicants.

Three factors of the bank's policy were then delineated, specifically: (1) should unlawful demonstrations occur, the bank will resort to injunctions and complaints for arrest, (2) the bank will not provide statistical information or sign agreements with a nongovernment agency, and (3) in any event the bank will follow a policy of equal employment opportunity.

The report then considered the policy and behavior of CORE. The group was accused of making appointments before the bank's first press conference and then failing to appear and saying at the same time to the press that "painfully long" but fruitless negotiations were taking place with the bank. The report concluded that CORE was "preparing their public for demonstrations" and that such conduct suggested "that some of the leaders of recent activities are more interested in demonstrations, disturbances and destruction of law than they are in jobs for members of minority groups."

The CORE organization was then accused as follows: (1) failure to provide, as agreed upon, a list of minority group organizations to help in finding applicants, (2) failure to find applicants, (3) "quoting out of context" to the press with "half truths and innuendoes" and thereby "giving a false impression," and (4) presuming that the bank was guilty of discrimination before facts or discussions had been established.

The statement declared that CORE's readiness to accuse the bank "smacks of the tactics polished to a fine art by extremists of both the far right and the far left. The system is to pick an opponent—the bigger the better—accuse him, and announce his guilt—and don't be too fussy about the facts. That is a tough system to beat . . . a type of witch hunting [that must be] identified and discredited wherever, or by whomever, it is practiced."

Declaring to the press that, having seen the material, the judgment was up to them, the statement continued that the bank "has no intention of being policed by . . . a self-appointed pressure group" in face of this threat to San Francisco and the state of California.

The statement to the press concluded with an affirmation of all cooperative efforts "in the common cause of real equality."

Following this and its other two press conferences, the bank received support from all the major daily newspapers.

On May 22, three days after the press conference, CORE began picketing several branches of the Bank of America throughout the state. A new item was added to their list of demands—that three hundred to eight hundred minority group applicants be hired within the month, providing that there would be a sufficient number of applicants and a sufficient number of jobs available through turnover without necessarily firing anyone. The picketing received first-hand press coverage during the first few weeks. The bank had representatives on hand in many locations to evaluate and "to help the press."[26] Branch managers continued to receive policy statements and guidelines on how to deal with the situation.

[26] Bank of America, June 1964 Press Conference, Stage III.

At a joint press conference on June 1, the Bank of America and the FEPC announced a memorandum of understanding (Appendix C) outlining: (1) the bank's submission of personnel data to the FEPC, (2) the ongoing review of the bank's implementation of an affirmative policy plus joint consultation concerning its effectiveness, and (3) periodic reporting by the FEPC to the public about pertinent personnel data and management action. The commission maintained the "right and responsibility to determine what information should be released in the public interest," although "unevaluated" personnel information was not to be disclosed. Any views the bank might have had concerning the validity of the FEPC analyses were to receive "serious consideration" before their release.[27]

The agreement on what personnel data should be submitted by the bank was a compromise between CORE's demands for statistical information and the bank's prior criteria on minority employment data. The data had to be broken down by ethnic group, by job class, by various geographic area designations, and by the percentage of total hires represented by each minority group. Detailed tallies of applicants and of hires, such as CORE enumerated, were to be conducted from time to time according to specific need by spot-checking and other methods.

As usual, the B of A's memorandum of understanding with the FEPC received widespread publicity and favorable editorial support hailing it as an agreement of far-reaching influence in the solution of minority problems.[28] Also, as usual, the editorial comment on CORE was neutral, nonexistent, or highly unfavorable. For example, in an editorial entitled "Against Bank Picketing," on June 11, 1964, the *Sacramento Observer* made the following comment:

> Although a lot of people may have been led to the opinion that the Observer is against CORE, this is not the case. . . . We remind them (CORE) not to make demonstrations, peaceful as they may be, the end instead of the means.[29]

In another editorial, "What Price Civil Rights," on June 3, 1964, the *Daily Commercial News* of San Francisco castigated CORE for its picketing against B of A and stated:

[27] Bank of America, June 1964 Press Conference, "Memorandum of Understanding Between California State Fair Employment Practices Commission and Bank of America National Trust and Savings Association."

[28] See "FEPC Accord Signed by Bank of America. Agreement Greeted as 'Historical Breakthrough' in Field of Employment," *Los Angeles Times*, June 2, 1964; "Bank, FEPC Sign Opportunity Pact" and "The Right Method," *Oakland Tribune*, June 2, 14, 1964; "Bank and FEPC Show the Way," *San Francisco Examiner*, June 3, 1964, p. 34; "The Right Way," *Los Angeles Herald Examiner*, June 3, 1964; and "Bank of America and Negro Jobs," *San Francisco Chronicle*, June 3, 1964.

[29] *The Sacramento Observer*, June 11, 1964.

It is difficult to believe that serious-minded California Negroes consider CORE as their true representative. It is difficult to believe they approve CORE's unreasonableness, its arrogance, its immature threats to the courts.[30]

On June 16, CORE held a press conference at which it was acknowledged that the FEPC "has a very valuable role to play in gathering this statistical information," although the commission had been unable to "pin the bank down to a specific agreement to hire any range or number of Negroes." Furthermore, it was stated that should the bank enter an adequate agreement with the FEPC rather than with CORE, picketing would be discontinued.

Several weeks later, the bank appointed its first black executive, E. Fred Morrow, as assistant vice-president.

Subsequent to B of A and FEPC agreement, CORE continued picketing throughout most of the summer, although public interest (as expressed in terms of newspaper and radio-television coverage) gradually declined. During this period, CORE sought further meetings with the bank, which the latter declined because CORE failed to meet the bank's demands: to renounce publicly its demand for statistical information and to sign an agreement on rehiring quotas with the bank. CORE also asked that it and the FEPC be associated in evaluating information furnished by the B of A. The FEPC did not grant this request.

On August 6, 1964, the Bank of America made its first report to the FEPC under the provisions of the Memorandum of Understanding. The data are summarized in Table 2.

Finally, CORE announced on August 31, 1964, that because the Bank of America had ended its discriminatory hiring practices, picketing would be discontinued.

TABLE 2

BANK STAFF: STATEWIDE TOTALS BY PRINCIPAL RACIAL AND ETHNIC GROUPS[1]
JULY 31, 1964

Total Staff	Negro	Oriental	Other Non-White	Spanish Surname	Other White	Total Minorities
28,856.6	826.1	640.5	531.6	1,841.3	25,017.1	3,839.5
In Percent	2.86	2.22	1.84	6.38	86.69	13.31

[1] Numbers refer to full-time equivalents and include part-time employees.
Note: Figures have been rounded off to the nearest hundredth.
Source: FEPC Report on Bank of America, September 1964, p. 6.

[30] Daily Commercial News, June 3, 1964.

PROGRESS IN EMPLOYMENT MADE BY MINORITY GROUPS AT THE BANK OF AMERICA

The FEPC released its evaluation of B of A's July report in September 1964, in which it affirmed that the bank was meeting its responsibilities as an equal opportunity employer in its recruiting, hiring, and training practices and that in spite of the difficulties of a large, complex organization attempting to achieve "complete implementation of a comprehensive new program in an extremely brief period,"[31] top bank officials were reported as having "cooperated fully" in taking "essential first steps" in administering an equal employment opportunity policy.

Table 3 presents a brief analysis of the commission's report.

The bank's statewide personnel figures were separated into four job classes. Although the proportion of total bank employees in Class 1 (initial entry positions, including clerks, typists, machinists, tellers) was 52.78 percent, and in Class 2 (first line supervisory positions) 27.21 percent, the proportions of total minority group members in these classes were 73.9 percent in Class 1 and 26.6 percent in Class 2.

Of the bank's total minority employees, 95.75 percent held jobs in these two classes, of the Negro employees, 98.85 percent. Of Class 3 (branch operations officer, lending officer, small branch manager, department head) and Class 4 (highest positions), 20.01 percent of all bank personnel were in these two categories compared with 0.45 percent of the minority group. Table 4 presents a summary of the data.

TABLE 3

COMPARISON OF MINORITY EMPLOYMENT FIGURES BETWEEN
APRIL AND JULY 1964

	April 1964		July 1964	
	Number	Percentage	Number	Percentage
Total Staff	28,553	100.00	28,856.6	100.00
White	24,213	87.15	25,017.1	86.69
Negro	635	2.22	826.1	2.86
Oriental	694	2.43	640.5	2.22
Latin Americans	1,942	6.80	1,841.3	6.38
Other Groups	399	1.39	531.6	1.84
Total Minorities	3,670	12.85	3,839.5	13.31

Note: Figures have been rounded off to the nearest hundredth. Figures compiled from FEPC Report on Bank of America, September 1964.

[31] FEPC Report on Bank of America, September 1964, p. 2.

THE BANK OF AMERICA

TABLE 4

BANK STAFF: STATEWIDE DISTRIBUTION BY JOB CLASS[1]
AS OF JULY 31, 1964

	Negro	Oriental	Other Non-White	Spanish Surname	Other White	Total
			Number			
Class 1	653.9	364.7	367.3	1,322.6	12,522.2	15,230.9
Class 2	162.7	243.8	135.3	425.7	6,883.8	7,851.2
Class 3	7.0	29.0	29.0	78.0	3,842.1	3,985.0
Class 4	2.5	3.0	—	15.0	1,769.0	1,789.5
TOTAL	826.1	640.5	531.6	1,841.3	25,017.1	28,856.6
Class 1A	233.7	101.9	75.8	295.4	5,141.1	5,847.9
Class 2A	116.9	132.4	63.3	220.8	2,491.0	4,024.4
			Percentage			
Class 1	79.16	56.94	69.09	71.83	50.05	52.78
Class 2	19.69	38.06	25.45	23.12	27.52	27.21
Class 3	.85	4.53	5.46	4.24	15.36	13.81
Class 4	.30	.47	—	.81	7.07	6.20
TOTAL	100.00	100.00	100.00	100.00	100.00	100.00

[1] For explanation of job classes see Appendix C, p. 173.

Note: Figures have been rounded off to the nearest hundredth.

Source: FEPC Report on Bank of America, September 1964, p. 8.

NEW HIRES

The bank refused to provide the FEPC with information on the *number* of vacancies or hires but would give only the *percentages* of hires in each of four major areas: San Francisco, Los Angeles, Sacramento, and San Diego. Since a comparison of percentage figures is meaningless without a knowledge of actual numbers hired, we have compared the "hire" percentages with those of applicants in two one-week periods in Los Angeles and San Francisco areas as reported by the bank. The data are presented in Table 5.

TABLE 5

COMPARISON BETWEEN BANK HIRES IN SELECTED AREAS AND TALLY OF
APPLICANTS FOR BANK EMPLOYMENT AT POINT OF FIRST INTERVIEW[1]

	Hires: Percentage by Racial or Ethnic Group for July 1964	Applicants Week 22–26 June No.	Percentage	Week 27–31 July No.	Percentage
Los Angeles					
Negro	18.41	85	22.30	56	28.43
Oriental	2.49	10	2.63	5	2.54
Other Non-White	1.99	13	3.42	5	2.54
Spanish Surname	18.41	108	28.35	40	20.30
Other White	58.70	165	43.30	91	46.19
TOTAL	100.00	381	100.00	197	100.00
San Francisco					
Negro	12.86	55	20.45	40	24.54
Oriental	3.57	12	4.46	6	3.69
Other Non-White	2.14	19	7.06	5	3.07
Spanish Surname	2.86	20	7.43	14	8.58
Other White	78.57	163	60.60	98	60.12
TOTAL	100.00	269	100.00	163	100.00

[1] Figures compiled and computed from data given in FEPC Report on Bank of America on pp. 10, 12.

BANK OF AMERICA

NATIONAL TRUST AND SAVINGS ASSOCIATION

SAN FRANCISCO HEADQUARTERS

R. A. Peterson, President   San Francisco 20, California
                                     March 12, 1964

The Chairman
Fair Employment Practices Commission
332 West First Street
Los Angeles, California

My dear Madam Chairman:

As you are painfully aware, San Francisco has been the scene of severe disturbances of public order caused by demonstrations designed to force employers to sign agreements with various groups.

It is the conviction of this bank that law and orderly processes must be maintained. It is the further conviction of this bank that it should not sign any agreement or furnish any reports on the racial characteristics of its employes to any nongovernment agency. Nevertheless, the bank recognizes that a sincere and dedicated attempt to improve the economic opportunities of minority groups has been and should continue to be part of its civic responsibility. We also recognize that there is legitimate reason for the public to be fully informed as to the bank's progress in discharging this civic responsibility.

The purpose of this open letter to you is to publicly affirm the equal opportunity employment policies of Bank of America N.T. & S.A. and to outline the practices which this bank will follow to provide a continuing program of assuring minority group members equal employment opportunities in the bank.

They are:

1. The management of the bank has for some time had an established employment policy as follows: "To employ personnel who are qualified to perform the duties which may be expected of them, and to do this without regard to their race, religious creed, color, national origin, or ancestry." This

148

statement is a quotation from the manual of instruction which is a standard item in every branch of the bank.

2. As in the past, FEPC Equal Opportunity signs will continue to be posted on all bank bulletin boards and places where employments are made.

3. As in the past, all classified advertising for employments placed by the bank will continue to carry the statement "An Equal Opportunity Employer."

4. When advertising for applicants in papers of general circulation, ads will also be placed in the Negro papers published in the same areas.

5. The bank will continue to endeavor to increase its input of qualified minority group personnel through contact with the minority specialists of the California State Employment Service. The bank will also continue to actively seek the assistance of minority group organizations in referring qualified personnel to us.

6. The bank will, within the next 60 days, and every 90 days thereafter, analyze its staff to ascertain the aggregate number of employes and the aggregate number of such employes who are of minority racial groups. Such information will be broken down into its components of Negroes, Orientals, Latin Americans and "other" and will be reported by area, e.g.:

   a) The state as a whole;

   b) Metropolitan Bay Area (San Francisco, Alameda, and Contra Costa Counties);

   c) The City of Los Angeles.

   The figures will be delivered to the offices of the Fair Employment Practices Commission in San Francisco, Los Angeles, and Sacramento so that this agency, which is charged with responsibility for enforcement of the Fair Employment Practices Act, may be fully informed on the status of the bank's staff.

7. Because our experience has clearly shown that a large proportion of minority racial applicants have not completed high school and cannot pass simple clerical tests, we cannot in good faith agree to the establishment of a definitive percentage of our employes who shall in the future be members of minority racial groups. However, we shall be glad at any time to cooperate with representatives of responsible minority group organizations and discuss specifically the progress being made and shall entertain such constructive suggestions as they may be able to offer to increase the

number of such employments. As evidence of the progress
the bank has made in this regard, you will be pleased to
know that a survey conducted this week in San Francisco
revealed that 15% of our employes in this city are members
of minority groups. A previous survey conducted one month
ago revealed that on a state-wide basis 11% of our employes
are drawn from minority groups.

In sending this open letter to you we hope we have demonstrated:

Our willingness to cooperate in providing opportunities for
members of minority groups.

Our dedication to the democratic processes and to law and
order.

That our policy refusal to sign agreements and provide reports
to nongovernment agencies such as the Ad Hoc Committee to
End Discrimination is not an attempt to hide our policies and
practices in respect to employment.

In common with all good Americans we are anxious to do all we
can to end the ugly specter of racial prejudice which has for too long
scarred our land. But also, as good Americans, we will not now or in
the future capitulate to illegal pressures of the type prominent in San
Francisco over the past weeks; and we are confident that we can
count on the full and effective support of law enforcement agencies
in the maintenance of this position.

Sincerely,
R. A. Peterson, *President*

APPENDIX B

Department of Industrial Relations
FAIR EMPLOYMENT PRACTICES COMMISSION
455 Golden Gate Avenue
San Francisco, California   94101

28 April 1964

California Chapters of the Congress of Racial Equality
Attention Mr. William Bradley, Bank of America Project Chairman
CORE San Francisco Chapter
1821 Fillmore Street
San Francisco, California 94115

Dear Sirs:

Your letter of 14 April 1964 posed a number of questions relating to the capacity of the State Fair Employment Practice Commission "to insure that an equal opportunity program planned by the Bank (of America) is fully implemented" if the Bank submits to us, as suggested, "pertinent personnel statistics relating to minority employment." Our answers are offered herewith, each one immediately following a restatement of your specific question, in the same order as enumerated in your letter.

1. "What kind of information would you need from the Bank of America in order to make a meaningful appraisal of its employment policy?"

Answer: We would need essentially the same information which we usually request of large employers when checking their employment patterns as to racial and ethnic composition. This would include approximate breakdowns of minority personnel in terms of Negro, Oriental, other Nonwhite, and Spanish-surname, according to major categories of position held and levels of compensation, main departments or other structural divisions, principal geographic areas, and perhaps selected branches within such areas. Concerning actual hiring processes, we would want to be informed as to normal person-

151

nel turnover in various categories, approximate numbers of minority applicants in given periods, recruiting sources and methods, and screening or testing procedures. Training programs and promotion practices would be of considerable interest. In general, we would wish to review the ways in which the Bank's equal opportunity policy is disseminated throughout its large organization, and the order of priority or emphasis which attaches to the implementation of this policy.

2. "Do you have the power to demand from the Bank of America in appropriate detail, and at regular intervals, all of the necessary data on recruitment, hiring, promotion, turnover, etc., and to independently verify such statistics?"

Answer: a) FEPC has the legal power to require such information only when engaged in investigation of a formal complaint or in a Commission-initiated investigation of apparent unlawful discrimination under Section 1421 of the FEP Act. When, instead, the employer is voluntarily cooperating with the Commission in a comprehensive review of his practices, looking toward strengthening those practices as may be indicated, we designate this process an "affirmative action," and there is normally no occasion to fall back on legal powers to secure meaningful information. Either the employer cooperates fully in this affirmative endeavor or it breaks down. In the event of such breakdown, there might be recourse, should the facts warrant, to a Section 1421 investigation. We hope and expect that the Bank of America contemplates, in the present instance, a fully meaningful, cooperative undertaking. b) Independent verification of such personnel information in exhaustive detail throughout an organization as large as the Bank of America would be well beyond our present staff capacity. It may be that spot checks or other techniques would suffice for all practical purposes, bearing in mind that the statistics, as indicated above, should be prepared according to specific categories which would be reasonably capable of review.

3. "Would such information be made available to the public? To CORE as an interested party? To an individual who had a complaint?"

Answer: Although our Commission has yet to establish policy which would permit a positive and explicit reply to this question, I anticipate that main information of this nature and our appraisal of it would be made available to interested parties, and perhaps to the general public as well. At present, the FEP Commissioner in charge of a given case may, in his discretion, release information about the case when this will serve a constructive purpose. We do not yet have precise guidelines, however, governing the degree of detail which may be appropriate to make public, or submit to interested parties, concerning a business or other organization which has been the subject of an affirmative action. It may well be—if we have been able to carry out a meaningful review of an employer's practices and personnel pattern, and if the public is already aware that FEPC and the employer are engaged in a program of this nature—that FEPC should issue one or more reports which would strike a mean between vacuous generalities and detailed raw data. Such reports should include careful appraisal of policy and practices, of progress made and further progress anticipated, of strengths and weaknesses, of trends in an evolving organization now giving special attention to its equal opportunity program. These questions, and the question as to whether detailed personnel pattern information may be released under certain circumstances, will be brought before our Commission at its next meeting. As for the individual complainant, our present practice is often to provide to him such limited information about the respondent's policies as will enable him to understand the basis on which the assigned Commissioner has closed his case.

4. "Do you have procedures for periodic review and analysis of the figures obtained?"

Answer: Periodic review of personnel pattern figures and other information bearing upon the status of the equal opportunity policy would of course be essential. I am unable at this time to make a positive statement as to our capacity to carry out periodic review and analysis of the Bank of America's practices, but we would surely endeavor to do so.

5. "Would you have the power to take affirmative action against Bank of America if the figures describing their minority group employment situation warranted it, on anything other than an individual case basis?"

Answer: a) Note first the FEPC now uses the term "affirmative action" in a different sense (see above) than suggested in this question. b) The question seems to imply that personnel pattern information of and by itself could constitute a basis for FEPC to compel an employer to change his practices. Generally, while we consider pattern information a relevant and often very significant reflection of an employer's actual personnel practices, it does not constitute, standing alone, conclusive evidence of unlawful discrimination. Weighed along with other facts and factors in a given situation, however, pattern information might well be persuasive in urging more effective implementation of non-discrimination policy. c) FEPC enforcement power may be exerted only in connection with formal complaints filed either by an aggrieved individual or by the Attorney General.

6. "Do you have adequate statutory authority to engage in such a project?"

Answer: Yes—as the general outlines of the project are described above, with some qualifications as mentioned.

7. "Do you have sufficient staff to adequately perform the work required for such a project without hampering the balance of the FEPC program now in operation?"

Answer: In the light of heavy present workload and the relatively limited size of our staff, undertaking a major new project as here contemplated would inevitably delay the resolution or completion of some pending cases (both individual complaints and Section 1421 investigations). Existing priorities would have to be shifted to some extent. We are hopeful, however, that budget augmentations urged by Governor Brown, now awaiting action by the Legislature, will be approved. If the Legislature so acts, FEPC will be in an improved position to engage in major affirmative actions.

8. "Would you be able to perform similar services for other large employers in the State of California upon request?"

Answer: As is implicit in preceding answers, such services could be provided only if staff capacity were substantially enlarged.

9. "Do you regard the action which you will take as a result of the voluntary giving of such statistics to FEPC as an effective substitute for the "Fair Employment Process Pact" being sought by the California Chapters of CORE with Bank of America or the one which the San Francisco Branch of the NAACP is seeking with Cadillac and the Automobile Dealers Association of San Francisco, and such . . . pacts as now exist between civil rights groups and Montgomery Ward, Sears and Roebuck, Littlemans Stores, Inc., Safeway, The West Bay Association of Food Industries, Inc., The San Francisco Retail Dry Goods Association, Mel's Drive-In, Lucky Stores and the Hotel Employers Association of San Francisco?"

Answer: FEPC's affirmative action approach, as sketched in part above, has long included main elements which are found also in the agreements to which you refer. As for the eventual results of such a program in terms of actual employment, we assume that CORE and other interested organizations or parties will, in due course, make their own judgments. At this writing we hesitate to prophesy or speculate. Among other things we do not know whether what we consider a meaningful approach will be acceptable to the Bank of America. And since we are not informed as to the extent of achievement to date under the various "pacts" referred to, comparative projections are hardly possible. But I can say that FEPC will not engage in, or remain active in, an affirmative action which does not give substantial promise, after expenditure of reasonable time and effort, of bringing about a truly strengthened equal opportunity program throughout the establishment concerned.

Please let us know if you wish additional information on any of the foregoing points. We shall advise you at the earliest possible time of any further expression which the FEP Commission may have after considering those of your questions which suggest the possible need for new or more explicit policy.

Finally, I wish to reemphasize the strong view of our Commission that affirmative undertakings of the sort discussed herein should comprise an increasingly important part of the FEPC program, so there may be significantly accelerated progress in bringing minority group Californians fully into the mainstream of our economic life. We earnestly hope that our agency will soon have sufficient staff to enable us to engage in such action on a scale commensurate with the urgent needs of our time.

> Sincerely yours,
> (MRS.) CARMEN H. WARSCHAW, *Chairman*

CHW:etc

cc: Mr. Chet Duncan, Western Regional Field Secretary, CORE
   Mr. Wester Sweet, Western Regional Legal Counsel, CORE
   Mr. Wilfred T. Ussery, National Second Vice Chairman, CORE
   Mr. Rudolph A. Peterson, President, Bank of America N.T. & S.A.

APPENDIX C

MEMO OF UNDERSTANDING

FULL TEXT OF AGREEMENT BETWEEN CALIFORNIA STATE
FAIR EMPLOYMENT PRACTICE COMMISSION AND BANK OF AMERICA
NATIONAL TRUST AND SAVINGS ASSOCIATION
JUNE 1, 1964

The Bank of America recognizes that a sincere and dedicated attempt to improve the economic opportunities of minority groups should continue to be part of its civic responsibility, and that there is legitimate reason for the public to be informed as to the Bank's progress in discharging this responsibility. In order to maximize its contribution to overcome the cancerous moral evil of inequities based on race, religion, or ancestry, the Bank believes that more than passive compliance with the letter of the fair employment law is essential—that a dynamic, comprehensive program of affirmative opportunity must be sustained on a high-priority basis. The Bank is deeply committed to such a program.

To these ends the Bank has expressed its willingness to confer with minority group organizations as to progress being made and to entertain their suggestions for improved practices, has accepted a number of such suggestions, has sought the counsel of the State Fair Employment Practice Commission (FEPC), and has offered to submit periodically to FEPC vital information reflecting the status and accomplishment of the Bank's affirmative opportunity program.

Recent discussions between the Bank and the Fair Employment Practice Commission have led to this Understanding, embracing three principal dimensions of the cooperative working relationship agreed to: 1) submission of significant personnel data to FEPC, 2) continuing review by FEPC of the Bank's affirmative policy implementation and joint consultation concerning its effectiveness, and 3) periodic public reporting by FEPC on pertinent aspects of the personnel data and management action in service of the foregoing objectives.

1. *Personnel Data to Be Submitted to FEPC Every Four Months*

a. In addition to total employment figures, racial or ethnic groups according to which reports of work force components will be submitted are: Negro, Oriental, other Nonwhite, and Spanish surname.

b. *By job classes.*

Class I. Normal in-hire or entrance positions generally designated as clerical. Typical positions are proof machine operator, credit checker, typist, PBX operator, statement clerk, safe deposit attendant, and teller. The teller position will be separately analyzed as a subgroup within the total. Approximately 50 per cent of all Bank personnel fall within Class I.

Class II. Included here are positions immediately senior to those in Class I, e.g., first-line supervisor, senior clerical, and note teller. This class comprises about 29 per cent of all personnel. In addition to the total, two sub-groups will be distinguished according to levels of responsibility.

Class III. The next higher 15 per cent. Typical positions include branch operations officer, lending officer, small branch manager, administration specialist, department head.

Class IV. The highest group, comprising about 6 per cent. Positions included are managers of intermediate to large branches, operations officers of major branches, heads of large administrative departments, administration specialists, supervisors of groups of branches, and senior management.

c. *By location.* State totals, plus each of 10 geographic areas exclusive of administration staff, and administration staff according to each of the three major locations in the San Francisco and Los Angeles areas, respectively. ERMA centers and district trust offices, although part of administration staff, will be reported for the areas in which they are situated, since their entrance staff is employed in the local market. In addition, the Bank will provide information relating to racial and ethnic distribution of personnel within the two major metropolitan areas.

d. *By job opportunities.*

1) For the first reporting period, the percentages of total hires represented by each of the component minority groups as follows: San Francisco and Los Angeles central hiring offices, Sacramento, and San Diego. It is understood that virtually all hires take place in Class I, except those which occur through the several training programs. The desirability of continuing this report with respect to Sacramento and San Diego will be reappraised by the Bank and FEPC after evaluation by FEPC of the first report.

2) For occasional, selected reporting periods: numbers of applicants and of hires, by racial and ethnic breakdowns, for selected cities or other areas.

3) For the formal training programs: numbers of entrants employed for these programs and successful completions, by racial and ethnic breakdowns.

e. *Applicant tallies.* Tallies of applicants at the point of first interview, by racial and ethnic breakdowns will be carried out from time to time, as requested by FEPC, for limited periods; e.g., one week. Initially, this will be done only at the central hiring offices in San Francisco and Los Angeles, later perhaps, in other locations. It is expressly understood that no such studies will entail any form of specification or designation of individual applicants by race or ancestry.

f.   If the further data or additional means of spot-checking or otherwise verifying certain types of information later appear to FEPC to be necessary or desirable, the Bank will cooperate in facilitating detailed examination of such data or augmenting its reporting.

g.   Apart from such statistical information, the Bank will keep FEPC advised as to any significant activities or developments relating to recruiting, training, upgrading, or other personnel processes which might have bearing on the general subject of this Understanding.

2. *Policy Implementation: Continuing Review and Consultation*

While the personnel data to be reported as described above are essential to the advancement of equal employment opportunity, such data alone will not provide an adequate basis for appraisal and strengthening of the Bank's overall employment practices. There will also be thorough-going study of all the policies and processes bearing upon recruitment, selection, training, and promotion of personnel, from which may emerge, in joint consultation, ideas and recommendations for increasingly effective practices. FEPC's examination of the Bank's practices affecting personnel will be as comprehensive as deemed necessary. The spirit in which this work proceeds will be that of a cooperative, affirmative endeavor, seeking full realization of the basic purpose of the Bank's policy on equal employment opportunity and of the intent of President Peterson's strong declarations on this subject.

In general, the main features of an affirmative program of this nature are set forth in the FEPC brochure, *Promoting Equal Job Opportunity: A Guide for Employers*. Features which, it is anticipated, will be applicable and useful in the Bank's program—to be supplemented by others resulting from experience, from consultation with FEPC, or from suggestions by concerned minority group organizations—are the following:

Policy. The Bank will continue to make every effort to ensure that its statement of equal employment policy as it affects hiring, promotions, training, and assignment carries the full force and effect of a major policy promulgated by the highest authority in senior management, and is carried out at all levels.

Recruiting. The Bank utilizes the services of the minority specialists in the various California State Employment Service offices throughout the State.

The Bank will expand its efforts to make its policies and personnel needs known to churches, school principals, teachers, counselors, and to other organizations, agencies and individuals which may provide communication or access to prospective minority applicants. Minority employees will be encouraged to refer qualified friends and relatives.

The Bank will participate with school districts in distributive education programs potentially leading to Bank employment and will provide speakers or other assistance to "Career Day" and similar activities.

Hiring. The FEPC employment poster is displayed at all Bank installations. Personnel, medical, and security procedures will be continuously reviewed to eliminate any possible discrimination, actual, inadvertent, or apparent.

Tests and standards have been and will be reviewed to make sure that they are valid for the positions, uniformly applied, and free of inadvertent bias. Special efforts will be made to ensure that personnel involved in hiring will be thoroughly aware of the problems of minority applicants.

Training. Special efforts will be made to recruit minority persons for training programs which lead to higher-skilled, supervisory, and executive responsibilities. Minority employees will be encouraged, along with others, to participate in American Institute of Banking courses, and will be counseled regarding methods of personal and career advancement.

Transfer and promotion. Promotional channels and decision-making will be continuously reviewed to make certain that minority employees have equal opportunity and are fully aware that advancement will take place on merit alone.

Advertising. Advertising of employment vacancies will be carried in minority news media among others and will emphasize the Bank's equal opportunity policy. Minority group persons will be among those portrayed in the Bank's general advertising in mass media.

3. *Public Reporting*

FEPC has the right and responsibility to determine what information should be released in the public interest and will accordingly prepare and issue occasional public reports summarizing and critically appraising main features of the Bank's equal opportunity policies and practices. Normally included, it is anticipated, will be discussion of areas of strength or weakness in the Bank's practices, with illustrative instances of progress or problems; appraisal of activities such as recruiting for entrance positions and for training programs; appropriate statistics and other supporting data and suggestions or recommendations which FEPC may wish to offer. It is FEPC policy not to disclose unevaluated personnel pattern information. Any views which the Bank may have as to the validity of FEPC's observations in a given report will receive serious consideration prior to its release.

MEMORANDUM OF UNDERSTANDING, June 1, 1964
signed by Mrs. Carmen H. Warschaw, Chairman,
Fair Employment Practice Commission,
and Mr. Jesse W. Tapp, Chairman of the Board,
Bank of America

"La Huelga o La Causa" (A)

California Farm Workers' Strike

Where is the Union now, friend, at the strike's end? Inside my heart, friend.

—MARSHALL DUBIN
Educational Director, Local 1199
Drug and Hospital Union, New York

On September 16, 1965, in Delano, California, the predominantly Spanish-speaking, Mexican-American, National Farm Workers Association (NFWA) joined with the AFL-CIO Agricultural Workers Organizing Committee (AWOC) in a strike against growers of table grapes. The growers were paying Mexican workers $1.40 an hour, per U.S. Department of Labor *bracero* program regulations, but refused to pay American workers more than $1.20 an hour.

AWOC began the strike on September 8; five days later the growers hired scab labor.[1] By September 20, both AWOC and NFWA were on strike.

---

[1] John Gregory Dunne, *Delano, the Story of the California Grape Strike* (New York: Farrar Straus & Giroux, Inc., 1967), p. 78.

The NFWA was no ordinary labor group, nor was its founder, Cesar Chavez, the usual labor organizer. In 1962, after ten years with Saul Alinsky's Community Service Organization, Chavez designed NFWA to operate as a combination welfare cooperative/union and to be the spearhead group for a civil rights movement. But Chavez differed from Alinsky on one notable, and unshakable, tenet: he took a nonviolent stance, maintaining that no union movement justifies the loss of one single human life, grower or worker. Toward its goal of bettering the lives of the thousands of poor, semiliterate, Mexican-American migrant farm workers in California and the Southwest, NFWA set up cooperative enterprises and welfare-type services for its membership of about two thousand families.

In the summer of 1965, AWOC (with predominantly Filipino-American membership) had successfully struck growers in the Coachella Valley over the same issue of discriminatory pay scales. There the hourly rates were: Mexican-American, $1.10; Filipino, $1.25; but bracero, $1.40. Parity was won for all at $1.40. When the growers farther north, around Delano, refused to pay equal wages, AWOC struck again and asked NFWA for help. Although Chavez felt that his association was not adequately prepared for a strike, or wanted one, and that it was premature for NFWA and might engender antagonism between Filipino- and Mexican-Americans, neither he nor his membership could refuse to join such a cause. The two organizations then merged and formed the United Farm Workers Organizing Committee under Chavez's directorship. Chavez himself said:

> We don't want to model ourselves on industrial unions. We want to get involved in politics, in voter registration, not just contract negotiations. . . . We have to find some cross between being a movement and being a union. The membership must maintain control; the power must not be centered in a few.[2]

A *San Francisco Chronicle* reporter noted the difference in this effort of farm workers to organize:

> This time—and this is what makes Delano significant—an alliance has been formed between two tightly knit community groups, and has given the strikers at least temporary unity and staying power rare in farm labor disputes.[3]

[2] Andrew Kokind, "Grape Pickers Strike," *New Republic*, January 29, 1966, pp. 12–13.

[3] *San Francisco Chronicle*, Dick Meister, November 9, 1965.

The Strike Begins

Chavez began the strike by sending registered letters to the thirty-eight growers in the Delano area asking for negotiations. None showed up for the meeting. A few days after the NFWA strike meeting on September 16, Chavez sought outside support from University of California and Stanford students, the Church, and such civil rights groups as SNCC and CORE. With this backing, NFWA began picketing.

> [Chavez] purposely did not picket certain growers, preferring to keep them for what he called his "safety valve." There was often work available at these ranches, and on those days, Chavez would pull pickets from the line and get them to sign on with the unstruck growers in order to earn a few days' wages.[4]

To replace those on strike, growers imported workers without telling them of the strike and deducted their full transportation cost from their first paychecks. Many workers, on learning of the strike, either joined the pickets or returned home.

The mechanics of picketing thirty-seven thousand acres of grapes was formidable. "It's like striking an industrial plant that has a thousand entrance gates and is 400 square miles large. And if that isn't bad enough, you don't know each morning where the plant will be, or where the gates are, or whether it will be open or closed, or what wages will be offered that day," a SNCC worker in Delano said.[5]

Violence was not confined to the growers, although the NFWA pickets had taken an oath of nonviolence. Assorted retributive measures were used against the growers, including:

> The Kern County sheriff's office discovered that Chavez supporters had purchased 4,000 marbles, which they were firing with slingshots at strikebreakers in the field. Rocks were thrown through windows in strikebreakers' houses, and picket signs set up on lawns reading "A SCAB LIVES HERE." One nine-year-old girl was told that unless her father came out of the fields, her house would be burned down.[6]

Both the growers and NFWA used unusual techniques to weaken each other's position. SNCC and CORE members would scout the vineyards in

---

[4] Dunne, *Delano, the Story of the California Grape Strike*, p. 84.

[5] Kokind, "Grape Pickers Strike," p. 14.

[6] Dunne, *Delano, the Story of the California Grape Strike*, pp. 24–26.

the morning to find evidence of work. The information would be radioed back to union headquarters and a caravan of roving pickets would be dispatched. Growers on their part would hide their workers in the middle of the fields so that they would not see the pickets. One grower cruised over Delano in his private plane and radioed the location of the picket caravan to his crew on the ground. Some other growers drove down their property line spraying the pickets with insecticide or fertilizer or gunned over the roads in tractors to raise dust.

But the violence was minimal; and despite all the efforts of the NFWA and its supporters, all but a few hundred acres were harvested. Profits were cut, however: importing labor was expensive, and unskilled workers caused excess spoilage. Distribution was difficult because trucks and San Francisco docks were picketed. The longshoremen's union refused to load grapes on a ship bound for the Orient. The Teamsters, who honored the strike in the fields, cooperated with the NFWA at the produce markets.

The Boycott and the March: Mixed Tactics

The strikers' next decision—a well-publicized nationwide boycott—was given a boost in December 1965 when the AFL-CIO passed a resolution supporting the strike. Another boost came from the UAW—after the AFL-CIO meeting, Walter Reuther went to Delano and appeared with Chavez. The AFL-CIO gave the joint strike committee $10,000, and the United Auto Workers and the Industrial Unions Department also gave financial support.

The first boycott target was one of the largest growers, Schenley Industries, Inc. Schenley's 3,350 acres of grapes in Delano contributed only a small fraction of its annual distilled spirits sales of $500 million (including wines from Delano grapes). NFWA workers and volunteers spread boycott news around the country by such ingenious tactics as a Boston Grape Party and a million leafllets distributed in New York City subways. The next boycott target was another giant, the DiGiorgio Corporation, with 4,400 acres of grapes on its Sierra Vista ranch near Delano. Of DiGiorgio's annual revenue of more than $230 million, the bulk came from canned foods and less than one-tenth from farming. Again the boycott was nationwide, but DiGiorgio denied any economic effects.

To intensify the pressure and garner additional publicity, Chavez staged a march from Delano to the state capitol in Sacramento. Well aware of the emotional impact of the Southern civil rights marches, Chavez decided the march should end with an Easter Sunday meeting with Governor Brown on the steps of the state capitol. Until then, both the state legislature and the governor had shown indifference to the strike.

In February 1966, the NFWA began signing up marchers for the 250-mile, twenty-five-day walk to Sacramento, which was to begin March 17. The march stopped at each town along the way to hold a rally to gain publicity and recruit new members. The marchers did not meet the governor—he kept to his announced plans and was out of town. While the march was in progress, however, mounting pressure forced Schenley to move. Lewis Rosensteil, then Schenley's board chairman and chief stockholder, ordered the company properties in Delano to be sold, but a lawyer advised giving in to NFWA demands for the sake of the company's image. On April 6, 1966, an agreement was signed that recognized the NFWA as bargaining agent for the Schenley field workers. Chavez, still on the march, ordered the full boycott effort swung against DiGiorgio.

DiGiorgio was a tougher target than Schenley. Its economic and political power was formidable, and its history was antiunion. Even DiGiorgio, however, hired a public relations team, but its campaign was not successful. Shortly after Schenley and Christian Brothers recognized NFWA as a bargaining agent, DiGiorgio stated that it was willing to have the field workers vote on the issue of union representation. Chavez, however, demanded recognition of the NFWA. DiGiorgio refused but left the door open for a vote and negotiation if the NFWA won the election.

At this point the Teamsters forsook their NFWA support and bid for the right to organize DiGiorgio workers. Teamsters—but not NFWA—were allowed to campaign on the ranch. "It's tough enough just fighting another union. But when the company and the union are working hand in glove, it's a hard combination to beat."[7]

After the vote on June 24, both sides claimed victory. Of the 732 eligible, 385 voted (281 for the Teamsters), but 347 heeded Chavez and did not vote. The strike continued. However, under pressure for a vote investigation, Governor Brown appointed an arbitrator, Dr. Ronald Haughton, who recommended that a new election be held August 30 under American Arbitration Association (AAA) auspices.

THE UFWOC AND A CONTRACT WITH DiGIORGIO

In need of greater organizing strength and more money, Chavez merged NFWA with AWOC into the AFL-CIO. The merged union, the United Farm Workers Organizing Committee, was to operate as part of and under the direction of the parent federation.

Strengthened by the merger, and aided by the AAA requirement that DiGiorgio provide lists of workers to *both* unions, UFWOC won a signifi-

[7] Dunne, *Delano, the Story of the California Grape Strike*, p. 153.

cant victory. Of 1,205 field workers voting (many of the seasonal workers were brought from as far away as Texas and Mexico), 530 voted for the AFL-CIO, 331 for the Teamsters, and 12 for "no union." The AAA challenged 332 ballots, largely on the grounds of eligibility. In the face of the growers' claims that field workers were not interested in a union and were harassed and victimized by labor leaders, the insignificant vote (12 of 1,205) for "no union" was noteworthy.

The victories at Schenley, DiGiorgio, and other scattered companies, although major, were by no means final. As Chavez pointed out, there were still 30 growers to go in the Delano area alone. Even at DiGiorgio it took 7 months to agree upon a minimum wage of $1.65 an hour, with a guarantee of 4 hours' pay if no work was available and a week's paid vacation for workers employed 1,600 hours a year. The minimum wage was raised to $1.70 in 1968, and workers who had been with the company for 3 years would get 2 weeks' vacation.

Truce with the Teamsters

Early in October 1966, Fred Perelli-Minetti, one of the biggest independent growers in Delano, gave the Teamsters sole bargaining power. Chavez refused to recognize the agreement and set up UFWOC pickets. The Teamsters, who knew that they were being used to stop UFWOC, discovered that to unionize farm workers they had to appeal to "la causa." Traditional trade union techniques were useless. Therefore, in January 1967, the Teamsters and Chavez worked out an agreement on almost every facet of farm labor organization. Perelli-Minetti was almost within UFWOC's grasp.

But the union power structure halted this agreement, to Chavez's dismay. Because UFWOC was not an independent union affiliated with AFL-CIO but an organizing committee of the federation, Chavez was subject to George Meany's decisions. Since 1957, when the AFL-CIO ousted the Teamsters, there have been no direct relations between the two unions.

The strike slowed as Teamsters and UFWOC traded allegations and growers watched. Finally in July 1967, again with the help of the clergy, an agreement was reached. UFWOC would have "jurisdiction over all field workers," while the Teamsters would have "jurisdiction over workers in canneries, creameries, frozen-food processing plants, dehydrating plants, and warehouses."[8] A number of California wineries immediately announced elections to choose the representing unions in the field and in the

[8] *Ibid.*, p. 173.

processing plant. But many growers held firm, and the Council of California Growers denounced the clergy for its union support.

During the fall of 1967, the UFWOC hiring hall dispatched workers to harvest more than ten thousand acres of grapes owned by Schenley, DiGiorgio, Goldberg & Company Packers, and Perelli-Minetti—all companies forced to sign contracts after bitter strikes. All workers were receiving a "respectable" wage and working under improved conditions:

> The lowest wage included in the contracts is $1.65 an hour plus $.15 for every box picked . . . and the base pay at most of the contract ranches is $1.80 plus the "incentive" or piece rate. The contracts include an additional $.05 or $.10 an hour contribution by the employer for health insurance, a life insurance program, unemployment insurance, a very strong grievance procedure clause, seniority rights, drinking water and toilets in the fields, rest periods, and a host of other details common to other industries.[9]

Despite these successes, setbacks almost overshadowed the gains. Joseph Giumarra and Sons, Inc., the largest table grape grower in the world, refused the union's and Governor Reagan's conservative State Conciliation Service's requests for elections. Giumarra workers struck on August 3, 1967. In retaliation, Giumarra employed a number of tactics and subterfuges, such as employing workers recruited by other growers and using more than fifty different labels owned by other growers in the area. Despite UFWOC complaints to the U.S. Food and Drug Administration, little was done. As a result, UFWOC boycotted all but DiGiorgio California table grapes in an effort to put greater pressure on Giumarra.

The community atmosphere was also hostile to the strikers. Friendly judges restricted picketing to one picket every fifty feet. Strikers were not allowed to visit strikebreakers in their homes, hand out leaflets, or even (for a time) use megaphones to reach workers deep in the fields. Local law enforcement agencies often acted as political obstacles by tending to side with the growers. In a survey conducted by the Marysville office of the California Rural Legal Assistance Program, it was found that 91 percent of the growers in Sutter, Yuba, Colusa, and Butte counties violated drinking water regulations and 98 percent violated sanitary and payday regulations. They also violated the regulation that workers be paid within seventy-two hours after they had been laid off or had quit. These findings were typical of the situation in the Delano fields.[10] Such violations were often ignored by local government regulatory agencies.

In an effort to curb the inflow of "green carders" (braceros), Chavez

---

[9] Doug Adair, "Cesar Chavez's Biggest Battle," *The Nation*, December 11, 1967, p. 627.

[10] *El Malcriado*, II, No. 4, April 15, 1968, 9.

went to Washington to persuade immigration officials of the need for a tougher enforcement of the laws prohibiting the illegal use of green card workers as strikebreakers.

Striking farm workers in other states (not all of them associated with UFWOC) ran into similar difficulties. In Colorado they struck the beet farms, in Michigan and Wisconsin the fruit groves, and in Texas the cotton and melon fields. The melon strike, run by UFWOC, achieved no results. A local judge in Texas outlawed all picketing in the melon strike, and hurricane Beulah destroyed 70 percent of the winter harvest in south Texas in 1967, crippling the union's activity there. In Texas it became a holding operation and worked on community organizing, voter registration, and the Giumarra boycott, giving its members whatever services and help it could afford.

The campaign against Giumarra met with difficulties other than grower opposition tactics. The UAW cut back its $7,500 a month, and although the AFL-CIO Organizing Department offered steady help, new sources of income were needed. The financial crisis forced a reduction in organizing and service activities. The UAW renewed its $7,500 a month, which augmented the AFL-CIO's $10,000, but the strike against Giumarra cost $50,000 a month. Help came from unexpected quarters. On May 20, 1966, a Supreme Court ruling relaxed restrictions by permitting a union to picket within a shopping center. Because of this ruling, "Don't Buy Grapes" signs became a familiar sight at supermarkets in major cities and their suburbs. The UFWOC also received strong backing in New York from the Seafarer's Union, which provided housing, food, and transportation for UFWOC members organizing the boycott in New York.

Even the most ardent supporters of grape growers conceded that UFWOC would eventually win the strike against Giumarra, as it had against diversified companies like DiGiorgio and Schenley, but supporters feared that the breakthrough with DiGiorgio might not prove permanent. The DiGiorgio contract had no "successor clause," and with sale of the land the contract would end. Both Schenley and DiGiorgio sold their table grape vineyards in 1969, leaving UFWOC with contracts with only six wine producers: Gallo, Christian Brothers, Masson, Almaden, Franzia Brothers, and Novitiate. The boycott itself became the strikers' main activity. Vineyard picket lines were all but abandoned; some strikers went back to work to ease the financial strain on the union; the workers and their families, on union salaries of five dollars a week, continued to wage probably the most extensive boycott in American labor history in more than thirty cities in the United States and Canada.[11] In 1969, boycott activity was expanded to two hundred United States cities and foreign ports.

[11] Dick Meister, " 'La Huelga' becomes 'La Causa,' " *The New York Times*, November 17, 1968, Sunday Magazine, p. 109.

The growers argued that unionizing workers was senseless in the face of increasing mechanization of farms and that, in fact, unions would only encourage automation. If and when mechanization came to the grape industry, Chavez believed, the union would be able to ensure the worker a share in the profits. "Our main concern is men, not machines," he said. "I'm not sure what effects automation will have in terms of man-power. Right now it doesn't make any difference. What does make a difference is that the farm worker has the same right as other Americans to bargain collectively with his employer. Unless the farm worker is represented, every future development in agriculture production will come, as in the past, at the expense of his human dignity."[12]

OBSTACLES TO ORGANIZING: THE GROWERS AND THE SOCIAL SETTING

The consolidated strike was directed against twenty-four growers in the Delano area. The largest growers, huge corporate concerns accustomed to a flooded labor market, were vehemently opposed to the unionization and felt that unions were traditionally their only real opposition to easily controlled labor costs. It is possible that they feared that an effective labor movement might result in congressional investigations of their land monopolies.

The small growers, whose forefathers had come a century too late in search of the American dream, were caught in a cost-price squeeze between the combined effects of large-grower efficiency and boycott pressure.

The primary characteristic of these small growers, also shared by the managers of the corporate farms, was their belief in paternalism. Even in the bitter struggle of the strike, they believed that their workers were happy and did not want a union.

> John Giumarra isn't sure the vineyard workers need a union, anyway. "You have to go slow motion to get less than $2.10 an hour. And it doesn't matter where they live they get free transportation. If they don't live around here we give them a place to stay, too. Absolutely free."[13]
>
> What is the problem? . . . The workers have always gotten along well with us. They make good money. Some have beautiful homes. They own cars. They are our neighbors here and we were getting along well until the troublemakers started.[14]

---

[12] "Squeezing California's Grape Growers," *Commonweal*, June 14, 1968, p. 374.

[13] Kokind, "Grape Pickers Strike," p. 14.

[14] Dunne, *Delano, the Story of the California Grape Strike*, p. 129.

The growers actually believed these statements in spite of overwhelming evidence to the contrary. Was it "good money" for a farm worker who was not given room and board to receive an average wage of $1.23 in 1966 while his counterpart in manufacturing received $2.71? Although the growers talked about the workers' "beautiful homes," a federal investigation committee discovered that over 80 percent of migratory workers lived in substandard housing. Growers called the workers "neighbors" in spite of the discrimination practiced against Mexican-Americans, even in Delano.

> Discrimination in Delano, as in all valley towns, is far more subtle than police charge sheets and segregated cemeteries. . . . Far more pervasive is the acceptance of the way the itinerant Mexicans are forced to live [which] is simply regarded as a fact of life in the Valley.[15]

Although the first line of grower defense against the farm workers' demands was economic, a study made by the Department of Labor estimated that "the cost of field labor to the California grower is only 2 to 5 cents on the dollar, depending on the crop. And, as Willard Wirtz has pointed out, even if growers doubled wages, they could pass on the increase to the consumers without raising prices very much."[16] To the individual grower, however, the difference might bring a loss. If, for example, he raised prices while other growers did not, he would lose his share of the market.

But this hardship plea was far from the only tactic: in action, growers were much rougher and much more direct. They harassed the strikers, turning off water and electricity in camps and evicting workers, scattering them and forcing many to migrate further. They bussed in scabs to work their fields. They suddenly supported a new union, the Kern-Tulare Independent Farm Workers Union, and some of the larger growers hired public relations firms.

In 1969, as the strike continued and as large-city politicians got into the act, the growers tried a new tack—the antiboycott boycott. It was estimated that the city of San Francisco would lose more than $1 million in convention business as agricultural associations changed the site of their annual meetings in protest against a resolution endorsing the strikers' boycott approved by that city's Board of Supervisors and signed by the mayor. The groups included the American Farm Bureau Federation, the California Grape and Tree Fruit League, the California Beet Growers Association, and the California Cattlemen's Association.[17]

---

15 *Ibid.*, p. 102.

16 James P. Degnan, "Monopoly in the Vineyards, the 'Grapes of Wrath' Strike," *The Nation*, February 17, 1966, p. 153.

17 *The Wall Street Journal*, April 7, 1969, p. 10.

And in March 1969, required reports submitted to the Office of Labor Management and Welfare Pension Reports (eight months late) disclosed that some large growers were secretly operating an organization disguised as a workers' group to undermine the UFWOC effort. The organization, the Agricultural Workers Freedom to Work Association, had been formed in May 1968 by a group of growers meeting to plan activities to combat the UFWOC, among them Giumarra senior and junior and the personnel manager of the DiGiorgio Fruit Corporation. Contributions were collected from more than twenty growers and farm supply firms; the Giumarras, DiGiorgio, and grower Robert Sarbovich provided office space and supplies and gave the general secretary and other officers of the association orders: ". . . spy on union members and supporters; halt or disrupt their activities, hold free picnics to get farm workers to listen to speeches against Chavez and UFWOC, wage a major propaganda effort and get growers to help recruit workers for the association . . . a key aim was 'to get headlines' and television coverage for statements that the union's strike against the growers and its related grape boycott were designed to force workers into the union."[18]

More than all the grower tactics, however, there were social attitudes and political and economic obstacles to the organizing of the farm workers that were far more difficult to overcome.

SOCIAL. Some resistance came from the grape workers themselves: Not unaware of their low social status, many never thought of themselves as being permanently in the farm labor force. Ethnic barriers were formidable, as were those between regular workers, foreign and interstate migrants, and part-time workers. Even among the farm workers themselves, differences in the kind of job—in the field or in the shed—were obstacles to community of interest.

Then there were the attitudes of society. Many people thought that their food was nurtured by the loving hands of the friendly small farmer and were unable to believe that agriculture was dominated by giant corporations that called themselves "agribusiness" and that agriculture was no longer a "sentimental way of life." The growers also chose to believe the myth. One grower lamented:

> I had a camp full of Filipinos, men who have lived there for 20–30 years. The wife of one of them used to take care of my children. They were like members of our family. We gave them a place to live all year long. And now they're sitting there in the camp on a sit-down strike. . . . I just can't understand it.[19]

18 *San Francisco Chronicle*, March 4, 1969, p. 4.
19 Eugene Nelson, *Huelga* (Delano, Calif.: Farm Worker Press, 1966), p. 33.

Another grower, who always considered himself a "good guy," made a similar statement:

> Our workers have never shown any dissatisfaction. We take good care of them. And most of these Mexicans like the arrangement of not working steady. It's the nature of these people to move from place to place.[20]

But if there existed deluded growers, there also existed many shrewd agribusinessmen who used the myth to frustrate effectively the organization of the grape workers. For example, many growers used the social stigma attached to wasting food by staging dramatic plow-unders for the press. This was generally quite effective in creating public outrage against the workers whom the farmers blamed for lost crops. Growers also resorted to the familiar "Red scare" tactic of calling union leaders "Communists" or "outside agitators."

Of course, the main opposition came from the large growers. The small growers, being quite familiar with their workers' problems, favored the movement.

> "The major opposition to agricultural unions in this state comes from the giants, the land monopolists . . . who own practically half the state," says Paul Taylor, emeritus professor of economics at the University of California and one of the nation's leading authorities on land tenure and agricultural water policies. "Since early in California's history, land monopolists have needed a flooded labor market, some kind of slave-labor situation to maintain their empires," Mr. Taylor says. "The land monopolists have always been afraid of labor. . . . Why, a really effective farm and urban labor movement here with power in Washington could bring about a series of Congressional investigations that might be the beginning of the end for these monopolies."
>
> When Walter Reuther spoke at Delano . . . the main substance of his talk was that he intended to call for a Congressional investigation of California land monopoly. It is interesting that not one major California newspaper or television station even mentioned this aspect of Reuther's speeches.
>
> Corroborating Dr. Taylor, Henry Anderson, editor of *Farm Labor*, a journal that supports the small farmer . . . writes that the amount of land owned by the monopolists is "impressive but the aggregation of economic power to which these landowners are tied through interlocking directorates is a great deal more impressive still." [For example, the] DiGiorgio Corporation . . . directorate interlocks with the Pacific Gas and Electric, Pacific Telephone and Telegraph,

[20] *El Malcriado*, II, No. 4, April 15, 1968, 3.

Bank of California, Union Oil, Fireman's Fund Insurance, in, to quote Anderson, "a relationship so close that it is rare even in the world of higher capitalism; DiGiorgio has four directors in common with the Bank of America."

These alliances illuminate the complaint of migrant minister James Drake, an aide of Cesar Chavez: "The little growers really want to help us with the strike; but they say if they dare recognize the union they better not try to get loans for next year's crop."[21]

Townspeople also opposed the strikers who they felt were giving their area a bad name. One such group was an organization called the Citizens for Facts from Delano.

> Its main function was to buff the image of the town, which had been, they thought, tarnished with malice aforethought by Chavez and the NFWA. The major thrust of the Citizens for Facts campaign was a fusillade of leaflets, broadsides, pamphlets, poster reprints, and letters to the editor suggesting obscure and tortuous links between Cesar Chavez and something which after a few weeks [came to be called] "the Communist conspiracy."[22]

Still another kind of opposition came from the local newspapers who were highly dependent upon, and pressured by, the growers. These newspapers consequently refused to print anything about the strike, especially anything that would be beneficial to the union cause.

Another obstacle was the role of other unions. Competition among various unions—the Teamsters, the NFWA, the AWOC—at first threatened to undermine the whole movement. Then the growers unsuccessfully attempted to set up a competing union.

ECONOMIC. The seasonality of the grape industry was an obstacle to successful organization. In Delano there was a fairly stable work force of about five thousand throughout the year, but during the harvest, thousands more workers were hired. The UFWOC, finding it difficult to organize migrating people, polled them through an affidavit system. Then the growers had almost complete economic control of the workers, even being their landlords.

The greatest economic obstacle had always been the availability of cheap labor. In the 1850s it was the Chinese immigrants, later the Japanese, then the flood of Mexicans fleeing the Revolution of 1910. Then came the Filipinos, to be followed during the depression by Dust Bowl refugees. With the labor shortage of World War II, the bracero program came into

---

[21] Degnan, "Monopoly in the Vineyards," p. 154.

[22] Dunne, *Delano, the Story of the California Grape Strike*, p. 110.

being and did not end with the war. Cheap agricultural labor was supplied through the provisions of Public Law #414, Section 214, of the Immigration and Nationality Act, which allowed Mexican nationals to enter the United States to work and then return to their homes as green card holders. The UFWOC newspaper, *El Malcriado*, described the plan this way:

> The green card system is really designed to allow immigrants to settle in this country. But the United States Immigration Service has created an administrative monster called the commuter system. . . . This allows Mexican workers to enter the country just to work and to return to Mexico. It has simply created a convenience to the growers, supplying them with cheap labor which will not remain in the country to plague them in the off season.[23]

Still another economic obstacle was the extremely high cost of organizing and running a strike.

POLITICAL. Despite a steady stream of bills in Congress, agricultural workers were excluded from the collective bargaining provisions of the NLRA and were not covered by minimum wage laws, unemployment insurance acts, or most Social Security benefits. Local courts often ruled against the workers, and bail procedures for growers and for workers were not equitable. One sheriff in Delano testified before a Senate investigating board that he had arrested the objects of threats—the picketers—rather than the threateners—workers in the fields—because "we just removed the cause of the problem."[24]

BACKGROUND ATTEMPTS TO ORGANIZE

Before the National Labor Relations Act was passed in 1935, the agricultural workers in the United States were one of many laboring groups powerless to control their economic situation. In every industry, including agriculture, workers attempted to raise their standards of living through the strength of the union.

No farm labor organization fully succeeded in its aims. The 1913 efforts of the Industrial Workers of the World failed. The Cannery and Agricultural Workers Industrial Union, backed by the Communist Party, failed in 1933. The Southern Tenant Farmers Union, beginning in 1934, merged with the AFL during World War II. The Filipino Agricultural Laborers

23 *El Malcriado*, II, No. 5, May 1, 1968, 9.
24 *AFL-CIO News*, March 26, 1966, p. 4.

Association gained limited success but was undercut by the bracero program. The 1947 AFL National Farmers Union attempts to organize resulted in such violence that further efforts were quashed. Then, in 1959, the AFL-CIO tried again, with AWOC, which merged with NFWA to become UFWOC. The continuing bracero program, formalized in 1951 by Public Law 78, further subdued farm labor organization.

In 1935, Congress passed the National Labor Relations Act. The purpose of the act was "to define and protect the rights of employers and employees, to encourage collective bargaining, and to eliminate certain practices on the part of labor and management that are harmful to the general welfare."[25]

Farm wages in California increased in the next few years, undoubtedly in large part because of union pressure. But "the elusive goal of a union contract with growers was never achieved . . . and large growers remained so firmly possessed of their medieval fear and hatred of unions that the huge DiGiorgio Fruit Corporation let its entire cherry crop rot at a loss in the hundreds of thousands of dollars rather than negotiate."[26] Other unions also made some progress, but it was far from spectacular. For example, in May 1961, the Teamsters Union announced that henceforth the field workers at Antle, Inc., one of the biggest lettuce growers, would be members of Local 890. But it was obviously a "sweetheart" contract, and the courts later threw it out.

These problems were further compounded by the nature of the workers as people. Many were illiterate, highly mobile, and skeptical—even distrustful—of union efforts in agriculture. Since the majority of the farm workers moved from job to job as the seasons changed and harvests rotated, few were willing to join an organization which might reap benefits for them only for a short time. In addition, some of the workers were reasonably content with their existence, having lived under comparable, or even worse, conditions throughout their lives.

The Grape Workers: Issues, Tactics, Position

In planning strategy for a strike for which he felt his group was unprepared, Cesar Chavez framed the issues in broader terms than the simply economic to gain the publicity and outside support he felt were necessary if there was to be any chance of success.

The first grievance was of course economic: at the time of the 1965

[25] Office of General Counsel of the National Labor Relations Board, A *Layman's Guide to the Basic Law under the NLRA*, 1964, p. 1.
[26] Nelson, *Huelga*, p. 18.

strike, the average wage of the workers was about $1.20 an hour plus a piece rate of 10 cents per lug of grapes picked. The piece rate might amount to 30 or 40 cents an hour extra for a fast worker. But even this rate applied only during the harvest season; during the pruning season, rates were lower, and during part of the year, there was no work at all. The average yearly income for the workers in 1965 was about $1,350, and 84 percent of them earned less than the $3,100 limit considered the poverty line.[27] The strikers were demanding $1.40 per hour plus 25 cents per lug. They also demanded enforcement of the standard working conditions prescribed by state law (for example, adequate field sanitation facilities), which were, in many cases, simply ignored by the growers.

The major demand, however, was for the right of collective bargaining, since landowners had continually refused to recognize worker organizations and demands. The NFWA platform stated that the workers

> . . . are not prepared to allow the growers to go on paternalisti-
> cally deciding what is good for the workers or what the workers really
> want or really need. They are asking to be treated as human beings—
> and to be granted at least the recognition that is granted the fertil-
> izers, machinery, and other factors in agribusiness. For the cost to the
> growers of all these items has risen in the last decade, but the cost of
> labor has remained almost stationary. The workers—and their tradi-
> tional passivity and lack of organization—have been taken for
> granted.[28]

It was on this plea for collective bargaining rights that the NFWA developed the moral issue with which Chavez hoped to gain public atten-tion and the support of the organized Church as well as of other groups.

In addition to Church support, which is discussed in "La Huelga o La Causa" part B, page 340, the NFWA received help from civil rights groups such as SNCC and CORE, which sent volunteers and equipment to help the grape workers organize an effective strike. Chavez had adopted a policy of nonviolence and had structured his movement along the lines of the civil rights movements; hence, the SNCC and CORE people were espe-cially valuable in teaching proper picketing and other protest techniques.

Financial support was still another problem: because of earlier political difficulties, the money that the NFWA might have obtained was not available. In the spring of 1965, Chavez had applied for a Poverty Program grant to train community organizers in money management, literacy train-ing, and family education. The proposal was on its way through the

[27] Martin Duberman, "Grapes of Wrath," *The New Republic*, December 2, 1967, p. 23.
[28] Michael Novak, "The Grape Strike," *Commonweal*, December 24, 1965, p. 367.

Washington maze when the strike began in Delano. Labor leadership in Washington consequently let the effort fail. Then, the Office of Economic Opportunity granted $267,000 for a community organization project, but because Chavez knew he could not separate the strike from the community organization, he asked OEO to keep the money until the strike was over. Delano Congressman Harlan Hagen, later defeated by Bob Mathias, took a different view of unionization in his home region: he flew to Washington and berated OEO officials. Moreover, Delano city councilmen (all white, although whites comprised only half the city's population) first voted themselves a nine-thousand-dollar raise as the official poverty board and then requested that Chavez's OEO grant be turned over to them. OEO, however, decided to keep the grant.

Partial rescue came in the person of Walter Reuther, who marched through the streets of Delano with Chavez and with Itliong of the AWOC. In a speech to the strikers, he said:

> This is not *your* strike, this is *our* strike. . . . If General Motors had to change *its* mind because of the auto workers, then the growers will have to change *their* mind. . . . We will mobilize every weapon we have and fight back, we will put the full support of organized labor behind your boycott and this is a powerful economic weapon. . . .[29]

The UAW then pledged $5,000 a month to the two groups, NFWA and AWOC, for the duration of the strike. The strikers' financial problems were by no means solved, however, and the problem of sufficient funds continued to plague UFWOC as the boycott of Giumarra continued.

The strike tactic generated additional publicity in the nationwide press as a result of the arrest of Chavez and two members of the clergy with some strikers, allegedly just for shouting "Huelga" at some scabs. Telegrams of protest were sent to Kern County authorities, and calls came in from major newspapers in cities all over the country. Assemblyman Phil Soto of La Puente demanded that the attorney general's office investigate police bias in the strike area. Then the Senate subcommittee on farm labor held hearings in the Central Valley, which were attended by such national political figures as the late Senator Robert Kennedy.

Publicity also helped the other UFWOC tactic, the boycott of table grapes on a nationwide—and sometimes even an international—basis. The strikers persuaded San Francisco longshoremen not to load grapes on ships. In cities in the East, local groups joined by UFWOC workers organized picket lines and met with officials of large supermarket chains to prevent the sale of table grapes. Millions of leaflets were distributed to consumers

[29] Nelson, *Huelga*, p. 121.

at shopping centers and in New York subways. By enlisting the support of all kinds of individuals and groups, Chavez's tactic of strike-cum-boycott-cum-social-movement gave the attempt by farm workers to organize a greater chance of success than any previous one.

Perhaps part of the success of the UFWOC and the movement was due to the personality of its leader, Cesar Chavez. Chavez, who had never been to Mexico, grew up in the labor camps and fringe towns of the farm valleys, and his life was typical of that of most Mexican-American farm laborers. However, in 1950, in San Jose, he met Father Donald McDonnell of the nearby mission church, who introduced him to the farm labor movement and to Fred Ross of the Community Service Organization (CSO), a new social service group of predominantly Spanish-speaking people which was trying to educate needy people to help themselves. CSO was headed by Saul Alinsky, who had spent years mobilizing ghettos across the country. Ross hired Chavez at a salary of $35 a week to help organize CSO chapters throughout the state. In a comparatively short time, Chavez had helped build CSO into a powerful organization with chapters in both California and Arizona, and by the late fifties he had become general director of the entire organization. "As head of CSO, Cesar Chavez involved the organization in a direct head-on confrontation with the power structure that gave it real meaning and that threatened to shake the foundations of the feudalistic elements in California's economy."[30] In one instance, finding that growers in one area were hiring braceros while domestic workers were being turned away, Chavez used traditional techniques (filing complaints with the Farm Placement Service, getting inspectors to visit, etc.) for several months without success and then had a group march, well-publicized by the press, which triggered a complete investigation of the Farm Placement Service, the resignation of its chief and two other men, and the dismissal of an assistant chief for accepting bribes from growers.

Later, however, conservative members of CSO refused to allow the organization to use its influence to help farm workers (as Chevez proposed), and Chavez in 1961 resigned from the CSO to devote his entire time to the farm workers. He also turned down a Peace Corps job as a $21,000-a-year director for four Latin American nations. Instead, he took a $1.25-an-hour job pruning grape vines in Delano and began spending all his spare time talking to farm workers, getting their opinions, and laying the groundwork for the Farm Workers Association which he organized in September 1962.

Chavez's personal dedication and his decision to found a movement rather than a union paid off by enabling farm workers to remain organized

[30] *Ibid.,* p. 50.

and unified and to use the economic, political, and social levers available to them to change their own situation. Of Chavez, one writer has said:

> He undoubtedly has a great deal of personal magnetism which is probably the single greatest key to his success. . . . He has an extremely tactful and considerate manner of giving orders so that one finds himself almost doing the thing required as if he had thought of it himself.[31]

International Grape Boycott Day

The farm union kept up the pressure of its grape boycott by declaring May 10, 1969, "International Grape Boycott Day." Chavez, confined to his bed for much of the preceding five months, wanted to revive the union's efforts. The demonstration that day was to focus on Safeway stores.

Safeway was the West's largest seller of table grapes, and the UFWOC's plan was to have students, union members, clergy, and minority groups picket the retail chain's stores to protest grape sales. According to a leaflet passed out by the picketers, "most Safeway directors sit as the directors of agri-business corporations which operate California's $4 billion farm industry." One of its directors was said to be on the board of a ranch being struck by the UFWOC. The leaflet went on to say that "Safeway has refused to discuss the issue of the boycott" and could not merely claim to be "caught in the middle" between growers and boycotters since it is "obvious" that the company itself "could bring the growers to the bargaining table." A Safeway spokesman said that "consumers should have the freedom of choice to buy whatever they want—and to force a supermarket operator to remove a product from his shelves would interfere with that right." The Safeway board said it favored President Nixon's proposed legislation which would allow consumers to buy what they wanted.

On May 10, eighteen California Safeway stores were picketed by as many as fifty people, and in New York City fifty to seventy-five demonstrators—all white youths—carried signs in Times Square. May 10 was a Saturday and the crowds were blamed on growers who had supposedly "packed" the markets with shoppers.

In addition to picketing Safeway stores, the UFWOC publicized International Grape Boycott Day by beginning a 100-mile march of union members from Indio in the Coachella Valley southeast to Calexico near the Mexican border where the union would attempt to convince Mexican workers not to come to the United States. In April, Chavez had an-

[31] *Ibid.*, pp. 51–52.

nounced his plans to extend the strike from the San Joaquin Valley to the Coachella Valley, only 90 miles from the Mexican border and its plentiful supply of green carders. He had originally sent pickets to Coachella in mid-1968 but soon withdrew them. One hundred and ten people showed up for the May 1969 walk which took eight days. Union leaders were somewhat pessimistic about their chances of convincing many Mexicans, and according to one official, "some of these Mexicans feed 20 people with their jobs across the border. . . . Maybe they're just too hungry to help us."

When UFWOC began striking in the Coachella Valley in June 1968, a large number of these green carders were brought in to break the strike, although their employment as strikebreakers was illegal. Nevertheless, the union continued strikes at twelve major vineyards. On July 2, Chavez announced that a picketing student had been beaten by a ranch hand and asked picketers to withdraw, saying, "I am sure we could win two or three contracts but someone's life is too dear a price to pay."[32]

In 1969, UFWOC used Mexican radio advertisements to keep green carders from breaking the strike. The growers responded by distributing leaflets. Prospects for the success of the strike appeared dim—only 3,000 workers were needed to harvest the crop, and even without the green carders there were 50,000 workers in the valley. Further dimming strike prospects were the two to three dollars per hour being paid. But if strike prospects were dim, those for the boycott were bright. Because of soil and climate peculiarities, the Coachella Valley fruit had little use other than as table grapes and could not easily be converted to wine and raisin use as could San Joaquin Valley grapes.

NEGOTIATIONS—"TOO BEAUTIFUL"

Returning to the Coachella Valley proved to be critical for the UFWOC, or so it seemed for a while. On June 13, ten of the biggest growers in the valley announced that they were willing to negotiate with the UFWOC—"tomorrow." A union official said, "It's beautiful—too beautiful. I can't believe it's finally happened. I always knew we'd win out, but it's been such a long struggle and we never knew when it would bear fruit."

Lionel Steinberg, cochairman of the growers group, said that "there could be a settlement in 48 hours if both sides pursue the matter. . . . The conference may make agricultural and labor history." The ten growers had made their decision reluctantly, however, saying they were "prepared

[32] "Farm Union Leader Urges End to California Strike," *The New York Times,* July 3, 1968, p. 24.

to meet in good faith with the union to attempt to bring peace to the table grape industry—and an end to the illegal, immoral boycott which is interrupting the flow of grapes from the farmers to the consumers."[33]

UFWOC optimism was high, for these growers produced one-third of both the Coachella Valley and the Arvin region of Kern County grapes—altogether about 10 to 15 percent of the state's table grape production. One union official felt that a settlement would be reached in two or three days, once the critical issue of the strike—recognition of the UFWOC by the growers—was out of the way.

The growers' group had asked the Federal Mediation and Conciliation Service in Washington, D.C., to arrange talks with the AFL-CIO union and had called on the President, Secretary Schultz, Senators Kennedy, Cranston, and Murphy, and local Congressmen John Tunney and Robert Mathias to "use their good offices to assist."

Steinberg, the growers' spokesman, encouraged the union when he said that although the strike had little effect, "it is costing us more to produce and sell our grapes than we are getting paid for them, and the boycott is the major factor in this ridiculous situation."[34] The State Department of Agriculture had recently released figures showing that sales had dropped 90,000 tons and prices $2.10 per ton in the two years of the boycott.

Despite UFWOC's Coachella victory, more than thirty other growers immediately stated that they would never submit to the union, although conceding that it had won a major victory. A spokesman said they would not "sell out" the American consumer or agricultural workers to Chavez's "coercive tactics." At the same time, the growers admitted that the boycott was a factor in their support for federal legislation to cover agricultural workers under the labor laws. (See "La Huelga o La Causa," part C, page 415, on government and politics.)

On June 26, the growers and the union exchanged written proposals for a contract settlement. On July 3, two more growers joined the negotiations, and others were expected to join despite the bitter friction that had developed between negotiating and nonnegotiating growers.

Lionel Steinberg, not only the growers' spokesman but a member of the State Board of Agriculture, wrote a letter to Alan Mills, head of the California Grape and Tree Fruit League, announcing his resignation from the league. He complained of the league's use of "misleading figures" in fighting the boycott. Steinberg wrote: "When you keep insisting everything is rosy and we should keep our chins up, I sincerely feel you are doing a disservice to the growers." Mills had cited increased production from the

[33] "The Week's News in Review," *San Francisco Chronicle*, Magazine Section, June 22, 1969, p. 5.

[34] Dick Meister, "Growers Regroup after Union Inroad," *San Francisco Chronicle*, June 12, 1969, p. 12.

Coachella Valley in the most recent harvest, but Steinberg said "every grape grower knows 1969 is going to be a bad season, and we are losing maybe 20 percent of our market because of the boycott." Mills, in his publicity, had ignored a "vicious cost price squeeze" the union had inflicted. Steinberg added that even though he believed the boycott to be "immoral and illegal . . . it is also a fact and we must recognize it and try to deal with it in a manner fair to both sides."[35]

The airing of the growers' dirty laundry brought out some statistics that provided a measure of the boycott's success. Spokesman Steinberg noted that in New York, Boston, and Chicago, grape prices had dropped as much as $1.50 from the $6.50 per box the previous year. He added that it cost some $700 per acre to cultivate grapes, but revenues down to only $300 per acre made for a net loss of $400 per acre.[36]

However, the most significant indication of the growers' loss was the suit for treble the alleged $25 million damages that the California Farmers Committee and eighty-one growers from all areas of the state filed against UFWOC in July. The suit was the first recognition by most growers that the boycott was succeeding. The growers said UFWOC had violated the Sherman Antitrust Act by unreasonably restraining trade by (1) coercing the growers and their workers to recognize the union as the workers' representatives, (2) using "intimidation" and threats of "financial ruin and other damage" on those retailers selling grapes, (3) entering into agreements with other retailers to halt the purchase of grapes, and (4) depriving consumers of the opportunity to buy grapes at a competitive price. The union's attorney called the suit a hoax.

Six months later the union was to enter a $112.5 million counter suit against the eighty-one growers, alleging that they were violating antitrust laws themselves and also committing infractions of the labor law by their attempts to keep workers from organizing. The growers' attorney said there was "no truth" to the counterclaim.

Meanwhile the July 1969 talks put the UFWOC in a dilemma as it was negotiating with only 12 percent of all California grape producers and the talks might becloud the previously clear boycott rule of "don't eat grapes."

How would consumers know which grapes were all right to eat? Any confusing procedures such as selling the nonboycotted grapes through previously boycott-supporting chain stores would dilute the boycott's effectiveness.

As negotiations slowed down, Steinberg recruited former California governor Pat Brown to help with the talks which by mid-July had reached

---

[35] Dick Meister, "Grower Quits Grape League," *San Francisco Chronicle*, June 28, 1969, p. 3.

[36] Dick Meister, "Brown to Enter Grape Talks," *San Francisco Chronicle*, July 12, 1969, p. 5.

an impasse. The major points of disagreement were wages ($2.00 versus $1.70 per hour), a union proposal to ban "chlorinated hydrocarbon" pesticides such as DDT, which can have latent poisoning effects on plants and animals, and a grower proposal that UFWOC not campaign against the use of pesticides.

Other issues were over the establishment of a union hiring hall and a stipulation that the union contract would have to be honored by the new owner if the vineyards were ever sold. Steinberg disagreed with the other growers and was ready to sign a union contract by himself, but the union turned him down. At one point, the growers wrote President Nixon asking him to appoint an investigative commission to recommend a solution to the dispute, but negotiations collapsed quickly.

The UFWOC and "La Muerte Andando"

A new issue came to the fore in 1969—pesticide poisoning of grape pickers—and UFWOC began claiming that pesticide poisoning from sprayed plants was so extensive that it should be considered an occupational hazard. Chavez said:

> We had no idea what this meant. We had heard about birds and bees dying from pesticides but we never connected it. It was not until the strike began and we set up a clinic that we began to see it was a serious problem. The real problem is that the workers don't even know how dangerous the stuff is. They call it dust or spray, but we call it poison. It's subtle death like quicksand. You don't know what's happening until it's too late.[37]

In January 1969, the union leader even offered to set aside wage and working-condition differences if the growers would discuss pesticide controls.

In March 1969, the union attempted to look at the Kern County pesticide records. The union said that these records were essential to its plans to launch a program for the treatment of the workers and to develop grounds for a possible suit alleging pesticide misuse. The county agriculture commissioner responded to the UFWOC allegations saying, "Agricultural pesticides and chemicals are a way of American life today. If it weren't for pesticides, we would be having a lot of worms in our apples and everything else." Several pesticide companies were successful in obtaining a preliminary injunction against the release of the records by saying that "trade secrets" would be released to the public.

[37] Stephen V. Roberts, "Change of Peril in Pesticides Adds Fuel to Coast Grape Strike," *The New York Times*, March 16, 1969, p. 46.

The union's concern was later vindicated in September 1969 and February 1970 when the California State Public Health Department announced several preliminary findings of a special study of pesticide poisoning. The first study cited "ample evidence" that official records of pesticide poisoning were unrealistically low. Officially, one per 1,000 farm workers was poisoned each year (out of about 250,000 California farm workers). The study said that pesticide poisoning might be as high as 150 cases per 1,000 farm workers. This rate was expected to increase because organic phosphates were replacing DDT. The official statistics were based on workmen's compensation claims only and hence did not include those who used their own or Medi-Cal money to pay for medical expenses or those who did not obtain medical help, which is sometimes not available. The study said that pesticide poisoning was preventable if proper industrial hygiene measures were taken. In August 1969, UFWOC bought some grapes in the District of Columbia and had them tested by an independent laboratory. The laboratory's report said that the residues of the pesticide Aldrin were eighteen times the allowable FDA levels. Senator George Murphy of California, a member of the Senate Subcommittee on Migratory Labor, asked that hearings be held concerning the alleged poisonings.

At the hearings in late September, Chavez said that pesticides were given a special name by the grape pickers—*la muerte andando*, "the walking death." He said, "Growers consistently use the wrong kinds of economic poisons in the wrong amounts in the wrong places in reckless disregard of the health of their workers in order to maximize profits." In addition to the three thousand California children requiring medical care each year after ingesting pesticides, "literally thousands of workers experience daily symptoms of chemical poisoning which include dermatitis, rashes, eye irritation, nausea, vomiting, fatigue, excess sweating, headaches, double vision, dizziness, skin irritations, difficulty in breathing, loss of fingernails, nervousness, insomnia, bleeding noses and diarrhea."[38]

Evidence at the hearings countered UFWOC's charges. Herbert L. Lay, Jr., an FDA commissioner, said that the FDA had purchased grapes from the same Washington grocery store and also from the growers' warehouses in California, had run tests on them, and could find no excess pesticide residues. Indeed, the commissioner said, the laboratory used by Chavez had misread the results of its own tests. The grower whose label appeared on the purchased grapes later stated that he had never used Aldrin. He said, "The Aldrin scare is no more than another effort to whip me into submission." The grower's statement was supported by the executive director of the Tulare County Farm Association who said that Aldrin had

[38] "Chavez at Senate Hits Pesticides," *San Francisco Examiner*, September 29, 1969, p. 8.

not been used on table grapes for six years and that even DDT had not been used recently.

Because the FDA disclaimed pesticide poisoning of grapes, Chavez and two hundred others picketed FDA offices and passed out leaflets stating that the regulatory body was "more interested in protecting the growers, not the consumers and workers" and was ignoring eight hundred deaths and eighty thousand injuries per year attributable to pesticide poisoning.

UFWOC IN THE TWILIGHT OF SUCCESS

In August 1969, the union won a pay increase and a new three-year contract with the Paul Masson Wine Company (including paid vacations, health benefits, and union shop rights). In November, Chavez conducted a nationwide tour to revive the boycott efforts set back by the Coachella negotiations. In early 1970, the union was involved in several court suits, one in response to the growers' $75 million suit, and the other *on behalf* of two small growers against California's largest grape growers, who supposedly used more than their fair share of federally subsidized water, thus driving small growers out of business.

The California grape harvest began in the Coachella Valley in the spring. Through the efforts of five Catholic bishops, talks were held between the UFWOC and forty Coachella growers. As a result, on April 2, 1970, it was announced that Lionel Steinberg and another grower had broken from the rest and had agreed to sign contracts with the union. By mid-April two more of the forty allowed their workers to vote the UFWOC as their sole bargaining agent. An AFL-CIO official pointed out that it would actively promote union-picked grapes while continuing the boycott against scab grapes.

By the end of May the bishops and the Federal Mediation and Conciliation Service promoted further talks which resulted in agreements between the UFWOC and "two of the state's largest and most influential" growers from the Delano area: Bruno Dispoto and the Bianco Brothers. Dispoto said he was "firmly convinced that Cesar Chavez and his union are here to stay," and he "wasn't going to tolerate another year of insecurity."[39] By early June the union had contracts with growers supplying 10 percent of the state's crop. Soon boxes of table grapes bearing the union label—"a fierce black eagle in a white circle on a red flag"—began appearing in supermarkets, and many growers waited to see how they would sell. Early reports showed that they were selling well. According to *Business Week*, "a

---

[39] "Big Grape Growers Sign with Union," *San Francisco Chronicle*, May 22, 1970, p. 3.

spot check of supermarkets in several cities suggests that boycotters, far from being confused by the new 'acceptable' grapes, are rechanneling their efforts to make sure that the grapes on sale are actually union-label fruit."[40]

By June 28 UFWOC had added nine more growers to its list, bringing union labels to 15–20 percent of the state's output. The next day Governor Reagan announced that the State Conciliation Service would be available to supervise secret elections to "enable farm workers to choose, if any, the union they wish to join," and fifty-two growers later announced that they were willing to start talks under the service's auspices. An assistant director of UFWOC replied, however, that "the time for elections has long passed." The union was feeling its strength and throughout the state (except for the Delano area) "growers were dropping like dominoes."

Delano was holding out for harvest time in mid-July. Yet on July 8 another "major breakthrough" occurred when a large Fresno grower signed a contract with UFWOC, and by the end of the month a tentative agreement was announced with twenty-six growers from Kern and Tulare counties bringing "virtually all" the state's grapes under union labels. The latter agreement was reached after two weeks of secret talks brought about by the "peace efforts" of the Catholic bishops responsible for earlier talks. Thus the newspapers were able to report on July 30:

> Delano, Kern County
> They began arriving early in the morning, brilliant red banners in hand, awaiting the word they had strained for almost five years to hear.
> As the more than 200 farm workers waited, they sang: "Nosotros venceremos, nosotros venceremos . . . we shall overcome, we shall overcome . . ."
> And their leader, Cesar Chavez, confirmed it. He signed before their eyes a labor contract with John Giumarra, the world's largest grape grower, and confirmed that the Delano grape strike was over. Won.[41]

The growers were as gracious as could be expected and John Giumarra, Jr., the growers' spokesman, said, "We're starting a new relationship here." Chavez predicted it would be a good relationship and said, "We were surprised to find that they did not have horns and they were surprised, I'm sure, to find out we don't have tails." Governor Reagan, however, called it "tragic" that the workers would not have a chance to vote on their union representation.

---

[40] "A Harvest Nears for Cesar Chavez," *Business Week*, June 27, 1970, p. 62.
[41] Dick Meister, "A Festive End to the Grape Dispute," *San Francisco Chronicle*, July 30, 1970, p. 1.

Encouraged by its success, UFWOC had begun organizing and leading strikes by plum, peach, and melon pickers. In these efforts, word of "la causa" had spread widely and had strengthened even the *strike* efforts of UFWOC, as one large fruit farmer discovered when his peaches needed thinning.[42] The Teamsters Union, however, had also been organizing farm workers and on July 28 announced that it had signed contracts which covered most farm workers in the Salinas Valley—the nation's "salad bowl." The AFL-CIO in turn threatened "all out war," and Chavez called the rival union's action a "Pearl Harbor type of sneak attack" against UFWOC, since the Teamster's "sweetheart agreement" was not as strict as the UFWOC demands. No vote had been taken by the workers as to which union should represent them. Soon thereafter Teamster contracts were signed in Santa Barbara County, and UFWOC filed suit against the Teamsters on behalf of Salinas workers who had been deprived "of free choice in the selection of a bargaining agent and negotiation of an acceptable collective bargaining agreement."

[42] "A Harvest Nears for Cesar Chavez," *Business Week*, June 27, 1970, p. 62.

III

———•———

CORPORATIONS,
THEIR DEPENDENCIES,
AND OTHER
SOCIAL INSTITUTIONS

A.
CORPORATIONS
AND
THE INDIVIDUAL

General Motors' Nadir, Ralph Nader

Corporate Economic Interests and Encroachment of an Individual's Privacy

When a trout rising to a fly gets hooked on a line and finds himself unable to swim freely, he begins with a fight which results in struggles and splashes and sometimes an escape. Often, of course, the situation is too tough for him.

In the same way the human being struggles with his environment and the hooks that catch him. Sometimes he masters his difficulties, sometimes they are too much for him. His struggles are all that the world sees and it naturally misunderstands them. It is hard for a free fish to understand what is happening to a hooked one.

—KARL A. MENNINGER

A *New Republic* news story[1] about Ralph Nader confirmed rumors and summarized three months of 1966 news accounts about an investigation into the affairs of the well-known auto critic. The article implied that some unnamed source in the automobile industry was behind the investigation. The allegations are abridged here.

According to Nader, on January 10, 1966, it was in the Kirkwood Hotel in Des Moines, Iowa, where he was testifying at the state attorney general's inquiry into traffic safety, that he first thought someone was following him. Later that month he began receiving annoying and unidentified calls on his unlisted telephone.

Senator Abraham Ribicoff's auto safety subcommittee invited Ralph

---

[1] James Ridgeway, "The Dick," *The New Republic*, March 12, 1966, pp. 11–13.

Nader to testify on February 10, 1966. On the evening before the hearing, harassing calls came with increasing frequency until 4:00 A.M.[2]

The subcommittee invited Ralph Nader to testify because he was campaigning to have automobile manufacturers remove design defects from their cars and to make them safer. On November 30, 1965, Nader's book, *Unsafe at Any Speed*, was published. It was "a meticulously documented (and as it turned out, best-selling) report on safety defects in Detroit's cars, primarily some of General Motors' early Corvairs."[3] The book criticized the industry's "over-emphasis of style, disregard for the safety of the driver and passengers, and engineering stagnation." *Unsafe at Any Speed* "received widespread and largely favorable reviews" and strengthened considerably the argument of auto-safety activists both on and off Capitol Hill.[4]

Nader made a great impression on the members of the subcommittee, and according to one staff member, "He [Nader] was a Congressional staffer's dream. . . . Nader wasn't selling anything . . . [and] he had the data—the names and phone numbers to substantiate everything."[5]

A series of events lent weight to Nader's conviction that he was being investigated. His landlady was asked about his promptness in paying bills. An attractive girl invited him to her apartment to discuss "foreign affairs with a few of her friends." Two men followed him from an airport. His old law school friend, Frederick Condon, was asked questions by an investigator supposedly representing a client who was thinking of hiring Nader. Other friends and associates were asked all kinds of questions by investigators from different agencies, *including whether or not he led a normal sex life, possible anti-Semitism, and political affiliations.*[6] A blonde in a

[2] According to *The New York Times*, "the callers were never obscene or abusive, he said.

" 'Mr. Nader?' a voice would inquire.

" 'Yes.'

"Then suddenly, as if to a child:

" 'Cut it out now! Cut it out! You're going to cut me off I tell you! Cut it out!' "

Nader said that the phone calls caused him to oversleep and hence he was late in giving his testimony to the subcommittee.

Walter Rugaber, "Critic of Auto Industry's Safety Standards Says He Was Trailed and Harassed; Charges Called Absurd," *The New York Times*, March 6, 1966, p. 94.

According to Ridgeway, *op. cit.*, ". . . on the evening of February 9, when he was trying to put the finishing touches on a prepared statement, Nader got half-a-dozen phone calls. A voice would say, 'Mr. Nader, this is Pan American,' and then hang up. Or, 'Mr. Nader, please pick up the parcel at Railway Express.' And finally, 'Why don't you go back to Connecticut, buddy-boy.' "

[3] "Meet Ralph Nader, Everyman's Lobbyist and His Consumer Crusader," *Newsweek*, January 22, 1968, pp. 65–73.

[4] Elizabeth Brenner Drew, "The Politics of Auto Safety," *The Atlantic*, October 1966, p. 95.

[5] "Meet Ralph Nader," *Newsweek*, January 22, 1968, p. 65.

[6] Ridgeway, "The Dick."

supermarket asked him to help her move some furniture (and asked no one else when he refused). By this time Nader thought that girls were being used to try to lure him into a compromising situation and that someone, most likely connected with the auto manufacturers, was attempting to dig up some sordid past episode to discredit him as a congressional witness.[7]

Employees of the New Republic, for which Nader had written articles, contacted Allied Investigating Service, which supposedly had questioned Nader's stockbroker. After much prodding, they denied investigating Nader. Management Consultants in Boston, which sent a representative to see Mr. Thomas F. Lambert, Jr., editor in chief of American Trial Lawyers Association (ATLA) publications—declined to discuss the matter. Vincent Gillen of Vincent Gillen Associates, however, admitted investigating Nader but would not name his client.[8]

The New York Times on March 6 stated that unnamed sources in the auto industry said the investigation was "too clumsy" to have been initiated by an automobile manufacturer and was probably done by other Nader targets in the "traffic safety establishment"—the National Safety Council or the American Association of Motor Vehicle Administrators. One informant added, "think of what a blunder it would be if a company was caught at it," and another said that if the manufacturers were doing it, Nader would not even be aware that he was being investigated. The major auto companies had special investigation bureaus for "high level security work" and preemployment investigations.[9]

On March 8, Senators Gaylord Nelson (D-Wis.) and Abraham Ribicoff (D-Conn.) asked the Justice Department to look into Nader's being "investigated by private detectives" and the late telephone calls since his appearance before a Senate hearing. Nader was scheduled to appear before the subcommittee again and Nelson said that "The clear implication of everything reported so far is that the automobile industry has hired at least three different firms of private detectives to shadow and investigate . . . a witness before a Congressional committee."[10]

Nelson added that both the auto makers and Congress should welcome

---

[7] Ibid., also see "The Nader Caper," Newsweek, March 21, 1966, p. 83.

[8] According to Ridgeway, "The Dick," Gillen said:
"I am a private investigator. We have hundreds of clients; we write thousands of reports, primarily on employment matters. I was asked by a client to make an investigation of Ralph Nader. I understand that he is an intelligent, articulate fellow. And my client told me he was considering him for an important job, to do research on something, I don't know what."

[9] "Investigation Asked," The New York Times, March 9, 1966, p. 38; "Ribicoff Summons GM on Its Inquiry of Critic," The New York Times, March 11, 1966, p. 18; "Critic of Auto Industry's Safety Standards Says He Was Tailed and Harassed; Charges Called Absurd," The New York Times, March 6, 1966, p. 94.

[10] "Investigation Asked," The New York Times, March 9, 1966, p. 38.

an investigation to "clear the air." Ribicoff stated that the incidents were "an apparent attempt to harass and intimidate a subcommittee witness," for which federal laws provide penalties of up to five years in jail and a $5,000 fine. The senator added, "no citizen of this country should be forced to endure the kind of clumsy harassment to which Mr. Nader has apparently been subjected since the publication of his book. Anonymous phone calls in the night have no place in a free society."[11]

On March 9, the vice-president and director of the Ford Motor Company, John S. Bagas, sent a telegram to Senator Ribicoff saying that the "Ford Motor Company has not been nor is it now directly or indirectly involved in any alleged investigation or harassment of Mr. Nader, nor has it any knowledge of or connection with the alleged incidents concerning him."[12] After the Ford statement was issued, newspaper reporters received denials from Chrysler and American Motors. General Motors would not comment. Put on the spot, GM spokesmen "shortly before 11 P.M. [and] after the first editions of most morning newspapers had been printed . . . delivered a statement to newspaper offices." The statement admitted that the company had directed the investigation.[13] Indications were that GM's president, James Roche, had not learned of GM's true involvement until late in the afternoon and had personally ordered that an admission be made:

> Following the publication of Mr. Ralph Nader's criticisms of the Corvair in writings and public appearances in support of his book . . . the office of its general counsel initiated a routine investigation through a reputable law firm to determine whether Ralph Nader was acting on behalf of litigants or their attorneys in Corvair design cases pending against General Motors. The investigation was prompted by Mr. Nader's extreme criticisms of the Corvair. . . . Mr. Nader's statements coincided with similar publicity by some attorneys handling such litigation. . . .
>
> The investigation was limited only to Mr. Nader's qualifications, background, expertise and association with such attorneys. It did not include any of the alleged harassment or intimidation recently reported in the press. If Mr. Nader had been subjected to any of the incidents and harassment mentioned by him in newspaper stories, such incidents were in no way associated with General Motors' legitimate investigation of his interest in pending litigation.
>
> At General Motors' invitation, Mr. Nader spent a day at the GM

---

11 *Ibid.*

12 "GM Admits Investigating Auto Critic," *Washington Post*, March 10, 1966, p. A7.

13 "Ribicoff Summons GM on Its Inquiry of Critic," *The New York Times*, March 11, 1966, p. 18.

Technical Center . . . early in January visiting with General Motors executives and engineers. . . .

Mr. Nader expressed appreciation for the courtesy in providing him with detailed information, but he nevertheless continued the same line of attack on the design of the Corvair. . . . This behavior lends support to General Motors' belief that there is a connection between Mr. Nader and Plaintiff's counsel in pending Corvair design litigation.[14]

Senator Nelson, "shocked" by the GM announcement, said that the investigation was "a pretty scandalous business"[15] and that he thought the auto safety subcommittee should determine if GM's law firm was in contempt of Congress. Senator Ribicoff said he would invite Roche, Nader, and the private detectives to testify before his auto safety subcommittee on March 22:

I have not discussed this matter with any of the parties concerned, but I suggest that they come before the committee to discuss the entire matter.

The safety of the American driving public is the basic issue before the committee. To this must now be added the additional issue of a witness's right to testify before a committee of the United States Congress without fear of character assassination or intimidation.[16]

Nader told the *New York Times* that he had not represented clients involved in Corvair litigations. A number of lawyers had asked him for Corvair information, but he had never been paid for it and had left his law practice "to pursue the cause of safer designed automobiles for the motoring public." Therefore, he asked GM to admit that it could not have evidence linking him with the Corvair lawyers.[17] GM implied in a *New York Times* story[18] that it could prove the case against Nader and that the proof would be presented before the Ribicoff committee.

---

[14] U.S. Congress, Senate, "Federal Role in Traffic Safety," *Hearings before the Subcommittee on Executive Reorganization of the Committee on Government Operations,* 89th Cong., 2nd sess., March 22, 1966, p. 1389.

As extensive use is made of the Senate Hearings, citations from this source will henceforth appear in the text set off by brackets enclosing page references.

[15] "Ribicoff Summons GM on Its Inquiry of Critic," *The New York Times,* March 11, 1966, p. 18.

[16] *Ibid.*

[17] "GM Acknowledges Investigating Critic," *The New York Times,* March 10, 1966, p. 1.

[18] "Ribicoff Summons GM on Its Inquiry of Critic," *The New York Times,* March 11, 1966, p. 18.

THE HEARING

On March 22, Senator Ribicoff's subcommittee conducted hearings into the investigation of Nader and, in spite of the confidence GM had displayed in its March 9 statement, the only case it proved was Nader's. According to *Newsweek:*

> The scene had all the fascination of a public whipping, and the huge old Caucus Room of the Senate Office Building was appropriately jammed with reporters, cameramen, television crews and Washington citizens. In the seats of power, ranged against a white marble wall, were a tribunal of Sen. Abraham Ribicoff's traffic-safety subcommittee. At the witness table was the president of the world's largest manufacturing company.[19]

The hearing had political overtones: It was good publicity for Democrat Ribicoff and only one of three Republicans on the subcommittee even showed up briefly. One subcommittee member, Robert F. Kennedy, recognized an old friend, Theodore C. Sorensen, who appeared but said little as Roche's legal counsel.[20]

Ribicoff sternly opened the meeting:

> There is no law which bars a corporation from hiring detectives to investigate a private citizen, however distasteful the idea may seem to some of us. There is a law, however, which makes it a crime to harass or intimidate a witness before a congressional committee.
>
> . . . [the] right to testify freely without fear of intimidation is one of the cornerstones of a free and democratic society. Any attempt to jeopardize this right is a serious matter.
>
> I have called this special meeting today to look into the circumstances surrounding what appeared to be an attempt by General Motors Corp. to discredit Mr. Ralph Nader, a recent witness before the subcommittee. . . . [GM] has admitted responsibility for undertaking a determined and exhaustive investigation of a private citizen who has criticized the auto industry verbally and in print [1380].

[19] "Private Eyes and Public Hearings," *Newsweek,* April 4, 1966, pp. 77–78.

[20] *Ibid.* Sorensen had been White House counsel under John F. Kennedy, and Sorensen's law firm was aiding GM's defense in the Corvair design suits. "Sorensen Expected at Nader Quiz Today," *Washington Post,* March 22, 1966, p. A2.

GM's POSITION

Mr. Roche testified as follows:

> Let me make it clear at the outset that I deplore the kind of harassment to which Mr. Nader has apparently been subjected. I am just as shocked and outraged by some of the incidents which Mr. Nader has reported as the members of this subcommittee.
>
> As President of General Motors, I hold myself fully responsible for any action authorized or initiated by any officer of the Corporation which may have had any bearing on the incidents related to our investigation of Mr. Nader. I did not know of the investigation when it was initiated and I did not approve it.
>
> While there can be no disagreement over General Motors' legal right to ascertain necessary facts preparatory to litigation . . ., I am not here to excuse, condone or justify in any way our investigating Mr. Nader. To the extent that General Motors bears responsibility, I want to apologize here and now to the members of this subcommittee and Mr. Nader. I sincerely hope that these apologies will be accepted. Certainly I bear Mr. Nader no ill-will.
>
> To the best of my knowledge . . . the investigation initiated by General Motors, contrary to some speculation, did *not* employ girls as sex lures, did *not* employ detectives using false names, did *not* employ Allied Investigation, Inc., did *not* use recording devices during interviews, did *not* follow Mr. Nader in Iowa and Pennsylvania, did *not* have him under surveillance during the day he testified before this subcommittee, did *not* follow him in any private place, and did *not* constantly ring his private telephone number late at night with false statements or anonymous warnings [1381].

Roche said that the investigation was initiated before Nader became a congressional witness and that it was wholly unrelated to the proceedings of the subcommittee and Mr. Nader's connections with them [1382].

He went on to say that no "derogatory information of any kind along any of these lines turned up in this investigation" [1383].

Roche also reiterated the company's right to investigate certain facts in relation to its defense of the one hundred Corvair design suits:

> *First*, to ascertain whether any actions for libel . . . should be instituted against members of the bar (including Mr. Nader) who publicly discussed pending or anticipated litigation; *second*, to ascertain whether any witness, or author of any book or article which might be offered as evidence in any court (including Mr. Nader) was

entitled to the legal definition of "expert"; and *third,* to ascertain whether [these individuals] . . . show bias, lack of reliability or credibility, [or] . . . if . . . they had a self interest in the litigation or had been attempting deliberately to influence public opinion [1384].

Roche said the company had the legal right and duty, in protecting its stockholders' interests, to make an investigation within the framework of these three points.

GM's president added that investigation into an individual's personal life, a very "uncommon occurrence" at GM, was usually for preemployment or possible embezzlement. It would be initiated by the general counsel, usually "in consultation with other executives familiar with the particular problem involved. But, if it were a serious enough matter, then it would be called to the attention of the other officials in the corporation, or perhaps some of our top committees" [1385–86].

Several members of GM's legal staff testified before the committee to explain in greater detail the necessity GM felt to investigate Nader.

INVESTIGATION STORY: GM'S VERSION

General Motors introduced its rear-engine compact car, the Corvair, in the fall of 1959, and by November 1965 the company had been plagued with over one hundred suits alleging injuries arising from Corvair failures due to basic design defects. Although GM had won two Corvair design suits, it settled another out of court (without admitting legal liability) because the jury's emotions had been aroused by gruesome photographs of the plaintiff's injury [1509–10].[21] This settlement further aggravated the situation as it was heralded in various news media "as a victory for the plaintiffs" [1408]. It was followed by a flood of letters from Corvair owners and GM stockholders. Thus the company became apprehensive that "false" publicity might adversely influence future cases.

By 1962, various attorneys and law firms (many of whom were handling Corvair cases) began exchanging information, and by 1965 they were speaking publicly about Corvair's design defects. In June and July 1965, Thomas F. Lambert, Jr., of ATLA suggested to those seeking more information about Corvair design that they contact a then unknown Ralph Nader:

---

[21] Ralph Nader's version of the reason GM settled is somewhat different from the company's version. GM discontinued the manufacture of the Corvair in May 1969. "The Last of the Troubled Corvairs," *San Francisco Chronicle,* May 13, 1969, p. 10.

We also suggest that you write to Ralph Nader, . . . Winsted, Connecticut. Ralph is a lawyer who has developed expertise in the area of automobile manufacturer's liability. Ralph has a substantial amount of information on the Corvair [1416].

According to Aloysius Power, GM's general counsel, the company wondered,

Who was this "lawyer" with whom the ATLA editor was on a first-name basis? At that time, Mr. Nader was not listed as counsel in any pending Corvair case. Where did he obtain such a "substantial amount of information on the Corvair," and how had he "developed expertise"?

Was he an engineer, a paid consultant to the ATLA Corvair counsel? Or was he preparing to file another one of these cases?

Practically all of the material he was using in his writings to attack the Corvair appeared to come from material collected or obtained by plaintiff's counsel in pending Corvair litigation [1420–40].

In addition, Nader wrote an article for the January 1965 ATLA magazine, *Trial*, outlining often overlooked sources of evidence of unsafe automobile design, and in October 1965 advance reviews and excerpts from the book began appearing in national magazines.

According to Power, pretrial investigation was crucial if they were to fight these pending cases effectively [1420–38].[22] The company must know how valid was Nader's claim to be an "expert," since expert testimony was vital in such cases. Second, had Nader violated Canon 20 of the Canons of Professional Ethics of the American Bar Association, which "condemns public discussion or statement by a lawyer concerning pending or anticipated litigation"? [1404]. Therefore, Power felt that an investigation of Nader was a "prudent and appropriate measure" to take. "In the light of the situation existing at that time, I could not have arrived at any other decision consistent with my responsibilities as the general counsel of General Motors" [1403].

On November 18, 1965, GM's legal department asked its product liability insurer, the Royal-Globe Insurance Company, if it had ever employed any private investigators in Connecticut who might have looked into Nader's qualifications. They had not, and a Hartford, Connecticut, investigator, Mr. O'Neill, was commissioned by Globe to "obtain whatever information he could with respect to his [Nader's] qualifications and whether or not he was a trial lawyer in Winsted, Conn." The report stated that Nader had only briefly practiced law in Hartford, that his family lived in nearby Winsted, and that he might be in Washington, D.C., although

---

[22] At the time of the hearings, GM had not lost any Corvair design suits.

no legal directory listed him there. No information as to his technical competence was uncovered [1439].

On December 22, 1965, Miss Eileen Murphy, who was working in GM's law library and who had earlier worked in Washington, phoned Richard Danner of Alvord and Alvord, a Washington law firm, to ask if he could recommend a good investigating agency for some "background information" on Nader. Danner in turn called Vincent Gillen in New York, president of Vincent Gillen Associates, Inc., to ask if he could handle an investigation covering several Eastern states. On January 11, 1966, Miss Murphy came to Washington and gave Danner what little information GM had obtained on Nader, reiterating GM's suspicions but adding that no compelling proof had been found [1515–16, 1524]. According to Power, Miss Murphy said the investigation should cover:

> Where does Mr. Nader live and where does he practice law if he is practicing? Had he been employed by the Federal Government? What other employment? Where is the source of his income? What were the details of his background that might affect his writings? Especially does he have any engineering background . . .
> What would account for the absence of objectivity unusual in a lawyer writing about the Corvair? Does he have any connection at all with ATLA or ATLA attorneys? Are there any indications that he might be working as a consultant to lawyers handling Corvair cases against General Motors? [1440–1516].

According to Danner, however, Miss Murphy also requested "a complete background investigation of Mr. Nader's activities." The instructions given were described by those agents actually investigating Nader: ". . . Our job is to check his life, and current activities to determine 'what makes him tick,' such as his real interest in safety, his supporters, if any, his politics, his marital status, his friends, his women, boys, etc., drinking, dope, jobs— in fact, all facets of his life" [1506].

Danner testified at Ribicoff's subcommittee hearing that he then told Miss Murphy that the investigating agency would have to use a suitable pretext as Nader would most likely learn of the investigation through the people being questioned. Danner also said that "all instructions to the investigative agency were to be handled by me, and all reports submitted by the agency were to be sent to me for transmittal to General Motors" [1440–42, 1516, 1524].

Gillen flew to Washington on January 13, 1966, to get his assignment from Danner. In his testimony before the subcommittee, Gillen said that it was the first time that he had heard of Nader. Gillen told Danner that if he were to ask questions about Nader's connection with Corvair cases, his expertise in safety, and his associates in the legal profession:

. . . the implication would be immediate, the onus would immediately be on General Motors if Nader heard of this, and I tried to dissuade them or told them "Are you prepared for what may happen, because you cannot investigate someone without their hearing about it talking to their friends." I told them right from the beginning.

Danner said, "Don't worry about it." So I did it as gently and discreetly and fairly to Nader as could possibly be done [1549].

Since it was necessary to conceal the nature of the investigation and the identity of the client, it was agreed that all information would be collected under the pretext of preemployment type of inquiry instigated by a company of a prospective employee.

In defending his belief that a preemployment pretext was the best strategy to use to get the desired information, Gillen told the subcommittee:

As you gentlemen are aware, whenever any investigation is made, people interviewed invariably jump to the conclusion that something is wrong with the person being investigated, especially if no reason for the inquiry is given. On the other hand, if people are told the person is being investigated for a position, no stigma is attached to the inquiry. We do it everyday [1525].

Danner told the Senators that Gillen and he had agreed that Nader was not to be placed under surveillance unless absolutely necessary [1517].

On January 17, Senator Ribicoff officially announced that Nader would be a witness at one of the subcommittee hearings on February 10.

On January 20, Gillen requested his Washington associate, D. David Shatraw, president of Arundel Investigative Agency of Severinia Park, Maryland, to investigate Nader, warning him "not to arouse the ire of Nader . . . it is important that interviews be handled with great discretion and under a suitable pretext" [1525].

From January 25 to January 27, Gillen's men conducted their investigation in the Winsted-Hartford, Connecticut, area. Gillen later said that all his men used their own names and identified Gillen as their employer (they didn't know who the real client was). No one in Connecticut could say where Nader was "except possibly in Washington." Little was discovered as to his sources of income or activities, so it was decided on January 26 that surveillance would be necessary. Shatraw began his end of the investigation on February 3, which according to Gillen showed that Nader's assertions to the press that he was harassed in January, if true, were not the result of Gillen's or Shatraw's work. One of Shatraw's men called an address that Nader had put on some legal papers many months before to "ascertain if anything was known of Mr. Nader. To his surprise, the landlady said he was rooming there but was not in" [1525–26].

On Friday, February 4, two Arundel Investigative Agency men began a surveillance on Nader, which because of the agency's heavy workload was ended the following morning. On Sunday, at 4:00 P.M., Gillen had two of his own men resume the surveillance and investigation in Washington. Gillen said that "all other surveillance and investigation in Washington thereafter was conducted by our own employees. We conducted no surveillance outside Washington" [1527].

On February 9, Danner suggested substituting "spot checks" for the unproductive and expensive surveillance. He thought a good time to pick up Nader would be directly after he testified on February 10. The "tailing" didn't begin until the eleventh at 11:00 A.M. when one of Gillen's men followed Nader into the new Senate office building but left when challenged by the guards. This ended the surveillance, but one man continued openly to interview Washingtonians about Nader. Newspapers reported the episode in the building on the thirteenth, saying that Gillen's men "clumsily" mistook a newspaper reporter for Nader (which Gillen denied). On the fourteenth, GM's Power, ex post facto, ordered the surveillance stopped [1543–44].

Gillen's man left Washington on February 18. Thus, Gillen said, the alleged incidents of women approaching Nader on Sunday, February 20, and Wednesday, February 23, were unrelated to his investigation. "Neither I, nor any of my former FBI colleagues, used any women during this investigation. I had no one, male or female, working on this case those days in Washington" [1528].

On February 28, Power instructed Danner to cease the entire investigation.

According to the testimony given at the hearings, Nader was investigated by various agencies for five or six days in mid-November 1965, and between January 25 and February 28, 1966. People from all walks of life who were even remotely connected with Nader were questioned. Frederick Condon and Thomas F. Lambert, Jr., wrote letters to the subcommittee and gave details of their interviews.

Condon, who had gone to law school with Nader, was at that time assistant counsel for the United Life and Accident Insurance Company of Concord, New Hampshire. Nader had dedicated his book, *Unsafe at Any Speed*, to Condon. According to Condon, Gillen came up to talk to him under the pretext of preemployment inquiries concerning Nader. However, the nature of his questioning made Condon suspect that Gillen was investigating Nader on behalf of some automobile company. Gillen asked questions slanted toward finding out if Nader was a homosexual. Gillen also inquired if Nader was anti-Semitic because of his "Syrian" ancestry—

(Nader is of Lebanese descent)—or had participated in or belonged to any left-wing organization. Condon thought that Gillen had a tape recorder in his attaché case as he was hardly taking any notes. Gillen, in his testimony, however, denied having any tape recorder with him and also gave a different version of his questioning of Condon. Gillen said that the sole purpose of his interview with Condon was to find out if Nader had ever had a driver's license, as official Connecticut records contained conflicting information and no one had ever seen him driving a car [1521–47].

Thomas F. Lambert, Jr., of ATLA publications wrote to Senator Ribicoff and described his interview with Mr. Dwyer of "Management Consultants." Gillen said that he had sent Dwyer on the interview. In response to Dwyer's questions, Lambert told him that it was

> our belief that Nader had done the best writing on unsafe design of automobiles of which we were aware . . . I [Lambert] suggested that Nader may have acted as a consultant to three very able and experienced trial lawyers who had handled or are currently handling Corvair cases. I suggested that he might be able to verify Nader's actual experience in such consulting work by directly contacting these three lawyers (David Harney, Los Angeles; Barney Masterson, Clearwater, Fla.; and Louis B. Davidson, Chicago) [7551–52].

Almost everyone denied using girls at any point or intending intimidation or harassment of any Senate subcommittee witness. Danner was unaware that Nader was to testify, and Gillen stated that the investigation would never have been initiated had he known that Nader was to testify. Furthermore, only two phone calls were supposedly made to Nader, neither during early morning hours. Gillen's reports were forwarded to Detroit by Danner, the final report being sent on March 14. Gillen was the only one in his organization who knew the real client's identity. Hence, he did not edit much irrelevant material from the investigators' reports. "To do so would have indicated the real client to my own staff. I even left in some rather harsh statements about General Motors and some of its officials" [1532]. Miss Murphy at GM received the reports. The company was billed $6,700.00 for the investigation [1539].

GILLEN'S PRETEXT: WAS IT ETHICAL?

Much of the subcommittee's attention was concerned with the questions asked Nader's friends and associates. Since a preemployment pretext was used, the investigators asked about things GM was supposedly not interested in. Gillen stoutly defended his investigative technique and denied any unethical practice or moral wrongdoing. Gillen said the motto of his company was "There is no substitute for quality and integrity. I stand on the quality of our reports. I submit my integrity to the scrutiny of all" [1532]. According to Danner, who hired Gillen, it was GM's idea that the investigation go into the "detail and background" of Nader's life, including anti-Semitism and marital status and the kind of girl friends he had. Danner said it couldn't have been his idea: He had never heard of Nader before Miss Murphy called him [1520–21].

Senator Robert F. Kennedy, a member of the subcommittee, questioned Gillen persistently on the use of the preemployment pretext, false names, and personal questions when Nader wasn't really being considered for a job. He was further concerned about harassing Nader. Gillen's position was that the objectives might differ but investigative methods for either objective were identical and did not constitute harassment. After all, Gillen said, pretexts "are used all the time. I know the government uses pretexts in connection with applicant investigations" [1519–20].

Gillen maintained that others were also investigating Nader a month before the subcommittee met. He suggested that the subcommittee find out who did vex Nader with phone calls, use girls as sex lures, and follow him in Iowa and Philadelphia. These were the real harassing agents [1550–51].[23]

Furthermore, our investigation uncovered absolutely no indication of any abnormality on the part of Ralph Nader. On the contrary, he obviously is an intelligent, personable young man.

The same thing applies to the questions regarding anti-Semitism. Virtually everyone we talked with in Winsted cautioned us not to attribute to Ralph the attitude and obvious feelings of some members of his family. In fairness to Ralph, we had to ask that question of all those with whom he associated during his adult life. I am happy to state that none of the people we interviewed believes Ralph Nader is anti-Semitic [1532].

The possibility of anti-Semitism was not the only thing Gillen felt it necessary to pursue "in fairness to Ralph." Nader's high school principal showed Gillen's men a yearbook which said, "Ralph Nader—woman hater." He said:

Now some people get the wrong impression about Ralph and this stuff. Do not pay any attention to it.

[23] "Critic of Auto Industry's Safety Standards Says He Was Tailed and Harassed," *The New York Times*, March 6, 1966, p. 94.

According to Gillen, "There is where it first raised its head and we had to pursue it in fairness to Ralph" [1549].

"What the hell's this 'fairness to Ralph'?" Kennedy barked. "You have to keep running around the country proving he's not anti-Semitic or not queer? Ralph's doing all right."[24]

Nader was not the only one to fall under the vast network of Gillen's operatives. Even Senator Ribicoff himself was checked to verify that he had never met Nader before he testified.[25]

GENERAL MOTORS' MARCH 9 PRESS RELEASE: WAS IT DELIBERATELY MISLEADING?

Another issue raised by the subcommittee hearing was the statement released by General Motors on March 9, in which the company admitted its responsibility for the investigation but said that it was limited to Mr. Nader's qualifications, background, expertise in car safety, and possible association with those handling Corvair cases against GM. Senator Kennedy, however, maintained that GM denied things that they were indeed responsible for and the statement "misled and in fact, was really, I might say, false" [1398].

GM's President Roche, in New York on March 6, saw the *New York Times* article describing Gillen's admission of the investigation. At the time, Roche was unaware of GM's instigation. On March 8, when Roche called his legal department in Detroit asking them to deny any GM involvement, he was told that GM was indeed responsible. He flew back to Detroit and with his legal staff worked on various drafts of the press release from 2:30 P.M. until 8:30 P.M. The mechanics of preparing it were such that it missed most morning papers' 10:00 P.M. deadline [1402]. While the release was being prepared, Roche's legal staff informed him that GM had hired Gillen, but he was not told of the preemployment pretext [1393]. In fact, Roche saw none of Gillen's reports before he signed the statement, and he relied entirely on the assistant general counsel, Mr. Bridenstine [1402]. Bridenstine assured Roche that the investigation was "made solely for the purpose of determining Mr. Nader's connection with the Corvair litigation" [1393].

GM's general counsel, Aloysius F. Power, who had originated the investigation, was out of town when the statement was prepared, and the

24 "Private Eyes and Public Hearings," *Newsweek*, April 4, 1966, pp. 77–78.
25 *Ibid.*

press release was read to him over the phone. He did not object to any inaccuracies even though he "was aware of the reports and the investigation . . ." [1397].

Roche admitted that the statement might be somewhat misleading and that he had learned a great deal about the investigation of Nader since the March 8 statement:

> But I thought our first responsibility was to put out a statement that admitted our responsibility for conducting an investigation. . . .
> As I indicated earlier, were I writing this statement, this press release, today, I think it would be in different language [1392].

Roche added, however, that there was no intent to mislead. Roche acknowledged that certain people on the GM legal staff were receiving reports and knew the full extent of the investigation. Senator Kennedy thought it was "terribly serious, almost equally unfortunate, if not more unfortunate, that General Motors permitted this statement to go out on March 9 which so misled the general public and misled members of Congress and the press of the United States . . ." [1399–1400].

Kennedy, however, was far from satisfied with this explanation. In speaking to Roche, he commented:

> What I don't understand is why people in your office would permit the release of a false statement. I mean, when you call in someone and say, we want to put the facts out, we want to be candid and honest with the general public. Because, nobody has a greater responsibility than General Motors. They are the leading corporation in the United States, they stand for something not only in this country but all over the world.
> Mr. Roche: This is certainly not like General Motors, Senator Kennedy, and I understand what you mean. This is a new and strange experience for most of our people with whom I am associated. And we do not like this kind of approach to a problem of this kind [1399].

Power also testified before the subcommittee, joined in Roche's apology, and said he thought the surveillance was ordered because the investigators thought it appropriate. According to Power, he had not read all available reports relayed by Mr. Danner, but he thought they contained nothing detrimental to Nader's character. However, they did "indicate that Mr. Nader had no educational background or work experience in the field of motor vehicle engineering or technical research, that he did not appear to have the background to qualify as an expert witness in Corvair design cases and that he was reported to have very little trial experience as an attorney" [1442].

The last report was sent to GM on March 14. According to Power, GM was wrong in having Nader followed, but he felt that the investigation was still "limited" and that the press release was not misleading. Power admitted that Nader's character was not helped by the intimate questions asked but thought that the seriousness of the charges against GM by Nader's book and articles should be kept in mind.

Only after extensive questioning by Senator Kennedy did Power say that maybe GM should have added after "initiate a routine investigation" the words "which developed into an intensive investigation" [1453].

Kennedy also relentlessly pursued the same line of questioning with Assistant Counsel Louis H. Bridenstine, who helped draft the March 9 statement. Bridenstine based that statement on "the people in the office who were working on the Corvair, and who knew about the investigation . . ." [1454].

The purpose of the statement was to admit GM's initiating an investigation but to disclaim instances reported by the press for which Bridenstine knew GM was *not* responsible [1457–60]. Bridenstine, who struck Kennedy as being evasive, said that the investigation was intended to be routine.[26] However, Senator Kennedy said:

> But that is not what you said [in the press release]. You didn't say the investigation was "intended." You state categorically that it was limited. . . . And, certainly anybody reading that statement would arrive at the conclusion that it was in fact limited and didn't go into all these other matters that had been reported in the press. Wouldn't you agree that it was misleading?
>
> Mr. Bridenstine: It certainly can be construed as that, sir, and if it will help us any, I will agree that it was misleading, but I will say it wasn't intended as such [1460].

Bridenstine knew that Nader had been followed, admitted that he should have known more about the investigations, but said that he did not have time to read the reports carefully.

Thus, the staff members at GM who initiated the investigation and who were responsible for it were not aware of its extent. The first report Gillen sent to GM via Danner stating that surveillance had taken place was on March 3. Power had heard about it on February 14, some eight days after it started, and ordered it stopped, but by then it was too late. But the very first report sent to GM, received midway during the surveillance, mentioned the possibility of surveillance as per Gillen and Danner's discussion, yet GM took no immediate action [1446, 1449, 1463].

Senator Ribicoff was curious why GM couldn't hire its own investigative

---

26 "Private Eyes and Public Hearings," *Newsweek*, April 4, 1966, pp. 77–78.

agency directly. Danner, who had never handled investigative work before [1518], was an intermediary in the truest sense—Gillen never spoke to anyone at GM, and Danner spoke only to Miss Murphy at GM. Gillen's reports were certainly detailed, but no one high in GM's legal hierarchy read them carefully. The multiplicity of links between Gillen and Roche certainly made for a large gap of ignorance [1521].

THE ISSUE OF AN INDIVIDUAL'S PRIVACY vs. CORPORATE POWER: NADER'S POSITION

The price paid for an environment that required an act of courage for a statement of truth has been needless death, needless injury and inestimable sorrow.

How much has this Nation lost because there are men walking around today with invisible chains?

The trademark of modern society may be the organization, but its inspiring and elevating contributions still flow from individual initiatives. Unless multiple sources of initiative and expression are kept open and asserted, the creative and humanizing infusions of a peoples' energies will atrophy.

Yet in a confrontation between an individual and a corporate organization, between myself and General Motors, if you will, the systematic immunities accrue to the corporation which has outstripped the law that created it. This problem of legal control over corporate action is one of increasing interest to a number of legal and economic scholars. I am responsible for my actions, but who is responsible for those of General Motors? An individual's capital is basically his integrity. He can lose only once. A corporation can lose many times, and not be affected. This unequal contest between the individual and any complex organization, whether it is a corporation, a union, government, or other group, is something which bears the closest scrutiny in order to try to protect the individual from such invasions.

The requirement of a just social order is that responsibility shall lie where the power of decision rests. But the law has never caught up with the development of the large corporate unit. Deliberate acts emanate from the sprawling and indeterminable shelter of the corporate organization. Too often the responsibility for an act is not imputable to those whose decision enable it to be set in motion. The president of General Motors can say he did not know of the specific decision to launch such an investigation. But is he not responsible in some way for the general corporate policy which permits such investigations to be launched by lower-level management without proper guidelines? The office of the general counsel can put forth a document outlining the limits of a "routine" investigation merely to protect the interest of the company's shareholders. A second shield in front of the corporate shield comes in the form of a law firm commissioned in the nonlegal task of hiring a private detective agency. In this case, apparently, GM did not wish to hire agents directly. The enthusiasms of their detectives, the law firm would have us believe, were unauthorized frolics and detours. Besides, the law firm could assume responsibility in the last analysis since there was little burden to such an assumption. Aside from the Federal statute under which this subcommittee is proceeding in this matter, there are few sanctions to protect the principle of privacy in American society against such new challenges largely unforeseen by the Founding Fathers [1466–67].

Nader said the investigation was indeed a harassment, to his family and to himself, for it sought "to obtain lurid details and grist for invidious use,"[27] and

it certainly took up a lot of my time and concern, and particularly concern over where was it going to end. One can possibly take harassing phone calls. One can take surveillance. But what is quite intolerable is the probings and what possibly might be done with these probings. One never has a chance to confront the adversary in a sense. It is faceless, it is insidious, and individuals, not only myself, can be destroyed in this manner, quite apart from discomfort. And so I was quite fearful of what was going to be the end of this. How was this information going to be used, and whether there was going to be even more overt foul play, perhaps of a physical nature.

I am not particularly sensitive to criticism at all. In fact, I probably have an armor like a turtle when it comes to that. I like to give and take. As an attorney, one is used to it. I don't intimidate easily, but I must confess that one begins to have second thoughts of the penalties and the pain which must be incurred in working in this area.

I think the thing that has persuaded me to continue in this area is that I cannot accept a climate in this country where one has to have an ascetic existence and steely determination in order to speak truthfully, candidly, and critically of American industry, and the auto industry. I think if it takes that much stamina, something is wrong with the enabling climate for expression in our country. I don't think it is generally wrong, but I think that we need to look into these areas and see how we can continually improve this climate. And it goes way beyond ideological considerations. This is not an ideological problem.

[27] "GM Apologizes for Harassment of Critic," The New York Times, March 23, 1966, p. 1.

This is a problem of individuals confronting complex organizations, whether they are complex organizations in the United States—corporations, labor unions or what not—or whether they are complex organizations in other countries of the world [1512].

The complex organization need not have the upper hand against the individual, Nader said. Improvement of public education in this regard can become "a built-in check" against invasion of privacy. According to Nader, protection of privacy involves social sanctions as well as legal penalties so that

> when somebody comes in and probes, and just flashes a badge without even showing it, people don't surrender and say, "I'll tell you everything." They will say, "Who are you? Who do you represent? Who is your client? Why are you asking these questions? What is your name? What is your detective serial number?" I am amazed how many people in this country are in a sense subtly restrained from that, as if they had better talk [1513].

Glancing at the thick sheaf of detective reports, Ribicoff told Nader, "You and your family can be proud. They have put you through the mill and they haven't found a damn thing wrong with you" [1513].

Nader stated that he did not represent clients involved in Corvair design suits or work for their attorneys. Nader in fact had said this to GM executives when he visited the Technical Center in January; apparently, involvement would have prohibited his seeing certain Corvair technical exhibits at the center. According to Nader, Bridenstine had indicated that he believed what Nader said. That GM's actions proved they did not take him at his word only demonstrated to Nader that

> General Motors' executives continue to be blinded by their own corporate mirror-image that it's "the buck" that moves the man. They simply cannot understand that the prevention of cruelty to humans can be a sufficient motivation for one endeavoring to obtain the manufacture of safer cars [1469].

Nader added that contrary to Roche's earlier statement, he was "singularly unimpressed" at GM's presentation, which included an "outrageously erroneous assertion" and "evasive responses" [1469].

As for the similarity of his writings and plaintiffs' language in design cases, Nader said these resulted from "a common design defect" in the cars. Indeed, some of Nader's material came directly from GM's patents and trade journals! [1507].

THE CASE IN RETROSPECT

Despite Nader's tormenting by the investigation and hearings, Ribicoff said he could not help "but feel that what this hearing has achieved will have a salutary effect on business ethics and also the protection of the individual" [1513]. Kennedy felt that Roche had raised his stature by appearing [1564]. Perhaps the most important results of the hearings were the auto safety laws. Kennedy said that were it not for Nader and Ribicoff, Congress would not even have considered an auto safety law [1515].

According to *The Atlantic*, the March 22 hearings

> did as much as anything to bring on federal safety standards. One Senator said, "Everybody was so outraged that a great corporation was out to clobber a guy because he wrote critically of them. At that point everybody said what the hell with them." Another Capitol Hill man said, "When they started looking in Ralph's bedroom, we all figured they must really be nervous. We began to believe that Nader must be right."[28]

As for Nader, the hearings made him front page material, the underdog miraculously defeating the giant automotive industry. According to *Newsweek*, "After his confrontation with GM, Nader's public image was more like that of a knight in shining armor." One auto man grumbled, "If GM hadn't beatified him, where would he be today?"[29]

Although the Justice Department decided that "criminal prosecution is not warranted in this matter" [1591], in November 1966, Nader filed a $26 million invasion of privacy suit in the Manhattan State Supreme Court of New York. He named General Motors, Vincent Gillen, Vincent Gillen Associates, Inc., and Fidelifacts, Inc. (a nationwide investigative firm for which Gillen holds the New York franchise).[30]

The papers filed in the suit said that General Motors "decided to conduct a campaign of intimidation, smearing and otherwise severely injuring [Nader],"[31] and subjected him to "harassment and intimidation [and] intruded into and invaded his seclusion, solitude and private affairs." The papers added that he had been "accosted by girls for purposes of entrap-

---

28 Drew, "The Politics of Auto Safety," p. 99.

29 "Meet Ralph Nader," *Newsweek*, January 22, 1968, pp. 65–66.

30 "Nader Sues GM for $26 Million," *The New York Times*, January 17, 1966, p. 35; and "Ralph Nader Sues GM over the Investigation Made of Him," *The Wall Street Journal*, November 17, 1966, p. 5.

31 "Ralph Nader Sues GM," *The Wall Street Journal*, November 17, 1966, p. 5.

GENERAL MOTORS' NADIR, RALPH NADER

ment and extortion" and that he had received phone calls "of a threatening, obnoxious and harassing nature." Furthermore, the defendants used "wiretapping, electronic or mechanical equipment . . . [for] eavesdropping" and interviewed his friends under false pretenses, casting aspersions on his "political, social, economic, racial and religious views, tendencies and possible prejudices" by questioning his integrity, "his sexual proclivities and inclinations; and his personal habits, such as the use of intoxicants, narcotics and the like."[32]

GM responded that it had no legal liability to Nader and that the courts would "vindicate" its position.[33] Gillen denied being concerned, saying the suit was "a lot of nonsense." He added that Fidelifacts, staffed by twenty-six former FBI agents in nationwide offices, "specialized solely in pre-employment investigations and had nothing to do with the case."[34] Nader said the suit was brought to "remedy a wrong inflicted upon one individual and the public interest, in the freedom to speak out against consumer hazards." Accordingly, any court awards would be used for the cause of auto safety.[35]

Meanwhile, as a result of a statement Gillen made to a Detroit newspaper, and unknown to GM, Nader brought a separate defamation of character suit against Gillen.[36] On the basis of Gillen's testimony in the suit's depositions, Nader's attorneys found information to make up "a list of more than 300 controversial statements about the facts in the larger suit against General Motors, and demanded that both Gillen and GM either confirm them or deny them." Within four of the twenty-nine days allowed to do so, Gillen responded. His response again made the Nader case front-page news and prompted Senator Ribicoff to ask the Justice Department to reinvestigate the possibility that perjury had been committed during his subcommittee hearings.[37]

GILLEN'S ALLEGATIONS

Gillen swore in the court papers that "General Motors caused the original version of the first page" of one of Gillen's reports to GM to be

"Nader Sues GM for $26 Million," *The New York Times,* November 17, 1966, p. 35.

Ibid.

Ibid.

Ibid.

"GM Aide Is Said to Assist Nader," *The New York Times,* February 7, 1967, p. 29; "Nader Again," *Newsweek,* February 20, 1967, p. 86; and Sidney Zion, "Ribicoff Seeking New GM Inquiry," *The New York Times,* February 6, 1967, p. 1.

Zion, "Ribicoff Seeking New GM Inquiry"; and "Nader Again," *Newsweek,* February 20, 1967, p. 86.

withheld from Ribicoff's subcommittee and substituted an altered version. The original version showed that the true purpose of the investigation was to "discredit" Nader and to "shut him up." Gillen cooperated with GM in changing the document as it "did not coincide" with GM's "announced purpose" for the investigation. Gillen added that he did not look into Nader's connection with Corvair suits but delved "deeply into [his] past and present life . . . covering all facets thereof, including his movements." The original version of the first page of his report on Nader was destroyed on Danner's request, and the new version stated that the primary objective of the investigation was to fill in missing details on Nader "with emphasis on anything showing prejudice against automobiles or their manufacturers, or any subsidy involved in his writings." Both the investigation and the preemployment pretext "had been approved by General Motors' legal department."[38]

Furthermore, Gillen said he secretly taped his first meeting with Danner (another former FBI agent) on January 13, 1966, when Danner gave Gillen his instructions. Danner allegedly told Gillen:

> They want to get something somewhere on this guy to get him out of their hair and to shut him up.
> He's Syrian, or something, and maybe you will find an anti-Semitic angle . . . that will be interesting to Ribicoff.
> There's something somewhere; find it so they can shut him up. His stuff is pretty damaging to the auto industry.

Gillen said that he had told GM, before the March 22 hearing, that he had recorded the discussion, but the company made no request for a transcript.[39]

Sometime after this interview, a letter written on blank stationery, signed "Eileen," complained about the investigation's progress and requested specific kinds of information—Nader's savings accounts, stocks, accidents, and driver's license.[40] According to the New Republic, "Eileen" was Miss Eileen Murphy, of GM's legal department, and the letter was the

[38] "Ribicoff Wants Study of Possible Perjury in GM–Nader Hearings," The Wall Street Journal, February 6, 1967, p. 4; and "Detective in Nader Case Says GM Altered Papers," The New York Times, February 5, 1967, p. 1.

[39] "Detective in Nader Case Says GM Altered Papers," The New York Times, February 5, 1967, p. 1. Perhaps GM did not request a transcript of the meeting between Danner and Gillen because Danner may have recorded it himself. In any case, Gillen's admission certainly is an indication of his tendency to use recording devices in his investigations. It was said during Ribicoff's hearing that such devices were not used in the investigation. See pp. 194 and 200 of this book.

[40] Ibid.

seven-page investigation "guide" Gillen referred to in his court statement.[41] The "guide" made no mention of Corvair litigation but suggested possible anti-Semitism, dope, and asked, "Does he drink?"[42] According to the *New Republic*, the letter was dated February 1966, addressed to Danner, and read in part:

> Dear Dick,
> . . . everyone is going overboard to impress us with what a great, charming, intellectual this human being is—Eagle Scout type. There are too many variances for this to be accurate. . . . What is his Army record? What did he do for six months in the Army? . . . He mentions an accident which happened a decade ago. *He saw* a child decapitated. See if this gem can be uncovered as to where, when or how he was involved. . . . Well, friend, have fun. . . .[43]

Gillen's court statement said that when he visited Detroit, shortly before the hearing, the company took the letter from him so that a copy would not fall into Ribicoff's hands.[44]

Gillen felt that one of the reasons for injecting anti-Semitism into the investigation "was to attempt to discredit Ralph Nader in the eyes of Senator Abraham Ribicoff, who is Jewish." He said that some members of GM's legal department thought Ribicoff and Nader had "some fairly close relationships" and they found it difficult to believe Ribicoff's statement that he saw Nader for the first time on February 10, 1966. Thus, Gillen was told to investigate the Senator's "credibility." In fact, when Gillen visited Detroit before the hearings, a GM lawyer "attempted to convince" him that he should deny any charges of investigating Ribicoff. Indeed, the night before the hearings, GM's Power, in getting Gillen to cooperate with GM, allegedly said, "I threatened to resign, but they're afraid to let me resign. If I can take this, you can take it too."[45] Power would not comment on Gillen's statements, saying, "It's unethical to discuss a case when it's at trial," referring questions to counsel representing GM in the suit.[46]

In the court statements, Gillen said that he had been conducting investigations for GM since 1959, including an investigation on entertainer Danny Kaye "to ascertain whether his morals, character and political be-

[41] James Ridgeway and David Sanford, "The Nader Affair," *The New Republic*, February 18, 1967, p. 16; and "Detective in Nader Case Says GM Altered Papers," *The New York Times*, February 5, 1967, p. 1.

[42] Ridgeway and Sanford, "The Nader Affair," p. 18; and "Detective in Nader Case Says GM Altered Papers," *The New York Times*, February 5, 1967, p. 1.

[43] Ridgeway and Sanford, "The Nader Affair," p. 18.

[44] *Ibid.*; and "Detective in Nader Case Says GM Altered Papers," *The New York Times*, February 5, 1967, p. 1.

[45] "Nader Again," *Newsweek*, February 20, 1967, p. 86.

[46] "Detective in Nader Case Says GM Altered Papers," *The New York Times*, February 5, 1967, p. 1.

liefs were suitable for identification with General Motors." Kaye, like Nader after him, received a good report. Gillen also helped with a two-year surveillance on a woman who said that she had had an affair with an officer of GM.[47] Also on Gillen's list were United Auto Workers officials and a civil rights worker "in whom General Motors was interested." In addition, Gillen looked into a Harlem antipoverty group which had charged GM with discrimination against Negroes in the company's hiring policies.[48]

GM's RESPONSE

The questions Nader's attorneys asked Gillen to answer were in the form of a "request for admission," which requires the other party to admit or deny certain statements under oath.[49] The same request was submitted to GM on January 25. Gillen signed the request within four of the twenty-nine days allowed for him to do so. Surprised at his speed in answering, GM asserted that he was in collusion with Nader against GM in the suit. Gillen filed the papers on a Friday and the next Monday, February 6, GM submitted court papers saying of Gillen's statements that "the most casual examination . . . makes it obvious that Gillen is cooperating."[50] The company then moved to strike the requirement for the "request to admit" citing it as improper, in violation of GM's rights, and not in line with established legal practice.[51] One week later, GM submitted court papers requesting that all suits involving Nader be merged, again charging Gillen-Nader cooperation. The company's stand was that the Detroit suit represented a vehicle for obtaining information against GM. Of Gillen's motive for collusion, the company's attorneys said that GM had advised Gillen the previous November that it could not commit itself to pay for his defense in the suit or to bear any of his losses. GM said, "That marked the end of any genuine effort on Gillen's part to defend himself . . . [beginning] fullest cooperation [with Nader]."[52]

---

47 *Ibid.*

48 *Ibid.*; and Ridgeway and Sanford, "The Nader Affair," p. 18.

49 "Detective in Nader Case Says GM Altered Papers," *The New York Times*, February 5, 1967, p. 1.

50 "GM Aide Is Said to Assist Nader," *The New York Times*, February 7, 1967, p. 29; and "GM Says Detective It Hired in Nader Case Now Helps Auto-Critic in Suit against Firm," *The Wall Street Journal*, February 7, 1967, p. 7.

51 "Ribicoff Wants Study of Possible Perjury in GM–Nader Hearings," *The Wall Street Journal*, February 6, 1967, p. 4; and "Nader Again," *Newsweek*, Feb. 20, 1967, p. 86; and "Detective in Nader Case Says GM Altered Papers," *The New York Times*, February 5, 1967, p. 1.

52 "GM Would Merge Nader–Gillen Suits," *The New York Times*, March 14, 1967, p. 35.

Gillen labeled GM's claims of cooperation as "ridiculous."[53] He said he had counterclaimed against Nader in the Detroit suit for $2 million and had counterclaimed against both GM and Nader in the New York suit—for $21 million each. Gillen asked, "Is that what they call cooperation? I'm suing Nader for $2 million in one suit and $21 million in the other." He said of the court papers filed recently that "I was simply telling the truth."[54]

Nader's attorney said of GM's charges, "If they're implying collusion or a deal of any kind, we flatly deny it. If General Motors wants to send a 'request to admit' on that, Nader will deny it under oath."[55]

MANEUVERINGS

A long series of pretrial maneuverings followed the company's February 1967 court motions, which were not concluded until July 1968. By this time, the court had rejected GM's claims of collusion between Nader and Gillen and had refused to throw out Gillen's allegations.[56] It was expected that the company would appeal these *pretrial* decisions to the U.S. Supreme Court.[57]

EPILOGUE

On August 13, 1970, General Motors and Ralph Nader announced an out-of-court settlement of $425,000 for Nader's $26 million invasion-of-privacy suit against GM. In announcing the settlement, Nader's spokesman said that the proceeds of the settlement, after deducting legal fees and expenses, will be used to establish a "continuous legal monitoring of General Motor's activities in the safety, pollution, and consumer relations area."[58]

[53] "GM Says Detective It Hired in Nader Case Now Helps Auto-Critic in Suit against Firm," *The Wall Street Journal*, February 7, 1967, p. 7.

[54] "GM Aide Is Said to Assist Nader," *The New York Times*, February 7, 1967, p. 29.

[55] *Ibid.*

[56] "Collusion Rejected in Two Nader Suits," *The New York Times*, July 6, 1967, p. 22; and "GM Is Rebuffed in Suit by Nader," *The New York Times*, July 6, 1968, p. 42.

[57] *Ibid.*; and "The Critic," *San Francisco Sunday Examiner and Chronicle*, February 23, 1969, A9.

[58] *The Wall Street Journal*, August 14, 1970, p. 4.

Bethlehem Steel Company and
the Woodroofe Incident

*To What Extent Can a Corporation Control an Employee's
Social and Political Activities?*

*The fundamental tendency of the bureaucratic mind is to turn all problems of politics
into problems of administration.*

—Karl Mannheim

On March 16, 1964, the Bethlehem Steel Company fired Philip B. Woodroofe, supervisor of municipal services at the Bethlehem, Pennsylvania, home office. The charge was that Woodroofe and his wife refused to comply with a company demand to resign from the Community Civic League, an organization to improve interracial relations. Woodroofe was a founder of the organization.

When pressed for an explanation, the company simply stated that Woodroofe had resigned and that it was not company policy to make statements on an individual employee's resignation. Woodroofe himself denied having resigned:

I have never submitted my resignation, nor have I been asked to submit one. . . . I was told I was through. . . . I was told I couldn't act as a private citizen, nor could my wife.[1]

This incident, which for a short time received national attention, brought into sharp focus the contradictions between a company's public posture and its private philosophy; the vulnerability of professional junior and middle-level managers—unprotected by unions or internal company due process against the arbitrary exercise of power by large corporations; and, still more important, the infringement of an individual's rights by the extension of the corporation's control over his actions in areas not directly connected with corporate activities.

THE COMPANY

Bethlehem Steel, the second largest steel company in the United States, dominates the economic and social life of the Lehigh Valley and the city of Bethlehem, Pennsylvania. It furnishes nearly 50 percent of the entire payroll of the town. Of Bethlehem's population of seventy-seven thousand, about one thousand are blacks, and a very small number are Puerto Ricans. (In the Lehigh Valley as a whole, with a population of two hundred and fifty thousand, about twenty-five hundred are blacks.) Schools have not been segregated, and there have been no civil rights demonstrations. There has been a problem of inadequate housing for the poor and a high rate of Negro school dropouts.[2]

Over the years, [Bethlehem Steel] has demonstrated its consciousness of the civic well-being of its home office city in many ways. It has invested heavily, without any prodding, in air pollution controls, in neutralizing the manufacturing effluents which it dumps into the Lehigh River, and in expending heavy sums to beautify the city by buying up eyesores and staving off blight along approaches or property not used for steel manufacturing. Besides, it has increasingly encouraged its people to participate in a wide range of civic activity, even to the point of giving one of its junior executives a leave of absence to run for Congress last year.[3]

[1] Joseph A. Loftus, "Bethlehem Puzzled by Dismissal of Steel Aide over Racial Stand," *The New York Times*, March 22, 1964, p. 10.

[2] *Ibid.*

[3] "The Woodroofe Incident," *Bethlehem Globe-Times*, March 20, 1964, p. 6.

In its management policies, however, the firm has long been regarded as one of the "most withdrawn and individualistic companies in a conservative industry."[4]

Bethlehem Steel is run by a board of directors made up entirely of company officers, without a single outsider. Situated far from the big steel centers, the "inbred and stratified social life" of the company executives centers on the Saucon Valley Country Club. To an outsider, the company "offers a cautious austere facade."[5]

> Bethlehem is noted for being stingy with titles but generous with salaries. With $2.1 billion in sales, it has only 10 vice presidents. United States Steel, with $3.6 billion in sales, has 77.
>
> The lowest-paid Bethlehem vice presidents received $113,866 last year, and the highest paid, John E. Jacobs, vice president for steel operations, drew $218,358. Mr. Cort, who was president and a director for five months, received $79,167 for the period, or payment at an annual rate of $145,000.
>
> Mr. Martin, in his capacities as president and vice chairman, drew $251,726, and Mr. Homer, as chairman, received $301,860.[6]

The style of management has been strictly individual and authority has clearly been centralized at the top. In its fifty-nine-year history the company has had only three chief executives. The first died in office at the age of seventy-seven. The other two retired after serving for eighteen and for seven years at the ages of eighty-one and sixty-eight, respectively. The fourth chief executive officer, Edmund F. Martin, took over on March 17, 1964, at the age of sixty-one, moving up from his former position as the vice-chairman.

Arthur Homer, the retiring chairman, has been regarded as one of the most commanding figures in the steel industry.

> He is a tall, lean simply-spoken man, whose demeanor has been described as that of an affable New England preacher. He enjoys a pipe and occasionally indulges in a little wit or whimsy.
>
> . . .
>
> At his quarterly press conferences in New York he stood at the door to the 15th floor conference room greeting reporters as they entered. He then took a seat alone on one side of a 30-foot table and fielded questions from the newsmen arrayed opposite him.

[4] John M. Lee, "1964: Year of Change for Bethlehem Steel," *The New York Times*, April 12, 1964, Sec. 3, pp. 1, 5.

[5] *Ibid.*

[6] *Ibid.*

Behind Mr. Homer, against the wall, sit all the directors. Only occasionally did Mr. Homer ask any of them to comment. During the conference, the directors' expressions seldom changed except to laugh at a Homer quip. There was no question of who spoke for Bethlehem.[7]

PHILIP B. WOODROOFE

Woodroofe, forty-five at the time of the incident, is the son of an Episcopal minister. He interrupted his studies at Lehigh University to enter the United States Air Force shortly after Pearl Harbor. He served in World War II and in the Korean conflict as a B-29 pilot and instructor. He left the service as a lieutenant colonel in the Air Force Reserve.[8]

In 1957, when he was director of residence halls at Lehigh University, he was hired to be Bethlehem's supervisor of municipal services. His duties at the company called for, among other things, cooperation in city planning.[9]

COMMUNITY CIVIC LEAGUE

In May 1963, the Right Reverend Arthur Lichtenberger, presiding bishop of the Protestant Episcopal Church in the United States, appealed to his church members to take positive action and assume responsibility in solving this country's racial problems. Mr. Woodroofe, an Episcopalian, took this appeal seriously and initiated informal meetings between local white and black leaders to develop the framework for an organization that could provide a forum where community problems could be brought into the open and discussed, thus avoiding the possibility of violent confrontation between various groups. Woodroofe took a leading role in mobilizing community support. As a result, the Community Civic League was formally organized on March 15, 1964, at the local YWCA. Participating were more than two hundred local citizens, including Bethlehem's mayor, H. Gordon Payrow, and a number of clergymen.

[7] *Ibid.*

[8] "Steel Company Ousts Municipal Aide," *Bethlehem Globe-Times*, March 17, 1964, p. 7.

[9] Loftus, "Bethlehem Puzzled by Dismissal of Steel Aide."

Woodroofe's Troubles with the Company

Two days before the organizational meeting of the league, Woodroofe was informed that his superiors were displeased with his involvement in league activities. According to a story in the *New York Times:*

On Friday, March 13, F. C. Rabold, manager of general services for Bethlehem Steel, said it had come to his attention through his superiors that Mr. Woodroofe was involved in the league. The instructions to Mr. Rabold were to "get me out" of the league, Mr. Woodroofe said.

One of Mr. Rabold's superiors is Russell K. Branscom, vice president for industrial and public relations. Nebraska-born, Mr. Branscom was graduated from the University of Alabama with the interfraternity award for outstanding service to the university. That was in 1935. He has been in Bethelehem since then.

Mr. Woodroofe was given until Sunday noon to make his decision. He talked with Mr. Rabold Saturday and was cautioned about the consequences of a wrong decision.

"Helen and I talked about exchanging places," she to go on the board of the league and he to be a rank-and-file member. "The company told me that wouldn't do," he said.

Mr. Woodroofe won an extension of the deadline until 4 P.M. Sunday so that he could talk to his friend, Bishop Frederick Warneke. The Bishop was away and Mr. Woodroofe gave his answer without that counsel. The answer was:

"Neither I nor Helen will disassociate ourselves from the Community League. What we started here is good. We must continue it."

Mr. Woodroofe said his superior's reply was: "I think you've made a mistake."

The company's view that the league would worsen rather than help the situation was conveyed to Mr. Woodroofe.

When Mr. Woodroofe reported for work Monday morning, Mr. Rabold told him, "I'm surprised that you are here."

"Do you mean to say really I'm through?" Mr. Woodroofe asked.

"Yes, you're through," was the reply.

"So I went to the board and punched my time card," Mr. Woodroofe said. He was through at 10:15 and left without cleaning out his desk.[10]

---

[10] *Ibid.*, p. 10.

The town was shocked and dismayed. The story made the national newspapers. The local papers during the next few days were full of angry letters from readers and editorials condemning Bethlehem Steel's action. Not a single word could be found in either the local or the national news media justifying or supporting the company's action.[11]

THE COMPANY'S POSTURE IN THE AFTERMATH

Bethlehem's press statement that Woodroofe had resigned was clearly unsatisfactory to the community. It refused to accept the company's statement in view of Woodroofe's charge that he was indeed fired. Consequently, in response to local inquiries, the company issued two statements denying that it was against employee participation in community affairs and insisting that Woodroofe's dismissal was based on a clear case of conflict of interest.

The first statement was issued on March 24, 1964:[12]

> [As far back as] in 1955, for example, our Chairman and Chief Executive Officer, Arthur B. Homer, addressing the Bethlehem Chamber of Commerce, emphasized that "our employees are encouraged to participate as fully as they can in the life of the community, as citizens, irrespective of their status with the company."
>
> This continuing policy was re-emphasized in a speech on March 16, 1960, by James V. Robertson, Manager of Community Relations, who said:
>
> ". . . Part of that job is encouraging employees—and I quote Mr. Homer on this—'to participate as fully as they can in the life of the community, irrespective of their status with the company.' "
>
> Also, in 1961, in management conferences held in all the steel plants, employees were again encouraged to participate as fully as they cared to in the life of the community, as citizens, irrespective of whether or not the company provides financial support for a particular organization's activities. That policy has continued without change to the present time.

A company spokesman also said that "the company would be glad, if invited, to designate an official representative to participate in the activities of the committee."[13]

[11] See *Bethlehem Globe-Times*, March 18, 20, 23–25, 27, 30, April 10, 1964; and *Allentown Morning Call*, March 27, 1964.

[12] "Company Says No Bar on Civic Activity," *Bethlehem Globe-Times*, March 25, 1964.

[13] "Steel Company Invites Bid to Interracial League," *Bethlehem Globe-Times*, March 24, 1964, p. 12.

The second statement, issued on March 25, 1964, dealt specifically with Woodroofe's dismissal:[14]

> As supervisor of municipal services of this company, Mr. Woodroofe participated as the official representative of the company in certain municipal activities. When he became identified with the Community Civic League, it was the company's belief that his position on matters coming before that organization would be viewed as an expression of the official position of the company. This type of activity did not represent an area related to his responsibilities with the company and the company believed it inescapable that misunderstandings would result.
>
> Therefore, although the company does encourage employees to participate in affairs of their local communities, the circumstances in this case were such—and Mr. Woodroofe was so advised—that there was a clear conflict between his official representation of the company in certain community activities and his participation in the League. Mr. Woodroofe chose to resign from the company.

In a later announcement, the company stated that Woodroofe was offered two other jobs with the company prior to his dismissal but that he refused to accept either of them.[15]

When asked to comment, Mr. Woodroofe said that he found it difficult to accept the company's statement at face value since it demanded that his wife also resign from the Community Civic League.[16] Mrs. Woodroofe added, "And I am on the Red Cross Board. I don't speak for the company there."[17]

COMMUNITY CIVIC LEAGUE'S RESPONSE

A league spokesman considered it an encouraging sign when Bethlehem Steel indicated interest in participating in the league's affairs. The Reverend R. Wakefield Roberts, the pastor of Saint John Zion Methodist Church and a member of the league's board of directors, said that he was positive that the league would extend an invitation to the company to join. He also stated that the board would adopt an official position on the Woodroofe incident.[18]

[14] "Steel Blames 'Conflict' in Woodroofe Case," *Bethlehem Globe-Times*, March 26, 1964.

[15] "Woodroofe Vetoed Two Other Jobs," *Bethlehem Globe-Times*, April 15, 1964, p. 1.

[16] "Steel Blames 'Conflict' in Woodroofe Case," *Bethlehem Globe-Times*.

[17] Loftus, "Bethlehem Puzzled by Dismissal of Steel Aide."

[18] "Steel Co. Bid to Interracial League," *Bethlehem Globe-Times*, p. 12.

The meeting took place on the evening of March 24, 1964. At the meeting the board turned down the company's bid to send an official representative to participate in the league's activities. In declining the company's request the board cited a provision of its constitution which limited the membership in the league to persons who were "willing to work as individuals towards improving conditions of minority groups in Bethlehem, rather than as representatives of any church, industry, business or profession."[19]

The board also unanimously decided not to take any official position on the Woodroofe incident. This was done at the suggestion of Mr. Woodroofe who requested that the board make no statement "public or private" as this "would not serve the league's purpose."[20]

On June 30, 1964, Philip Woodroofe resigned from the board of directors of the league as he planned to move to New York where he had reportedly accepted a real estate job. However, he retained his membership in the league.[21]

[19] "Civic League Fails to Offer Steel Bid," *Bethlehem Globe-Times,* March 25, 1969.

[20] *Ibid.*

[21] "Woodroofe Resigns Seat on Civic League Board," *Allentown Morning Call,* July 1, 1964.

Motorola v. Fairchild Camera

The Case of C. Lester Hogan, et al.

All that clearly appears is that he undertook to use in his new employment the knowledge he had acquired in the old. This, if it involves no breach of confidence, is not unlawful; for equity has no power to compel a man who changes employers to wipe clean the slate of his memory.

—JUSTICE FRANCIS M. SCOTT
in *Peerless Pattern Co.* vs. *Pictorial Review Co.*
(147 App. Div. 715, 132 N.Y.S. 37)

On August 8, 1968, C. Lester Hogan resigned from Motorola, Incorporated, to join Fairchild Camera and Instrument Corporation. At the time of his resignation, Mr. Hogan was a director and executive vice-president of Motorola and general manager of the Semiconductor Products Division. His new position was as a director and president of Fairchild. Soon after Hogan resigned, seven other top men in Motorola's semiconductor division joined him at Fairchild,[1] and by the end of September, another fifteen executives left Motorola.[2]

On August 27, 1968, Motorola filed a civil suit in the Federal Court in

[1] *Motorola, Inc.* v. *Fairchild Camera and Instrument Corporation, et al.*, Civil Complaint No. 6808, U.S. District Court, Arizona, August 27, 1968, as amended by the Court Order of September 18, 1968, pp. 6–20.

[2] "The Fight That Fairchild Won," *Business Week*, October 5, 1968, p. 113.

Arizona charging Fairchild and seven other defendants with antitrust violations, unfair competition, interference with advantageous personnel relations, and unjust enrichment. Motorola sought relief in terms of compensatory and exemplary damages and also asked that Hogan and the other defendants hold in "constructive trust" (read, returnable to Motorola) all profits they derived from Fairchild. Named as codefendants were the wives of Hogan and of the seven other defendants for the reason that the financial benefits allegedly gained by the defendants "are or may constitute community property for which said defendants must account to plaintiff and as to which a constructive trust is prayed to enforce the rights of plaintiff therein."[3]

The Defendants

1. Fairchild Camera and Instrument Corporation
2. C. Lester Hogan and Audrey Hogan
3. Leo E. Dwork and Bea Dwork
4. Eugene A. Blanchette and Valerie Blanchette
5. George M. Scalise and Dorothea Scalise
6. Andrew A. Procassini and Jean Procassini
7. William A. Lehner and Ella Lehner
8. Thomas D. Hinkelman and Winnie Hinkelman
9. Wilfred J. Corrigan and Sigrun Corrigan

Motorola's Specific Charges: Against Fairchild

1. Fairchild knew, or reasonably should have known, that Hogan and the seven other defendants were key members of the top management team of Motorola's Semiconductor Division; had harmonious relations with Motorola's management; and had each executed stock option contracts with Motorola which stipulated remaining in Motorola's employ for one year [24]. Its solicitation and employment of Motorola's key management employees in the Semiconductor Division would tend to restrain and lessen competition in the semiconductor industry, inasmuch as the wrongful wholesale defection of part of the latter's top management team to a

---

[3] Extensive use is made of Motorola's Civil Complaint No. 6808. Citations from this source henceforth appear in the text set off by brackets enclosing page references.

competitor might well seriously weaken and render less effective Motorola's competitive position. This restraint of and injury to competition between Motorola and Fairchild violates the laws of the United States. "The products of both Motorola and Fairchild are sold and move in and are a part of the interstate and foreign commerce of the United States" [25,31].

2. Despite this knowledge, Fairchild enticed these defendants into breaking their employment relationships with and fiduciary duties owed to Motorola [26].

3. As part of this wrongful scheme, Fairchild expected that Hogan would directly and indirectly solicit the key employees—that is, the remaining named defendants, and others—to break their employment obligations with Motorola by leaving Motorola in a body and without notice and becoming employees of Fairchild. Furthermore, as part of this scheme, Fairchild authorized Hogan to induce Motorola employees to join Fairchild and for this purpose gave him written forms of stock options [26,30].

MOTOROLA'S SPECIFIC CHARGES: AGAINST HOGAN

In the middle of July 1968, after Fairchild approached him for the first time, Hogan assured Motorola that he was not interested in changing employers and that he intended to honor his commitment to Motorola. This was a misrepresentation, however, according to Motorola, as Hogan suddenly advised Motorola on August 7, 1968, that he was resigning and submitted his written resignation the next day, to be effective immediately. Without his employer's knowledge, Hogan had negotiated with one of Motorola's largest competitors in the semiconductor industry with intention to defect and to "take his 'team' of top management people in the Semiconductor Division with him." To accomplish this, Hogan met with his codefendants individually and in groups on various occasions between early July and August 7, 1968, in Maricopa County, Arizona [28–29].

MOTOROLA'S SPECIFIC CHARGES: AGAINST HOGAN AND HIS CODEFENDANTS FROM THE SEMICONDUCTOR DIVISION

1. Motorola charged that Hogan, Dwork, Corrigan, Blanchette, Hinkelman, Procassini, Scalise, and Lehner knew, or should reasonably have known, that the lavish salary increases and other financial benefits offered by Fairchild were

for the purpose of obtaining for Fairchild access to the trade secrets and "know how" of Motorola known to said employees by reason of their employment by Motorola for use by Fairchild. Each of said employees knew or should have realized that their knowledge and familiarity with said trade secrets and know how was so intertwined with their personal engineering and other skills that use by and disclosure of Motorola's trade secrets to Fairchild would be inevitable and unavoidable if said employees undertook to discharge and carry out duties for Fairchild which were similar to their duties while employed by Motorola [30].

2. These defendants were part of the top management team of Motorola's Semiconductor Division. As such, they were privy to trade secrets,[4] information concerning Motorola's research, new product development, current products, pricing, and other policies in the highly competitive marketing of semiconductor products, both in the United States and abroad. They also had access to the confidential information supplied to the company by Motorola's customers for product research and development. These defendants had been informed and were aware that such information or know-how was confidential and was the sole and exclusive property of Motorola, could be used solely for the benefit of and in the cause of business for Motorola, and was to be kept confidential for a period of two years after any termination of employment with Motorola [3].

3. Each of the individual male defendants had executed an agreement with Motorola with respect to inventions and other proprietary information, and these agreements were in force at the time of their unilateral resignations [3–4].

4. In March 1968, each male defendant was granted substantial salary increases and additional valuable stock options, in consideration of which he agreed, in writing, to remain in Motorola's employ for a period of one year from that date [20].

---

[4] The definition of trade secret as used by Motorola in its complaint (p. 9) and accepted by Fairchild and the other defendants in their answer to Motorola's complaint is as follows:

A trade secret may consist of any formula, pattern, device or compilation of information which is used in one's business, and which gives him an opportunity to obtain an advantage over competitors who do not know or use it. It may be a formula for a chemical compound, a process of manufacturing, treating or preserving materials, a pattern for a machine or other device, or a list of customers. A trade secret is a process or device for continuous use in the operation of the business. Generally it relates to the production of goods, as, for example, a machine or formula for the production of an article. It may, however, relate to the sale of goods or to other operations in the business, such as a code for determining discounts, rebates or other concessions in a price list or catalogue, or a list of specialized customers, or a method of bookkeeping or other office management.

It may be a device which is patentable but it need not be. It may be a device or process which is clearly anticipated in the prior art or one which is merely a mechanical improvement. It must at least be novel to the person receiving the disclosure.

5. The defendants knew that their resignations without notice would constitute a wrongful breach of their employment obligation with Motorola [31].

6. They also knew that Fairchild would obtain, by its wrongful conduct, a top-management team of great value to Fairchild and the loss of such a team could be seriously damaging to Motorola as a competitor of Fairchild [31].

7. These defendants, between August 9 and August 14, 1968, wrongfully left Motorola to accept jobs with Fairchild. Furthermore, *these defendants' new jobs with Fairchild covered the same areas of responsibility as those of their previous jobs with Motorola* [31].

8. Motorola also charged that, since

It is impossible to separate out and segregate the amount of said inducements which might be considered as legitimate, if said defendants had not been under an employment obligation to Motorola, and hence the entire gain is infected with the evil purpose which actuated the offers by Fairchild.

Each therefore holds these gains as property secured by wrongful acts damaging to Motorola, as constructive trustee for Motorola [emphasis supplied] [31].

NATURE OF RELIEF SOUGHT BY MOTOROLA

Motorola asked the court that: 1. Fairchild, Hogan, and the other male defendants be enjoined from employing or agreeing to employ any present employee of Motorola and from soliciting, urging, or permitting the male codefendants to disclose or utilize any trade secret or information of Motorola and its customers in discharge of their duties as employees of Fairchild [36–37].

2. Hogan and other male defendants be enjoined from disclosing or utilizing, for the benefit of Fairchild, any trade secrets or confidential information of its customers gained while employed by Motorola [37].

3. All male defendants and their wives be enjoined from selling, encumbering, or otherwise lessening the monetary value of each of said defendants' financial gains and rewards realized by accepting employment from Fairchild. That these defendants are to hold all "illicit gains made by them from Fairchild" as the price for breaching their agreements with Motorola as a "constructive trustee for Motorola and requiring that the same be paid over to Motorola" [38].

4. Motorola be awarded judgment "against *Fairchild and Hogan* for such damages compensatory and exemplary as the court may determine as

appropriate to make Motorola whole and to deter other corporations and directors and officers thereof . . ." [emphasis supplied] [38].

SUBSTANTIATION OF CHARGES BY MOTOROLA

To substantiate its charges against Fairchild and other defendants, Motorola made the following points:

1. Both Motorola and Fairchild are manufacturers and sellers of semiconductor products and other devices and instruments that use these products. Motorola and Fairchild compete with each other in interstate and foreign commerce for the distribution and sale of these products.

2. Motorola is a pioneer in the electronics industry, including the semiconductor field, and is recognized as such nationally and internationally.

3. Motorola has expended large sums of money on research and development in electronics, including the semiconductor field, and has maintained a large staff of scientists, engineers, and technicians. As a result of these activities, the company has developed certain novel products and processes which are trade secrets and are maintained as proprietary information in the operation of the Semiconductor Division.

4. All male defendants had been part of Motorola's Semiconductor Division. Within that division their duties and responsibilities were such that they had access to, and were familiar with, these trade secrets [6–20]. The brief job descriptions of these defendants, at the time of their resignations, will clarify this point:

C. LESTER HOGAN. As director and executive vice-president of Motorola, Inc., he was privy to, and had knowledge of, Motorola's corporate trade secrets. As general manager of the Semiconductor Division, he was familiar with all its trade secrets and knew of its product mix, marketing policies, and long-range plans for product development and marketing.

LEO E. DWORK. Vice-president of Motorola, Inc., and director of Products and Operations Group within the Semiconductor Division. Prior to an organizational change four months before the resignations in April 1968, Dwork reported directly to Hogan. Dwork was manager and director of discrete semiconductors, with some minor exceptions, and had supervisory and management direction and control of all research and development and manufacturing of these products. He was responsible for the activities of the Applied Sciences Group which performed basic research for both discrete semiconductor products and integrated circuit products; for overall management of quality control; for the important Materials Department which supplied materials for product manufacture throughout the entire division. Dwork was chairman of the division's Patent Committee and as such reviewed and had access to all new invention and patent disclosures emanating from all division departments; received confidential information on the various aspects of Motorola's basic research, product development and manufacturing, and marketing. Further, defendants Lehner and Procassini reported directly to Dwork.

WILFRED J. CORRIGAN. As director of Products Groups, he was in direct charge of product development and manufacturing operations pertaining to the majority of discrete semiconductors and related products and applications, which product area provides a large dollar volume of sales to Motorola at the present time.

EUGENE A. BLANCHETTE. As director of Integrated Circuits Operation, he was in direct charge of product development and manufacturing operations pertaining to integrated circuits and related products and applications. Blanchette had full knowledge of all of Motorola's integrated circuitry manufacturing equipment processes and technology much of which, including trade secrets, marketing and customer information, was confidential.

WILLIAM C. LEHNER. As manager of Equipment and Plant Operations, he had overall responsibility for designing, engineering, building, maintaining, and calibrating all special manufacturing and testing equipment used by Motorola in its Semiconductor Division.

ANDREW A. PROCASSINI. As director of Reliability and Quality Control, Procassini had frequent occasion to confer personally with Dwork, Corrigan, Lehner, and Blanchette with respect to quality control aspects of the entire Semiconductor Division. He was also responsible for translating customers' specifications (generally considered as confidential) to Motorola's format of specifications. Procassini had intimate knowledge of customers' special reliability requirements, which were also highly confidential.

GEORGE M. SCALISE. As general manager of Semiconductor Division, European Operations, he had knowledge pertaining to all of the manufacturing and marketing operations, including, importantly, knowledge concerning the products that are or can be sold in the greatest volume and profitability in the European market. Additionally, Scalise had participated in the long-range planning of both manufacturing facilities and marketing in the European area.

THOMAS D. HINKELMAN. As director of Planning and Production Control, he was responsible for preparing long-range plans and recommendations with respect to capital expenditure requirements of the Semiconductor Division projected over a five-year period. He also participated in new-product planning for the European market and was responsible for process-ing all requests from all departments within the division for capital ex-penditures on a day-to-day basis. Hinkelman was also responsible for inventory control and warehousing operations in the domestic Semicon-ductor Division. In this capacity he had detailed knowledge of the volume of product types that Motorola manufactures.

Events Leading to the Resignations from Motorola

Motorola maintained that relationships between the company and its top-management personnel were harmonious and that the latter worked together smoothly as a team. Moreover, the company contended that, as late as March 1968, each male defendant was granted a substantial salary increase, stock options, participation in Motorola's profit-sharing plan, and a host of other benefits which the company considered "as fair and reason-able compensation for their services to the company, and as a proper and fair inducement for said defendants to perform their corporate functions competently and loyally and as fiduciaries to their employer Motorola" [20]. In return for these benefits, each defendant agreed in writing to remain with Motorola for at least one year from the date of the agreement. Thus Motorola implied that it clearly was the injured party and an inno-cent victim of the unfettered greed of the male defendants and of the ruthless and unprincipled temptations offered by Fairchild to entice these employees of a competitor to break their agreements with their employer in a manner that was tantamount to personnel raiding.

However, it appears from other accounts that things may not have been that smooth at Motorola and, although Fairchild did indeed make a very tempting offer to Hogan, it is not at all clear that he or the other male defendants would have stayed with Motorola for long even if Fairchild's offer had not been forthcoming.

Hogan joined Motorola's Semiconductor Division in 1958 when it was beset with start-up problems and had annual sales of less than $5 million. Prior to joining Motorola, Hogan had taught physics, had a fine technical background, and understood the making of semiconductors. He was able to build a superb organization at Motorola by attracting good men and keeping them together. Although he had no previous business experience, he lost no time in acquiring this knowledge under the guidance of vice-chairman Daniel E. Noble (who had hired him) and other Motorola people. Under Hogan's leadership, the Semiconductor Division took off and, in 1967, the division's sales amounted to $230 million, with profits of $30 million. In 1968, the company for the first time passed Texas Instruments (the perennial leader in the semiconductor industry) to become the biggest producer in the United States.[5]

Despite the tremendous success achieved under his guidance, Hogan became disenchanted with his job. He felt that Motorola's top management had not recognized his and the division's outstanding performance: He claimed that he had received only one voluntary raise during his ten years with the company. He also felt demeaned because he had to report to three other executives—Chairman Galvin, Vice-Chairman Noble, and President Elmer H. Wavering. The first confrontation between Hogan and the company came about in January 1968. At that time, Hogan was offered the presidency of General Instrument Corporation, a manufacturer of semiconductors and electronics with headquarters in New York. Although he turned down the offer, he used it as a lever to force Motorola's management to offer him and his staff greater salaries and benefits.[6] It might be noted that these were the increases granted the staff in March of that year which Motorola cited in its suit as an example of its generosity.

In the case of Hogan,

Motorola offered Hogan an increase in salary from $80,000 per year to $90,000 per year, which increase was effective with his January 16, 1968 check, and also agreed to give him a stock option for 10,000 shares of Motorola stock which amount was substantially above the stock option policy of Motorola. (Subsequently, by mutual agreement, to avoid emphasizing the fact that Hogan received the very large stock option as compared with other officer employees, the option was reduced to 9,000 shares.) [In return Motorola received] Hogan's assurance and promise that he would remain in the employ of Motorola for at least a year and that he would not either entertain or accept any offers from other companies during such period [23].

The incident, however, left the relationship between Hogan and Motorola's Chairman Gavin somewhat less than friendly. Furthermore, "Hogan, who until then had netted only $239,000 from previous stock options, made a discouraging discovery: The new stock options were useless because he lacked the money to exercise them, and he could not afford the interest on a loan to do so."[7]

While these events were taking place at Motorola, Fairchild—once the darling of the semiconductor and electronics industry—was experiencing difficulties due to a diversification program that had not been successful. In 1967 its chairman had resigned, sales had fallen 10 percent from the previ-

[5] "The Fight That Fairchild Won," *Business Week*, October 5, 1968, p. 107.

[6] *Ibid.*, p. 112.

[7] *Ibid.*, p. 113.

ous year's, and the company incurred a loss of $7 million. During the first half of 1968, Sherman M. Fairchild, the largest stockholder of Fairchild Camera, took over the chairmanship of the company as an interim measure. The active management was given to a four-man committee. However, the committee system failed and conditions deteriorated further. To keep the situation from worsening, Sherman Fairchild and his advisers started looking for a new president. Feeling that they needed a man experienced in the semiconductor industry, they offered the job to the president of a small company in this field. To make the job more attractive, Fairchild considered spinning off the semiconductor division into a separate company. When this man declined the offer, Hogan became the next choice. On June 25, 1968, Robert N. Noyce, group vice-president in charge of the semiconductor and instrumentation divisions at Fairchild, called Hogan and made an appointment for Walter Burke, a board member and personal financial adviser to Sherman Fairchild, to meet Hogan in Phoenix. According to a story in *Business Week:*

> Hogan jumped to the conclusion that Burke wanted to talk about a Motorola license for planar technology and readily agreed to the visit. Motorola is the only major semiconductor maker that has not licensed this important Fairchild process, and Hogan feared that Fairchild would sue for patent infringement. . . . [Instead] Burke offered Hogan a job—though it was somewhat vague in detail. Hogan, though receptive, turned it down.[8]

In the meantime, Noyce, who wanted to quit Fairchild Camera and start his own semiconductor company but had agreed to stay—at Sherman Fairchild's urging—until a new executive was found, decided that he could wait no longer. His lawyers had warned him of a possible conflict of interest if he continued to work with Fairchild while planning to start his own company. Consequently, on June 28, 1968, Noyce resigned formally, thus forcing Sherman Fairchild to act immediately. According to *Business Week:*

> A week later, Sherman Fairchild himself visited Hogan at his home in Phoenix and offered him a job—this time as president of Fairchild Camera. Hogan said he was dedicated to his career at Motorola and added that stock options were pie in the sky if one didn't have the money for them. His decision was left in abeyance.
>
> A few days later, when Hogan called to decline the job, Sherman Fairchild unfolded a new offer, complete with a personal loan to pay for the stock options. . . .

[8] *Ibid.,* p. 112.

Meanwhile, Noyce paid a visit to Hogan and frankly spelled out the strengths and weaknesses of Fairchild Camera for his benefit.[9]

The offer, as disclosed to Motorola by Hogan, contained substantially the following terms:

1. Hogan would become director and president of Fairchild and his annual salary would be increased from the $90,000 paid him by Motorola to $120,000.
2. Upon becoming an employee of Fairchild, Hogan would be put in a position to reap an immediate financial gain of $250,000 either by a cash payment or immediately realizable stock options.
3. Hogan would receive a stock option on 90,000 shares of Fairchild at approximately $60 per share, and Sherman Fairchild would loan Hogan $5,400,000 for up to ten years, without interest, to enable Hogan to exercise this option. If the stock value slipped below the option price, Hogan was to have the right to repay the loan by surrendering the stock at the option price. (A 6 percent loan for the same sum and duration would be worth $324,000 per year or $3,240,000 at the end of ten years.)
4. Fairchild would move the main office headquarters from Syosset, New York, to Mountain View, California, so that Hogan could live near San Francisco according to his preference.
5. Hogan would have the right to select the Board of Directors of Fairchild with the promised assistance and cooperation of one or more of Fairchild's major stockholders [27–28].

Hogan was persuaded to accept the job because of the challenge of being the No. 1 man and because, for once, he could be financially independent. He accepted the offer on August 3, 1968.

According to *Business Week:*

On Aug. 7, Hogan turned in his resignation to Noble, the Motorola executive who had hired him in 1958. Noble was hurt because he had not known that Hogan had reopened negotiations with Fairchild after having once turned the company down. He urged Hogan to reconsider and to talk to Galvin.

The next day in Chicago, an annoyed Galvin feared another ploy to raise salaries. He started the conversation by discounting Hogan's contribution to Motorola's success. Annoyed, Hogan spelled out Fairchild's deal and compared it to what he felt was Motorola's parsimony. The meeting grew more acrimonious. It finally ended

9 *Ibid.*

with Galvin accepting Hogan's resignation and telling him not to return to the plant, not even to pick up his own checkbook, which Hogan had left in his desk.[10]

DEFENDANTS' REPLY TO MOTOROLA'S CHARGES

Fairchild and Hogan denied that there was "any wrongful raid upon plaintiff's employees."[11] Hogan maintained that, contrary to Motorola's allegations, his staff had visited him at his home, requesting him to take them with him to Fairchild. This, according to Hogan, took place over the weekend *following* Motorola's announcement of Hogan's resignation. The desire to leave Motorola was so great and so widespread that Hogan turned down seven or eight men for each one he accepted.[12]

Moreover, Fairchild contended that Motorola

> does not come into court with clean hands in that it has solicited and induced highly skilled and knowledgeable employees of its competitors, including Fairchild, to terminate their employment and work for plaintiff and has then obtained and used the trade secrets and confidential business information of said competitors; accordingly, the plaintiff is not entitled to equitable relief herein and may not maintain this action.[13]

According to *Business Week*, personnel raiding is common practice in the semiconductor industry. When Motorola was struggling to develop its semiconductor division, it hired eighteen engineers from General Electric, and every other company in the industry has done much the same thing.[14]

Hogan and the other male defendants denied any wrongdoing in resigning from Motorola. Although they were granted certain stock options in March 1968, not exercisable for one year from that date, they were compelled to execute an agreement in connection with accepting such stock options. The defendants alleged that such instruments, which compelled an employee to remain in the

> employ of Motorola for a stated period of time, are null and void and have no effect by reason of lack of valuable consideration for such

10 *Ibid.*, p. 113.

11 "Complaint and Answers," *Motorola, Inc. v. Fairchild Camera and Instrument Corp., et al.*, Civil Action No. 6808, U.S. District Court, Arizona, p. 11.

12 "The Fight That Fairchild Won," *Business Week*, October 5, 1968, p. 113.

13 "Complaint and Answers," *Motorola v. Fairchild*, p. 52.

14 "The Fight That Fairchild Won," *Business Week*, October 5, 1968, p. 106.

promise, failure of consideration and lack of mutuality of obligation and remedy.[15]

Under this agreement Motorola was not obliged to employ the individual defendants for any definite period.

Fairchild, Hogan and the other male defendants contended that Motorola presented no evidence to prove that any trade secrets had or would be violated by the defendants and that any of their actions were or would violate antitrust laws as being in restraint of competition or unfair trade practices.

The defendants contended that Motorola was not the real party allegedly injured because part of the trade secrets referred to were those of Motorola's customers, who had not joined Motorola in this complaint. Therefore, the plaintiff had, in any event, failed to comply with Rule 19(c) of the Federal Rules of Civil Procedure.[16]

MAJOR DEFENSE

In addition to denying Motorola's charges, Fairchild and the other defendants rested their defense by attacking the basic premise of Motorola's contention that an employee can be forced to work for a given company, or not at all.[17] According to the defendants:

If, as seems to be the position of plaintiff, a highly skilled and knowledgeable employee of plaintiff may not be employed by or work for a competitor but must remain an employee of plaintiff or not work at all, then in effect said employee would be placed in involuntary servitude in violation of public policy and in violation of Section 1, Amendment XIII of the Constitution of the United States; accordingly, plaintiff is not entitled to equitable relief herein and may not maintain this action.[18]

As of this writing, the case had not come up for trial.

[15] "Complaint and Answers," *Motorola* v. *Fairchild*, p. 31.

[16] *Ibid.*, p. 53.

[17] It might be noted that such a practice, with few exceptions, is legal and prevalent in the sports profession, which is exempt from U.S. antitrust laws.

[18] "Complaint and Answers," *Motorola* v. *Fairchild*, p. 52.

B.
CORPORATIONS
AND
THE STUDENTS

---◆---

Dow Shalt Not Kill

*Dow Chemical Company's Manufacture of Napalm and
Confrontation with Students on College Campuses*

*The main thing . . . is that the rebellion start off by despising make-believe. . . .
If we behave like the other side, then we are on the other side. Instead of changing
the world, all we'll achieve is a reflection of the one we want to destroy.*

—JEAN GENET
"The Balcony"

Students at the University of Wisconsin staged mass demonstrations
against on-campus job recruiting by the Dow Chemical Company on
October 17 and October 18, 1967. Early the second morning more than
two hundred students marched to the Commerce building where Dow was
holding its interviews. The "sit-in" students packed the three stories of the
building and in effect took the Dow recruiter prisoner to prevent him from
interviewing job applicants. Dow manufactured the chemical napalm, used
in the Vietnam War, and according to one observation, "to some of
today's youth, that's like waving a red flag at a bull."

The recruiter was freed at 10:00 A.M., but the students remained and
addressed their demands to the university administration. Evan Stark, a
teaching assistant and graduate student in sociology, shouted through a
bullhorn to the assembled students to propose a "tentative agreement"

with the university administration's "protection and security" department. "We'll get out of the building if Dow leaves permanently," he said. Another student added, "We don't want them back tomorrow, Friday, or next week." In reply, the university's chief of protection and security told the students, "There is no deal. I'm here to tell you that this is an unlawful assembly and that you are to disperse or be arrested." At this point the students "began to harass the police," according to one inspector.

For the police to move students out of the building was not easy. Many locked arms as soon as the officers arrived, making it very difficult to pry them apart. One witness said that some police had "confronted the students, clutching their night sticks with both hands," and most met with resistance as students threw themselves to the floor or grabbed at police helmets and eye protectors or kicked at their abductors. Some protesters threw bricks and stones. "One girl, painted and decorated like a flower child, was dragged to the police van." Some three hours after the demonstration began, police cleared the remaining students from the building with tear gas. Sixty-five persons, including three policemen, were injured, apparently none seriously, but only nine students were arrested.

Eight hours after he had originally refused the student demands, Chancellor William H. Sewell announced the cancellation of Dow interviews until he could meet with the faculty the next day. However, Sewell also said that the university would prefer charges, would suspend the leaders of the sit-in, and would refer their cases to student conduct committees. Two days later students pressed for a more permanent ban of Dow recruiters by picketing campus buildings and calling for a boycott of classes. Their efforts met with little success.

The controversy spread beyond the campus and shook the walls of the Wisconsin capitol; on October 20, the state senate began investigating the incident. The lower house voted to cut out-of-state enrollment to reduce the numbers of student radicals, many of whom came from New York and Chicago, including Evan Stark.

Feelings of legislators and ordinary citizens rose to a frenzied pitch. Some directed charges of brutality at the police. Others were convinced that the demonstration was Communist instigated. Consequently, there was an investigation to see how many of the demonstrators belonged to the W. E. B. Du Bois Club or to the Students for a Democratic Society (SDS). The result of the investigation, however, was that Wisconsin did not have a Du Bois Club and that the local chapter of the SDS did participate in the demonstration but did not organize it. In fact, a special group, the Ad Hoc Anti-Dow Committee, was formed "because no student group wanted to sponsor the affair."

By mid-November the university had begun to take action against student leaders of the demonstration. On November 15 it announced that

Evan Stark had been dropped from the university payroll, had been re-lieved of his teaching assistant duties, and would face disciplinary action.

The Wisconsin protests climaxed the almost coast-to-coast demonstra-tions at college campuses against the Dow Chemical Company. In a sense, it was ironic that Dow was picked as the symbol of the ugliness of the whole Vietnam War. Dow was not a major producer of war materiel. The products of hundreds of other companies—aircraft, helicopters, guns, ammunition—accounted for an immeasurably larger number of civilian and military casualties in Vietnam. Nor was napalm a major money-maker for Dow Chemical. The napalm business represented less than half of one percent of the company's total sales of almost $1.4 billion in 1967, and its contribution to profits was even lower. Dow's business with *all* branches of government came to less than 5 percent of sales.[1]

Dow Chemical—History and Background

Dow Chemical was founded in 1897 by a young chemist, Herbert Henry Dow, to make chlorine bleach. Dow as a student had rented a barn in 1890 and "hooked up a home-made rope drive from the steam engine of a flour mill, reactivated an idle brine well nearby," and demonstrated a new electrolytic process for extracting chemicals from brine. During the periods of major protest Dow Chemical made more than eight hundred products, and although few of these were directly intended for the ultimate con-sumer, the Dow name was familiar to many Americans.

Headquartered in Midland, Michigan, Dow Chemical in 1966 was the United States' fourth largest chemical company and employed more than thirty-six thousand persons in sixty-three United States and foreign locations.

Although accounting for less than 5 percent of sales, at that time Dow's Government Affairs Department was engaged in a wide variety of activ-ities. Dow did work for the government in virus cancer research, artificial kidney development, waste and water treatment, and space research. The chemical giant also sold chemicals, metals, plastic materials and products,

---

[1] For the Wisconsin-Dow Chemical story, see especially James Ridgeway, "On Wis-consin Faculty and Police vs. Students during Anti-Dow Chemical Demonstrations," *The New Republic*, November 4, 1967, pp. 8–10; "Anti-War Protest Ends in Violence," *The New York Times*, October 19, 1967; Lawrence J. Lasser, "Dow Chemical Com-pany," case study for classes at the Harvard Business School, 1968; "Madison Calm Again," *The New York Times*, October 21, 1967; Richard Stone, "Escalation—Now It's the Protesters," *The Wall Street Journal*, December 7, 1967; "Wisconsin Ousts Protester," *The New York Times*, November 16, 1967; Ellis N. Brandt, "Napalm—Public Relations Storm Center," *Public Relations Journal*, July 1968, pp. 12–15; H. D. Doan, "Dow Will Direct Its Efforts Toward a Better Tomorrow," *The Dow Diamond*, No. 4, 1967, Dow Chemical Company, Midland, Michigan.

Dow Chemical Company Statistics

(Millions of Dollars)

	1965	1966	1967	1968	1969
Sales	1,176	1,310	1,383	1,653	1,797
Earnings	108	122	132	136	149
Earnings per share (in dollars)	3.58	4.06	4.36	4.51	4.91

pharmaceuticals, and agricultural and consumer items to the Defense Department. Since 1951 the company had operated a classified weapons facility for the AEC at Rocky Flats, Colorado. Dow Catalytic Department was offering facility services to NASA at the Kennedy Space Center.

During this time all but one of Dow's sixteen-man board of directors was an operating officer. Carl A. Gerstacker was chairman and Herbert D. Doan was president. Doan was the grandson of the company's founder, and although dedicated to keeping company research and products in the forefront of technology, the "pervading philosophy" of the company was much the same as it had been in Herbert Dow's day. "If you can't do a thing better than it's already being done, why do it?" Company literature attributed Dow's growth to its traditional "will to progress," teamwork, and research.

Dow's contributions to educational institutions in grants, gifts, and services were $1.4 million in 1967, $2.3 million in 1968, and $3.2 million in 1969.[2]

Dow and Manufacture of Napalm

Napalm, first developed at Harvard University in 1942, burns on impact and adheres to all kinds of surfaces. It is dispersed either through flame throwers on the ground or through bomb canisters dropped from airplanes. Many countries have used it, including the United States in World War II, in the Korean conflict, and in Vietnam. In 1964, coincident with the large-scale United States involvement in Vietnam, air force scientists developed a much more adhesive formulation by adding polystyrene to the gasoline and benzene components. They called this improved product napalm B. Dow Chemical, a leading producer of the plastic raw material

[2] For the history of Dow Chemical Company, see "The Dow Chemical Company, Background Information," Public Relations Department, Dow Chemical Company, Midland, Michigan, March 27, 1967; and Dow's *Annual Reports*, 1966–69.

polystyrene, was asked to bid on a contract for napalm B manufacture. Although Dow had never manufactured napalm of any sort, its components were so simple that its production would be "bathtub chemistry."

The original decision to bid on the napalm contract was made by Dow's Government Affairs Department, not by the board of directors, because napalm was not going to be one of Dow's major products and at the time there was no antinapalm publicity. The air force had asked the company to bid on the product, and according to one official, "we had the capability to fulfill it" and so "we bid on it."[3]

History, Nature, and Extent of the Protest Movement

The first sign of protest against napalm appeared in 1965 when some residents of Redwood City, California, sought a municipal referendum against granting a construction permit to United Technology Center (UTC). The plant's critics, who had obtained more than three thousand signatures, considered napalm to be "an inhuman weapon."

Dow felt that the UTC issue was primarily local in nature. It was not until March 1966, when an article in the *Wall Street Journal* said that the April annual meeting of napalm manufacturer Witco Chemical would be picketed, that Dow began to worry. Nothing happened at Dow's annual meeting in early May, but a few weeks later Dow sales offices in Rockefeller Center in New York City attracted seventy-five protesters. Picketers carried signs, handed out leaflets urging shoppers to boycott Dow products, and charged, "Napalm burns babies. Dow makes money!" The Women's Strike for Peace and the Citizens Campaign against Napalm participated in the demonstration. This was Dow's first demonstration. On the same day Dow's napalm plant at Torrance, California, was picketed by members of the Students for a Democratic Society (SDS) and the Victory in Vietnam association.

In August 1966, there were protests in various parts of the country to commemorate the atomic bombings of Hiroshima and Nagasaki. Some college and noncollege groups used this occasion to demonstrate against Dow both at the company's Torrance plant and at the Rockefeller Center sales offices. The New York protests resulted in twenty-nine arrests and received nationwide publicity.

---

[3] See Lasser, *op. cit.*; and Doan, *op. cit.* Dave Coslett, Public Relations Department, Dow Chemical Company, Midland, Michigan, is the source of much information through a personal interview with the author.

The College Campus

Wayne State University was the first college to have demonstrations. This was in October 1966. Soon thereafter, picketers at Cornell attempted to debate with the Dow recruiter, who refused: "Anything I may say will be construed as company policy." At Princeton the SDS argued heatedly with the university president in an attempt to get him to comply with their demands to ban Dow. He refused, and students once again took up the picket sign. Almost half the protests in 1966–67 were on the West Coast, including demonstrations at UCLA and Berkeley which followed the pattern of publicity, administration resistance to student demands, and student picketing. Violence occurred only at the University of Wisconsin and was caused by only five of the sixty demonstrators present. The largest demonstration, with three hundred pickets, occurred at the University of Chicago.[4]

Dow's second encounter with demonstrators, at the University of Wisconsin, is an example of what Dow recruiters met with during the 1967–68 school year. According to Dow's public relations manager, the 1966 protest was "accidental," but at the 1967 protests the students, who were protesting violence in Vietnam, seemed to be seeking it on campus.

> To us it seems that Wisconsin is a pretty confused place. But this has set the pattern for subsequent demonstrations. Earlier this year it was apparent that Wisconsin's would be the general pattern of demonstrations this year as compared with last. Last year there were demonstrations, but for the most part they were passive. Now we see that they are going to be violent just as the peace movement in general has become more violent as compared to last year.[5]

During the fall of 1967, protesting students at the University of Illinois kept a Dow recruiter isolated in a room for five hours, and on October 24 students at the University of Minnesota staged a "sleep-in against Dow on the carpeted floor of the plush Regents Room of the University." More than fifty students sat-in outside and eventually moved to the placement director's office. A brief fight broke out between the demonstrators and the pro-war students.

[4] For broader coverage of the campus situation, see newspapers and periodicals for the period, especially *The New York Times, Newsweek,* and *New Republic.*

[5] Lasser, "Dow Chemical Company," p. 12.

On October 25, two hundred to three hundred Harvard and Radcliffe students kept a Dow recruiter imprisoned in a campus conference room for nine hours. At the time this was the college record. The students jammed the adjacent corridors and picketed outside the building carrying signs reading "Dow Shalt Not Kill" and "Napalm—[President] Johnson's Baby Powder." The crowd, which had linked arms to bar the doorway of the conference room to prevent the Dow recruiter from leaving, was nevertheless good-humoured and responsible. Harvard deans and faculty members were allowed to go to and from the interview room at will. The dean read "to the group Harvard's regulations forbidding 'unauthorized demonstrations.'" The students demanded that all recruiting by the Dow Chemial Company be prohibited and that no disciplinary action be taken against them. Although the university did not agree to the demands at that time, the demonstrators did not interfere with the recruiter's tasks—he was trapped in the chemistry building during the afternoon, but he had conducted all but one of the scheduled interviews that morning.

A somewhat different approach was taken at nearby MIT. Three days before recruiters were scheduled to begin interviews (November 6), sixty interested faculty members met with students who urged them to support the demonstration against Dow. Most of the sixty faculty felt, however, that civil disobedience "would be a mistake in the circumstances." The students maintained a nonviolent and nonobstructive sit-in outside the Dow interview offices throughout the first day of interviews anyway.[6]

> As a further ploy, seven SDS members had signed up for interviews with Dow. They asked the interviewers whether they believed that they were war criminals and, less melodramatically, whether they felt any moral conflict in working for a firm which makes profits from a product whose only use is to inflict pain. Throughout the interviews the demonstrators acted politely and treated the Dow men more in sorrow than in anger; "I hope you'll change your mind," said one co-ed at the end of her half hour. Indeed, the whole demonstration was notable for the restraint on both sides; lively discussion between pro and antiwar demonstrators never degenerated even into slogan shouting.[7]

Meanwhile, some of the faculty members who had refused to participate in the demonstrations quickly organized a forum on "Napalm, Vietnam, and the University" to be held November 6, the day the recruiters were to

[6] "Dow Day at MIT," *Technology Review*, MIT Alumni Magazine, December 1967, pp. 54–55.

[7] *Ibid.*

arrive. Came the day, and the forum, planned only two days previously, was met with overflow crowds in the school's 1,200 seat auditorium. On hand to express their views were the MIT president, the chairman of the faculty, Dow's director of Industrial Relations, and a physician from Massachusetts General Hospital.

On November 20, two thousand students at San Jose State College in California also staged demonstrations against Dow on campus recruiting. The college vice-president called in police after the students "ignored continuous requests to peacefully demonstrate." When a busload of helmeted officers arrived, "the students jeered and a few barred the administration building entrance with a chain. When orders to disperse were ignored, a flying wedge of officers forced their way through to the entrance. Later, the police donned gas masks and tossed tear gas canisters into the crowd." Twenty students were taken into custody. The action inspired California's Governor Reagan to warn, "Once it has been established who is to blame, those persons should be punished . . . severely disciplined and subject to expulsion." Ignoring the governor's warning, as many as five hundred demonstrators marched the following day through a student-faculty meeting and picketed the college administration building.

Also on November 20 the recruiter for Dow Chemical of Canada, Ltd., was confined in the University of Toronto's placement office for two hours. The aftermath of the Toronto demonstration may be unique: The student council president sent a letter to the recruiter apologizing for "any inconvenience" he had been subjected to. The letter was sent following a unanimous decision by the student government.

Demonstrations at UCLA in late November caused Dow recruiters to postpone interviews for one week, and demonstrations during the fall of 1967 also occurred at Boston College, Boston University, the University of Iowa, and New York University.

At Columbia University, antiwar students circulated a petition to have Dow banned from recruiting. However, at the last minute, of three potential candidates, two doctoral students canceled their interviews and the third notified the placement office that he would be "out of town all day," causing the company to cancel its visit. A company spokesman said he thought it was the only time in 1967 that the company itself had canceled a visit to a university.

In the fall of 1968 protests began to wane. There was no trouble at the University of Minnesota or even advance recruiting publicity as there had been the year before. The company canceled interviews on a number of campuses because "there just weren't enough sign-ups to make it worthwhile," one recruiter said. Student radicals on one campus interpreted the cancellation as "the demise of Dow Chemical." At Harvard, where the student newspaper urged that an open meeting be held to question Dow on its policies, the chemistry department decided to limit the meeting to graduate students and postdoctoral fellows in chemistry. The company's visit to the campus was postponed indefinitely until the department "resolved the details of the meeting." When Dow visited the University of Wisconsin, one hundred students picketed, but 1967's violence was replaced by a mere heckling of police guarding the recruitment office. An interesting event did occur at Wisconsin which seems to be part of a trend among scientists and engineers—the bread and butter of Dow's recruitment effort. According to the *New York Times:*

> Members of the Science Students Union attempted to explain to the engineering students their opposition to the use of "scientific technology for destructive purposes and the manipulation of scientists by large corporations."
> A year or two ago, such attempts by protesters were usually greeted with ridicule, but this year several engineering and science students listened and agreed with the members of the S.S.U.[8]

Protests against Dow in the fall of 1968 also occurred at the University of Notre Dame, the University of Connecticut, Emory University, and Colorado State University.

In the struggle with the protesters, the recruiters may have had the last laugh in the fall of 1969. One of the demonstrations, at Notre Dame in late November, resulted in the suspension of five students and the expulsion of five others, but they were too late—Dow had stopped making napalm six months previously.

Stockholders' Meeting

On May 9, 1968, Dow's annual meeting was subject to widely publicized protest. An article in the *Wall Street Journal* reported that:

> About 300 college students and clergymen wearing black arm bands picketed the company's annual meeting, took their antiwar views to the homes of Dow employees, had a confrontation with Dow's top executives and then sent a delegation into the annual meeting itself.
> But their efforts to change Dow failed. Housewives slammed their doors on the picketers. Top officers of the company gave them a

8 "Campus Protests against Dow and the Military Found Waning," *The New York Times,* December 1, 1968.

polite brush off. And nearly all the 1,150 shareholders and employees who crowded the meeting sided with management.[9]

The meeting itself was limited to shareholders, employees, and newsmen, yet five protesters who qualified for attendance confronted Gerstacker during the meeting.

> [Gerstacker] charged the protesters' attempts to embarrass Dow have clouded the real issue—ending the war in Vietnam. "Companies don't start wars, and companies can't end them" he asserted.
> "You are talking to the wrong people; if you want to stop the war why aren't you talking to legislators," Mr. Gerstacker asked. Later the chairman said, "I want the war over, too."

The chairman concluded the meeting with an emotional defense of Dow.

> "You can harass us. You can hurt us—and I think you have. We won't strike back at you because we respect your right to dissent. But . . . as long as our democratically elected government sends draftees to die in Vietnam, we're going to support those men." His remarks drew extended applause from the partisan audience.[10]

More Protest

In addition to protests at Dow offices in Midland, San Francisco, and New York (as many as five hundred people), several Dow employees received abusive phone calls and letters after their promotion notices appeared in the paper. One public relations official received a letter notifying him he was to be tried as a "war criminal." According to a company report of March 1968:

> [Dow] has received several thousand letters from individuals protesting the use of napalm in Vietnam, and threatening to boycott our consumer products because of our connection with that weapon. Such letters continue to arrive in Midland at a rate of about two hundred each month. Only a scant handful of letters praising our contribution to the war effort have been received.[11]

[9] Kenneth C. Field, "Dow Chemical Meeting Backs Production of Napalm; Antiwar Protesters Rebuffed," *The Wall Street Journal*, May 9, 1968.

[10] *Ibid.*

[11] R. J. Williams, "Attitudes toward the War, the Use of Chemical Weapons, and the Dow Chemical Company," Marketing Research Report, Dow Chemical Company, March 1968.

Analysis of Campus Demonstrations

In the fall of 1967, a survey by the National Student Association (NSA), a loose nationwide union of college student governments, revealed that Dow demonstrations were the focus of more demonstrations than any other organization or concept. In many instances the Dow protests were associated with other demands, most of which were focused on the recruiting efforts of governmental agencies, government defense contract work with the university, and general antiwar demonstrations. Due to the similarities between the Dow protests and the other campus demonstrations, no loss of generality results from a study of all protests.

The survey was compiled from information in more than 2,100 newspaper articles supplied by a clipping service. The study included 62 schools (34 public, 28 private), including all those so far described. Only those demonstrations were included that had more than 35 participants or "which produced strong administrative reaction or which had a persuasive effect on the campus."

The demonstrations described in the study "were sponsored, initiated, and led by students *at* the campuses, and not by national or regional groups such as the anti-war mobilization. All focused on a social, political, or educational issue, and for example did not include panty raids, or football rallies." The NSA study also revealed that of seventy-one demonstrations on sixty-one campuses during the fall of 1967, twenty-seven (or 38 percent) of them were protesting Dow Chemical recruitment.

The NSA study gave the breakdown of reasons cited for demonstrations being held:

	Demonstrations	*Percentage*
Dow Chemical Company recruitment	27	38
Armed Forces recruitment	8	12
Governmental agency recruitment	6	8
Defense Contract work on campus	6	8
Compulsory ROTC	3	4
Pro- or Anti-Vietnam War	7	10
Black Power and racial integration	4	6
Student Power	6	8
Miscellaneous	4	6

The NSA study gave a breakdown of changes in disciplinary citations determined by January 1, 1968:

	Initially		After Appeal or Pressure		
	Number	Per-centage		Number	Per-centage
Admonition	171	23	(All at Harvard)	171	23
Censure	10	1	(Two schools)	10	1
Warning	35	5	(All at Berkeley)	35	5
Probation	330	45	(Eleven schools)	399	54
Suspension	152	21	(Nine schools)	60	8
Expulsion	39	5	(Three schools)	32	4
Rescinded			(Two schools)	30	4
	737			737	

Unspecified disciplinary citations rescinded without proceedings 251
Number of demonstrators arrested by civil authorities 477
(this is 3.3 percent of all students involved in demonstrations)
Number of demonstrators who had civil charges dropped as of
January 1, 1968 95
(this is 20 percent of all students who were arrested)

A *Wall Street Journal* article said the consensus among university administrators and faculty was that campus demonstrations were led by hardcore student extremists who

> . . . aren't worried about whom their tactics will alienate. In many quarters their idealism and faith in democratic processes have evaporated. A 24-year old Berkeley anti-draft organizer comments cynically that teach-ins and pickets are exercises in "civics-class morality." The pacifist ideal of "speaking truth to power," says Frank Bardacke, a 27-year old Berkeley obstructionist, "is completely ineffectual." The new idea is speaking power to power.[12]

These small groups of protest leaders could attract other, not quite so radical, students to participate in a given demonstration. At Berkeley, according to one administrator, a group of 150 "seriously imbued with the idea of ersatz guerilla tactics" can expand to 200 who "are willing to face probation for rules violation" which can expand to 2,000 willing to participate in "disruptions if they can get away with it" and [if] the police aren't "forced to toughen up." This out of a campus of 29,000.

At Wisconsin a core of 300 "new left" students could turn out "momentary" support of 2,500 out of a 33,000 enrollment. Only 15 of the 300 core

[12] Stone, "Escalation—Now It's the Protesters," p. 16.

were "obstructers," according to one Wisconsin professor. However, leftist strength was irregular, and the 2,500 could, overnight, drop to only several hundred.

It was probably true that most students on campuses supported the right of Dow Chemical and other corporations and agencies to recruit on campus. This was demonstrated by the letter of apology from the University of Toronto to the campus Dow recruiter. At San Francisco State College, a student vote indicated that the majority of students supported Dow's right to recruit.

Who were the students who protested against Dow Chemical? More than likely they were the same ones who were in the limelight in other campus protests. The Students for a Democratic Society, for example, were credited by the NSA study with sponsoring 21 percent of the demonstrations on college campuses in the fall of 1967 (not all of which were against Dow).

Why did students protest? Some said because students, unlike most people, were not afraid to face up to the horrors of reality such as napalm. Other observers, including many faculty members, saw the protests as excuses for exerting "student power." Considering the large number of students involved in demonstrations, both opinions might be correct. John Fischer, writing in *Harper's*, probably spoke for many academics, administrators, and journalists when he said the protests were not caused by incompetent administrators, the "malaise of Vietnam," or the "vague epidemic of student unrest which seems to be sweeping the world." These were important but not the main ingredients as they alone "could not produce such widespread disorders." Fischer said students' "deep sense of grievance" was due to the short-changing of liberal arts education since World War II. Government money has tended to support the professional fields, science, and engineering while the liberal arts and humanities have been starved for funds.

The "tragedy" of these grievances was compounded as they were held by the "best students in the best universities. They have considerable talent for leadership—a talent which they are all too likely to use, in their frustration and disgust, to disrupt the university which has failed them."[13]

Free Speech and Protest

The anti-Dow protests accused the company of immoral action by producing napalm. However, a number of observers accused the students themselves of "immorality." Typical of this reverse flow was an editorial by

[13] John Fischer, "The Case for the Rebellious Students and Their Counter-revolution," *Harper's*, August 1968, pp. 9–12.

a California radio station about anti-Dow San Jose State College demonstrations:

> The riots at San Jose State College exceeded the law and did so on a premise that is both false and unfair to all college students preparing to become productive citizens. A militant minority indulged in twisted thinking, to the detriment of the student majority and at the expense of the California taxpayer.
>
> Let us set the record straight. Those students who issued an ultimatum to this nation's fourth largest chemical firm failed in their homework. They did not dig out some key facts; thus they blamed the wrong people.

The editorial cited Dow's contribution to California education:

> It donates $20 million a year to California colleges and universities, in scholarships, research grants and aid-to-education projects.[14]

Additionally, Dow's role as one of California's largest taxpayers helped "foot the bill for preserving free education." Even Dow protesters drank water made pure by Dow chemicals. Dow was "essentially peace oriented" and had developed "the only one-shot measles vaccine in the world." This breakthrough in two years had safeguarded 18 million American children against nerve disorders and hearing defects. "It also developed the only artificial kidney within the reach of the common man."

> This, or any other American company so closely involved with students on our campuses as well as soldiers on our war fronts deserves better treatment than it got at San Jose. And the students who elect to work for such a firm must enjoy continued free choice to do so.[15]

The Dow Recruiting Effort

Up until 1966 Dow college interviews were conducted by employees who took time out from their regular jobs to recruit on campus. In 1966, because of company growth and competition from government and educators for college graduates, Dow reorganized its program so that it had 15 full-time recruiters, plus the regular 250 technical and professional employees who spent a week outside their usual jobs interviewing students on

---

[14] "Setting the Record Straight," KGO Radio (San Francisco, ABC-owned station), editorial by E. F. McLaughlin, general manager, November 25–28, 1967.

[15] Ibid.

campus. This intensification of recruitment effort increased the total number of interviews from 11,156 in 1966–67 to 13,634 in 1967–68.

	1966–67	1967–68
Schools visited	300	339
Recruiter man days	1,360	1,558
Interviews per man day	8.2	8.75
Write-in applications	5,258	6,905
Campus demonstrations	55	133
Campuses affected	55	113
Interviews per man day where incidents occurred	N.A.	8.5
Man days affected by demonstrations	N.A.	362
Interviews held during campus demonstrations	N.A.	3,079
Campus interviews	11,156	13,634

Fewer than twenty interviews were canceled by Dow or campus authorities because of demonstrations.

With few exceptions, the on-campus placement center was a post-World War II phenomenon which protected both companies and students. It was impractical to interview off campus, particularly when women candidates were involved. An academic atmosphere protected both candidate and company: a motel did not. Encouraging campus placement centers helped keep the U.S. Employment Service from invading every campus—which was its aim—with consequent tax savings. Placement centers maintained files of company literature for student perusal and advised applicants about suitable companies. Going off campus, then, undercut the placement people who gave both students and companies the most help.

Furthermore, Dow felt that hiring only those with experience—an increasingly common practice—in effect bought loyalty from someone else. Then what was to prevent employees from leaping at the next higher offer? Dow deemed it better to hire directly upon academic completion, maintain a good working environment, and keep long-term employees.

Interestingly, opinion at Dow was divided on the effect of demonstrations on the quality of students being interviewed and hired. This latent protest effect was certainly one of the most profound and most difficult to measure.

Dow management held that napalm demonstrations may have cost the company the equivalent of the next inventor of nylon, but Dow recruiters, who were closer to the campus scene, were less concerned. They maintained that they were seeing higher-quality students, perhaps as a silent counterprotest to the demonstrators, perhaps because more students were aware of Dow's breadth of chemical activity.

But according to one recruiter:

> I admit there is a good possibility that the really imaginative, top-notch guy is leaning toward the demonstrators. Even with our company, out of a few thousand scientists involved in research I bet there aren't 25 who I'd call the real top ones. Of this group, I'd say maybe 80 percent are liberal in politics. . . . These are men interested in pure research and interested in the human problem. . . . Of course, we are not looking for, nor would we ever want to hire all of the people in the top five or ten percent of their class even if we could get them. The genius is such an individualistic guy that he just doesn't fit in here. . . . Of sixty Ph.D.'s we hire every year we couldn't stand all geniuses even if we could get them. . . . We don't want too many top guys. The genius stands out as being different and being kooky.
>
> If you rated all the people we speak to every year on a scale of one to five, I spoke to one student at Berkeley last year who would at least be a six. But he was a nut. The system here can only accept someone like that once every few years. There is a way to do things here and these guys just often don't fit in. They wear cowboy boots and plaid shirts, and retreat to their laboratories.
>
> Appearance is important here, because the supervisor will think differently of the scientist because of the way he looks. If his boss doesn't like cowboy boots, then he isn't going to think very highly of the guy.
>
> Of course, the company is moving to be able to handle individualists. Ten years ago we couldn't take them at all. Today we are changing. Today we realize we have to meet people's needs. Ten years ago only two or three men in the whole company could look at a man and no matter what he looked like accept him on the merits of his work. Ten years ago if a scientist came in here wearing sandals he would have been fired. Today it is probably OK.
>
> But still, this change has got to be gradual. So we don't really want the top five or ten percent at all. Maybe one or two, so if these are the only ones we are scaring away, the napalm probably doesn't mean very much.[16]

The effects of controversy on recruiting are made even more difficult to evaluate by the belief of many that the "creative individual" is an outdated concept in scientific discovery: a team approach toward research is most common now. Indeed, projects are so large and require so many interdisciplinary skills that the narrowly specialized scientist is less and less able to make important discoveries on his own. The question thus became not was Dow losing the creative individual to the protesters but was the scientist

[16] Lasser, "Dow Chemical Company," pp. 27–32.

who worked well as a team member likely to be the type who was "unwilling to brave" the scorn of his fellow students. Not everyone had to be a Nobel laureate to work at Dow, "a strong engineering candidate might have a C-plus average and be a "good, hustling, clean cut guy who wants to go out and do a job!" Even more subtle was the possibility that the bright student, faced with a bewildering array of recruiting companies and insufficient time to interview all of them, might cross Dow off his list because it was too much bother to brave the picket line.

Thus it was a difficult decision for the company to make whether or not to remain on campus, but the full-time recruiters decided to remain and Doan backed them up.

Dow's Evaluation of Campus Protests and Their Effect on Recruitment Effort

In July 1968, a member of Dow's Consumer Products Marketing Research Section, R. D. Kent, issued a report on a fifteen-campus study of faculty and students which had been conducted in May. Since there was intensive competition in the recruitment of graduates, the company was "naturally curious whether the participants in these demonstrations are a small, highly organized, vocal minority or whether they are spokesmen reflecting the attitudes of the majority of the academic community."

The report concluded that if the protesters represented a majority opinion, an immediate effect of Dow's "merchant of death" role would be a diminished ability to recruit new personnel and a long-term effect would be a diminished sales volume as students moved on to positions of influence on buying both consumer and industrial products. The report said that the protesters did not, in general, speak for the majority of students and faculty, but their opposition against the war was greater than that in the general population. Dow was well known on campus as a napalm manufacturer, but little antagonism was expressed specifically toward the company, and a majority of students interested in a business career said they would work for Dow. However, Kent noted in the report that the majority of students and faculty were troubled by the Vietnam War, many were willing to support the cause in which they believed, and Dow was the most widely known manufacturer of war material. "For this reason," said Kent, "I feel we cannot rest on our laurels, but must continue to conduct a vigorous corporate PR program designed to communicate these facts about this company which will help the campus community to perceive our positive contributions to society and civilization."

The report also noted that 90 percent of the students felt that all recruiters should be allowed on campus, but 2.5 percent would ban Dow. Seventy-five percent of the students would go through a demonstration to complete a scheduled interview. The report noted that "Dow must communicate to students and faculty the fact that it is not a war oriented company, or possibly face severe problems in the future."

Dow's Recruiting Policy

Dow decreased the number of schools it visited in 1968–69, primarily because most of the dropped schools did not really have many graduate students in the needed disciplines. A number of schools, such as Purdue, dropped Dow, but even there the university president questioned the dean's decision. By November 1967, five universities had canceled or had postponed interviews, but the company felt that some of the visits would be rescheduled. Dow also dropped a number of schools because they would have put it on the defensive.

Dow and many other corporations recognized a growing disinterest among college students in working for private industry; they seemed to prefer the challenges of research in academia and in government. To appeal to student desire to make important social contributions, Dow and its competition filled their recruiting brochures with salesmanshiplike phrases: "Are you dedicated to change for the better? We are! . . . We are looking for young men and women who want to help our company change the world for the better." During the 1968–69 school year, Dow, Goodyear Tire and Rubber, and Motorola sponsored a series of open letters between their chief executives and students which appeared in campus newspapers across the country as full-page advertisements.

Public Relations

Once the decision to make napalm was firm, the Public Relations Department made the big decisions on company strategy in the controversy. It handled all inquiries from the news media and although recruiting belonged to the Industrial Relations Department, PR had a full-time liaison man with them.

Top management, including President Doan, was kept in constant touch with Public Relations and its decisions. Beginning in November 1967, the department issued a "round-up sheet" whenever anything happened on the napalm issue. This sheet, issued daily if necessary, circulated to the president, the board of directors, the executive vice-president, the personnel concerned with recruiting, and the Industrial Relations and Public Relations departments. This round-up sheet was only one of Dow's efforts to keep communications open. Another device was the "napalm school" where the entire public relations staff of the company gathered in Midland (whether their key concern was napalm or not) and spent a whole day discussing the matter. Both the chairman and president of Dow took part in the discussions.

The department distinguished two distinct phases of Dow's public relations effort. The first could be characterized by the company's feeling that napalm was such a small part of its activities and that the protests were so isolated that it "couldn't see too much to be gained by trying to encourage publicity." The second phase could be characterized by the realization that a more "activist" strategy would have to be taken.

Phase I began in March 1966 when the *Wall Street Journal* announced that the annual meeting of another napalm manufacturer, Witco Chemical, was to be picketed. Public Relations then prepared a statement for the chairman of the board to issue if Dow's annual meeting in May became the scene of any demonstrations. The annual meeting was held without incident so the statement was not issued until Dow's office in New York City, and its plant in Torrance, California, were picketed.

During the summer of 1966 students from various midwest colleges converged on Midland for the "August Days of Protest" and asked to speak with President Doan about Dow's napalm policy. A PR official, Dave Coslett, felt that there was no question but that Doan should meet with them; however, if he met with them on the day of the demonstrations it would give "the whole affair a traumatic moment of confrontation between the group and the president" and the students "would benefit in terms of greater publicity from such a confrontation." The company pointed out that "if they wanted to talk to the president, there were very legitimate ways to do this. They didn't have to come up and stage a strike or stage a picket line in front of the building in order to get to talk to the president. All they had to do was write and ask for an appointment and we would try to set one up." When the students did picket the Dow offices, Coslett signed them up for an interview and two weeks later he and Doan met with four members of the SDS. Also present was the editor of the local newspaper who was invited in the hope that a viewpoint different from the students' would emerge from the meeting.

As it turned out, the only press coverage of the meeting was in the students' *University of Michigan Daily*. Coslett thought some of Doan's statements had been taken out of context, but overall "I wouldn't say they grossly distorted what he had to say. . . . I don't think he convinced them of anything, but he certainly answered their questions."

Phase II began when the events in the fall of 1967 caused Dow to develop a new public relations strategy.[17] Student protests ceased being local issues and became a national concern. Dave Coslett of Dow's Public Relations Department said, "All of a sudden it had become a national news roundup story." Calls came from about a dozen different media—the *Wall Street Journal*, the *Chicago Tribune*, UPI, *Time*, *Business Week*, and radio and television networks.

To prepare Dow recruiters for the inevitable onslaught of questions about napalm, the Public Relations Department put together a press kit which contained background information on Dow, a list of products manufactured by the company (to demonstrate napalm's small role compared with that of such products as the measles vaccine and the artificial kidney), statements by military leaders concerning the need for napalm in Vietnam, and physicians' reports on the extent of napalm damage to Vietnamese civilians. Any questions were to be referred to the Public Relations Department in Midland, and to facilitate this the press kit included phone numbers. During Phase II, when Dow for the first time felt the urgency of presenting a stronger public image, President Doan became the chief spokesman for the company. And when the *Wall Street Journal* offered to publish an article presenting Dow's side of the controversy, the offer was gladly accepted.

Another Phase II PR effort was to keep Dow employees informed on the napalm issue through employee publications which presented such items as letters from the military in Vietnam stating that napalm had "saved their lives."

At the same time that the press kit was issued, Jack Jones, West Coast director of Dow's public relations, adopted a policy of making personal appearances on campuses likely to be scenes of trouble. According to Coslett, "he had more problems on the West Coast than we had elsewhere." Soon Midland followed Jones's example and began sending PR men to other campus locations. Coslett said, "The local media would usually have only the protest side of the story. They seldom had any information from Dow. And where we sent PR people generally they received very good local press coverage."

Dow also sought more opportunities to speak on campus but avoided debating the napalm issue, not wanting to be a "defender" of United States Vietnamese policy. Dow wanted to clear up misunderstandings about itself, its operation, and what a corporation could actually do to influence its government's policy.

Coslett said that public relations heard very little from Dow employees

[17] Dave Coslett, Public Relations Department, Dow Chemical Company, Midland, Michigan. Interview with the author.

about the controversy, nor did any resign in protest, as they had been publicly urged to do. This indicates, perhaps, that most of them were behind the official company policies although they doubtless represented all shades of opinion. According to Coslett, Dow was the kind of company where employees could be against the manufacture of napalm. "There is a great deal of respect for individual opinion here. The employees are free to take stands that conflict with company stands and they do . . . and I guess there have been a few isolated instances where some employees have joined in some of these protest marches, which is fine."

Coslett felt that overall the press (including television) did not exaggerate in its coverage of the protests and was "fairly levelheaded." The company collected press clippings representing a large spectrum of viewpoints (including the *Daily Worker*). Perhaps the greatest compliment was paid by the business editor of the *Toledo Blade*. "No matter from which side the controversy is viewed, the Dow PR department has set a classic example of how such a delicate situation can be professionally handled."[18]

Consumer Products Boycott

Although only 3 percent of Dow's sales came from its consumer products, some of them, such as Saran Wrap and Handi Wrap, were well known. Company officials thought that a boycott of these products "was an obvious club for those seeking to 'punish' Dow for its manufacture of napalm." Only the reaction to Dow recruitment was more vocal.

The first attempts in the boycott originated at a San Francisco Bay Area consumer cooperative grocery store. The store told Dow that its products would be identified so that "those who oppose the use of napalm may know whether or not they are purchasing your product." This action was in response to a petition signed by 250 of the store's member-owners. The petitioners and the company were allowed to post position statements on the store's bulletin board.

In New York City a "Down with Dow" committee was formed to picket supermarkets, asking customers to join the boycott. Boycotters handed out leaflets depicting an Asian mother holding her burned child. The leaflets described the horrors of napalm, listed Dow's consumer products, and told shoppers, "If you buy Dow products, you help kill. DO NOT buy Dow products—buy substitutes as long as Dow makes napalm." Attached to the leaflets were coupons to give to grocers, urging people to write to Dow's

[18] Sam Allen (Business Editor), "Dow Plays It Cool on Napalm Production Protest," *Toledo Blade*, May 12, 1968.

vice-president (and gave the address) or join one of six scheduled peaceful demonstrations at different supermarkets.[19]

Reported the company's consumer marketing man:

> Two years ago we started receiving letters from consumer products customers. A few were from ministers who claimed to represent congregations of thousands of people. Others threatened a campaign of chain letters. We received a few letters from prominent people such as Hollywood entertainers. Despite this, and despite threats and talks of extensive boycotts, this year [1967] all of our consumer brands are selling ahead of plan. . . .
>
> Saran Wrap, which has been the product most frequently singled out for attempted boycott, is 6½ percent ahead of plan now.
>
> Though it is true that we don't know how much better than this sales might have been had there not been the napalm problem, our sales forecasts aim for absolute realism and historically are very accurate. Six and a half percent is a substantial and unusual increase over plan.[20]

Dow even singled out the Berkeley Co-op, one of the stores mentioned previously, to see how sales were being affected. Although the store was adjacent to that hotbed of student radicalism, the University of California, and even though Dow's products were marked as being made by the manufacturer of napalm, sales did not drop.

Public Relations Director E. N. Brandt said that not only did the boycott fail but "some kind of backlash may be at work." The PR department pointed to the case of a buyer for A&P stores in New York who had not previously featured Dow products. Following the initial boycott publicity, however, he advertised Saran Wrap as a loss leader. The consumer marketing manager for Dow said that this reflected the buyer's reaction to the protesters and to his having a son in Vietnam. He also said that most of their trade was with older people who were, if anything, pro-Dow and pro-napalm.

If there were a backlash it would almost be impossible to assess its impact.

STOCKHOLDERS AND PHYSICIANS

Consumer products were not the only products subject to boycotts. The *Wall Street Journal* reported that Dow "concedes that its drug salesmen

---

[19] "Down with Dow," consumer boycott leaflet (photo of mother and burned child), New York City, "Down with Dow" committee.

[20] Lasser, "Dow Chemical Company," p. 13.

have run into some resistance from doctors in the San Francisco Bay Area. One peace group has urged a boycott of Dow's measles vaccine, and some pediatricians actually have stopped buying it."[21]

There also were attempts to encourage investors to sell their Dow Chemical stock in protest. However, in mid-1968 Dow's treasurer reported that "only a couple dozen" stockholders had told Dow they were selling their stock for such reasons.

Some letter writers said they would not cash their Dow dividend checks until the company stopped producing napalm: Two of these writers owned only one share each—worth fifty-five cents in quarterly dividends. One trust account manager threatened to have the Securities and Exchange Commission order Dow to cease its napalm manufacturing. The treasurer did not answer that letter. Some churches eliminated Dow stocks from their portfolios and a number of universities were pressured to do the same. One stock analyst visited Dow's treasurer to see if the company was going to change its napalm policy. The analyst thought Dow stock was important for his client's portfolio but was ordered to sell his large block of stock after the Dow visit. Although the napalm issue had no observable effect on the stock price, most of Dow's financial people were somewhat concerned. The treasurer said:

> Whether our stock will develop a defense image or a defense stock orientation as a result of our close association with napalm is definitely a problem. As far as the professional investment advisor is concerned, I am not worried. Perhaps the analyst will ask today what percentage of our business is defense products where he didn't before, but he will receive an answer and not be concerned. The small investor is another question.
>
> My personal reaction is that I don't like to see the company get an image which causes people to sell stock. I don't like the "leper complex." I don't know who has been selling stock if anyone has. In short, I am doing nothing different because of this.[22]

Indeed, the only company communications to stockholders regarding napalm were statements in the quarterly shareholder's letter. Standard letters "signed" by the president or chairman were sent in response to complaints.

One public relations official said, "There has been no great outcry of protest from stockholders," but this did not mean an absence of protest. In the first half of 1968 Dow stockholders declined from ninety-five thousand

[21] W. Stewart Pinkerton, Jr., "Merchants of Death; Charge Plagues Firm That Makes Munitions," *The Wall Street Journal*, August 21, 1967, p. 1.

[22] Lasser, "Dow Chemical Company," pp. 16–17.

to ninety thousand, and the company's director of public relations said, "the company feels this may in part be ascribed to the napalm situations."

CORPORATE MORALITY

Dow itself did not need to make napalm, and the effort could easily have been taken over by the government, but Dow's President Doan said:

> Why do we produce napalm? In simplest terms, we produce it because we feel that our company should produce those items which our fighting men need in time of war when we have the ability to do so. . . .
>
> All of the debate in the world about how we got there or how we get out is proper and right in its place but it doesn't change the fact that we are there nor the fact that our men are there and need weapons to defend themselves.[23]

For more than a year Dow's position in regard to napalm was represented in Chairman Gerstacker's statement prepared for May 1966:

> The Dow Chemical Company endorses the right of any American to protest legally and peacefully an action with which he does not agree.
>
> Our position on the manufacture of napalm is that we are a supplier of goods to the Defense Department and not a policy maker. We do not and should not try to decide military strategy and policy.
>
> Simple good citizenship requires that we supply our government and our military with those goods which they feel they need whenever we have the technology and capability and have been chosen by the government as a supplier.
>
> We will do our best, as we always have, to try to produce what our Defense Department and our soldiers need in any war situation. Purely aside from our duty to do this, we will feel deeply gratified if what we are able to provide helps to protect our fighting men or to speed the day when fighting will end.[24]

Herbert Doan said, "I never had any personal qualms about the production of napalm but the demonstrations brought the question into sharp focus." The president added that he personally was against using napalm on civilians but that he felt no more obligation to find out the end use of one Dow product than of all the others.

[23] Doan, "Dow Will Direct Its Efforts toward a Better Tomorrow."
[24] Brandt, "Napalm–Public Relations Storm Center," p. 14.

Despite the company's reluctance to take a position on the use of napalm in Vietnam, assorted evidence pointed out that, as far as possible, it was indeed confined to military uses and GIs considered it an effective weapon.

Protesters widely distributed reprints of photographs of Vietnamese children burned and disfigured, allegedly by napalm. Dow labeled these as propaganda, but since such stories had a measure of credibility a number of voluntary civilian medical teams visiting and working in Vietnam investigated the claims. The best known of these was led by Dr. Howard A. Rusk who reported his findings in the *New York Times* in March 1967. Rusk's team visited civilian hospitals ranging from isolated mountain dispensaries to large provincial hospitals in combat zones. Rusk said:

> To many Americans, Vietnam is a distant and devastated country filled with children who have been burned by American napalm bombs.
>
> This picture is simply not true.
>
> The very nature of the fighting in Vietnam has made civilian casualties inevitable. . . .
>
> Certainly there are burned children and adults in Vietnam.
>
> This writer personally saw every burn case in the twenty hospitals he visited. Among them was not a single case of burns due to napalm, and but two from phosphorous shells.
>
> There have been cases of severe burns from napalm, but the numbers are not large in comparison to burns due to accidents.
>
> Of the scores of American physicians queried, many had not seen a single case of burns due to napalm and others had seen but a single case. For every case of burns resulting from war there are scores of cases of burns resulting from gasoline.[25]

Rusk believed that stories and photographs alleging napalm burns originated with farmers and villagers who used gasoline instead of kerosene in their cooking stoves. Since inflation had driven up the price of regular fuel, many Vietnamese bought or pilfered stolen gasoline. Their inexperience in its use frequently led to tragic burns.

Dow often received letters from civilian physicians working in Vietnam stating they had seen none or only a few napalm burns. Of the first 500 reports filed with the American Medical Association by physicians in its Volunteer Physician for Vietnam program, less than 2 percent even mentioned napalm. A special medical team sponsored by the government's Aid for International Development, composed of distinguished physicians from around the country, reported to President Johnson in September 1967 that

[25] Howard A. Rusk, M.D., "Vietnam Tour I, Reports of Many Children Burned by American Napalm Are Challenged," *The New York Times*, March 12, 1967.

"we saw no justification for the undue emphasis which had been placed by the press upon civilian burns caused by napalm. A greater number of burns appeared to be caused by the careless use of gasoline in stoves."[26]

However, these physicians saw only the wounded—an effective weapon would theoretically leave few wounded among its casualties. Some observers of the war reported that voluntary physicians saw only a fraction of the civilian wounded. The Princeton University student newspaper stated:

> Neil Sheehan estimated in the *New York Times Magazine,* October 9, that the present civilian death rate is 1,000 per month, based on the number of war wounded treated—but he continued in the next sentence, "The number of wounded handled by the medical teams, I believe from my own observation, is merely a fraction of the total." The House Foreign Affairs Committee released a higher figure in a report of March 17, 1966. Napalm is the principal reason these casualties are so high.[27]

Dave Coslett of Dow said that no one was sure of the true facts of napalm usage but the protesters based their argument on faulty evidence. "We have done further investigation that would tend to show that there has been a tremendous amount of propaganda about the uses of napalm, that under pretty close medical surveillance don't stand up at all. This has been an issue that has been blown out of all proportion by propaganda, so that the indiscriminate use of napalm is, in fact, *almost* a myth."

The company received a multitude of letters from GIs fighting in Vietnam stating their appreciation of the job napalm did in protecting their lives against the Viet Cong.

> A Congressional Medal of Honor winner has written, for instance, "War and killing is not at all pleasing to anyone. The infantry in Viet Nam fights to win and *stay alive.* We need and are thankful for napalm."
>
> An Army enlisted man writes: "The war would not end if companies such as yours suddenly refused to manufacture napalm and other military supplies."
>
> An infantry captain: "Your napalm has saved the lives of countless American soldiers."
>
> Fourteen GIs signed a letter including this comment: "The effectiveness of napalm in saving U.S. lives is overwhelming."
>
> And a Marine Corps lieutenant: "War is never a pleasant form of existence, but we believe we are here to further the cause of peace,

---

[26] Howard A. Rusk, M.D., "Vietnam Medicine I, Visiting American Team on Its Return, Reports to Johnson on Napalm Burns," *The New York Times,* October 1, 1967.

[27] Lasser, "Dow Chemical Company," p. 6.

and stem the tide of communism. Napalm is just one of the instruments which we must use to support ourselves."

One Army soldier lamented: "It is unfortunate that many protesters think more of the lives of the Viet-Cong than the lives of American servicemen. I know from experience; I used to be a protester until I understood what the goals of many protesters are, and they are not just to stop the war in Vietnam! I am ashamed that I was at first so blind."[28]

Even former Secretary of Defense Robert S. McNamara wrote to Herbert Doan: "In trying circumstances, your company and the individuals who have faced these incidents have conducted themselves in exemplary fashion. I commend you and your employees for the contribution they are making to our commitment in Vietnam." The use of napalm, "a military necessity," did not bring Dow any great profit. McNamara continued,

> Our contracting procedures insure that there can be no profiteering. . . . The protesters who attempt to interfere with recruiting efforts by any company as a form of protest against either a military weapon or the war in Vietnam are misdirecting their efforts. These are matters of military policy and foreign policy over which private industry has no control. Along with you, we deplore the isolated instances where demonstrations have gone beyond mere protest to the point of interfering with the rights of students to discuss employment opportunities with any prospective employer in whom they may be interested.
>
> Your employees and stockholders should be aware that your company is performing a service for our armed forces—a service that plays a vital role in protecting our fighting men.

Dow has declined to take a stand on the morality of napalm and that of the war itself. The company *has* stated its belief, however, that the government itself is moral. In effect, the company said that a "moral" government fighting an immoral war using an immoral weapon is an impossibility, or if it is, it should not be recognized.[29]

The framework used most frequently to judge a corporation's position on the morality of its government is the Nuremburg war trials. Of these, Doan has said:

[28] Letters cited in Doan, "Dow Will Direct Its Efforts toward a Better Tomorrow."

[29] Dean Wakefield, Dow's public relations director for the Eastern Region, in a debate at New York University is alleged to have said that napalm is no more reprehensible than dozens of other weapons. See Steven V. Roberts, "Dow Aide Defends Sale of Napalm. Tells Students Vietnam War Is Not a Moral Issue," *The New York Times*, November 28, 1967.

But what of the argument that we are no different from the [WW II] German industrialists who "just followed orders"?

We reject this argument on several points. First, we reject the validity of comparing our present form of government with Hitler's Nazi Germany. In our mind our government is still representative of and responsive to the will of the people.

Further, we as a company have made a moral judgment on the long-range goals of our government and we support these. We may not agree as individuals with every decision of every military or governmental leader but we regard these leaders as men trying honestly and relentlessly to find the best possible solutions to very, very complex international problems. As long as we so regard them, we would find it impossible not to support them. This is not saying as the critics imply that we will follow blindly and without fail no matter where our government leads us. While I think it highly improbable under our form of government, should despotic leaders attempt to lead our nation away from its historic national purpose, we would cease to support the government. But I can foresee this happening only if through resort to anarchy we prevent the functioning of democratic processes.

Our critics ask if we are willing to stand judgment for our choice to support our government if history should prove this wrong. Our answer is yes.[30]

On another occasion, Doan said:

If [the government] is not moral then it should be changed. If it is a moral government, then we must allow some latitude and some mistakes. If I believed that the government is immoral, then I would try to do something about it. But if accidents happen with the use of napalm, or if inaccurate stories circulate, then I see no reason to change our position. Our company has a responsibility to act like a good citizen.

We want our company to try to raise the standard of living in the world. We can't do everything. We can't run to Vietnam to check on how napalm is being used. We just have to conclude that this is a moral government and that this is a moral society. The only thing we can do as corporate citizens is to say the government is trying to do the right thing and the best thing.

I guess, if something should happen and China ended up ruling the world, and I was forced to answer "Yes" as to whether I was responsible for the manufacture of napalm I would be branded a war criminal.

The only situation in which I could conceive of Dow's refusing to

[30] H. D. Doan, "Why Does Dow Chemical Make Napalm?," *The Wall Street Journal*, December 8, 1967.

manufacture napalm was if I judged the government to be basically immoral. I think Hitler was, for example. But as long as there is a freely elected government and a free press which provides that there will be a moral government, I can't conceive of such a situation.[31]

Being caught between the needs of the government and cries of "Merchants of Death" placed Dow in an unusual position; the whole controversy, according to Doan, "is a stinking, lousy, goddam mess. None of us likes war. None of us likes to be called murderer."

Dow submitted its bid and received its first contract to produce the chemical in 1965. The company used its plant in Torrance, California, to blend the napalm B component, and the work required only ten people. The air force contract was for $6.5 million. Since then, the average contract had been about $5 million a year. The 1969 contract, which Dow lost, was for $9.2 million. Dow claimed that it would have been more profitable to sell the polystyrene on the open market than to continue to use it as a napalm component. According to industry sources, napalm B offered a big outlet for polystyrene. In 1966, Dow made about 4,550 tons of napalm B per month, with polystyrene contributing about one-half of that weight. Coincidentally, early in 1966, after the development of napalm B, when it became clear that there would be a new demand for polystyrene, the company raised its tank car price of polystyrene from nine to ten cents per pound. The public relations director for the West Coast called industry's speculation on why the company raised its prices "irresponsible speculation."

United Technology Center, a subsidiary of United Aircraft Corporation, was the main napalm B contractor—100 million pounds per year—at the time Dow began manufacturing. But UTC was the object of numerous protests in 1966 (people prevented shipments by lying down on railroad tracks, and so on), so it did not submit a bid to the air force in 1967. Other producers also withdrew, and in 1967 Dow became the sole producer of napalm B, although some companies continued to make conventional napalm.

When the protests first began to be felt, in March 1967, Dow's board of directors spent two full days discussing the issue. The board included both "doves" and "hawks" and all felt the issue to be a question of morals; some even consulted their clergymen. According to Doan:

> One board member raised the issue in a very forceful way. He wondered whether we should be doing this at all. A debate exposed many arguments pro and con. The doves considered this a foul weapon and said that they had recently read that many civilians were

[31] Lasser, "Dow Chemical Company," pp. 22–23.

being killed by it. They asked how we could supply a weapon such as this which was so bad.

The questions received very open-minded treatment. There were no set positions. It was a very open debate. Frequently the board broke into small groups for very intense discussion. Members talked back and forth. At the end of the meeting, with nothing firmly decided, but with three or four members looking as if they might take a stand against napalm, everyone went home and must have had a very troubled sleep. The next morning each of these men individually came to my office and said that after careful and troubled consideration they agreed that the company should continue what it was doing. I am not sure of any exceptions on the board today; maybe one at most.[32]

One board member said, "If we believe our government is a democratically chosen government—and we do—then we have to support that government when it asks for our help. The really terrible thing for us to do would be to deprive those boys, who have been democratically drafted to go to Vietnam, of the weapons they need. We're not going to do that."[33]

Since then the board has discussed the protests, the letters from the public, and the appropriate answers, but never with the idea of taking another vote on the issue.

During late November 1967, a press report quoted Chairman Gerstacker as suggesting that Dow not continue to manufacture napalm after its present contract ran out. The report was frequently discussed in relation to the Dow controversy, but soon after it appeared Gerstacker said, "Our bid for the next napalm contract has already been submitted. . . . My remarks were intended to mean only that I cannot commit my company at this time to a course of action for the indefinite future [and] should not be interpreted to mean that there has been any change in our present policy or in our determination to produce napalm."[34]

For all the publicity regarding napalm B it was ironic that when, in October 1969, President Doan mentioned on television that Dow had lost the napalm contract the previous May, the news media ignored his remarks. However, in mid-November, when Chairman Gerstacker made a similar statement in answer to a reporter's question after a speech in Los Angeles, the item was picked up and made the headlines. Reporters then called Midland to ask Doan why the company hadn't tried to "take itself off the hook" by making the announcement earlier. Doan replied, "We're

[32] Ibid.

[33] Brandt, "Napalm—Public Relations Storm Center," p. 15.

[34] "Dow Seeks to Deny It Might Get Out of Napalm Business," The New York Times, November 24, 1967.

making no noise about it because we win and lose contracts all the time. We don't think it's newsworthy." Dow's president denied overbidding the $9.2 million contract, saying, "We did not raise the price despite the fact that our costs had gone up."

In a later communication to the author, Public Relations Director Brandt explained Doan's statement by saying that the company had not wanted to place "undue emphasis" on its loss of the contract to avoid giving the impression that the company "had caved in or chickened out" or had "even radically changed its policy in regard to napalm," or "that the protest elements had won a great victory." Brandt said any feelings by the students that they had forced Dow out of the napalm business ignored the company's "harsh policy" that it "will bid on napalm again when the government asks for bids."

C.
CORPORATE DECISIONS AND THEIR EFFECTS ON URBAN COMMUNITIES

—◆—

The Milwaukee Braves, Atlanta

Indiscriminate Moving of Sports Franchises

But while the nation as a whole benefits from the prompt shift of resources from old to new uses, the employees and the communities directly involved may, temporarily, be adversely affected. From the viewpoint of both social equity and economic efficiency, these people should not be asked to bear by themselves the full burden of such adjustments unaided.

—ROBERT S. McNAMARA
Secretary of Defense under
Presidents Kennedy and Johnson

The cliff-hanger 1957 World Series ended on a triumphant note for the Milwaukee Braves' fans. Lew Burdette won the final game by shutting out the New York Yankees for the second time in four days. Milwaukee went wild and the team was greeted "with the wildest welcome ever given a series champion."[1] *Life* magazine called Milwaukee's unabashed enthusiasm for its team "the most refreshing thing in baseball in years."[2]

The Braves had moved to Milwaukee in 1953 when the city built them a new county stadium at a cost of $8.5 million.[3] Since moving to Milwaukee

---

[1] "Beer City Goes on Binge," *Life*, October 2, 1957, p. 97.

[2] *Ibid.*

[3] "Fighting for Pennant. Atlanta-Bound Braves Feel Milwaukee's Ire," *The Wall Street Journal*, August 27, 1965, pp. 1, 16.

267

the team had had tremendous financial success. Attendance peaked at 2,050,000 in 1956.[4] In winning the pennant the Braves drew 2,215,404 spectators, ending a five-year period in which they netted $1,857,602—a close second to baseball's best, the Brooklyn Dodgers. In the succeeding years the team had its problems on the field, and these problems were magnified at the turnstiles. Attendance sagged to 766,921 in 1962, 770,000 in 1963, 910,911 in 1964, and 555,584 in 1965.[5] It would be difficult to determine whether the cause was simply the fickle baseball sports fans or just that enthusiasm for major-league baseball was wearing off in Milwaukee.[6]

During this period of decline there was also trouble in the front office. Reversals in other ventures had caused the Perini Corporation, the owner of the Braves, to suffer overall net losses. In the baseball division of the corporation, even though $8 million had been invested in developing new talent, little return had been realized. Trades did not go well; the team did not do well. The declining performances of pitching stars Lew Burdette and Warren Spahn made even them expendable. In 1962, the Perini Corporation finally sold the franchise to a group of Chicago businessmen for $6 million. Perini had enjoyed little popularity in Milwaukee as owner of the Braves, but he was well liked in comparison with the new group. It is putting it mildly to say that they were not well received. One reason was that they were from Chicago, and Chicago is a dirty word in Milwaukee. Another reason was that the Chicagoans, being a group, could correctly be called a syndicate, a word that carried nefarious connotations associated with certain underground Chicago activities. The new owners could sense the hostility of their new town and being "aware that they were looked upon as interlopers from Chicago . . . attempted to court their factory town. The management's wives traveled up to the games, and their husbands nervously jested that they lived in a southern suburb of Milwaukee. Commuting [though] wasn't enough."[7] The syndicate had problems

---

[4] Steven M. Lovelady, "Baseball at Bat," *The Wall Street Journal*, March 22, 1966, pp. 1, 18.

[5] "Wail of Two Cities," *"Time*, February 4, 1966; William Leggett, "Atlanta You Can Have the Rest, Leave Us Eddie Mattress Our Hero," *Sports Illustrated*, April 26, 1965, pp. 24, 90, 92–93.

[6] It might be noted here that falling attendance was not confined to the Milwaukee Braves alone but was common to all of professional baseball. For example, in 1948, with 16 teams in 10 cities, major league baseball drew a total attendance of 21.4 million people—an average attendance per game of 17,000. In 1962, with 20 teams in 17 cities, the total attendance was 21.6 million people, or 13,200 per game. The picture would look all the more dismal if this lag in attendance were compared with increased attendance for other professional sports, notably football, or the rise in population, i.e., the potential audience. "Baseball: Another Business Facing Change," *U.S. News and World Report*, August 12, 1963.

[7] "Home Are the Braves: In Atlanta, a Divorce from Milwaukee," *Look*, May 3, 1966, p. 62.

other than public relations. Of the $6 million paid for the club, two-thirds had been borrowed. In the words of a Milwaukee investment broker, "there are damn few businesses you can leverage up to this point and be successful. A corollary is that there is precious little time to wait for profits or woo fans back to the ball park."[8]

The syndicate put six local people on the board of directors and then attempted a stock issue among Wisconsin residents. It failed miserably— less than 10 percent of the 115,000 shares were purchased outside the syndicate, which had to buy up the rest. Another loan of high interest was required. In the parlance of the game, the "squeeze" was on.

It was apparent at this time that something had to be done. The person who considered all the alternatives would probably have included moving the franchise as a distinct possibility. However, if this inclination had even crossed the syndicate's mind, it was not evident by their public actions. Far from moving, in 1964 the club put on what the newspapers called the best selling job ever done in Milwaukee. Players made personal appearances to promote ticket sales; there were discount prices and "buck" nights. Although the attendance in 1964 thereby increased to 911,000 up from 770,000 in 1963, the discounts and increased promotional expenses prevented any increase in revenues in the succeeding year.

Rumors of a move had floated about the baseball world all during the 1963 season. Though no site in particular was mentioned, it was not often overlooked that Atlanta was erecting a new major league stadium. Almost as if it were part of the selling campaign, the chairman of the board, William C. Bartholomay, announced at the start of the 1964 season that "We are positively not moving. We are playing in Milwaukee whether you're talking of 1964, 1965, or 1975."[9] This seemed at first a firm enough commitment, but certain events of the ensuing year provided more than enough reason for doubt.

The *Milwaukee Journal* reported that small packages were being sent by the Braves to Atlanta. The explanation given was that they were just "old programs." Later, the *Journal* discovered that a complete inventory had been taken. "Routine," explained the Braves' management. The final blow to the credibility of Bartholomay's statement came with the *Journal's* exposition that a local company was under contract to build a giant Braves-head emblem, presumably for use on a major league baseball scoreboard. When the emblem was discovered shortly thereafter gracing the new Atlanta stadium, queries began to become quite pointed.[10]

After the close of the 1964 season, amid increased rumor and accusation, the syndicate announced that it would move the franchise to Atlanta.

[8] *Ibid.*

[9] *Ibid.*

[10] "Like Gone with the Wind, Braves Take Atlanta," *Life*, April 22, 1966, p. 77.

National League officials approved the move by a vote of nine to zero. The decision made Milwaukee, with a population of 741,300, "the only one among the country's dozen biggest cities that does not have either a big-league baseball team or a professional football team."[11] However, in view of threats of lawsuits and breach of contract by Milwaukee officials, the Braves decided to continue in Milwaukee for one more year—1965— before moving to Atlanta.[12]

LEGALITY OF THE MOVE

Milwaukee was not to be contented with this sop. In August 1965, Milwaukee County accompanied the state of Wisconsin in a suit "charging the Braves and the other nine teams in the National League with illegally and monopolistically depriving Milwaukee of its major league franchise."[13] In another suit, filed separately in the federal courts by the state of Wisconsin, the state argued that the United States Supreme Court should override its previous decisions exempting big league baseball from the Sherman Antitrust Act.

LEGAL PRECEDENTS. Professional baseball has a long history of immunity from the antitrust laws which were first established by the Supreme Court in 1922 in the case of *Federal Baseball Club of Baltimore Inc.* v. *National League of Professional Baseball Clubs, et al.*[14] and concerned a member of a weak third baseball league. The suit charged that the American League was conspiring to monopolize baseball business and was in violation of sections 1 and 2 of the Sherman Antitrust Act. The jury agreed with the plaintiffs and awarded them damages in the amount of $800,000. The appellate court, however, reversed the lower court's decision, holding that baseball was not engaged in interstate trade and commerce and was there-fore not subject to the antitrust laws. The Supreme Court concurred with Justice Holmes, saying: "The business is giving exhibitions of baseball, which are purely state affairs."[15]

---

11 "Baseball: Case Dismissed," *Time*, August 5, 1966.

12 "Home Are the Braves," *Look*, p. 62.

13 "Wail of Two Cities," *Time*, February 4, 1966, p. 81.

14 "The Sherman Act, in section 1, declares every contract, combination or conspiracy 'in restraint of trade or commerce among the several states . . . to be illegal,' and in section 2, condemns every person who shall monopolize, or attempt to monopolize, or combine with others to monopolize, that trade or any part thereof." *National League of Professional Baseball Clubs, et al.,* v. *Federal Baseball Club of Baltimore, Inc.,* 269 Fed. 681, at p. 684.

15 *Ibid.*, p. 208.

Although the precedent set in the *Federal Baseball* case was modified somewhat in subsequent cases to allow individual players to seek damages under the antitrust laws where their "livelihood and pursuit of happiness in the sports world were subject to group boycott,"[16] its essential features remain intact even today. Nor was the immunity granted to professional baseball extended to other professional sports, the Supreme Court maintaining that:

> The issue confronting us is, therefore, not whether a previously granted exemption should continue, but whether an exemption should be granted in the first instance. And this issue is for Congress to resolve, not this court.[17]

In response to increasing judicial pressure to clarify the position of professional sports in general or baseball in particular, the House of Representatives conducted hearings in 1957 to clarify the various issues relative to the applicability of antitrust statutes to professional sports. Appearing as witnesses before the House subcommittee, the commissioners of the baseball, football, basketball, and hockey leagues supported the exemption of organized sports from antitrust laws maintaining that:

1. Sportive leagues were different from all other industries in that the owners were not competitive with one another;
2. Their present practices had been in operation for many years, were indispensable for the proper functioning of the business, and were these practices to be declared illegal, the leagues would be faced with insurmountable difficulties of operation;
3. Without their present practices, especially in relation to "player draft," they would be unable to function in that wealthy teams would obtain the best available talent, which would prevent competitive playing strength.[18]

The House subcommittee report issued in May 1958 contained three views.[19] The majority supported the view that the sport leagues should be subject to the antitrust laws with courts granting exemptions for those practices which were "reasonably necessary" to maintain balanced "com-

---

[16] *Gardella* v. *Chandler*, 172 F.2d 402 (2d Civ. 1949).

[17] *United States* v. *International Boxing Club*, 348 U.S. (1955) p. 243.

[18] Maxwell Keith, "Development in the Application of Antitrust Laws to Professional Sports," *Hastings Law Journal*, November 1958, p. 119.

[19] U.S., Congress, House, "Applicability of Anti-trust Laws to Professional Team Sports," Report from House Committee on Judiciary to Accompany H. R. 10378, 85th Cong., 2d sess., 1958, May 13, 1958.

petitive playing strength" between different clubs and also to preserve confidence in the honesty of the sport contest. A minority wanted complete exemption from the antitrust laws for organized sports, while a third view maintained that sport contests are not trade in business and therefore do not come under the purview of antitrust laws.[20]

The House did not accept the doctrine of "reasonably necessary" and instead passed the Walter Bill which exempted professional sports from antitrust laws where their practices involved:

1. Equalization of competitive strength.
2. The employment, eligibility or selection of players, or the reservation or assignment of player contracts.
3. The right to operate within specific geographic areas.
4. The regulation of rights to broadcast and telecast reports and pictures of sports contests.
5. The preservation of public confidence in the honesty of the sports contests.[21]

The passage of the House bill was followed by Senate hearings before the Judiciary Committee Subcommittee on Antitrust and Monopoly. The subcommittee voted to table the bill and no action was taken before the Congress adjourned.

The legal proceedings that arose from the announcement of the Braves' move had legal implications that went far beyond the question of whether the Braves should be allowed to move or not; they involved the National League, the American League, organized baseball's contractual processes, and even the question of what is and what is not interstate commerce.

The lawsuits filed by the state of Wisconsin and Milwaukee County contended that the owners and management of the Braves and the National League had violated federal and state antitrust laws by trying to move the Braves to Atlanta without providing a replacement franchise for the city of Milwaukee. Suits were filed in both the circuit court of Milwaukee and a federal district court. Both suits demanded that the National League either expand the league and give Milwaukee a new franchise or allow a group of businessmen in the city to purchase the Braves from the owners to keep the Braves in Milwaukee. The suits also asked that the Braves be restricted from playing in any other city until one of the alternatives had been met.

In April 1966, Judge Elmer W. Roller of Wisconsin Circuit Court ruled

[20] Keith, *op. cit.*, p. 135.
[21] H. R. Rep. No. 10378, 85th Cong., 2d sess., 1958.

that the National League had violated Wisconsin's antitrust laws by moving the Milwaukee-based Braves to Atlanta "with the result that trade and commerce within the State of Wisconsin have been substantially restrained." He fined each of the ten teams in the National League $5,000 plus costs. The league itself, which was a defendant in addition to the individual teams, was fined $100 for costs. The court also ordered the league to either (1) bring the Braves back or (2) give Milwaukee a new team.[22] The ruling came a day after the Braves opened their 1966 National League season in Atlanta before a crowd of 50,000 spectators. While Judge Roller was finding against the National League in Milwaukee, an Atlanta judge, Sam McKenzie, was ordering the Braves to honor their contract with the Fulton County Stadium Authority (Atlanta), which meant that the Braves could not return to Milwaukee. The effect of these two conflicting decisions was not immediately apparent, but they implied that the Braves would not be able to play anywhere in the 1966 season. This would have thrown the rest of the league into chaos, financially damaging the other nine teams and perhaps destroying the Braves.

One Milwaukee attorney, Dominic Frinzi, made a personal attempt, quite apart from the action by the county and the state, to use the legal machinery of the state to harass the Braves. He incorporated himself in the state of Wisconsin as "Atlanta Braves, Inc.," in a maneuver designed to coerce the Braves organization to operate legally with their former corporate name, "Milwaukee Braves, Inc.," or face a challenge as to the legality of all the games that the Braves played under the new corporate name. His attempt, however, was unsuccessful as the attorney general of the state, Bronson C. La Follette, branded the action irresponsible and it was never brought to trial.

In analyzing the approach taken by Milwaukee, it is important to note that they did not directly attack baseball on the grounds that it was an illegal monopoly. They did point out that "league decisisons and limits on franchise locations are a conspiracy in restraint of trade,"[23] but they did not pursue these points to any length as to do so would have been tantamount to saying "baseball is an invidious monopoly, and we are suing to make sure we keep a piece of the action."[24] The plaintiffs were willing to acknowledge that baseball was in fact a legal monopoly but that it was illegally using its monopoly powers. Judge Roller's court concluded that the Braves had acted "surreptitiously and deceitfully." In his decision, Judge Roller said that "the refusal of the National League and the failure of the

[22] *State of Wisconsin* v. *Milwaukee Braves, Inc., et al.*, 144 N.W. 2d at p. 7.

[23] *The Wall Street Journal*, March 22, 1966, p. 18.

[24] *Ibid.*

American League to issue a franchise to Milwaukee County . . . was a concerted refusal to deal in restraint of trade and commerce within the State of Wisconsin."[25]

The Atlanta Braves and the National League appealed Judge Roller's decision to the Wisconsin Supreme Court. The state supreme court agreed with Judge Roller's reasoning, but not with the decision—which they reversed on the grounds that "baseball should be considered interstate commerce."

In reversing Judge Roller's decision, the Wisconsin Supreme Court stated:

> It is evident that the activity of major league baseball, spread through eight states in the National League and nine states and the District of Columbia in the American League is interstate commerce. Any suggestion to the contrary in 1922 in the *Federal Baseball* case, infra, has been effectively overruled in the subsequent decisions explaining the exemption enjoyed by organized baseball, hereinafter discussed, and those cases now make it clear that organized baseball is interstate commerce and Congress may therefore regulate it. [p. 11]
>
> The history of judicial action and legislative inaction with respect to organized baseball at least suggests a federal policy of approval of the existing structure, and the question readily arises whether there is a conflict between state and federal policy, so that the state policy must yield. [p. 12]

The Wisconsin Supreme Court in citing various United States Supreme Court decisions seemed to indicate that although operating conditions in professional baseball in 1953 might have changed since the days of the *Federal Baseball* case of 1922, it was up to Congress to decide whether or not to include baseball within the federal antitrust laws.[26]

With this decision a serious conflict between various courts was avoided, but also, perhaps for a long time, an opportunity was lost to discuss and resolve the anomalous situation of professional baseball in relation to the communities in which the teams play. The issuance of an enforceable permanent injunction by Judge Roller against the Braves would have made them liable for large financial penalties under Wisconsin law. The "full faith and credit" clause of the Federal Constitution would have had the effect of some state courts enforcing the Wisconsin ruling while others followed the Georgia court ruling by ordering the teams in their respective

---

[25] "Baseball Braves Ordered to Return to Milwaukee," *The Wall Street Journal*, April 14, 1966, p. 6.

[26] *State of Wisconsin* v. *Milwaukee Braves, Inc., et al.*, 385 U.S. 990, 31 Wis. 2d 699, 144 N.W. 2d 1.

states to play in either Milwaukee or Atlanta, depending upon the judgment that they were enforcing.

Moreover, an extension of the antitrust laws to baseball would have meant that the league could not place any restrictions on the number of territorial locations of franchises. Clearly, this would have created havoc if the league had been deluged with a multitude of new teams. Furthermore, such a decision would have meant the end of the reserve clause in the player contracts. The reserve clause provides that once a player has signed a contract with one team, he may not go out on the player market to seek employment with another team.

The result of this decision was to give the Braves unfettered latitude in whatever action they wanted to take, as far as moving was concerned. This is the situation that prevailed as the suit in federal court failed to come to trial; no further litigation was forthcoming, and abuse of baseball's favored position and special privileges is still unchecked.

THE ECONOMIC LOGIC: THE BRAVES, MILWAUKEE, AND ATLANTA

From the viewpoint of the public and the courts, the special privilege accorded professional baseball carries an assumption that there are compensating advantages and that public interest is better served by protecting baseball from competition and keeping the various clubs economically healthy and balanced in strength. The questions therefore that need answering are whether there is such a need for protection for baseball and whether baseball has abused its special position.

The Braves contended that they were not misusing their monopoly power but that adverse economic conditions forced them to move. In addition to the continuous loss in attendance at the gates, the Braves were also facing competition from two Chicago teams for the Milwaukee baseball dollar. These factors, combined with the highly leveraged financing of the organization, placed the Braves in a financial squeeze. The allegation that this resulted in a considerable net loss was a major controversy of the case. At best, though, profits were substantially reduced. The owners testified in court that they had indeed lost money—$3.5 million from 1963 through 1965.[27] The Braves offered this information as economic justification for the withdrawal from Milwaukee. In doing so, they were attempting to show that their action was not a capricious use of monopolistic power but a reasonable course of action taken by an organization facing financial disaster.

27 *The Wall Street Journal*, March 22, 1966.

The Braves maintained that the revenue resulting from low attendance was not sufficient to keep the team out of the red; hence, they insisted that the area was economically unproductive for their organization. The management claimed that the club would have to draw one million two hundred thousand spectators in Milwaukee to break even, and one million four hundred thousand spectators to earn a reasonable return. The chairman of the board, William C. Bartholomay, claimed that normal revenues had been so slight in past years that only the sale of players in the farm system had prevented losses from being tremendous.[28]

However, a group of Milwaukee businessmen contended that a baseball team could be profitable in Milwaukee with attendance of only eight hundred thousand per year.[29] Moreover, the state and county testified that the Braves' alleged losses were on paper only, arising from the use of unconventional accounting methods. Unlike the practice of other major league clubs, the Braves were charging off scouting costs as current expenses rather than capitalizing and amortizing them over a period of years. However, in their briefs to the Wisconsin Supreme Court both parties to the case agreed that "had scouting expenses been capitalized . . . as sound accounting methods would require, the Braves would have shown a net income of approximately $170,000 in 1963 and $151,000 in 1964."[30] The difference in yearly net income would have put the team into the black. This certainly made Bartholomay's minimum attendance figure and his contention that the club was losing money subject to question. From Milwaukee's point of view, the club chose to leave the area even though it had been shown to be "economically productive."[31] However, the use of this term by the Milwaukee businessmen seemed to indicate merely the absence of a net loss. Obviously, the board of directors of the Braves had an entirely different definition in mind. This definition becomes clearer when we consider the potential economic gains in operating in Atlanta compared with operating in Milwaukee from the viewpoint of the Braves' management.

Atlanta had been considering major league baseball since 1960, when the Georgia legislature approved a stadium authority. Nothing much happened, however, until Ivan Allen was elected mayor of Atlanta in 1963. His first attempt at courting a major league team floundered when he found that not everything Charles Finley (owner of the Athletics) promised had the sanction of the league. Atlantans maintained that the owner of the

[28] Selling assets is a dubious means of earning income. If, in fact, there was wholesale unloading of players in the farm system, it seems unlikely that much, let alone the substantial profits intimated in the testimony, could have been realized.

[29] This group of businessmen attempted to purchase the franchise in 1964 but were unsuccessful as they were far short of the necessary capital.

[30] *State of Wisconsin* v. *Milwaukee Braves, Inc., et al.*, 144 N.W. 2d at p. 6.

[31] *The Wall Street Journal*, March 22, 1966, p. 18.

Athletics had promised them the team if Atlanta would provide a stadium. Undaunted, Atlanta went shopping for another team with Arthur Montgomery, chairman of the Stadium Authority and head of the Coca-Cola Bottling Company, as the man in charge. To his amazement, he found in his friend Delbert Coleman, one of the new owners of the Braves, a willing listener. To the Braves, Atlanta was indeed an attractive place. In the words of general manager Jon McHale: "We looked at other cities, but there was a hub of 500,000 with 18 million people in the market area. Atlanta is the center of shopping and transportation in the Southeast." No sooner did the Atlantans return home than plans began to unfold. Surveys were taken to determine how great an attraction major league baseball would be. Also surveyed was the reaction to integrated seating—all answers were favorable. The architects chose what they thought were the best points of all other stadiums. The result was an $18 million amphitheater seating fifty thousand for baseball and fifty-seven thousand for football, with provisions for a dome and air conditioning to come later. To Atlanta, the acquisition of the Braves meant thousands of new jobs directly connected with the team itself, jobs and revenues associated with the new concessions and with the radio and television broadcasts, and many jobs created in all fields of the expanded economy. For the city the presence of the team meant greatly increased tax revenues, more tourist dollars, and another major attraction for business and industrial firms.

The deal was further sweetened by Atlanta. The city agreed to indemnify the club in the event of any lawsuits—the entire cost of the Braves' defense was borne by Atlanta. The city also completed the stadium in the record time of fifty-one weeks, resulting in bonus payments of $700,000 to the contractors. Another factor was the lucrative television contracts with commitments of over $1 million in advertising from Coca-Cola and Gulf Oil alone. In comparison, the other side of the coin was dull indeed. Milwaukee simply did not have the dazzling commercial economy of Atlanta. As the court found, the northern city did provide radio and television revenues, which compared favorably with other teams in the league. However, these failed to approach the exclusive rights to a seven-state area that Atlanta offered. Atlanta was a bustling, growing, dynamic city with one new freeway after another reaching out to all the southeast. Milwaukee, its economy based on heavy industry, had finished its growth long ago: "Now, smoke from aging factories grays downtown buildings. Land for expansion is hard to find amid the cramped streets, and the population statistics are static. Nearby cities compete for new business. While prosperity surrounds gritty Milwaukee, the city must fight to hold what it has."[32] Add to this the hostile fans, competition from three nearby

[32] *Look*, May 3, 1966, p. 62.

teams, and declining attendance, and the economics of the move was more than justified.

That Milwaukee's interests were ignored in the whole affair is undeniable. The deal between the Braves and Atlanta was "sealed by a handshake in Chicago in March 1964"[33] after secret negotiations and was denied by the Braves even after their agreement with Montgomery. Leaks of the agreement were as abundant as the Braves' vehement denials. Though Atlanta had had some financial problems, the stadium construction was not long delayed. In addition, amid the denials, "someone" indemnified William McKechnie, owner of the minor league Atlanta Crackers, in the sum of $200,000 for his franchise in the International League.

Commenting on the indifference of the Braves' owners and the National League toward Milwaukee, an editorial in the *Wall Street Journal* on August 1, 1966, stated:

> Far from cooperating with the local businessmen anxious to assume the risk of maintaining a franchise in an abandoned town, the owners in effect decreed that the city will not have a team. Even a legally sanctioned monopoly such as a patent licensee cannot operate so arbitrarily.
>
> More disturbing is the sport's player draft, which, with no thought of consent from the individual concerned, assigns a single team rights to a potential player. The wage for such a prospect is held way down by such a draft.[34]

The pursuit of profit with no regard for the fans was further evinced by the Braves' owners in their radio and television broadcasts of the Braves' games. During the 1965 season, Atlanta received nineteen of the Milwaukee Braves' games on television and another fifty-five on radio. Compared with this, no games were televised in Milwaukee and only a last-minute $110,000 radio contract enabled the games to be broadcast to Milwaukee fans.[35]

The Washington consulting firm of Robert A. Nathan estimated the cost to Milwaukee at "$18 million in income, 2,600 jobs and more than $600,000 in tax revenue."[36] These are only the costs that can directly be attributed to the move. The indirect costs are infinitely more difficult, if not impossible, to measure. For example, how many firms chose not to locate in Milwaukee after it became a non-major league city? What were the associated costs in terms of jobs, income, and tax revenue? What were the losses to hotels, restaurants, and other retail establishments?

[33] *Ibid.*

[34] "Baseball's Illogic, an Editorial," *The Wall Street Journal*, August 1, 1966, p. 8.

[35] *Sports Illustrated*, April 25, 1965, p. 24.

[36] *The Wall Street Journal*, March 22, 1966, p. 18.

It should be noted that these effects should not totally be attributed to the Braves' management. The National League sanctioned the move. Ostensibly, its view was that "its special monopolistic position in no way obligates it to even consider anything like economic damage and social loss to a vacated city, while it pursues its own profit and convenience."[37]

The economic costs notwithstanding, Milwaukee suffered a severe social loss. In one year Milwaukee changed from a prestigious city whose name was on the lips of millions of baseball fans to a virtual nonentity among large cities. Many fans mourned the loss of their city's "status symbol," and one fan in particular articulated the feelings of a great many of the burghers of Milwaukee: "It was the first time Milwaukee was major league in anything."[38]

In Atlanta, there was similar feeling. Arthur B. Montgomery of Coca-Cola said, "The true worth of a major league team is what it does for the posture of the city. You're either a first rate or a second rate city. Major league baseball with pro football makes us first rate, puts us ahead of other cities with more population."[39]

This left Milwaukee with another problem—what to do with the $8.5 million county stadium that had been built expressly for the Braves. Ben Barkin, one of the businessmen in Milwaukee pushing for the retention of major league baseball, verbalized the social injustice that certainly many others also felt: "It's the responsibility of organized baseball to take a good look at what it has done to Milwaukee. Now we're left with a stadium built by taxpayers' dollars . . . baseball can't be business one day and holier-than-thou the next."[40]

The Braves, and baseball in general, drew little sympathy from the nation's sports writers who characterized the Braves as pure economic opportunists. For example, Rick Young of the *New York Daily News* said that the Braves "moved in like a gay young blade, ravished the land and are about to move on to other parts where money is fresher and suckers riper."[41]

Although the people of Milwaukee were having their franchise stolen by Atlanta, they were reluctant to attempt to steal someone else's. Said E. B. Fitzgerald, one of the leading Milwaukee businessmen, "In view of our displeasure at the stealing of our own franchise, we're not in a good position to steal someone else's."[42]

---

[37] *The Wall Street Journal*, August 1, 1966, p. 8.

[38] "Fighting for Pennant, Atlanta-Bound Braves Feel Milwaukee's Ire," *The Wall Street Journal*, August 27, 1966, p. 16.

[39] *Look*, May 3, 1966, p. 64.

[40] *The Wall Street Journal*, August 27, 1966, p. 16.

[41] *The Wall Street Journal*, March 22, 1966, p. 18.

[42] *The Wall Street Journal*, April 27, 1966, p. 1.

Prior to the Braves' move to Atlanta, the civil rights actions and desegregation of the city were instrumental in gaining favor with the league. Despite this, Alabama-born Henry Aaron was not overjoyed at the prospect of returning to the land of cotton. Other black players likewise preferred the more liberal attitudes of the North and regarded the move with some apprehension. Again the Braves' management seemed to place economic considerations above all else.

It thus appeared that Milwaukee would have to wait for an expansion of the baseball leagues before it could hope to gain another franchise. Undoubtedly, Milwaukee baseball fans were disappointed when in 1968, the major leagues, in only their second expansion since World War II, awarded American League franchises to Kansas City and Seattle and National League franchises to Montreal and San Diego.[43]

But history was destined to repeat itself. Although the American League said that the Seattle Pilots would remain in Seattle for a long time, after months of wavering and court actions, one week before the opening day of the 1970 baseball season, the Pilots announced that they would be leaving Seattle for Milwaukee. The team would be known as the Brewers, and even though it was only a second-year expansion team, it would be the first for Milwaukee in five years. Brewers' stockholders were almost all Wisconsinites and the team had a twenty-five-year lease on County Stadium at a rent of one dollar a year (provided attendance did not exceed 1 million). The owners of the team, having learned from past mistakes, secured a $1.2 million-per-season five-year radio and television advertising contract with Schlitz beer.[44]

Peter Carry said in *Sports Illustrated* that by the second home game, "Not only had baseball come back, but excitement over the game had come with it." Although "the welcome for the Brewers seemed remarkably subdued, . . . the reticence appeared to indicate greater sophistication rather than less enthusiasm." Ticket outlets were mobbed, and "In the first 10 days of season-ticket sales, the Brewers sold over 4,000, nearly double the Braves' total in their first year."[45]

The Pilots claimed last place in their division in the 1969 season and as Brewers they stayed there during the beginning of the 1970 season.

---

[43] Golenpaul, Dan, ed., *Information Please Almanac, Atlas and Yearbook*, 1969, 23rd ed. (New York: Simon, 1968), p. 824.

[44] Peter Carry, "Milwaukee Is Falling in Love Quietly This Time," *Sports Illustrated*, April 27, 1970, pp. 50–52.

[45] *Ibid.*, p. 52.

D.
CORPORATIONS
AND
THE NEWS MEDIA

---❖---

A.B.C. + I.T.T. ≟ Free Press[1]

News is nothing more than any other thirty minutes of TV programming, and when it starts getting bad ratings it's going to go off the air.

—ANONYMOUS OBSERVATION

Journalists were never intended to be the cheerleaders of a society, conductors of applause, the sycophants. Tragically, that is their assigned role in authoritarian societies, but not here—not yet.

—CHET HUNTLEY

INTRODUCTION AND BACKGROUND

What exactly is the public interest in the news media? This question is open to many interpretations, but the news media themselves use the criterion that news be covered "fairly," with no one business, government, or interest group controlling media coverage.[2] Competition among enterprises engaged in the communications business insures the use of technological improvements and up-to-date services and helps to minimize the influence of any one group. Likewise, the public interest is served by

[1] Title adapted from Eileen Shanahan, "Comment: Merger Issue. A.B.C. + I.T.T. = ?," *The New York Times*, July 30, 1967, Sec. 4, p. 5.

[2] S. Prakash Sethi, *Business Corporations and the Black Man* (San Francisco: Chandler Publishing Co., 1970), Chap. 6.

corporations with sufficient financial resources to assume risks in introducing new processes and techniques and in expanding into pioneer communications fields.

The following case concerns the thwarted merger between two communications companies, ABC and ITT. In the events surrounding the proposed merger the issues involved in defining the public interest in news broadcasting were thoroughly scrutinized, with implications not only for the immediate question of the conformity of the merger to government regulations but also for the long-term issues of control, autonomy, and quality performance of broadcasting enterprises.

Background of ABC and ITT

International Telephone and Telegraph (ITT) is one of the largest conglomerate corporations in the world. Since its formation about fifty years ago, it has primarily operated as a holding company for foreign telephone equipment and operating companies.[3] With interests in at least sixty-six countries, ITT is engaged in domestic and foreign manufacturing, the operation of telecommunications utilities, and financial and other service activities. A leading international record carrier, ITT also claims to be the world's largest manufacturer of telecommunications equipment.[4] Of its domestic manufacturing activities, about 40 percent is done under government contract related to space programs and defense. Sixty percent of its net income comes from abroad and, according to the company, it has "extensive investment and responsibility in the economies and societies of the countries in which it operates."[5]

In 1959 ITT hired Harold Geneen as president. To balance the corporation's domestic and international operations, Geneen activated a vigorous policy of growth, primarily through the acquisition of domestic industries, including Alexander Hamilton Life Insurance, American Universal Life Insurance, Avis Rent-A-Car, and Aetna Finance Company. The goal of

---

[3] "Dissenting Opinion of Commissioner Nicholas Johnson," Part IV of *ABC-ITT Merger Proceedings*, Federal Communications Commission, Washington, D.C., rev., December 21, 1966, p. 15.

[4] *Ibid.*, "Dissenting Statement of Commissioner Robert T. Bartley," *ABC-ITT Merger Proceedings*, Part II, pp. 2–3.

[5] *Ibid.*, Part IV, pp. 8, 11, 21. For example, directors of foreign ITT subsidiaries include three legislators, a former premier, and foreign ministry employees. Eventually seven of fifteen board members of the Chilean subsidiary will be government appointed [pp. 19–20].

The Indian government owns 75 percent of one ITT company, and the company cannot sell any of the stock to an Indian or to a citizen of a country not approved by the Indian government.

doubling sales and earnings in the first five-year period was achieved, and ITT's acquisitions have continued unabated. Much of the success of ITT's growth policy has been attributed to Geneen and the taut system of control that he exerted over ITT's previously autonomous operating managers.

The American Broadcasting Companies, Inc., is a child of the government's concern for the maintenance of freedom of the press. In response to the Federal Communications Commission's (FCC) chain broadcasting rules of 1941, the Blue Network Company, one of two networks owned by the Radio Corporation of America (RCA), was offered for sale and was purchased by Edward J. Noble, who created the "American Broadcasting Company." ABC has since substantially increased its operations and by 1966 owned 399 theaters in thirty-four states, five television stations (most ABC affiliates are independently owned as per government regulation), and six AM and FM stations in the top ten broadcasting markets. ABC is capable of reaching 93 percent of 50 million American homes with television sets and 97 percent of those with radios.

In addition, ABC subsidiaries produce records on six different labels, publish three farm newspapers, and distribute filmed television programs to stations, networks, and advertisers. ABC is active in foreign markets through a wholly owned subsidiary which acts as program purchasing and sales representative for foreign stations in twenty-five nations.[6]

HISTORY OF THE MERGER

On December 3, 1965, ITT publicly announced that the two companies had met several times and agreed that ABC would be merged into ITT as a wholly owned subsidiary with control passing from ABC stockholders to a new group composed of both ABC and ITT stockholders.[7]

The two companies entered into the agreement on February 14, 1966, and on March 31, 1966, ABC filed the necessary applications with the FCC for its approval of transfers of licenses for ABC broadcasting stations to the new ITT subsidiary corporation. Proxy statements describing the details of the merger were sent to the shareholders of both companies who voted overwhelmingly to approve the merger.

In July 1966, the FCC requested information from the presidents of ABC and ITT regarding the proposed future operations of the new broadcasting company. Replies were soon received by the commission, which then accepted the bulk of the data as authentic and accurate statements of

---

[6] *Ibid.*, Part II, Attachment A; Part IV, pp. 12–15.

[7] *Ibid.*, Part IV, p. 85.

fact. The FCC then ordered that a hearing before the full seven-member commission be held on September 19, 1966; any party interested in the case could appear and be heard at that time.

As in all merger cases, the FCC considered the possibility of potential antitrust effects, and in keeping with policy, maintained a continuing liaison with the Antitrust Division of the Department of Justice with regard to the case. The division itself had been independently collecting data on the case since the two companies' first announcement but continually put off the commission when it requested Justice's views. Thus the department made no statement regarding the matter prior to the FCC's hearing on September 19, 1966, did not appear at the hearing, and commented only that it had the matter under study.[8]

It was not until November 3, after the commission had notified Antitrust Division Chief Donald Turner that an FCC decision was imminent, that Turner replied that there was a "sufficient possibility of significant anticompetitive effects"[9] which could result from the merger. He suggested that the commission hold off its decision until the department had arrived "at a final decision on the anticompetitive aspects of the merger."[10] The commission then asked the division to make a more definite statement and notified it that it was preparing to issue its decision on December 21, 1966. The commission noted, however, that whereas a Justice Department report would be significant, it would not be binding.[11]

Finally, on December 20, 1966, Turner submitted to the commission the Antitrust Division's decision that the department did not have the grounds to seek to block the merger in court, but it saw a number of possible anticompetitive consequences in the proposed merger that the FCC should explore.

The commission, having been prepared for weeks to act on the proposed merger, approved it the next day, noting that the questions Justice raised had already been carefully considered. The commission also criticized the Justice Department for waiting as long as it had before expressing its views.

[8] *Ibid.*, "Memorandum Opinion and Order," Part I, pp. 1, 2, 5.

[9] *Ibid.*, Part IV, p. 80.

[10] *Order on Petition for Reconsideration*, Federal Communications Commission, February 1, 1967, Part I, p. 2.

[11] *ABC-ITT Merger Proceedings*, Part I, pp. 1, 5; Part IV, pp. 80–84.
This was the first time that the Justice Department had sought to intervene in a case involving FCC's handling of broadcast properties. Traditionally, the courts had recognized that in the regulation of broadcast media considerations other than competition should also prevail in the general public interest. For exmple, in the case of FCC v. RCA Communications, Inc., the court agreed with FCC that "encouragement of competition as such has not been considered the single or controlling reliance for safeguarding the public interest." 346 US 86 (1953).

The commission's vote was four to three, with Commissioners Bartley, Cox, and Johnson dissenting.

Promptly following the commission's decision, the Justice Department, in a Petition for Reconsideration, asked the FCC to review its decision and to hold a full and evidentiary hearing (which had not been done earlier) and to permit the Antitrust Division to participate as a party.[12] The department hinted that if the FCC did not reopen the case, it might bring suit under Section 7 of the Clayton Act to nullify the merger on anticompetitive grounds.[13]

On February 1, 1967, the FCC ordered ABC and ITT to delay the merger until a reconsideration hearing had been conducted.[14] The companies called the department's intervention an "unprecedented attack" on the commission's competence and urged the FCC to reject the department's allegations.[15] The FCC said that the delaying action was taken because of the unique status of the Justice Department and the particular nature of the case but pointed out that this procedure set no precedent whatsoever. The commission further indicated that Justice would have to supply it with documentary evidence to support its charges.[16]

The commission held a thirteen-day hearing during April 1967, in which the Justice Department was a party. The commission again approved the merger on June 22 and the vote was again four to three with the same dissenters.[17]

Subsequent to this second approval, the Justice Department appealed the case to the United States Court of Appeals in Washington, and the unlikely happened: the U.S. (Justice), as it were, was opposing the U.S. (FCC) in a court case.[18] Prior to a court decision, however, ITT withdrew from the ABC merger agreement on New Year's Day, 1968.[19] The merger agreement had given either party the right to cancel after New Year's Eve. ITT exercised this option because it felt that terminating the

[12] *Order on Petition for Reconsideration,* February 1, 1967, p. 4.

[13] *ABC-ITT Merger Proceedings,* Part I.

[14] "Dissenting Opinion of Commissioners Robert T. Bartley, Kenneth A. Cox, and Nicholas Johnson," *The ABC-ITT Merger Case Reconsideration,* Federal Communications Commission, June 22, 1967, p. 135.

[15] Eileen Shanahan, "Merger Defended by ITT and ABC," *The New York Times,* February 24, 1967, p. 1.

[16] *Order on Petition for Reconsideration,* February 1, 1967, pp. 3–4.

[17] *The ABC-ITT Merger Case Reconsideration,* June 22, 1967, Sec. 2, pp. 137–138.

[18] "ITT-ABC Merger Is Held Up by Federal Court," *The New York Times,* July 22, 1967, p. 53.

[19] Jack Gould, "ITT Calls Off ABC Merger Bid," *The New York Times,* January 2, 1968, p. 1.

merger would best serve the interest of its stockholders as the stock price of ABC had tremendously risen during the long delays plaguing the merger. The potential cost to ITT of the merger had risen from $380 million to $660 million.[20]

Some Key Issues

It would be impossible to present all the issues involved in the proposed merger, but some of the most important are discussed below.

During the first hearing, the majority of the commission was of the opinion that since ITT and ABC were not competitors in any market, the merger would not increase the concentration of control in the broadcasting industry, hence it would not have anticompetitive effects. Indeed the merger would benefit the public interest for three reasons. First, the increased financial resources available to ABC through ITT would result in better programming. ABC's financial need was great. Although NBC and CBS had been very profitable operations, ABC had been in the red for the past four years. Second, ABC stated that more cash would better its competitive position with respect to the other networks, and ITT promised to help in this area. Third, ITT had decided to attempt to make technological advances in UHF broadcasting, an area that would help the network to be more competitive with CBS and NBC.

Some observers felt that one reason for ABC's enthusiasm for the merger was the fear that a prominent industrialist, Norton Simon, was attempting to take control of the company. Simon had begun buying ABC stock in March 1964, and by July 1964 he was the largest single stockholder with 9 percent of the company's outstanding stock. It was rumored that he wanted a seat on the network's board of directors. Speculation abounded that ABC wanted to merge (which would dilute Simon's ownership percentage) to prevent his control of the company.[21]

Both the Justice Department and the dissenting commissioners raised another issue. The original hearing had consisted of only two days of oral hearings before the commission *en banc*, and not before an examiner who customarily heard the arguments. The FCC felt this to be a more direct and public way to study the issues. However, the antagonists said that the commission had "failed to conduct the type of full hearing required by the

---

[20] "A Broken Engagement for ITT and ABC," *Business Week*, January 6, 1968, p. 24. It is not obvious that those objecting to the merger will be completely satisfied as ABC is still merger minded. Wall Street matchmakers have suggested Xerox, Singer, Litton Industries, and Sears Roebuck as possible suitors for the network.

[21] *ABC-ITT Merger Proceedings*, Part I, pp. 8–13; Part IV, pp. 15–17.

Federal Communications Act of 1934"[22] and had not given sufficient warning for those opposed to the merger to prepare their arguments. Indeed, no opposing arguments were made.[23]

The antagonists felt that the merger would eliminate ITT as a potential independent entrant into broadcasting. They said that ITT was one of the relatively few firms with the resources, technical capability, interest, and incentive likely to make a significant contribution to diversification in broadcasting and to activities directly competitive with broadcasting. The merger would reduce the likelihood of such occurring. It was said that ITT had been considering entering the broadcasting industry prior to the merger agreement. Without the merger, the argument ran, ITT would have entered TV broadcasting on a significant scale.[24]

The same argument was said to apply to ITT's CATV and Pay-TV efforts. If the merger were approved, ITT would probably drop its efforts in this area as CATV would conflict with ABC's broadcasting aspirations.[25] That is, the company would have an interest in the *status quo* technology and would be less interested in research and development aimed at promoting Pay-TV and CATV. Merger opponents rejected this on the grounds of ABC's financial needs. They said that open-market financing was available and that despite ABC's rapid approach to the debt limit, the limit could probably be extended. Furthermore, ABC's deficient performance was not due to insufficient funds but to operational difficulties.[26] Finally the opposition accused ABC and ITT officials of making misleading and erroneous statements and of lacking general candor while testifying.[27]

The commission majority replied that ITT's decision to merge with ABC came *after* its decision not to enter the broadcasting industry and *after* it had begun moving out of CATV. In addition, the majority held that there were "hundreds" of other companies capable of doing valuable

[22] *Ibid.*, Part I, p. 4. According to dissenting Commissioner Johnson, the commission was not originally planning to hold hearings at all as the outcome had "been a foregone conclusion." Only Commissioner Bartley's insistent request for "a full evidentiary hearing" led to the compromise "oral hearing" [Part IV, p. 2].

[23] Department of Justice, *Proposed Conclusions and Brief*, May 29, 1967, p. 82. See also *ABC-ITT Merger Proceedings*, Part IV, Sec. 2, pp. 68–70.

[24] *Ibid.*, p. 87. See also *The ABC-ITT Merger Case Reconsideration*, June 22, 1967, pp. 43–47.

[25] CATV, or Cable TV, transmits programs by telephone wires rather than by air and usually increases the number of stations available to a particular area. James Ridgeway, "The Voice of ITT," *The New Republic*, July 8, 1967, pp. 17–19.

[26] *The ABC-ITT Merger Case Reconsideration*, Sec. 2, June 22, 1967. See also *Proposed Conclusions and Brief, op. cit.*, April 29, 1967.

[27] *The ABC-ITT Merger Case Reconsideration*, Sec. 2.

research and development in broadcasting technology and that the merger would induce ITT to do research that might benefit ABC.[28]

The three commissioners who wrote the minority opinion disputed ITT's statement that it had decided not to enter the broadcasting industry, citing an offer the company had made to an independent television station. Also, if the merger were allowed, ITT would pursue research in general broadcasting which could help ABC, but it probably would not do research on Pay-TV and CATV, media competitive with ABC's general broadcasting. On the other hand, if the merger were prohibited, ITT would be one of the most likely contributors to Pay-TV and CATV technology.[29] Also, ABC should not look to ITT for help with its cash flow problem as ITT documents had projected a net cash flow *from* ABC to the parent company.[30]

THE ABC-ITT MERGER AND THE INDEPENDENCE OF THE NEWS MEDIA

The primary issue of this case, and indeed one of the primary issues of the merger agreement, was the degree of autonomy that ABC would maintain as a wholly owned subsidiary of ITT. ABC President Goldenson, in an interdepartmental letter sent before the agreement, stated:

> While I cannot at this time discuss the details of these continuing negotiations, I thought you would like personally to know that a prerequisite of any proposed merger, as far as I am concerned, will be the continued autonomous management and operation of American Broadcasting Companies, Inc., and its divisions and subsidiaries.[31]

ABC later won assurances from ITT that it would remain autonomous under its present management and Goldenson's leadership. Doubts were expressed, however, that ITT President Geneen would stand idly by as a titular head of "that third network" after a record of wanting the top position in everything he did.[32] Shortly after the agreement was made,

---

[28] "Opinion and Order on Petition for Reconsideration," *The ABC-ITT Merger Case Reconsideration*, Federal Communications Commission, Washington, D.C., June 22, 1967, Sec. 1, pp. 14, 38.

[29] *The ABC-ITT Merger Case Reconsideration*, June 22, 1967, Sec. 2, pp. 13–14, 43–45.

[30] *ABC-ITT Merger Proceedings*, Part IV, p. 10.

[31] Gene Smith, "Defines Merger Proposal," *The New York Times*, December 3, 1965, p .55.

[32] Gene Smith, "New Role Looms for IT&T Chief," *The New York Times*, December 3, 1965, Sec. 3, p. 1.

Wall Street observers anticipated "that the strong personalities of Mr. Geneen and Mr. Goldenson will clash and that the ITT image will intrude heavily into ABC, particularly in programming."[33]

In any case, the merger agreement provided that ABC would retain its own independent board of directors and management, with some cross representation on the two boards, for at least three years. During those three years, however, matters of major ABC importance were to be submitted to the ITT board before becoming effective.[34]

The FCC Majority Opinion

The majority opinion in the FCC's first ruling of December 1966 pointed out that the key issue of the proposed merger was whether the extensive business interests of ITT might influence ABC's broadcasting activities, and particularly whether there would be any commercial influence on the journalistic function—the reporting of news and news commentary—or on the selection, scheduling, or treatment of public affairs programming. The majority recognized the large stake our society has in preserving the freedom of broadcast stations and networks from the intrusion of extraneous private economic interests upon programming decisions. Thorough, fearless, and unbiased collection, dissemination, and analysis of news is, they said, crucial to a free society. There is widespread and growing reliance by the public upon broadcast sources of news and news commentary and upon public affairs programming and other kinds of informative programming. They were, therefore, attentive to the positive assurances that both ABC and ITT gave the FCC and the public on this score.

The majority opinion affirmed that the commission's own criteria for freedom of the press would not be violated by the merger because of ABC and ITT's repeated assurances that ABC would operate as a substantially autonomous subsidiary and that ABC's operations as a broadcasting licensee would not be affected by the commercial, communications, or other similar interests of ITT. Both ITT and ABC officials were examined at length on this matter, and the assurances and representations set forth were considered sufficient guarantee that the autonomy of ABC's news department was not in jeopardy.[35]

[33] Gene Smith, "Personality: The Empire Builder at I.T.T.," *The New York Times*, December 20, 1966, Sec. 3, p. 3.

[34] "Dissenting Statement of Commissioner Robert T. Bartley," Part II, *ABC-ITT Merger Proceedings*, FCC, December 21, 1966, p. 8.

[35] *Ibid.*, Part I, p. 10.

As to the hazard of alien influence on the broadcasting operations of an American subsidiary of ITT, the majority opinion stated that:

> We know from our experience in the regulation of communications that many of our large broadcasting licensees and the two other television networks also have substantial foreign interests, including subsidiary corporations in many countries. We have seen no evidence at any time that any of these foreign interests have influenced any of the programming presented in this country. There is no reason to assume or suspect that any such influence will occur in the case of ITT.
>
> Nothing of which we are aware in the history of ITT's operations abroad or in the United States suggests that it has ever been or would in the future be neglectful of its loyalties or responsibilities as an American company, or that aliens associated in the ownership and management of overseas ITT companies would by some sinister and unexplained means exert influence upon the interests of the United States broadcast public.[36]

The Dissenters

The key difference between the majority and minority opinions was in regard to the *possibility* of dangers resulting from the merger as opposed to the *probability* of such. The minority was concerned with the *"potential* conflict of interest between the business interests which comprise ITT and ABC's broadcasting responsibility to the public, especially in news and public affairs," while the majority was concerned with the *likelihood* of such. This is why dissenting Commissioner Johnson felt that it was ITT and ABC's burden to show that the merger was in the public interest, and not as the majority felt, that any merger is in the public interest unless proof to the contrary is brought forth.

Johnson said:

> ITT as owner of ABC constantly will be faced with the conflict between its profit maximizing goals—indeed obligations to shareholders—which characterize all business corporations, and the duty to serve the public with free and unprejudiced news and public affairs programming. The issue is both whether anything damaging to ITT's interest is *ever* broadcast, as well as *how* it is presented.

The number of such potential conflicts is "endless." How, for example, is ABC to report foreign affairs when 60 percent of ITT's earnings is from

---

[36] *The ABC-ITT Merger Case Reconsideration,* June 22, 1967, Sec. 1, pp. 16–17.

foreign subsidiaries and investments? More specifically, how should ABC report on the possible nationalization of ITT property in foreign countries? (It has occurred in eight countries.) In the past, ITT has encouraged such laws as the Hickenlooper amendment calling for reduction of United States aid in countries not paying for nationalized property. How should ABC News view such laws in the future? How should the network report widespread dissent movements in Brazil if the government outlawed reports favorable to the dissenters? "Would anyone in ABC News be inclined or feel free to propose the show in the first place?," said Johnson. "Would they be able to withstand suggestions from within or without ITT that ABC news' resources might better be used on other assignments?" How should ABC report government defense and space policy when space-related contracts account for 40 percent of ITT's domestic income? Or, how should the network view truth-in-lending legislation while parent ITT operates several finance companies?

The mere promise of ITT officials that they would not interfere with ABC news and public affairs programming was not sufficient, Commissioners Johnson and Bartley asserted. Both Goldenson and Geneen might be out of a job tomorrow, but the corporation would continue. "These assurances are given by men—and we are turning these broadcast properties over to corporations," which would continue to influence the public after present officials were gone.

Even assurances by present management would not guarantee the independence of ABC during their periods in office:

> Subtle pressures on ABC officials to serve ITT interests cannot be eliminated by the most scrupulous adherence to formal independence for ABC and its editorial staff. ABC personnel will, on their own initiative, consider ITT's interests in making programming decisions. Institutional loyalties develop. These are often reinforced by the acquisition of stock in the employing company—now ITT stock, not ABC. And most important, it will be impossible to erase from the minds of those who make the broadcasting decisions at ABC that their jobs and advancement are dependent on ITT.[37]

With awareness of ITT's foreign interests, even the most conscientious news official would be less objective than he would be if ABC remained unaffiliated, and he would not forget that his future in the company could be affected by his handling of ITT-sensitive issues. Thus, the threat was less that items would be filmed, killed, or slanted, as that ideas or new coverage would never even be proposed. It was also possible that materials

---

[37] All these quotations will be found in *ABC-ITT Merger Proceedings*, Part IV, pp. 6, 18, 20–22, 24–29. See also Part II, p. 4.

would be considered that were in essence simply public relations pieces for ITT or its interests. These were real threats, but the more probable abuse was that newsmen might overcompensate by stressing or suppressing developments embarrassing to ITT. Whichever way the programming leaned, the public would suspect that ITT interests governed ultimate selections. "The risks which this suggests are of a kind that should be taken only with the greatest caution and only with a showing of extraordinarily compelling countervailing benefits."[38]

Johnson added that ITT is like most companies that spend "vast sums to influence its image and its economic relations—through advertising, public relations, and Washington representation."

Are we to accept, on the parties' own self-serving assurances, that although ITT may continue to exert pressure as an advertiser on the programming of CBS and NBC, it will exert none as an owner on the programming of ABC?

I am afraid I must concede that the assurances we have been provided—that ITT will be totally oblivious to the image created for it by its own mass media subsidiary, ABC—simply strain my credibility beyond the breaking point.

It seems elementary to me that the only real way to find adequate safeguards for the public's interest in programming integrity is to give attention to the structure of the industry, not to assurances, albeit sincere, of interested parties who may be gone tomorrow.

[Thus] the best we can do is to try to provide as much insulation as possible for the industry's programming from extraneous economic considerations. The worst we can do is to encourage mergers like this, which expose businessmen to the daily temptation to subvert the high purpose and indispensable role of the broadcast media in a free society.[39]

Bartley, who agreed with Johnson that industry *structure* was paramount, in his dissent referred to other cases in which nonbroadcast corporate interests have intruded into broadcast operations. For example, RCA-NBC exerted pressure on Westinghouse to "swap stations in Cleveland and Philadelphia so RCA could have an outlet in Philadelphia where its laboratories were located."[40] Bartley concluded that "as bankers think like bankers, I believe we can expect that corporate conglomerates will think

[38] "Dissenting Opinion of Commissioners Robert T. Bartley, Kenneth A. Cox, and Nicholas Johnson," *The ABC-ITT Merger Case Reconsideration*, Federal Communications Commission, Washington, D.C., June 22, 1967, p. 85.

[39] *ABC-ITT Merger Proceedings*, Part IV, pp. 28, 30.

[40] *Business Week*, January 6, 1968, p. 14.

like corporate conglomerates rather than like objective professional broad-casters."

The majority did not feel structure to be that critical, as it did not

. . . treat the matter as closed. It demands "eternal vigilance" by all broadcast licensees and will receive our continuing scrutiny for indication that our reliance upon the assurances and safeguards set out on this record was not warranted.[41]

To the majority's promised scrutiny, Bartley retorted:

What tools do they have to make the vigilance meaningful? . . . Such policing would be a near impossibility. When such eternal vigilance demands our continuing scrutiny of the particular situation, I believe the better course is to protect the public interest by not allowing it in the first place.

The majority pointed out, however, that since the beginning of broad-cast licensing, the commission had licensed enterprises involved in a vast number of activities. Proposals excluding particular business interests (such as those in foreign countries) could not now be adopted unless they were applied to other cases, which would require the FCC to restructure the broadcasting industry, in turn requiring the FCC to refuse to renew licenses held by other networks and by numerous large conglomerate corporations. The majority said that such actions would not be in the public interest. But Bartley was suggesting this restructuring of the indus-try when he said, "This merger presents the Commission with the very basic and fundamental question of whether licenses should be granted to corporations involved in business other than broadcasting."

ITT Pressure on News Media

In April 1967, the FCC held hearings on the Justice Department's re-quest for a reconsideration of the merger. During these hearings, ABC President Goldenson testified that the president of ABC-News would still have unquestioned authority over news programming and his decisions "wouldn't have to be cleared with anybody."[42] ITT President and Chair-man Geneen testified before the commission that his company had "abso-

---

[41] All the quotations will be found in the following sequence in *ABC-ITT Merger Proceedings*, Part II, p. 4; Part I, p. 10; Part II, p. 13; Part I, p. 18; Part II, p. 14.

[42] Fred L. Zimmerman, "Managing the News?," *The Wall Street Journal*, April 17, 1967, p. 18.

lutely no intention of interfering in any way with the content of news programs" on ABC. The "composition and status" of ABC's board of directors would be unique among ITT subsidiaries, and present "operating personnel and general policies" would be continued. Geneen said, "We have considerable confidence in ABC's management or we wouldn't have entered into the merger."

This confidence in ABC's management, it turned out, was not unconditional. Geneen's original position was that, as a member of ABC's new board and executive committee, he would refrain from voting on matters likely to involve conflict of interest. However, the *Wall Street Journal* reported that Geneen, under pressure by an FCC attorney, admitted "it would be his duty to vote on all matters before ABC's board or executive committee." ITT would have the final say in the network's programming and selection of ABC directors. Geneen also said other "matters of major importance" would need his company's approval.[43]

Only a few days after Geneen testified that his company would not unduly influence ABC's news programming, an article in the *Wall Street Journal* quoted three reporters who said ITT officials had requested them to alter news stories in various ways. The article gained wide publicity for the issue of freedom of the press in the proposed merger.

The *Journal* Article

The *Wall Street Journal* article of April 17 quoted one reporter as saying, "It's incredible that guys like this want the right to run ABC's news operation." This criticism was in response to an ITT representative's complaint to the reporter's editor about his articles.[44]

A public relations official of ITT said, "We've been dissatisfied with some of the coverage. . . . Some of it has been incomplete and unfair." Indeed, by late February, various company officials had complained about the coverage of the *New York Times*, the Associated Press, United Press International, the *Wall Street Journal*, and the *Washington Post*. According to the *Wall Street Journal*:

> The complaints were made through calls and letters to reporters and editors, and at meetings with editors here [Washington, D.C.] and in New York. Occasionally factual inaccuracies were alleged, but more often the complaints were that reporters weren't writing bal-

---

[43] "ITT Says Its Control of ABC Won't Alter Network's News Policy," *The Wall Street Journal*, April 17, 1967, p. 3.

[44] Zimmerman, "Managing the News?," p .18.

anced accounts or were obtaining information from unreliable sources.

Eileen Shanahan, who had been covering the proposed ITT-ABC merger for the *New York Times*, said that in January two ITT officials came to see her to complain about an article and to suggest "in imperious tones" that the *New York Times* carry the full text of a long FCC order issued that day. Later on, a third ITT representative telephoned her, criticizing an article and saying that the subject matter "wasn't worth a story." Miss Shanahan said, "He questioned my integrity and that of the *Times*." The official in question, in denying Miss Shanahan's allegations, said he only "objected to one or two sentences."

Morton Mintz of the *Washington Post* found ITT's Public Relations Department's actions "rather unusual" when they first called him in November 1966 to suggest that he cover a certain congressman's speech which was expected to be favorable to the merger. Mintz replied that he was busy and did not intend to cover the speech. At that point the ITT representative asked to speak to the editor and executive vice-president of the *Post* who, however, never mentioned this to Mintz.

A UPI reporter said he was subject to "an obvious economic threat" from ABC, a big customer of the press service's radio and television news reports, after various stories he wrote concerning the merger appeared. Jed Stout, another reporter from UPI, said that John Horner, Washington, D.C., director of news media relations for ITT, telephoned him and cited a *Wall Street Journal* article dated February 6, which stated that the Justice Department would bring ITT to court if the FCC did not rule against the proposed merger. Stout said, "As I interpreted it he was asking me to write a story 'knocking down' the Journal piece. I declined to do so."[45]

The night that the FCC announced another delay of the ITT-ABC merger to hold further hearings regarding the Justice Department's evidence, a Washington-based AP reporter, Stephen M. Aug, was dictating the story over the phone. As he was in the middle of his sixth paragraph he was told that ABC had seen the story over the AP wires and had called from New York requesting he change his first paragraph.[46] Network officials wanted the paragraph changed from the FCC "ordered" a delay in the merger to the FCC "suggested" a delay. Aug refused to change the wording.[47]

[45] *Ibid.*; see also "ITT Inquiry Calls Three Reporters," *The New York Times*, April 20, 1967, p. 28.

[46] Zimmerman "Managing the News?," p. 18; see also Fred P. Graham, "3 Reporters Allege Pressures by ITT about Their News Coverage of Its Merger Plan with ABC," *The New York Times*, April 21, 1967, p. 45.

[47] Graham, *op. cit.*

REACTION TO THE *Wall Street Journal* ARTICLE

Two days later, on April 19, the Justice Department requested the FCC to subpoena three of the reporters quoted in the article, Messrs. Aug and Stout, and Miss Shanahan, to "explore matters raised by a *Wall Street Journal* article Monday, reporting on efforts to affect press coverage of these proceedings and the independent news judgment" of these reporters and their organizations.[48] According to the department such "alleged pressure" might be improper[49] and might be related to the company's promise not to interfere with ABC news coverage.[50] The FCC chief examiner complied with the department's wishes.[51] Also, an FCC Broadcast Bureau attorney said the bureau intended to call on John Horner, the ITT official mentioned in the article, to testify before the commission concerning his reported activities.[52]

The reporters were reluctant to give information to other reporters until after their testimony. Miss Shanahan did say, however, that the *Journal* article was "correct, as far as it went—there was more."

Horner issued a statement saying:

> . . . we have made no effort to manage the news. We at ITT believe wholeheartedly in the right of free speech and we have the greatest respect for members of the press and other news media. Historically, the company has been able to communicate its views to the press without any difficulty.
>
> As a publicly held company, we regard it as our duty to supply the fullest information possible on news stories and when occasional errors occur, to assist correspondents in correcting the record. In so doing over many years, we have enjoyed excellent cooperation from the media.

The day the subpoenas were issued, James Hagerty, an ABC vice-president who had been President Eisenhower's press secretary, said it would be "impossible" for ITT to influence ABC news coverage—and "if it did I would resign."[53]

---

[48] "Reporters Are Subpoenaed for Hearing on ABC-ITT," *The Wall Street Journal*, April 20, 1967.

[49] *The New York Times*, April 20, 1967, p. 28.

[50] Graham, "3 Reporters Allege Pressures by ITT," p. 45.

[51] *The New York Times*, April 20, 1967, p. 28.

[52] *The Wall Street Journal*, April 20, 1967.

[53] *The New York Times*, April 20, 1967, p. 28.

The Reporters Testify

The three reporters testified at hearings held on April 20. Stout of UPI added greater detail to the allegations made in the *Wall Street Journal* article of April 17.[54] He said Mr. Horner had talked to him in February about the *Journal* article of February 6 and had asked him about the *Journal's* sources of the rumor that the Justice Department would probably challenge the merger in court if the FCC approved it. The article was not free to name the officials who had given the information. Stout, who regularly covered the Justice Department, said at the hearings that Horner "asked me to make inquiries in the Department of Justice as to whether or not this decision [to go to court] had [actually] been made." Stout refused Horner[55] and told the FCC he had never before received such a request.[56]

ITT had already complained to the *Wall Street Journal* about the February 6 article. The *Journal* said of the complaint that

Mr. Horner said then that it was a "speculative story" and that it didn't seem right for the Journal to print "speculative" stories.

He said the Journal shouldn't write stories having an adverse effect on the stock market. He noted that ABC stock had dropped $4.50 a share the day after the article was printed. The same day, however, ITT common stock rose $1.625 a share.

ITT succeeded in getting the Justice Department to send the company a telegram stating that a decision hadn't been made on whether to take the case to court. ITT itself promptly issued the telegram to the press. But a Justice Department official told the Journal privately that the telegram to ITT shouldn't be construed as a denial of the Journal's report.

Mr. Stout said that Horner telephoned him again concerning the *Journal* article, calling its author a "hipshooter" and saying "there had been a great deal of inaccurate reporting on the merger." Also, Stout's own reporting came under fire. On February 3, two of his superiors discussed his "choice of words" in a story concerning the merger proposal. They explained to him that "there have been complaints received from officials of

[54] Graham, "3 Reporters Allege Pressures by ITT," p. 45.

[55] "Reporters Tell FCC That ITT, ABC Tried to Influence Press Coverage of Merger," *The Wall Street Journal*, April 21, 1967, p. 10.

[56] Graham, "3 Reporters Allege Pressures by ITT," p. 45.

ABC about the accuracy of the story." The reporter's superiors told him the phrase in question was not accurate.[57]

Miss Shanahan testified that ITT representatives had contacted her five or six times. During one brief encounter, an official, whose identity the reporter did not remember, talked to her of a recent development in the merger case favorable to ITT saying, "I expect to see that in the paper, high up in your story."[58]

On February 1, at about 8 p.m., Edward Gerrity, senior ITT vice-president for public relations, and another ITT official delivered a company statement to Miss Shanahan's office.[59] According to the reporter, Gerrity indirectly requested to see the story Shanahan was then writing, which she thought he should have known was "an improper thing to ask a reporter." He asked if her paper was going to run the text of a recent FCC statement criticizing the Justice Department for being late with its evidence in the case. Shanahan thought that document insufficiently important, but Gerrity asked in an "accusatory and certainly nasty" tone, "you mean you did not even recommend the use of text?" Shanahan said, "He badgered me again to play up favorable developments in the case." Gerrity also inquired if she had been following the stock market prices of ITT and ABC. Shanahan told him she had not[60] and later told the commission that "he asked if I didn't feel I had a responsibility to shareholders who might lose money from what I wrote. . . . I told him no.[61] . . . My responsibility was to find out the truth and print it."[62]

Gerrity then asked if she was aware "that Commissioner Nicholas Johnson was working with some people in Congress on legislation that would forbid any newspaper from owning any broadcast property."[63] (The *New York Times* owns an AM-FM radio station in New York.) When she told him she was unaware of such a bill he replied, "I think this is some information you should pass on to your publisher before you write any more about Commissioner Johnson's opinions."[64]

During the hearings the *Times* reporter identified one of the congressmen alleged to be working with Johnson as Senator Gaylord Nelson of

[57] *The Wall Street Journal*, April 21, 1967, p. 10.

[58] *The ABC-ITT Merger Case Reconsideration*, June 22, 1967, Sec. 2, p. 29.

[59] *Ibid.*; see also *The Wall Street Journal*, April 21, 1967, p. 10.

[60] *The ABC-ITT Merger Case Reconsideration*, pp. 29–30. See also Graham, "3 Reporters Allege Pressures by ITT," p. 45.

[61] *The Wall Street Journal*, April 21, 1967, p. 10.

[62] *The ABC-ITT Merger Case Reconsideration*, June 22, 1967, Sec. 2, p. 30.

[63] *Ibid.*

[64] *The Wall Street Journal*, April 21, 1967, p. 10.

Wisconsin.[65] In response to this testimony the FCC later issued a statement saying:

> Commissioner Johnson will have no statement to make on this charge, at this time, while the merger case is under consideration by the Commission. Neither Mr. Johnson nor any other official Commission spokesman has ever talked with any person at any time about legislation prohibiting newspaper ownership and no change in that policy is now under consideration.[66]

Johnson later personally denied "collaboration" with Nelson, and Nelson denied ever having met Johnson.[67] According to the July 8, 1967 issue of the *New Republic*, *Variety* discovered that ITT public relations officials had given the same story about Senator Nelson to reporters for the *Milwaukee Journal* which owns a radio and TV station. The newspaper, however, discovered that the ITT information was incorrect.[68]

According to the reporter's testimony, later in February the Justice Department filed its report with the FCC and Miss Shanahan wrote an article on the department's evidence.[69] John Horner then told her that her coverage of the merger "has been unfair right from the beginning."[70] According to Horner the most objectionable part of her recent story was her statement that the department would take the merger to the courts if the FCC did not reopen its hearings. Horner said the department "had issued a statement saying that it would not go to court." The Times reporter asked him to read her that statement which she testified only said that "the Department had not decided what it would do if the Commission refused to reopen the hearing." When she said that he had "improperly characterized" the statement, Horner again told her her reporting was unfair, a remark that angered her. According to her colleagues, she yelled at Horner[71] that he had insulted not only her but also her editors and she hung up the phone.[72] Miss Shanahan then called the Justice Department and inquired about the statement Horner had read to her over the phone. As it turned out, such a "statement" had never been

65 *The ABC-ITT Merger Case Reconsideration*, Sec. 2, June 22, 1967.
66 *The Wall Street Journal*, April 21, 1967, p. 10.
67 *The ABC-ITT Merger Case Reconsideration*, Sec. 2, June 22, 1967.
68 Ridgeway, "The Voice of ITT," pp. 17–19.
69 *Ibid.*, p. 31.
70 *The Wall Street Journal*, April 21, 1967, p. 10.
71 *The ABC-ITT Merger Case Reconsideration*, Sec. 2, June 22, 1967.
72 *The Wall Street Journal*, April 21, 1967, p. 10.

released—the information was a private communication to the company from the department.

Continuing her testimony, Miss Shanahan said that during one of the commission's earlier hearings she had missed a brief portion of the testimony. Upon her return Horner informed her of what she had missed. He supposedly told her, in an "insistent and nasty" tone, that "I expect to see headlines just as big on this one as on what happened the other day,"[73] presumably referring to an article that Horner considered unfavorable.[74] Miss Shanahan said a similar incident had only happened once in her five years with the *Times*.[75] Her editor, she said, also told her that this was uncharacteristic of the paper's previous contacts with the company.[76]

Prelude to Decision

During the April 20 hearings, ITT counsel attempted to question the reporters about their sources within the Justice Department,[77] on the grounds that the company was "entitled to show that the Department of Justice has had conversations with the press [also]. This bears directly on ITT's efforts to get two-sided coverage." However, the hearing examiner sustained a Justice Department objection of immateriality.[78] The ITT lawyer himself then objected on the grounds that ITT and ABC were being denied their right of free speech in getting their side of the merger to the public while secret government sources were allowed to present their own side.

In general, ITT spokesmen would not comment about the testimony after the hearings were over, but James Hagerty of ABC said he accepted Aug's statement that someone from the network had asked him to change a story before it was finished but that the company was unable to determine who made the call.[79]

On April 21, the president of ABC News, Elmer Lower, testified before the commission. In reference to Hagerty's reported statement that he would resign if ITT attempted to influence the network's news policies, Lower said, "I think I would hear about it before Mr. Hagerty did and I

---

[73] *The ABC-ITT Merger Case Reconsideration*, Sec. 2, June 22, 1967.

[74] Graham, "3 Reporters Allege Pressures by ITT," p. 45.

[75] *The ABC-ITT Merger Case Reconsideration*, Sec. 2, June 22, 1967.

[76] Graham, "3 Reporters Allege Pressures by ITT," p. 45.

[77] *Ibid.*

[78] *The Wall Street Journal*, April 21, 1967, p. 10.

[79] Graham, "3 Reporters Allege Pressures by ITT," p. 45.

would be out the door ahead of him." According to Lower, no one of his superiors in the ABC hierarchy had ever exercised any control over the network's news programming, and he did not expect any change in this policy in the future.[80]

Arguments of both sides in the merger case continued until June 2 when ITT concluded its oral arguments with assurances that "the independence of ABC programming from any other ITT commercial or similar interest shall be inviolate."

According to the attorneys for the two companies, the "built in guarantees of independence for ABC news"—sections of the merger agreement and internal policy documents signed by ITT President Harold Geneen—answered "the major issue the Justice Department relies on" in attempting to prevent the merger. Accordingly, any changes in this policy would be communicated to the Commission.[81]

The Justice Department maintained, however, that the commission would not "find it possible to monitor . . . on a day to day basis," ITT's pledge of a hands-off policy.

In answer to questions from the commission, ITT attorneys said that the company's actions regarding attempts to influence the news coverage of the merger hearings "were more than the normal kind of public relations [in] one or two instances" and did not represent company policy.

Commissioner Johnson asked if the FCC could believe that ITT "will follow higher principles with ABC," with whom it had economic influence, than with reporters such as those covering the FCC hearings, over whom it had no control. ITT counsel replied that the company now had "a greater sensitivity and a greater awareness" of the need for a free press.[82]

FCC's "Reconsidered" Opinion[83]

On June 22 the FCC announced its decision to allow the merger. The commission agreed with ABC News President Elmer Lower that the greater financial resources available to ABC if the merger took place "would increase, rather than decrease, the independence of the news

[80] "A.B.C. Station Aid on Merger Urged," *The New York Times*, April 22, 1967, p. 36.

[81] "ITT Gives Pledge on News Policy," *The New York Times* (special), June 3, 1967, p. 63.

[82] *Ibid.*

[83] All quotations in this section will be found in Federal Communications Commission, "Opinion and Order on Petition for Reconsideration," *The ABC-ITT Merger Case Reconsideration*, June 22, 1967, Sec. 1, pp. 30, 31, 34.

gathering organization." Without ITT's finances, the commission stated, the network would not be able to equal the "cultural programming innovation, news and public affairs expansion" necessary to compete with the other two TV networks, CBS and NBC.

The commission added that "news and public affairs programs are not profitable and that the ability of a television network to produce and present such programs depends in large part on its financial prosperity and resources." The majority opinion cited Mr. Fred Friendly, former head of CBS News, as saying that NBC, with the financial strength of RCA behind it, was in a more advantageous position regarding the type of non-profit public service programming it could present and initiate.

Thus since ABC was not as highly profitable as NBC and CBS, "it is obvious that ABC is at a tremendous disadvantage."

> Finally, that the heightening of competition between the networks will serve the public interest needs no exposition. Therefore, based on our knowledge of the industry and the present network situation, we find on the supplemental record that there will be a significant benefit to the public interest in this respect.

In regard to ITT's and ABC's alleged pressuring of news reporters, the commission cited only one instance of improper conduct. In general,

> there is no evidence that either ITT or ABC did any more than ask reporters covering the proceeding to be factually accurate in their reporting. It is clear that there was some difference of viewpoint as to what the significant facts were, and this difference persists among the parties, counsel, reporters, and others concerned with the case. There is no impropriety in approaching the press to inform or to attempt to correct supposed inaccuracies. All of the reporters testified that this is a common, even daily, occurrence for reporters. The Commission's own 'fairness doctrine' is premised on the right to do just this with respect to broadcast reports of news and commentary concerning controversial matters.

Only Gerrity's relating of false information to Miss Shanahan was cited as "improper" and only an "isolated incident."

The majority dismissed Justice's fears of ITT pressure on numerous grounds, including (1) "the Commission's experience with similarly situated enterprises in the industry," (2) "the past performance of both applicants as long time licensees of the Commission," and (3) the fact that "the area of broadcast reporting of news and public affairs is a field in which the Commission has experience and special competence and in which the Department has no special qualifications."

DISSENTING OPINION[84]

Commissioners Bartley, Cox, and Johnson dissented from the FCC majority opinion in the reconsideration. The actions of the two companies with regard to alleged pressuring of news reporters and other incidents

> show the disdain in which ITT holds the Commission, and other persons and institutions in our society, seen as bothersome obstacles in the way of their merger or other ITT design. Such conduct is relevant to the credibility of ITT's self-serving statements generally, and especially its assurances to this Commission of its regard for the integrity and independence of ABC programming decisions and of its sense of responsibility in making commitments to this Commission as a broadcast licensee.

The minority opinion characterized ITT's "treatment and attitude towards the working press reporting these proceedings [as] shocking."

During reporters' testimony before the FCC, it was brought out that ITT public relations men had at various times called reporters at their homes; "Such repeated remonstrances and requests, and the willingness to contact the reporters at home indicate a zealousness which we believe, at least, an unusual evidencing of extraordinary sensitivity to press treatment."

The incident involving Gerrity and Shanahan

> evidences (1) overbearing behavior generally, (2) an insensitivity to the independence of the press, (3) a contempt for the proper functioning of government, (4) either a willingness to engage in deliberate misrepresentations of fact, or incredible naïveté in accepting and spreading unsubstantiated rumor, and (5) an attitude completely accepting the propriety, indeed the inevitability, of news reports reflecting the extraneous economic interests of a reporter's friends or employers.

The conduct of John Horner, ITT's head of PR in Washington, and other officials in pressuring Miss Shanahan regarding the Justice Department "statement"

> demonstrates an abrasive self-righteousness in dealing with the press, a shocking insensitivity to its independence and integrity, a willing-

[84] All quotations in this section will be found in Federal Communications Commission, "Dissenting Opinion of Commissioners Robert T. Bartley, Kenneth A. Cox, and Nicholas Johnson," *The ABC-ITT Merger Case Reconsideration*, June 22, 1967, Sec. 2, pp. 27–29, 31, 33, 34–37, 40.

ness to spread false stories in furtherance of self-interest, contempt for government officials as well as the press, and an assumption that even as prestigious a news medium as The New York Times would, as a matter of course, want to present the news so as to best serve its own economic interests (as well as the economic interest of other large business corporations). Despite this, ITT offered no rebuttal of any of the testimony of Miss Shanahan.

The minority opinion went on to say that it was not clear if the ITT public relations department had acted on its own or "was ordered, encouraged, or merely condoned by the top management of ITT. The least that can be said is that the officials involved presumably thought they were acting in accord with the wishes or policies of top management, or in the interests of the corporation." Indeed, ITT merely characterized the Public Relations Department's behavior as "overzealous," and no apologies or reprimands were made public. Even if public relations was acting outside of company policy (and ITT did not make this clear), "ITT would then be left with the fact that it cannot guarantee ABC's autonomy. If it cannot control its own senior vice president's conduct it has little hope of controlling lesser officials and employees."

The minority opinion also cited previous instances in which ITT allegedly had behaved illegally or improperly. In one, the company acquired an international carrier and transferred control of it from one subsidiary to another, before the required FCC approval, *then* sought the commission's permission to perform an act already accomplished. Another instance was cited in which ITT, even though it had not yet been merged with ABC, used the economic pressure of its advertising accounts to influence other corporations to benefit the network. The behavior of ITT lawyers during the supplementary hearings was also characterized as "high-handed," and reference was made to a company lawyer's telephoning a Justice Department witness

and, in a two-hour conversation, tried to get him to change three sentences in the testimony which he was proposing to give. On cross examination, when asked if he felt he had been pressured, his first reaction was: "It depends, I am fairly tough, but two hours on a telephone, you know. I don't know. You can interpret that in your own way."

The opinion cited the chief hearing examiner's characterization of ITT lawyers' behavior as "improper" when they were delivering notes to witnesses who had not yet testified and who were excluded from the hearing room by order of the examiner himself. ABC lawyers were also accused of proffering witnesses with "positively misleading information" and making no attempt to set the record straight.

In regard to ITT's behavior with respect to the news media and FCC witnesses, the three commissioners said:

> ITT officials performed these acts and displayed these attitudes in a period which should have been filled with incentive for the most exemplary behavior because of the company's assurances about ABC's freedom from news management and pressure. Certainly it is likely that never again will there be such a depth and immediacy of public scrutiny of ITT's posture in this regard. Yet, with full knowledge of this public attention, ITT not only failed to match its assurances about the future with its deeds of the present, but actually conducted itself in a deliberate manner that gives these assurances a distinctly hollow ring. If ITT behaved this way with the spotlight on it, how much credibility can be given to assurances that ITT would not be led to similar conduct when the pressures, subtle and overt, can be transmitted with a minimum of visibility and accountability? It is not unreasonable, therefore, to believe that ITT would evidence similar disdain for ABC as a press medium, whether arising from such misguided managerial élan or conflicting business goals inherent in its conglomerate and international operations.
>
> In our view, this recurrent conduct on the part of ABC and ITT officials and attorneys has gone far beyond the bounds of natural prejudice and advocacy. The examples are far more numerous than we have recited. . . . We cite this deeply disturbing pattern of behavior because we believe it makes it impossible to approach the self-serving testimony of applicants' officials with anything but skepticism. And it is that testimony which constitutes a major part of the majority's "justification" for this merger.

SHADES OF RALPH NADER

On July 8, the New York Times and the New Republic reported Eileen Shanahan as saying that John V. Horner had been making inquiries about her "professional and personal life."

> She said that three different persons, two of them her former employers, had told her of the inquiries and that in one of the cases she had been told that Mr. Horner had made a telephone call whose sole purpose was to inquire about her.[85]

[85] (Special to The New York Times), "Reporter on Times Says ITT Made Inquiries about Her," The New York Times, July 8, 1967, p. 22.

After hearing from the second person approached, Miss Shanahan contacted ITT's counsel for the FCC hearing and "demanded that the investigation be stopped." The attorney called her the next day and said that he did not think there had ever been a "systematic investigation" and that no further inquiries would be made anyway. According to Horner, there was, and there had been, no investigation. He admitted that Miss Shanahan's name might have come up in "normal chitchat" with people, but no inquiries were made that were not "entirely normal, clean and above board." Horner said he "couldn't say" if he had contacted her former employers as "I don't know who her former employers were."[86]

On September 7, the *New Republic* said that ITT had been investigating, through third parties, the personal life of James Ridgeway whose articles in that magazine had been critical of the proposed merger.[87] One of the third parties was James Mackey, a researcher for *Army Times* of Washington, D.C. According to the *New Republic*, Mackey called the magazine's offices and asked

> what sort of articles did [Ridgeway] write, how often did they appear, how long had he worked there. . . . What was his height and weight, what restaurants did he frequent, did he drink, was he married, . . . was his wife a reporter. Did she help out with his work, was he friendly with the other employees (Does he say good morning), did the editor care much for him and so on.

Later on, Mackey said that one of ITT's advertising agencies had asked him to "find out anything, everything I could about a guy named James Ridgeway." Mackey had never done this before, but his newspaper depended heavily on its advertisers and wanted to please their ad agencies.

Ridgeway questioned Mackey who replied, "This is all above board as far as I know. Gee, don't think your name is Ralph Nader or anything like that." An ITT representative told Ridgeway, "We're not conducting any investigation of you, and we have no reason to . . . I don't know anything about the *Army Times*. It seems to me that if you have an argument with somebody, it's them not us."[88]

In a letter in the September 30, 1967 issue of the *New Republic, Army Times* Vice-President William F. Donally said that Mackey "undertook the investigation . . . entirely on his own and without authorization from

---

[86] *Ibid.*

[87] Eileen Shanahan, "Justice Department Disputes Faith Shown by FCC in Its Approval of ITT-ABC Merger Proposal," *The New York Times,* September 8, 1967, p. 30.

[88] "ITT's Press Relations," *The New Republic,* September 16, 1967, pp. 6–7.

Army Times or anyone connected with *Army Times*" and was dismissed for his "incredible behavior."

Donally said it was his opinion that neither ITT "nor anyone else" authorized the investigation. Mackey, according to the vice-president, refused to discuss the matter with his former employer, though the *Times* continued to try to get an explanation from him.

According to Donally, the newspaper was "totally unaware" of Mackey's investigation and had "never done any investigation of any individual for anyone: not for advertisers, not for editors, not for anybody."[89]

JUSTICE RETURNS

Also on September 8, the Justice Department brought the FCC decision to the court of appeals on the grounds that the commission could not insure that ITT would maintain a hands-off policy regarding ABC News if the merger were to take effect. According to the department, any attempt to "enforce" ITT's promise not to influence ABC public affairs and news programs for its own interest was an "impossibility" and "would come dangerously close to the kind of program censorship which is barred by the First Amendment and the Communications Act."[90]

The company also came under fire. "It is plainly absurd to think that the FCC will receive advance written notice [as ITT promised] before ITT tries to kill an ABC documentary or before ABC officials on their own, shelve subjects which would be embarrassing or detrimental to ITT." The Justice Department also challenged the commission's contention that ITT did not differ from RCA as a television network parent company, although RCA had extensive business with foreign countries. Unlike RCA and CBS:

> ITT is, in origin, a foreign operating company and its predominant source of profit overseas is in the sale of telecommunications equipment.
> Since the postal, telephone and telegraph functions in other countries are almost invariably performed by governmental entities, ITT's position in these markets is largely dependent upon its success in dealing with the officials of governmental or quasigovernmental bodies.
> [Thus] ITT could have strong motivation to use a news medium

[89] "The Ridgeway Caper," *The New Republic*, September 30, 1967, p. 36.

[90] All quotations in this section will be found in Shanahan, "Justice Department Disputes Faith Shown by FCC," p. 30.

affirmatively to promote certain of its investments, by showing officials or programs of a foreign government in a favorable light.

Dangers exist in that "internal corporate pressures" and "subtle influences" may result "in avoidance of subject matter, blunting of criticism, the treatment of controversy in a noncontroversial manner, because of the economic interest of the company."

The Justice Department attacked the FCC majority opinion's statement that there was only one "isolated" instance of improper conduct in regard to ITT's pressuring reporters covering the hearings. Indeed, certain activities of ITT officials were "outrageous conduct" and were central to "the very matter" of the Justice Department's worry over "ITT's assuming responsibility for ABC's news and public affairs activities."

The FCC filed its brief with the court of appeals during the first part of October and said the Justice Department erred in its contention that the commission could not enforce ITT's promise that it would not interfere with the network's news and public affairs programming.[91]

The merger was canceled by ITT on January 1, 1968, before the court of appeals had made its decision.

[91] "ITT Scores Suit to Block Merger," *The New York Times*, October 3, 1967, p. 28.

Eastman Kodak Company (B), Rochester, New York

Conflict with a Minority Group—FIGHT: The Role of the News Media

The media report and write from the standpoint of a white man's world. The ills of the ghetto, the difficulties of life there, the Negro's burning sense of grievance are seldom conveyed. Slights and indignities are part of the Negro's daily life, and many of them come from what he now calls the "white press"—a press that repeatedly, if unconsciously, reflects the biases, the paternalism, the indifference of white America. This may be understandable, but it is not excusable in an institution that has the mission to inform and educate the whole of our society.

—Report of the National Advisory
Commission on Civil Disorders (1968)

From the very beginning the news media played an important part in the Kodak–FIGHT controversy. Both protagonists were aware of the role mass media could play in informing and influencing public opinion. The news media were therefore an important variable for Kodak and FIGHT, and the strategies of the two parties were carefully designed to *manipulate* and *use* the media to their best advantage.

Would the Kodak–FIGHT altercation have received national attention had not radio and television, wire services, national newspapers, and magazines covered Stokely Carmichael's visit to Rochester, Minister Florence's

309

press conferences, and the demonstrations at Kodak's annual stockholders' meeting? The news media apparently played an important role in bringing the issue before the public. Furthermore, it is becoming apparent that the media's role in molding public opinion is increasingly critical in similar situations and that all parties to a conflict must consider the media before deciding on a course of action.

The news media are of interest in this case because to some extent they helped to create the news they reported. FIGHT's attempts to make its disagreements with Kodak a nationwide controversy were aided by the media. Several times throughout late 1966 and the first half of 1967, Florence was able to win support among various segments of the American public because he kept the issue at a controversial level. This strategy, to a large degree, accounts for the often bizarre manner in which FIGHT's spokesmen and supporters acted before television cameras to attract public attention. By focusing solely on its sensational aspects, the news media chose to elevate the controversy to a national level and at the same time distorted and exaggerated its impact.

The conflict between Kodak and FIGHT was covered nationwide by the major news services and by national magazines and journals of all types and political persuasions. Although events were reported throughout the controversy, national coverage was heaviest immediately after Kodak repudiated its agreement with FIGHT and at the time of the stockholders' meeting in Flemington, New Jersey.

THE LOCAL NEWS MEDIA[1]

The only English-language daily newspapers in Rochester—the *Democrat & Chronicle* and the *Times-Union*—are both part of the Rochester-headquartered Gannett newspaper chain and are both published by Paul Miller, president of the chain.[2] Before the FIGHT–Kodak controversy

[1] The accounts of coverage by local television and radio stations reported in this section were indirectly obtained through newspaper reports and magazine articles.

[2] Gannett Co., Inc., is a chain of newspapers and radio and television stations located in small and medium-size cities primarily in the northeastern states. It has 30 newspapers (29 owned and one affiliated) with circulation ranging from 6,500 to 218,600. In addition, Gannett owns AM radio and VHF television outlets in Rochester and Birmingham, New York; AM-FM radio outlets in Danville, Illinois, and Cocoa, Florida; and a VHF television outlet in Rockford, Illinois. Of the two Rochester newspapers, the *Democrat & Chronicle* is published mornings and Sundays (circulation 142,794 and 218,586 respectively), and the *Times-Union* is an evening paper (circulation 143,855). See *Ayer Directory of Newspapers and Periodicals, 1967* (Philadelphia: N. W. Ayer and Son, 1968); *Broadcasting Year Book, 1968* (Washington, D.C.: Broadcasting Publications, 1968), p. A-112; *Editor and Publisher Year Book, 1968* (New York: Editor & Publisher Co., 1968), p. 312.

erupted, the Gannett chain had a reputation for progressive thinking and constructive work in the area of civil rights. In 1962, the *Times-Union* published an updated version of a 1960 series under the title "Winds of Revolt," which showed "how badly the Negroes were housed in a city famous for its homes, its trees and lilacs, its culture, its generosity, and its depression proof economy."[3]

In 1963, Paul Miller assigned Gannett's executive director, Vincent Jones, to investigate the different ways Northern cities were coping with racial unrest and urban crisis. More than forty editors and reporters contributed to the investigation, and more than one hundred articles were prepared and distributed within a year, starting in July 1963 under the general title of "The Road to Integration." This series won journalism's highest award, the Pulitzer Prize, the first ever awarded to a group or chain.[4] The same series won a Brotherhood Award from the National Conference of Christians and Jews.

However, when the Board for Urban Ministry invited Saul Alinsky to Rochester, Gannett raised a strong protest. The reaction probably reflected the views of publisher Paul Miller who, since 1966, had led a one-man crusade against FIGHT, church organizations supporting FIGHT, Saul Alinsky, and all other persons sympathetic to FIGHT.

The *Times-Union* and its radio and television affiliate WHEC dispatched a three-man team to Chicago to study the operations of Alinsky's Industrial Areas Foundation in the Woodlawn section of Chicago. The outcome was a three-part series in the paper and two one-hour television documentaries during prime time. According to Vincent Jones,[5] "both sides praised these presentations as objective and informative."

However, neither this series of articles nor the opinions expressed by local clergy changed any minds at Gannett. As Jones put it:

We have tried to keep our feet on the ground and to pursue a moderate, practical policy. . . . The invitation [to Saul Alinsky] was issued by the Council of Churches without first consulting the community. Because of the way it was handled, and a belief that Alinsky's controversial methods would do more harm than good, the *Times-Union* questioned the whole project. It was a moderate editorial stand, but left no doubt of the newspaper's belief that the move was risky at best.[6]

[3] Vincent S. Jones, "How Rochester Reacted," *Nieman Reports*, June 1965, pp. 16–17.

[4] *Ibid.*

[5] *Ibid.*

[6] *Ibid.*

Miller's wrath was directed as much, if not more, against the Rochester Area Council of Churches (RAAC) as it was against FIGHT and Saul Alinsky. According to an article in the *New Republic*:

> At a church breakfast in late 1966, Miller was once more belaboring the ministers for "sneaking" the organization past responsible citizens, and bringing into their midst this "ill-mannered tiger" [Alinsky] to preach "his hate."
> "Rochester, New York, is not Rochester, Alabama," said Miller, who sounds like an undertaker. "We have primarily a refugee problem, not a racial problem." How inappropriate it was, he went on, for church people to cultivate in Negroes the idea that in Rochester as in the South, they must take something away from somebody to make progress. Miller recommended to the ministers an article in the December *Reader's Digest* entitled "Are We a Nation of Hoods?" It provided a valuable perspective on the teachings of Jesus.
> "If the organization you finance be continued," he said, "why not see that it gets a name somewhat less offensive to the total community. How about W-O-R-K instead of F-I-G-H-T, how about L-O-V-E, how about T-R-Y, how about D-E-E-D-S?"[7]

Again in January, Miller made an editorial attack in the *Times-Union* on those of the clergy who had supported FIGHT. The editorial, entitled "The Gulf between Pulpit and Pew—One Layman's View," drew a large number of letters to the editors of both papers, and most of the letters were critical of FIGHT and its supporters. However, it was not so much the letters as how they were headlined that reflected the bias of the editorial staff and management.

The two papers gave extensive coverage to Kodak and generally accorded front-page space to its press releases. Again the titles were invariably pro-Kodak or anti-FIGHT. The newspapers' coverage on FIGHT's activities and its position was small compared to that on Kodak or to that accorded FIGHT by the national news media. This bias was carried further into 1967 when an editorial in the *Democrat & Chronicle* of June 16, 1967, entitled "Council's Defense," derided the attempt of the Rochester Area Council of Churches to defend their support of FIGHT.[8]

Gannett newspapers were not the only media that did not like Alinsky and FIGHT. As noted in part C of the Kodak study (page 324), radio

---

[7] James Ridgeway, "Attack on Kodak," *New Republic*, January 21, 1967, pp. 11–13.

[8] "Alinsky Defends Black Power" and "Kodak Reviews Record on Job Talks with FIGHT," *Rochester Times-Union*, October 24, 1966 and September 21, 1966; "FIGHT Vows New Push for Kodak Jobs," "Kodak Questions FIGHT Job Demands," and "Council's Defense," *Rochester Democrat & Chronicle*, October 26, 1966, September 8, 1966, and June 16, 1967.

WHAM canceled a free hour it had been giving to the RACC. In an editorial attack on the council, reported in the *New Republic*, WHAM said:

> Thinking members of Rochester area churches have admitted many times over that the solution to the plight of any minority cannot be solved overnight—that demands are one thing, but that people do not become economically equal just because the various members of the Christian faith would have it that way. More realistically, members of the human race must prove their capacity to compete and to want to be part of the community.[9]

FIGHT's only local outlet was WBBF, which Kodak people called "the Voice of FIGHT." This station presented FIGHT's publicity releases as news copy and made no attempt to give Kodak's viewpoint to listeners.

Coverage by the wire services and the nationally prominent newspapers was quite extensive, and most leading metropolitan dailies reported the conflict at its various high points, many relying on the wire services for their information. The biggest coverage by the press, radio, and television was accorded the stockholders' meeting. The proceedings of the meeting, the demonstrations outside the auditorium where the meeting was held, and the pronouncements of the spokesmen for Kodak and FIGHT were reported by all of the national television networks, radio stations, and newspapers across the country. The only other occasion when network television cameras visited the scene was to record Stokely Carmichael's visit to Rochester in January 1967.[10] The role of television seems to have been crucial to Minister Florence's strategy. To some extent he was able to use television networks to escalate the issue to national prominence, and he believed that only in this way could he pressure Kodak into conceding FIGHT's demands.

To get a better idea of the emphasis given to the Kodak–FIGHT controversy, it is necessary that we make a detailed analysis of the nature and extent of coverage accorded the incidents by various news media.

The *New York Times*, perhaps the most influential newspaper in the country, was constantly on the scene. Starting with the first FIGHT convention in June 1966, the paper continuously reported the story as it developed. Immediately after Kodak's repudiation of the agreement of December 20, the *Times* published a long article, followed by four more related articles in January 1967 (three in the first week alone), two in

[9] James Ridgeway, "Saul Alinsky in Smugtown," *New Republic*, June 26, 1965, pp. 15–17.

[10] The account of coverage by network radio and television described here was gathered only indirectly through a study of the press reports.

February, nine in April, and three in May. The coverage thereafter declined in quantity but was adequate for reporting all the relevant news.

A close reading of the *Times* coverage reveals certain interesting points. First, the reporting was carefully balanced and "objective." John Kifner, who did most of the reporting, as well as Edward Fiske and M. J. Rossaut, presented opposing views in every story. The captions for different articles were either neutral or balanced to give equal billing. Nevertheless, the complete lack of the interpretive articles or in-depth analyses generally associated with this paper is striking. Not a single editorial was written on the controversy which had vast social implications and had received so much national attention. Moreover, the reporting appeared to be somewhat indifferent, in that it was confined to merely quoting the spokesmen for Kodak and FIGHT. (As will be shown in the following section, the *Wall Street Journal* did the best investigative job of reporting although it printed fewer stories than the *Times*.)

The *Washington Post* presented the other extreme. Nicholas Van Hoffman made no secret of where his sympathies lay. In a long article on January 9, 1967, entitled "Picture's Fuzzy as Kodak Fights FIGHT," he blamed Kodak for a large part of the conflict. In colorful language he suggested that the Kodak management was "out of focus" and hinted darkly that if the situation did not improve soon, "Negroes may again be out on the streets shooting, and not with Brownie Instamatics!"[11]

Among the national news magazines and general periodicals that covered the story at various times were *Time*, *Newsweek*, and *U.S. News and World Report*. Of the three, *Newsweek*'s coverage was more extensive, with sufficient interpretive material to enable readers to see the conflict in its proper perspective. However, there was no expressed opinion by any of the magazines.

In contrast, the national magazines with liberal leanings were full of interpretive articles by well-known writers. The *New Republic* carried two articles by James Ridgeway, "Attack on Kodak" and "Saul Alinsky in Smugtown." The *Reporter* had two articles, one by Barbara Carter entitled "The FIGHT against Kodak" and the other by Jules Witcover entitled "Rochester Braces for Another July." The *Atlantic* had an article by William C. Martin entitled "Shepherds vs. Flocks, Ministers vs. Negro Militancy." While most of these articles listed the contributions made by Kodak to Rochester's civic causes, they minimized their real value in the light of changing social conditions. These authors also faithfully reported Kodak's position but berated its rationale and were generally pro-FIGHT in their writings.

The conservative magazine *National Review*, in an article entitled "The

---

[11] "Picture's Fuzzy as Kodak Fights FIGHT," *Washington Post*, January 9, 1967.

FIGHT-Kodak Fight" by Dorothy Livadas, took a strong pro-Kodak position and largely blamed "the starry-eyed churchmen," Saul Alinsky, and Florence for aggravating racial tension in Rochester. The article implied that most Rochester blacks wanted "no part of FIGHT" and suggested that Saul Alinsky was a man who "capitalized on the plight of the downtrodden and made a hero of himself while exploiting their misery."[12]

In a personal interview, a Kodak public relations executive expressed the conviction that the company's position in the controversy was not being fairly reported in the national press:

> It always makes good copy for David to be throwing a stone at Goliath. If Minister Florence were anywhere in the vicinity, the reporters would go after him to say something and he would take full advantage of this opportunity. . . .
> The problem was primarily local in nature until the stockholders' meeting when, despite the 116 newspaper people present, the national press reported the thing so poorly that most people who read the account that appeared in a local paper hadn't the slightest idea what it was all about except that Kodak was having some trouble with Negroes.

According to an article by Raymond A. Schroth in the magazine *America*, "Kodak officials are still smarting from stories by James Ridgeway in the *New Republic* (January 21, 1967) and by Nicholas Van Hoffman in the *Washington Post* (January 9, 1967), in which Kodak claims to be misquoted."[13] In an interview with Schroth, Kodak spokesmen again repeated this charge.

THE BUSINESS NEWS MEDIA

The Kodak–FIGHT controversy was of special interest to the business community as businessmen all over the country were asking themselves, "Will this happen to my corporation?" Alinsky himself saw Kodak as just the beginning of a pattern of attacks by racial minorities against outmoded corporate behavior.

The business news media covered the controversy extensively as news, provided their readers with in-depth analyses and interpretive articles, and also wrote policy editorials. The opinions of most business magazines ran from sympathy for Kodak to extreme hostility toward FIGHT in terms of both its objectives and its tactics.

---

12 "The FIGHT–Kodak Fight," *National Review*, June 27, 1967, p. 683.
13 "Self-Doubt and Black Pride," *America*, April 1, 1967, p. 502.

The news coverage by the *Wall Street Journal* was perhaps the best of any newspaper in the country. For example, it was the *only* newspaper to report that after the Kodak repudiation, Mr. Florence offered to amend the agreement in any manner acceptable to Kodak or even to scrap it if Kodak officials would jointly announce with him on television their willingness to cooperate with FIGHT "to get more jobs for Negroes."[14] This was indeed an important concession by FIGHT, asking to do only what the company had said all along that it was willing to do. Yet Kodak officials turned down FIGHT's offer.

Why did FIGHT not choose to publicize Kodak's refusal? Florence was desperate after Kodak's repudiation and was probably willing to go to great lengths to salvage at least something from the situation. He might also have realized FIGHT's lack of staying power in a long contest. However, after his turndown Florence kept this incident quiet for fear it would appear to his followers as a "sellout" and would show lack of courage and militancy on his part. Kodak was not interested in publicizing the event because it would make the company look stubborn and unreasonable and would refute all the pro-cooperation propaganda it had been making in public.

The kind of coverage given the Kodak–FIGHT controversy by the business news media is exemplified in some of the story titles and excerpts from these stories:

The *Wall Street Journal*: "Eastman Kodak Accuses Rochester Rights Groups of Pushing for Power," "Kodak Refuses to Restore Negro Job Pact; Rights Group Vows 'War' against Concern," "Eastman Kodak and Negro Group Reach Compact to Work in Harmony," "Kodak's Ordeal: How a Firm That Meant Well Won a Bad Name for Its Race Relations," "Kodak Announces Plan to Help Slum Dwellers Start Own Business."[15]

Business Week: "The Fight That Swirls around Eastman Kodak," "Kodak and FIGHT Agree to Agree," "What the Kodak Fracas Means."[16]

Fortune: "And Kodak Will Ask, 'How High?'" (a reference to Stokely Carmichael's inflammatory statement in his Rochester press conference on January 19, 1967).[17]

Factory: "There's a FIGHT in Kodak's Future."[18]

Barron's National Business and Financial Weekly: "Who's Out of

[14] Earl C. Gottschalk, Jr., "Kodak's Ordeal: How a Firm That Meant Well Won a Bad Name for Its Race Relations," *The Wall Street Journal*, June 30, 1967, pp. 1ff.

[15] *The Wall Street Journal*, January 9, 1967; April 26, 1967, p. 7; June 26, 1967, p. 9; June 20, 1967, pp. 1ff.; November 20, 1967, p. 15.

[16] *Business Week*, April 29, 1967, pp. 38–41; July 1, 1967, p. 22; May 6, 1967, p. 192.

[17] *Fortune*, June 1, 1968, p. 78.

[18] *Factory*, June 1967, p. 69.

Focus? A Note on the Harassment of Eastman Kodak" (an attack on FIGHT and the church organizations supporting FIGHT).[19]

Reviewing Kodak's handling of the situation, *Business Week*[20] commented that after the second meeting, "Kodak was admittedly sidestepping FIGHT's demands. . . . [No] major company could remain union free in New York State, as has Kodak, without considerable skill at evasive tactics." On Kodak's repudiation of the agreement, *Business Week* said: "While the agreement clearly ran counter to what Kodak had insisted all along, disavowing it weakened the company's position." Quoting an executive, the same periodical stated: "At least one executive thinks Kodak's lack of labor negotiating experience explains some of its clumsiness. 'Union negotiating teaches you when your name is on something, you have got an agreement.' "

Fortune, on the other hand, confined itself to quoting Kodak spokesmen and wrote:

> Two days later, Kodak declared that the agreement was "unauthorized" and unacceptable. Chairman William S. Vaughn subsequently issued a statement saying that Mulder . . . had acted "through an overzealous desire to resolve the controversy."[21]

Barron's National Business and Financial Weekly[22] presented the extreme end of the continuum on anti-FIGHT opinion. In an article on May 1, 1967, it stated: "Legally and morally, however, the company could not make the commitment demanded by FIGHT." *Barron's* thought Kodak had a lot to learn about labor relations: "If anything, it has taken not too hard a line, as its radical critics aver, but too soft. The presence on the pay roll of an executive who failed to grasp the elementary principles cited above suggests as much."

Although some of the business magazines recognized the need for change in corporate behavior and suggested more positive action in the area of assistance to minorities, most of them were editorially critical of FIGHT and its supporters.

In an editorial entitled "What the Kodak Fracas Means," *Business Week* called the Kodak–FIGHT conflict the forerunner of similar conflicts. The editorial further stated:

> The demand that Kodak simply put to work whatever Negroes FIGHT produces is preposterous. . . . It is not the business of any

[19] *Barron's National Business and Financial Weekly*, May, 1967, p. 1.

[20] *Business Week*, April 29, 1967, pp. 38–41.

[21] *Fortune*, June 1, 1968, p. 78.

[22] *Barron's*, May 1, 1967, p. 1.

corporate management to run a public welfare establishment. Efficient production of goods and services is the name of the business game. Personnel policies that are violently inconsistent with profitability violate one of the private corporation's cardinal rules. Management must retain its rights to hire, fire, promote, and assign work in ways that serve business objectives.[23]

The editorial urged business to understand and appreciate the objectives of civil rights groups in Rochester—the main objective being blacks—but said that "hiring unskilled Negroes cuts into profits, at least in the short run," and argued that "business must be paid for undertaking what is in the end a public responsibility." It exhorted civil rights groups to abandon their militancy and warned them that like the Wobblies and the Knights of Labor, "they will get nowhere unless they avoid inflicting serious injury on the effective operation of private business in this country. . . . Black Power won't work any better than did labor power, when directed at radical objectives."

In another article *Business Week* commented:

Alinsky—and FIGHT—are intent on using Kodak to press their conviction that corporations must assume more responsibility for the poor in their communities than business customarily takes on. Says Alinsky: "American industry had better recognize—and some do— that they have a special obligation. . . . [The] Kodak situation dramatically reveals that today's ghettobound, militant urban Negro may generate even more problems for business than the civil rights struggle in the South created."

No business would find it easy to keep pace with Alinsky's fast-moving, bare-knuckles style of civil rights campaign. . . .[24]

Kodak's dealings with FIGHT, in fact, starkly dramatize the clash of modern radical black tactics with well-meaning but traditionalist business attitudes.

An editorial in *Fortune* described FIGHT's action at the stockholders' meeting as a harassment and described the Kodak–FIGHT situation so that businessmen would understand "what the battle is really about." The editorial agreed that

Many U.S. industrial corporations are failing to move fast enough to help Negro applicants qualify for employment. No company can be expected to "create instamatic jobs," as Minister Florence has said Kodak should. But in one way or another, industry should try to help

[23] *Business Week*, May 6, 1967.
[24] *Business Week*, April 29, 1967, pp. 38–41.

unskilled and uneducated Negroes who want jobs to qualify for jobs. What makes FIGHT's "war" against Kodak appalling is that Kodak has recognized its obligations here. It is hard to imagine a worse way for Negro organizations to try to beat down employers.[25]

The clergy's desire to support better job opportunities was good, but *Fortune* questioned their use of stock voting proxies to achieve these objectives. However, in the Kodak case, a proxy for FIGHT was not a vote for blacks but a vote for giving FIGHT power. "And that cause imposes no moral claim upon churchmen or businessmen or anybody else."

Barron's rebuked Kodak for its softheadedness in dealing with FIGHT and questioned the logic of the concept of social responsibility for corporations:

The time has also come to do a little soul-searching with respect to corporate responsibility. Companies want to be good citizens, and, by providing jobs, paying taxes and the like, they generally succeed. However, management is the steward of other people's property. It can never afford to forget where its primary obligations lie.

[The] company policy as outlined in a 1966 Management Letter . . . speaks of going beyond selection of the best qualified person, to seeking "to help the individual who lacks the necessary qualifications to become qualified."

More suited to a sociology text than a corporate manual, the Letter adds: "Industry must look less critically at the individual's school record and work experience and more at his potential." Throughout the protracted dispute with FIGHT, Kodak's executives have chosen to ignore repeated provocations, insults and lies, an excessive forbearance which has merely incited their tormentors. In the corporate realm, as in any other, appeasement is a losing game. For Kodak and the rest of U.S. industry, it's time to stop turning the other cheek.

The clergy is in bad company. In taking issue with the employment policies of Eastman Kodak, moreover, the churchmen stand on very shaky ground.[26]

THE RELIGIOUS PRESS

The religious press not only actively participated in informing its audience about the Kodak–FIGHT conflict but also contributed to molding the opinion of the nationwide clergy. Generally speaking, it supported the

[25] *Fortune,* June 1, 1968, p. 78.
[26] *Barron's,* May 1, 1967, p. 1.

stand taken by national church organizations in assisting FIGHT and also supported FIGHT's demands against Kodak.

In an editorial entitled "Economic Leverage of the Churches," *America*, the national Catholic weekly, supported the stand taken by Protestant groups in withholding their proxies from the management of Eastman Kodak and further asserted:

> Anyone who believes that it is morally reprehensible to buy the products of a firm that discriminates against colored workers must hold that passive, uncritical ownership of the firm's securities is also wrong.
>
> It must be admitted, however, that in many cases it simply has not occurred to managers of church funds or purchasing agents to use their economic power for moral goals. Like other investors, they have single-mindedly sought security and a satisfactory rate of return. Similarly, purchasing agents have felt that they discharged their duties when they obtained goods and services at a favorable price.
>
> All this leads one to wonder why a theology of consumption and investment for modern market societies has not been more intensively cultivated. The humbling fact is that before the civil rights movement challenged God-fearing people to practice what they preach, most of us in transacting business performed as economic men. Or, which is nearly as bad, we absentmindedly followed the rule attributed to the late Henry Ford: "Whatever is good business is also good morals."[27]

The *Episcopalian* echoed similar views[28] as did the *United Church Herald*, which commented on the involvement of the churches in the Kodak–FIGHT conflict:

> Nor will the role of the churches in these developments go unnoticed. The Christian community often has been called the conscience of America but seldom has its voice been heard so clearly. Such a role is bound to be controversial—especially when the church challenges the intentions of its own members. But in a nation where the structures of power are increasing rapidly in size and influence, the corporate body of Christ must speak its convictions and may occasionally need to flex its muscles.[29]

The Belgian *Chronicles and Documents* commented in an editorial on the economic wealth of the church and its possible uses:

[27] "Economic Leverage of the Churches," *America*, May 13, 1967, p. 714.
[28] "Church vs. Kodak: The Big Picture," *Episcopalian*, June 1967, pp. 43–44.
[29] "Rare Days in Any Month," *United Church Herald*, August 1967, p. 23.

But, have the Church administrators always been aware of the duties imposed by the possession of this wealth? In countries where the economy rests greatly on private initiative, shouldn't it be necessary that the Church herself show some initiative, and set an example wherever the possession of certain resources gives her the right to be present? The Kodak case shows very clearly the positive role that the ecclesiastic structures could play in a business concern.[30]

The religious press, however, did not unanimously support church involvement in racial problems, issues of job discrimination in general, and FIGHT in particular.

The *Christian Century* for one did not agree with either FIGHT or its church supporters and editorialized:

But one wing of the clergy—greatly and properly concerned and determined to do something, even if it is the wrong thing—gulp and swallow what in the opinion of many of us is a highly dubious nostrum. Moreover, this minority is enraged by those of us who, having studied the Alinsky method closely and for a long time, resolutely refuse to gulp and swallow. What amazes and puzzles us is not Alinsky—he declares himself most forthrightly—but the hypnotic effect he has on some members of the clergy.[31]

In another editorial, entitled "Episcopal Editor Denounces Saul Alinsky," the *Christian Century* concurred with the opinion of another Alinsky critic, Carroll E. Simcox, editor of the *Living Church*, by saying:

And Simcox, with whom we are not always in agreement, said a great deal more to which we found ourselves tapping our feet, including his statement: "I don't want one nickel of my church offering ever to find its way to anything that this man Alinsky administers or even comes near, and if I learn in advance that it has an Alinsky-related destination I won't offer it."[32]

The editorial policy of *Christianity Today* also did not support FIGHT. In "Church Leaders Put the Squeeze on Kodak," the paper cautioned:

Members of denominations backing FIGHT must consider whether their churches should be so deeply involved in big business, and whether their stock voting power should be used to harass responsible private enterprise. . . .

[30] "The Church and Capitalism," *Chronicles and Documents*, Brussels: Auxiliaire de la Presse, S. A. Bureau voor Persknipsels, N. V., 1967.

[31] "Alinsky Denounces Reconciliation," *The Christian Century*, July 5, 1967, p. 861.

[32] "Episcopal Editor Denounces Saul Alinsky," *The Christian Century*, November 15, 1967, p. 1452.

Every Christian must be committed to equal-employment opportunities for men of all races. But race is not the only issue in the
Rochester controversy. The basic issue in all agitation aroused by the
Saul Alinsky forces centers on changing the economic structure of our
nation. Church members should repudiate and withhold financial
support from leaders who back such rabble-rousing causes. All Christians should become involved in the Church's foremost enterprise,
sharing with men poor in spirit the unsearchable riches of Christ.[33]

In another editorial, "A Fight Church Officials May Regret,"[34] *Christianity Today* said:

Denominational officials are rendering a great disservice to the
cause of Christ and the betterment of the Negro's status in American
life by supporting the Saul Alinsky FIGHT organization in its calculated controversy with the Eastman Kodak company. . . . In its zeal
to aid the Negro, the Church must exercise care that it does not
promote organizations that sow disruption and seek political power
while professing to help the less fortunate.

The *Presbyterian Journal* was perhaps the most vocal and vociferous in
its attack against those clergy who sympathized with FIGHT or supported
their churches' involvement in seeking economic justice for the poor. In a
strange indictment of FIGHT supporters, it said:

*Notice that the people on whose behalf the Church was called to
picket were not necessarily Christians.* No. The Church merely considered that its mission was to decide between two contending
factions in a business dispute, and join the picket lines across the
nation against one faction. [Emphasis added.][35]

Dr. L. Nelson Bell, in an article in the *Presbyterian Journal*, stated his
views on the blacks. They sounded like an echo of the apologetics of the
segregationists of a (hopefully) bygone era. Among other things, he stated:

Perhaps Eastman Kodak Co. has been too slow in making use of all
available labor. On the other hand, some may be demanding "rights"
for which they are not equipped. We do believe the Church in its
eagerness to promote civil rights may have omitted an even greater
duty—the promotion of a sense of responsibility which can only be
attained by hard work.[36]

[33] "Church Leaders Put the Squeeze on Kodak," *Christianity Today*, April 28, 1967,
p. 1.

[34] "A Fight Church Officials May Regret," *Christianity Today*, May 12, 1967.

[35] "Re: Church Strikes and Boycotts," editorial, *Presbyterian Journal*, March 8, 1967.

[36] L. Nelson Bell, "Church Activities Have Gone Wild," *Presbyterian Journal*, March
8, 1967.

The Black Press

The Kodak–FIGHT conflict was covered for the black press by the Negro Press International. Its reporting—quite sparse compared with other special-purpose media—was confined to the statements made by the spokesmen for FIGHT and Kodak on different occasions during the dispute. The only black paper of national repute, the *Chicago Daily Defender* (national edition), carried a total of eight stories on the dispute, only three of which related the background in any detail. The paper also carried an editorial entitled "Economic Justice."[37] However, this editorial was devoid of any statement of position or philosophy by the editors or publisher of the newspaper and was just a brief summary of events.

Crisis, the official organ of the NAACP, published only one article on the problems of Rochester, Arthur L. Whitaker's "Anatomy of a Riot,"[38] and carried two short news items ("NAACP Hits Rioters" and "Rochester NAACP Aids in Bringing Peace to Riot-Torn City") in the news section under the heading "Along the NAACP Battlefront."[39] The news items appeared in the August–September 1964 issue. Mr. Whitaker's article appeared in the January 1965 issue and preceded the Kodak–FIGHT conflict by at least six months.

[37] "Economic Justice," editorial, *Chicago Daily Defender*, nat. ed., May 20–26, 1967, p. 10.

[38] "Anatomy of a Riot," *Crisis*, January 1965, pp. 20–25.

[39] Along the NAACP Battlefront," *Crisis*, August–September 1964, p. 470.

E.
CORPORATIONS
AND
THE CHURCH

Eastman Kodak Company (C), Rochester, New York

Conflict with a Minority Group—FIGHT: The Role of the Church

The church is not an impersonal edifice, although all too often it seems that way. The church is what we have made it. The dilemma is that while its mission should be the righting of wrongs and the active pursuit of the great Judeo-Christian values, we have instead made it for the most part a force for the status quo.

—JOHN D. ROCKEFELLER, JR.

The activities of the church[1] played a very important role in the Kodak–FIGHT controversy. It was an agency of the church that was instrumental in bringing Saul Alinsky to Rochester and thus creating FIGHT. Moreover, it was the local clergy who provided FIGHT with its initial momentum and sustained it in the early stages. Even after FIGHT was a going concern, the church was one of its strongest supporters at both local and national levels. Protestant and Catholic church organizations consistently supported FIGHT, although their membership was predominantly

---

[1] Church is defined here as all organized Christian religious organizations in the United States.

This case material has been adapted from S. Prakash Sethi, *Business Corporations and the Black Man* (Scranton, Pennsylvania: Chandler Publishing Company, 1970). Copyright © 1970 by Chandler Publishing Company. Used by permission.

white. These groups were under constant pressure, especially at the local level, to disengage themselves from this controversy. Obviously, it was not the most usual activity for the church to engage in. Although members of the clergy had been involved in civil rights actions in the South and had participated in sit-in demonstrations and peace marches, their action in Rochester was unprecedented in many ways. It involved a deliberate attempt at organizing local minorities through techniques that were unorthodox and unacceptable even to some of the most liberal groups in the United States. These techniques carried with them the potential for violence. In a city like Rochester, which had been the scene of race riots, this action seemed particularly foolhardy. It was sure to incur the displeasure of a majority of the town's citizens who were, after all, church members and had the right to ensure that the churches satisfy their spiritual needs rather than become rabble-rousers.

Why then did the church become involved in the controversy? To understand this, we must realize that in Rochester the various elements of the church, ranging from the Rochester Area Council of Churches to the individual ministers and priests, had somewhat different, at least short-run, objectives and more often than not were subject to different pressures or allegiances.

The Board for Urban Ministry was the organization originally responsible for inviting Saul Alinsky and his Industrial Areas Organization to Rochester with a view to encouraging organization among the local minorities and giving them a new voice in representing their views to the city and its establishment. The board realized that this action might not be acceptable to the city's other powerful and equally well-meaning groups because of Alinsky's reputation as a radical. To understand the board's action it is necessary to consider the circumstances and the source of the board's authority.

The Board for Urban Ministry was a semiautonomous offshoot of the Rochester Area Council of Churches (RACC). Although the RACC endorsed the board's action, it was the board and not the council that was actually responsible for bringing Alinsky to Rochester. The distinction between the two, often overlooked, is strategically important. As William C. Martin, writing in the *Atlantic*, put it:

> The Council is composed of more than 200 member congregations and is ultimately answerable to them. The Board for Urban Ministry is composed of representatives from eight denominations and is thus not directly answerable to individual churches. According to the policy of the two organizations, the Board could have invited Alinsky without the Council's approval, but the Council was not obligated to poll its member churches as to their desires in the matter.

The Board for Urban Ministry issued the invitation to Alinsky and led in providing his fee. Over half the fee came from church agencies such as the Presbyterian Board of National Missions. Much of FIGHT's most articulate support at Flemington came from similar denominational offices. These agencies and their staffs are ultimately responsible to a constituency, but even if that constituency opposes a policy decision strongly enough to try to countermand it, it is likely to move too late or hit the wrong target.[2]

THE ATTITUDE OF THE NATIONAL CHURCH ORGANIZATIONS

Only during the past twenty years or so have American churches become conspicuous in causes against race prejudice and economic inequality. Thus the National Council of Churches went on record in 1954 as working against those forms of economic injustice that are expressed through racial discrimination.[3] It is also on record in support of equal employment opportunity for all,[4] the use of nonviolent demonstrations to secure social justice,[5] the elimination of segregation in education,[6] and the prevention of discrimination in housing.[7]

The use of economic pressure in racial issues was specifically proposed and approved in a background paper prepared for the National Council of Churches:

> We believe it is of primary importance that Christian people everywhere recognize that what may be called bread-and-butter injustice can be equally as devastating to human life and well-being as civil injustice, if not more so, largely because bread-and-butter pursuits are so necessary to the maintenance of life. Because these forms of injustice are so closely related to habit, local mores, and man-to-man

[2] William C. Martin, "Shepherds vs. Flocks, Ministers vs. Negro Militancy," *Atlantic*, December 1967, pp. 55–59.

[3] National Council of Churches of Christ in the United States of America (NCCCUSA), "Christian Principles and Assumptions for Economic Life." Resolution adopted by General Board, September 15, 1954.

[4] NCCCUSA, "Christian Influence toward the Development and Use of All Labor Resources without Regard to Race, Color and Religion or National Origin." Resolution adopted by General Assembly, December 9, 1960.

[5] NCCCUSA, "The Church and Segregation." Resolution adopted by General Board, June 11, 1952. Also see "Resolution on the Sit-In Demonstrations." Adopted by General Board, June 2, 1960.

[6] NCCCUSA, "Statement on the Decision of the U.S. Supreme Court on Segregation in the Public Schools." Adopted by General Board, May 19, 1954.

[7] NCCCUSA, "The Churches' Concern for Housing." Resolution adopted by General Board, November 18, 1953.

relationships, they can only partially be opposed or regulated by law or civil authority.[8]

The General Board, therefore, resolved on June 8, 1963:

> When other efforts to secure these rights do not avail, to support and participate in economic pressures where used in a responsible and disciplined manner to eliminate economic injustice and to end discrimination against any of God's people based on race, creed, or national origin.[9]

The National Council of Churches has gone even further by recognizing that the churches' own purchases must be based on other than strictly economic criteria. The basic philosophy of the council was very well articulated in the policy statement adopted by the General Board on September 12, 1968:

> The institutional church enters into the economic life of society in a variety of ways. . . . The economic activities and financial transactions of the church total many billions of dollars annually. As a result, the church is inevitably involved in the exercise of substantial economic power. . . . We reaffirm that all economic institutions and practices are human structures conceived and designed by men; that they affect the conditions and quality of life of persons, many of whom cannot exercise any control over their functioning. . . . The market system which characterizes the American economy is one such institution. When the church approaches the marketplace in its role of purchaser of goods and services, it inevitably becomes a participant in an intricate network of economic forces involving ethical issues, policies and decisions. . . .
> Most purchasing decisions by the church involve a selection among competing vendors. Such factors as quality, performance, convenience and price—conventional determinants of most purchasing decisions—although relevant to the economic activity of the church, are not sufficient criteria for its selection among vendors. The nature of the church requires that as an economic institution it also consider the social impact of its purchasing decisions in terms of justice and equality. . . .
> In cases where injustice is found to exist, the church should make vigorous efforts through moral persuasion to secure correction of the

---

[8] NCCCUSA, "Background Paper of Information Relating to Resolution on the Use of Economic Pressures in Racial Tensions." Prepared by Department of Church and Economic Life in consultation with Department of Cultural Relations of Division of Christian Life and Work, June 9, 1963, p. 5.

[9] NCCCUSA, "The Use of Economic Pressure in Racial Tensions." Resolution adopted by General Board, June 8, 1963.

abuses. . . . Where such measures prove to be inappropriate in securing justice, or where past experience demonstrates that these means alone are ineffective, the church is not only justified, but in faithfulness to its nature, is required to give its patronage to sources of goods and services which it finds to have policies and practices that better serve social justice. . . .

When such action is taken, the church is free and indeed may be impelled, as a form of witness, not only to inform the vendors involved but also to announce publicly the nature of its action and the reasons for it.[10]

The problem of the church's concern for economic issues and its involvement in conflicts where it is not a direct party has another dimension which is equally explosive: the choice of strategies. The National Council of Churches has supported the use of nonviolent methods in securing economic justice for minorities.[11]

However, what should the church do if nonviolent and peaceful means do not succeed? When is a violation of man-made laws justified if there is a superior law of conscience? Economic pressures can be used not only by the church but also by other groups that the church is opposing. If these measures by the church can be justified because of the righteousness of the cause, how can they be condemned when used by other groups if the latter are equally honest in their belief of the justness of their cause and are not motivated by bigotry, selfishness, or prejudice? The mere existence of power, be it legal or implied, is not enough justification for its use. However, if ends are to be used as criteria for legitimizing means, the church as a party to the conflict has no more right to proclaim that its values are the "justifiable" ends than have the other parties to the conflict.

The National Council of Churches, recognizing some of these issues, justified its approach thus:

Use of economic pressures also involves the possibility of violence. Though violence may sometimes result from an action, this possibility does not necessarily call for opposition to such action, particularly on the part of those who seek to use non-violent economic means to eliminate or decrease discrimination.[12]

The council also recognized that there might be occasions when a company might lose its regular clientele if it were to cater to the special needs of a particular group. It thus argued that such a company was only an

[10] NCCCUSA, "The Church as Purchaser of Goods and Services." Policy statement adopted by General Board, September 12, 1968.

[11] "The Use of Economic Pressure in Racial Tensions," NCCCUSA, June 8, 1963.

[12] "Background Paper of Information," NCCCUSA, June 9, 1963.

innocent bystander, not the offending party, and should therefore not be subjected to economic pressures by the church. These measures might involve yet another party—those people who give tacit support to discriminatory practices of some businesses by not actively opposing those companies and their activities and by continuing to patronize them. Notwithstanding, the council maintained:

> These factors make more difficult, but no less necessary, the understanding of and resistance to the use of economic pressures as a means to enforce racial discriminations or oppression. They serve to highlight the importance of looking with broad historical perspective at the full sweep of economic injustice which the victims of economic injustice now seek to remove, or at least alleviate through the use of economic pressures being made against them.

> It is, therefore, no wonder that the board was more in tune than the council with the trends of national church organizations and more willing to use less conventional approaches to solving the problems of Rochester's minorities. The board was assured of the support of the National Council of Churches in view of the latter's public statements and official resolutions favoring the use of economic pressures and other direct action to promote the cause of the minorities. Moreover, financial independence and only indirect representation of the local churches insulated the board from local pressures and in a sense made it insensitive to the feelings and desires of the local clergy and citizens.[13]

In inviting Alinsky, the board knew that it was creating "an atmosphere of controversy,"[14] but the ferocity and, to some extent, the direction of opposition were unexpected. The RACC and its member congregations came under immediate attack from media and laymen alike. The local newspapers accused the council of bringing in "outsiders" and troublemakers and of supporting militants who were intent on creating unrest among the people of Rochester. As reported in the *New Republic*, the city's most powerful radio station, WHAM, an ABC affiliate, in an editorial warned that

> If the clergy persisted in bringing Alinsky into town then the ministers must start paying $275 for the hour-long Sunday morning church service the station had been broadcasting free. WHAM said Alinsky was a "troublemaker." . . . The Council held its ground

---

[13] *Ibid.*

[14] "The Fight That Swirls around Eastman Kodak," *Business Week*, April 29, 1967, pp. 38–41.

against WHAM and the Sunday morning radio program was cancelled.[15]

Commenting on the intensity of local hostility to the council's action, the same observer stated:

> In the face of this intensive barrage, many laymen found themselves in a quandary over the role their pastors and denominational leaders were playing. For weeks, representatives of the Board for Urban Ministry and the Council of Churches spent their evenings interpreting the realities of life in the ghettos and the dynamics of the Alinsky approach to groups of troubled laymen.[16]

It was easy and perhaps spiritually comfortable for most of the educated, suburban, affluent laymen to support their clergy's involvement in social action, as long as it did not go beyond the discussion stage and as long as any action was confined to peaceful methods of protest. However, these parishioners could not reconcile themselves to the idea of their clergy being involved in an open struggle for power between different groups in the community. The lack of precedent, the absence of a clear-cut philosophy, and the feeling of uncertainty about possible achievements further added to the laymen's confusion and frustration, as reflected in the nature and intensity of their response. There was a widespread cancellation of pledges —sometimes running into thousands of dollars. William C. Martin reported: "Resentment of church involvement ran so high in some congregations that church leaders would not pass out brochures presenting FIGHT's request for third-year funding until after the annual pledge drive."[17]

There was a serious question as to how long clergymen could function under such strain and still maintain their sanity. One minister, tormented by threats and telephone calls, took his own life; the calls were then made to his wife.[18] Others were victims of anonymous letters circulated among the congregations and of telephoned threats against their families. A minister who had been attacked for supporting FIGHT found that the lug bolts had been taken off the wheels of his car.[19] In a large number of cases parishioners simply stopped talking or being friendly to their clergymen. William Martin, writing in the *Atlantic*, commented:

---

[15] James Ridgeway, "Saul Alinsky in Smugtown," *New Republic*, June 26, 1965, pp. 15–17.

[16] *Ibid.*

[17] Martin, "Shepherds vs. Flocks," pp. 55–59.

[18] Jules Loh, Associated Press Feature Story for Sunday A.M. papers, April 23, 1967.

[19] James Ridgeway, "Attack on Kodak," *New Republic*, January 21, 1967, pp. 11–13.

The loss of members and money affects a minister because they are tangible signs of his professional "success," however much he may wish they were not. But the confusion, bitterness, and hostility that he sees in his people cause him the greatest pain. In [one] case, members made a point of telling the minister's children that the church could never make progress until their father left. In some churches dissident laymen organized attempts to get rid of the offending minister. In others, leaders withheld salary increments or warned the pastor not to spend too much of his time in activities related to FIGHT.[20]

The resentment of the local citizenry against the Rochester Area Council of Churches was even more vocal and violent. According to William Martin:

Letters and telephone calls—some reasonable, others obscene and threatening—poured into the council office. Numerous churches and individuals decided to "teach the council a lesson" by lowering or canceling contributions for the coming fiscal year. One church, recognizing that FIGHT was only one part of the council's activity, raised its contribution $500, but accompanied its pledge with a letter strongly critical of the council's stance. Others were not so charitable. At the final tally, the council's annual fund drive for the coming year missed its goal by $20,000. Ironically, the attempt to punish the council has had no effect whatever on FIGHT, which has in fact been guaranteed third-year funding by the various denominational bodies and church agencies, nor on the Board for Urban Ministry, which is also funded denominationally and has never been more secure financially.[21]

CHURCH ACTIVITIES AFTER THE AGREEMENT OF DECEMBER 20

When the executive committee of Kodak's board of directors repudiated the agreement signed by John Mulder, the RACC found itself in a worse dilemma than ever before. The community was already hostile to RACC's earlier actions, and any support of FIGHT would further intensify the conflict. FIGHT's actions immediately following the repudiation did not help. On January 19, 1967, against the advice of many of his supporters, Minister Florence invited Stokely Carmichael to Rochester. In his speech

---

[20] Martin, "Shepherds vs. Flocks," pp. 55–59.
[21] *Ibid.*

Carmichael made inflammatory statements against Kodak, Rochester, and every other organization that did not agree with FIGHT.

The council was really concerned about the danger of the situation getting out of hand; yet it could do nothing but support FIGHT's cause since it felt that Kodak had indeed broken a promise which the other party had accepted in good faith. The council's hand was further forced when Kodak took full-page ads in the local newspapers to publicize its reasons for rejecting the agreement. The council wanted to avoid a further deterioration of the situation, but it could not desert FIGHT's cause without losing all the work done so far and perhaps permanently discouraging the minorities from putting any faith in the white man's promises. The council took double-page ads in the papers urging Kodak to honor the agreement and at the same time asking FIGHT to support Kodak's training programs. However, with supporters of both factions having raised community passions to a high pitch, the council's appeal to patience and reason was lost in the hysteria, while its support for FIGHT was overblown. The reactions were predictable though unfortunate.

DENOMINATIONAL DIVISION OF OPINION OF FIGHT

The controversy caused division among individual denominations in the Council of Churches. Stokely Carmichael's visit prompted six of Rochester's eighty Presbyterian churches (FIGHT's largest church supporters) to consider withdrawing their support of FIGHT while their parent body's Health and Welfare Association condemned Kodak.[22] The Episcopalians were reportedly the second-largest church supporters of FIGHT. In response to criticism of FIGHT by the Gannet newspapers, the bishop of the Episcopal diocese of Rochester appointed a committee to "assess FIGHT and to determine," by April 1967, "whether the diocese which has already contributed $19,000 should continue its support."[23] The third-largest church group, the Baptists, decided to continue their contributions, but a third of the delegates voted against the proposal.[24]

The Reverend Elmer G. Schaertal, pastor of the Lutheran Church of the Redeemer, openly dissented with the council's stand in a letter to the *Rochester Democrat & Chronicle*. Schaertal equated the disrespect for authority that was sweeping the country with that of FIGHT for Kodak:

[22] Barbara Carter, "The Fight against Kodak," *Reporter*, January 21, 1967, pp. 28–31.

[23] Raymond A. Schroth, "Self-Doubt and Black Pride," *America*, April 1, 1967, p. 502.

[24] "And Kodak Will Ask, 'How High?'" *Fortune*, June 1, 1967, p. 78.

. . . the disrespect sweeping our country of youth, of college students, of ministers, and leaders like Adam Powell and James Hoffa for the law and courts and of FIGHT for Kodak which is the most community minded company that I know. . . . The demands of FIGHT call for a special privilege because of color. . . . This seems crazy to me and would do great harm to both company and all the workers who would resent the man coming in by paternalistic power rather than qualifications for the job. If one asks why Florence and FIGHT are so insistent in this, one can only answer that it is for power and would be used in that way rather than for benefit of workers, or company or Rochester. . . . As to the Council of Churches and the denomiations supporting FIGHT, I do not believe the majority of either their ministers or their people are in sympathy with the stand their leaders have taken or the support they have given.[25]

Several other ministers used their pulpits to advocate reason and even some rethinking on the part of the church. However, none took as harsh a stand as Mr. Schaertal. One minister said that many church people were "facing the future with some misgivings" and that "we must find our way back to the true image of the church and lessen the gap between clergy and laity." Another minister commented that "part of the reason why we have this controversy and the strong difference of opinion within the church is that we are in new times and the church is facing new and greater issues for which we have no sharp guidelines from the past." Another minister asked that Kodak and FIGHT "call it a draw," saying that the struggle was "like that between the elephant and the whale, which are different animals living in different environments and moving in different worlds."[26] Some ministers, even had they wanted to, could not support FIGHT because of individual circumstances, such as age, health, or special situations in their churches.[27]

There followed a spate of letters to the newspapers by irate citizens opposing the church's stand on the controversy. Many strongly supported Mr. Schaertal's views. Few, if any, sympathized with the position taken by the Rochester Area Council of Churches. Here is a representative sample of the comments made by some of the readers:

I commend Pastor Elmer Schaertal for expressing his opinion so clearly in his letter to the D. & C.

[25] Elmer G. Schaertal, "A Pastor Speaks Up for Kodak," *Rochester Democrat & Chronicle*, January 15, 1967.

[26] "Pastors Refer to FIGHT Case," *Rochester Times-Union*, January 23, 1967.

[27] Martin, "Shepherds vs. Flocks," pp. 55–59.

In the long run more could be accomplished if everyone were allowed to devote full time and attention to his own problems. Eastman Kodak to the business of manufacturing and selling its products, FIGHT to sending its people to the proper place—the school—for education, the Rochester Area Council to preaching the Gospel.

The local crusading knights of the cloth, johnny-come-latelys in the civil rights bandwagon, cloaked in their spiritual aura of infallibility, are quite ready to order others to place their houses in order according to their views, integratively speaking, but have woeful shortcomings in their own houses of worship.

Every day we read that more and more people believe that religion is becoming less meaningful. Therefore, why don't preachers either return to the pulpit and extol an almighty and just God, or leave the church to campaign for Minister Franklin Florence, Saul Alinsky and other radical dissidents under their own names. Let those disenchanted clergy look about them. Hardly an area in or about Rochester has not benefited from the Eastman Kodak Company. There isn't a major company in the United States with a more liberal and higher standard of employment ethics.[28]

The expression of resentment and dissent also took other forms. The president of the Council of Churches (a Kodak employee) and two directors of its board (one of whom was a Kodak employee) resigned from the council in protest.

Fundamentalist and Evangelical churches kept out of the Kodak–FIGHT controversy, perhaps because of theological conviction. These groups believed the primary function of the church was to prepare individuals for life after death and saw no relationship between socioeconomic and religious issues. The deed of one church specifically prohibited the discussion of social or political issues anywhere on church property. According to William Martin:

Some are simply not aware of what is going on in their city. One insisted that Negroes "are basically a happy, satisfied people who like to work as servants and live in a haphazard way." He doubted many in his church would object if Negroes tried to become members, "but, of course, if too many came, then we'd start a colored work." Another admitted he was not too well informed about FIGHT, but he hoped Hoagy Carmichael would not get to be its president. Most, however, are as concerned as their more liberal colleagues but cannot reconcile conflict tactics with their understanding of the gospel. "We feel," one evangelical minister said, "that you will never get rid of

28 "The Ordeal of the Black Businessman," *Newsweek*, March 4, 1968, p. 34.

slums until you get rid of the slum in men. You have to start with the individual man, and you don't start by teaching him to hate."[29]

THE POSITION OF THE CATHOLIC CHURCH

For the most part, the Catholics (not represented in the Protestant Council of Churches, of course) steered clear of the Kodak–FIGHT dispute. However, on January 3, 1967, when the turmoil in Rochester was at its peak because of Kodak's December 20 repudiation, Bishop Fulton J. Sheen asked the Reverend P. David Finks—a FIGHT sympathizer—to advise him on the problems of the poor by appointing him an episcopal vicar of urban ministry. Finks was a member of FIGHT's advisory council and was on the executive board of Friends of FIGHT at the time of his appointment. Bishop Sheen admitted that the appointment was "a very unusual step" but said, "I do not follow traditional methods, except in the faith." He also raised the possibility of strong cooperation with other faiths "even to the sharing of houses of worship . . . in poor neighborhoods." According to the *New York Times:*

> Spokesmen for the Roman Catholic diocese declined to say whether the priest's appointment was connected with the current controversy between the Negro group and the Eastman Kodak Company. They commented that the letter naming Father Finks to the post speaks for itself.[30]

Speaking before the city's Chamber of Commerce on January 23, 1967, Bishop Sheen said:

> As the Church had to learn that the world was the stage on which the gospel was preached, so the world has to learn that the inner city is the area where the secular city will find God. Could not all the industries of the secular city begin to give a proportion of their blessing to the inner city—not just "tokens" but something more substantial? The whole world looks at Rochester, . . . but it does not see the city's beauty: it sees the blemish on its face.[31]

Father Finks expressed his views on FIGHT and his philosophy on religion and church in an address to the Pittsford-Perinton Council on Human Relations:

[29] Martin, "Shepherds vs. Flocks," pp. 55–59.
[30] "Sheen Appoints a Vicar for Poor," *The New York Times,* January 4, 1967, p. 4.
[31] Schroth, "Self-Doubt and Black Pride," p. 502.

Those seeking social justice for the have nots of this world should support a viable community organization of minority groups dedicated to bring about the necessary social change. The most viable group here is FIGHT. . . . Christianity is not a mere belief or ritual, but is basically living like Christ did. We will be judged on whether we respond to the urgent call for social justice. . . . Tensions are necessary and can be used creatively in making the democratic process work. . . . Members of the clergy have been chaplains of the establishment too long.[32]

THE PART PLAYED BY NATIONAL CHURCH ORGANIZATIONS

Florence was quite successful in his appeal to various organizations to withhold their proxies from the management and also to boycott Kodak's products and demonstrate against its plants in all parts of the country. At the Kodak stockholders' meeting in April 1967, seven of the eight dissenting groups, which represented forty thousand of the 80.7 million outstanding shares, were religious organizations. Although the stock represented by these groups was but a small fraction of the total, it would be misleading to measure the impact only in terms of the number of shares. Unlike FIGHT, these organizations were well-established institutions representing a large number of churches. They had access to the public forum which, though not equal to that of business institutions, was quite important. Kodak—or for that matter any other business corporation— could not afford to treat the voice of this group as representing merely one-half of one percent of their stock.[33]

Bishop Dewitt, who represented the Episcopal Church at the annual stockholders' meeting, read a statement prepared by the church's executive council for the press. This statement perhaps sums up the feelings of many other churchmen who were also present at that meeting:

Possession of power conveys the obligation to use that power reasonably. Corporations—and indeed investing churches—must measure the responsible use of their resources by social as well as financial yardsticks. . . . We stand with Negro communities in their real grievances and their urgent need for organizational power to participate in an open society. And we stand with the management of

[32] Chuck Boller, "Priest Backs FIGHT," Rochester Democrat & Chronicle, February 2, 1967.

[33] For example, the Episcopal Church has 3,340,759 members in 7,547 churches and the United Church of Christ has 2,067,233 members in 6,957 churches. John Kifner, "2 Churches Withhold Proxies to Fight Kodak Rights Policies," The New York Times, April 7, 1967, p. 1.

corporate enterprises which seek to manage their affairs for the well-being of the total community.[34]

FIGHT's request for national demonstrations against Kodak's plants was not enthusiastically received by some of the church organizations. In an editorial entitled "Re: Church Strikes and Boycotts," the *Presbyterian Journal* rejected that church's activities in the area of community organization:

> For those who see the church as an organization existing for the purpose of helping achieve certain needed social, economic and political objectives (in much the same way Kiwanis Clubs work for the betterment of boys generally) these developments are a logical outgrowth of their concern. But for those who still hold to the Scriptural mission of the church, to win men to salvation in the Lord Jesus Christ, these developments must be viewed as radical departures from the assignment given the church by her Lord.[35]

The same editorial reported that the Nashville Presbytery, when asked to support Project Equality, which involved sponsoring official boycotts of businesses that did not practice fair employment, turned it down by a vote of two to one.

FIGHT's popularity waned somewhat among the clergy when Florence escalated his demands to Kodak and threatened to start a nationwide demonstration that summer. The Rochester Area Council of Churches, in its first official criticism of FIGHT, passed a resolution criticizing the organization's intemperance and urging a cancellation of a candlelight demonstration.[36] Church pressure, as well as lack of interest in Florence's planned demonstrations, may well have speeded the "reconciliation" between FIGHT and Kodak on June 23, 1967.

Kodak officials were also not happy with the stand taken by the RACC in the Kodak–FIGHT controversy. During an interview with the author, some Kodak spokesmen expressed the opinion that the RACC's involvement in originally hiring Alinsky kept it from objectively assessing the company's side of the dispute. This bias spread to other churches locally and to the communication the RACC had with the National Council of Churches. As evidence of this bias, the Kodak men stated that in only a handful of instances across the country did clergymen attempt to look into the Kodak side of the story. Even when Kodak officials tried to present the

---

[34] "Church vs. Kodak: The Big Picture," *Episcopalian*, June 1967, pp. 43–44.

[35] "Re: Church Strikes and Boycotts," editorial, *Presbyterian Journal*, March 8, 1967.

[36] Martin, "Shepherds vs. Flocks," pp. 55–59.

facts as they saw them, their efforts were rebuffed by the clergy.[37] Kodak spokesmen gave the impression that the RACC was not only primarily responsible for creating FIGHT and for the resulting tension in the community but also largely instrumental in engaging the National Council of Churches in the conflict and in generating adverse national publicity and reaction against Kodak.

THE RAMIFICATIONS OF CHURCH INVOLVEMENT

Where has the involvement between Kodak and FIGHT left the church? The Rochester Area Council of Churches certainly has not won any kudos for its efforts from any group in the community. In fact, as the Reverend Paul R. Hoover pointed out, "the loudest condemnation of the RACC's actions has come from inner-city citizens of all races."[38] The dissatisfaction of the community's affluent is reflected in the financial problems of the RACC. Referring to the slump in the council's financial support, the *Rochester Democrat & Chronicle* said that it indicated disillusionment with sponsorship of FIGHT and disappointment in an approach to helping blacks based on acrimony and upheaval rather than on goodwill and orderly processes. The newspaper further said that it would be more in keeping with reality "if the Council just admitted a misjudgment and went on from there."[39]

According to one observer, one of the key factors in the Rochester situation was the presence of a closely knit group of activists in the Board

---

[37] Kenneth Howard of the Industrial Relations Department, Eastman Kodak Company, said in an interview with the author that a "member of the Presbyterian clergy in Missouri was urged to send us a telegram by a clergyman in New Orleans. The clergyman in Missouri called Kodak to hear our side of the story. I had a long talk with him and sent him some information. He never sent the telegram to Kodak.

"The amusing sideline to this is that I am also a graduate of a divinity school. In the middle of this network of communications, we discovered that a former very close friend of mine in the divinity school was sending out his literature to clergymen all over the country. So I called him and said that I had heard he was interested in the Rochester situation and asked him whether he had ever visited Rochester and he said 'yes, oh yes.' So I told him that since I was also involved in this issue from the other side, it might be worthwhile if we got together sometime and talked about it. I pointed out to him that I believed there were certain inaccuracies and half-truths that were being circulated about Kodak and that I was sure he wouldn't want to be a party to them. But he never called me, he never came to see me, he wouldn't send me a copy of what he sent out around the country. This was typical of the whole problem. He wasn't in the least bit interested in knowing the facts."

[38] Paul R. Hoover, "Social Pressures and Church Policy," *Christianity Today*, July 21, 1967, pp. 12–14.

[39] "Council's Defense," *Rochester Democrat & Chronicle*, June 16, 1967.

for Urban Ministry who were instrumental in inviting Alinsky and also in attracting like-minded ministers from the local clergy. This group did not share the apprehensions of the local people nor did it identify with their objectives. Those in the group believed themselves to be working for a great cause and had a different and more radical outlook as to what ailed society and how it could be cured. Equally important in their indifference to the local pressures was the fact that their personal advancement and goal achievement depended on satisfying a peer group that was national in character and was not likely to be influenced by the opinions of the Rochester power elite.

Reviewing the situation in Rochester, the Reverend Paul R. Hoover wrote in *Christianity Today:*

> The frightening events in Rochester have left behind two tragic consequences: (1) a growing lack of confidence in churches and church leaders, not excluding inner-city ministers whose motivation and actions over the years were hardly open to question; and (2) a growing fear of what the future may hold in view of the reckless threats of members of the FIGHT organization at the Kodak annual meeting in Flemington, New Jersey. . . . Part of the soul-searching on the part of ministers, particularly those working within the city, centers on how long they can physically and mentally stand the pressures that stem from the difference in attitudes and professional experiences between the suburban congregation and the mission-oriented inner-city congregation.[40]

[40] Hoover, "Social Pressures and Church Policy," pp. 12–14.

"La Huelga o La Causa" (B)

California Farm Workers' Strike: Where Does the Church Fit In?

Occasionally, the voices raised against the pope's power are also raised to demand that his power should be used . . . to stop the war in Vietnam, and generally to turn the church inside out to suit the protesters' own vision of what it should be like. Some of those who shout loudest about the abuse of power in the church, might, in fact, be rather ugly customers if they themselves ever got hold of that power.

—JOHN HOGAN,
Religion and Education Editor of the *Irish Times*

The church was involved in the fate of the farm workers before UFWOC (United Farm Workers Organizing Committee) was organized. During the early sixties, the National Catholic Rural Life Conference was one of the more vocal groups which had demanded stiffer controls on United States farmers' importation of Mexican workers under the bracero program. Despite stiff opposition from the agribusiness interests, the Congress, bowing to public pressure, refused to extend the bracero program and allowed it to lapse on December 31, 1964.

From the very beginning, the movement to organize the farm workers in California had a strong religious emphasis. Cesar Chavez himself is deeply religious, and most Mexican-Americans are devout Catholics. The cross was carried to the fields and in the forefront of marching groups. Masses were held in the open air for the strikers. Despite this religious emphasis,

340

the institutionalized church was slow to support Chavez's group actively. It was 1965 before the churches realized the impact Chavez was having on labor in the Delano area. Until that time, only small groups, independent leaders, and the California Migrant Ministry of the National Council of Churches—which had openly been supporting the organization of farm workers for years—were active.

Chavez's timing was just right. The civil rights movement in the South had gained national recognition and sympathy; the nation was trying to build its Great Society; and many citizens were becoming more aware of injustices that were occurring close to their personal spheres of experience. Church groups—Catholic, Protestant, and Jewish—which had been experiencing a renewal and a reevaluation of their own social roles, collected food and money for the strikers, informed their congregations of the issues, and dispatched clergymen and parishioners who marched, picketed, and were even arrested with strikers. The Northern California Council of Churches, a Protestant group, adopted the strike as the main activity of its Migrant Ministry.

The Protestant Church

One of UFWOC's most loyal supporters was the organized church. However, this support had never been unanimous, and there was reevaluation in some religious circles of the issue of church involvement in the table grape boycott. This reflected the uncertainty in the minds of many religious leaders and of much of the general church membership on what the role of the church should be. The difficulty was in deciding whether the church was responsible to its members or to a higher moral order determined by high-ranking officials in the church hierarchy. The Reverend Wayne C. Hartmire, Jr., director of the California Migrant Ministry, stated the implications of this problem in the recent situation:

> There is no doubt that Protestant churches have a traditional commitment to social justice. But that tradition has been betrayed time and again by silent acceptance of injustice and by elevating institutional self-preservation above the needs of suffering men and women. In Delano in 1966–67, local churches continued that betrayal, but other Christians rallied to the cause of the striking grape-pickers.[1]

From the outset, Chavez counted on the support of the church. It

[1] Linda L. Tooni, *Farm Labor Organizing 1905–1967, a Brief History*, New York, National Advisory Committee on Farm Labor, 1967, p. 50.

was a foregone conclusion that he would be aided by the California Migrant Ministry, an adjunct of the Division of Home Missions for the National Council of Churches . . . [which] had for years been intimately connected with farm labor problems. But Chavez was also convinced that he would get other, less institutional clerical support. . . . "I've been making friends with the clergy for sixteen years, ever since I was with the CSO. How could the Catholic clergy stay out of this one? All the Mexicans are Catholic. . . ."[2]

When the strike first began in Delano, in 1965, the Migrant Ministry, under the auspices of the Northern California and the National Council of Churches, immediately supplied staff members and secured assistance from other church groups. The Delano Ministerial Association and some of the local Catholic clergy severely criticized these actions and denounced or ignored the grape strike. These clergymen found themselves caught between two opposing forces. The Catholic priests had in their congregations both the predominantly Mexican-American fieldworkers and many of the growers who were of Italian or Yugoslavian descent. Conversely, the Protestant clergy was faced with the actions of its National Council while the local congregation was predominantly made up of white Anglo-Saxon conservatives who sided with the growers. The clerical predicament was compounded by fiscal jeopardy—dissident Catholic growers and Protestant conservatives could withhold a major source of church income, their contributions. However, the Council of Churches continued its support, and there appeared to be an economic backlash against that organization from at least part of its constituency.

> The Fresno [California] Council of Churches, facing a $6,000 deficit on a $20,000 budget, dismissed its only two staff members. Economic and other pressures have followed council support of the area grape pickers' strike.[3]

In the immediate area of the conflict, at least, it seemed that the authority of the Council of Churches was losing some respect.

The issue of clerical support split clergy and congregations alike: Clergy who depended for financial support on the growers and Anglos but whose congregations were predominantly Mexican sometimes tried to stay "neutral" by calling the strike purely an economic problem of no concern to the church and sometimes declared their opposition to the workers' demands. Churchmen from outside the area, however, began to give Chavez support

[2] John G. Dunne, *Delano, the Story of the California Grape Strike* (New York: Farrar, Straus & Giroux, Inc., 1967), p. 84.

[3] David E. Kucharsky, "The Grape Debate," *Christianity Today*, October 11, 1968, pp. 41–43.

in direct defiance of their superiors, and as criticism from both within and without began to mount, the Catholic Church was forced to take a position.

The publicity generated by church involvement and controversy was considerable, bringing the strikers what they needed: The chance to gain support from wide segments of the public. Students—especially from Stanford and the University of California—worked as volunteers. From San Francisco and Los Angeles came food donated by businesses and labor unions, particularly the United Auto Workers.

The Reverend James Drake, of the California Migrant Ministry, one of the first religious leaders to participate actively in the movement, became Chavez's right-hand man. Since the beginning of the strike in September 1965, there had been a steady flow of religious leaders and laymen volunteering to help; but the church hierarchies and church policy had remained for the most part "neutral." The local priests around Delano, either too old to comprehend the changes or caught in the crossfire of the parishioners who gave financial support (the growers) versus the parishioners who filled the churches for services (the workers), opposed the movement or ignored it in the hope it would disappear. They were not really sure it was, in fact, a church problem.

THE CATHOLIC CHURCH

Support from the Catholic Church did not come as quickly or was it ever as extensive as the backing from the National Council of Churches. Whereas the NCC assigned its Migrant Ministry to assist the strikers, there was no similar directive issued from the Catholic hierarchy. Instead, priests and nuns, acting as individuals, began volunteering their services. They marched in picket lines and in processions, celebrated mass for the fieldworkers, and, on occasion, were arrested. The Catholic bishops, who could no longer remain aloof, came out in full support of the strike. The precedent had been set by the Second Vatican Council in its evaluation of the social role of the Catholic Church. The primary document of the council, the Pastoral Constitution on the Church in the Modern World, states as follows: "Among the basic rights of the human person must be counted the right of freely founding labor unions." The document also reaffirmed the traditional teaching of the church of the right to strike if necessary.

At the height of the conflict, California's eight Roman Catholic bishops made a plea to a Senate subcommittee in Washington for an investigation into farm labor problems. They also asked for an amendment of the federal labor codes to extend to farmers and their employees all the rights given to workers in other industries. Accordingly, the first statement by a Catholic bishop on the subject of the grape strike reflected these beliefs. Bishop A. Donohoe of Stockton, spokesman for the bishops, gave full support to the strike and appealed for full collective bargaining rights for the fieldworkers.

An important event of 1968 was the release of a Statement of Farm Labor by the National Conference of Catholic Bishops which represents all the Catholic bishops in the United States. This important document addressed itself to the problems of both the farm worker and the grower, especially the small family farmer. It recognized the grower's difficulties, such as mounting costs and foreign competition, and even suggested that it was the grower's duty to help form associations to protect himself and his interests. In analyzing the rights of the worker, the National Conference specifically asked Congress

1. To include farm workers under the National Labor Relations Act,
2. To include farm workers more effectively under a national minimum wage which would insure them a decent standard of living, and
3. To include farm workers under the national unemployment insurance program.[4]

The statement reaffirmed what the church considered its moral duty—to speak out on controversial issues even though this might alienate some people. Thus the Catholic Church faced the same problem that the National Council of Churches faced in Delano and in Rochester over the FIGHT–Kodak affair. In discussing tactics available to the strikers, the document stated that "the strike can still be a necessary, *though ultimate*, means for the defense of the workers' own rights, and the fulfillment of their just demands."[5] (Emphasis supplied.) There was no endorsement of the boycott which was the primary tactic being used at the time the statement was drafted. In fact, there was even the implication that the boycott was not a justifiable tactic.

Even though the National Conference of Catholic Bishops did not endorse the boycott, individual bishops had. In April 1969, the diocese of Pittsburgh donated $1,500 to provide materials for promoting the boycott in its area. In that same month the diocese of Davenport officially urged its

[4] National Conference of Catholic Bishops, "Statement on Farm Labor," November 13, 1968.
[5] *Ibid.*

parishioners to support the boycott. The two bishops of the San Francisco Bay Area followed the precedent set by the National Conference—they supported the strike while not officially backing the boycott. Archbishop Joseph T. McGucken of San Francisco, in a June 1969 statement, emphasized the necessity for the Catholic Church to be involved in the strike on the side of the fieldworkers. Bishop Floyd L. Begin of Oakland believed that the growers' refusal to allow impartially supervised elections questioned their integrity and that this refusal induced more people to support the boycott. All the California Roman Catholic bishops supported the strike without officially endorsing the boycott. Not all Catholic priests would go this far, however. Monsignor Roger Mahoney of the diocese of Fresno, who was subjected to much pressure from his area, stated at the beginning of 1969:

> Individual priests who align themselves with one side or the other do not speak for the Catholic Church. We endorse neither UFWOC nor the growers and seek a solution favorable to both.[6]

However, in the summer of 1969, Catholic priests in Delano had been given permission to speak out in favor of the farm workers' right to form a union. Many of the young priests believed that neutrality in this issue was nothing but supporting the *status quo*.

Although the National Conference of Catholic Bishops failed to endorse the boycott, the National Council of Churches' general board was able to pass a resolution supporting the boycott, but not without much difficulty, in October 1969. The issue divided the board and required two days of debate. Even then the resolution had to be amended before it was passed. The resolution, as passed, was as follows:

> That the National Council of Churches, including its several units, refrain from the purchase or use of California table grapes until such time as union recognition and assurance of good faith collective bargaining are granted by the California growers.[7]

This resolution was passed a day after the same board had officially adopted a major policy resolution endorsing the use of economic boycott as a legitimate exercise of a given group's power to effect desirable social changes. This stand was far more daring than that of the Catholic bishops and had much to say as to the role of the church in society. Prior to this, the NCC had primarily used political channels to effect social change, but now the economic realm was open. The NCC planned to increase its

6 Gene Logsdon, "The Wrath of Grapes," *Farm Journal*, February 1969, p. 63.
7 Kucharsky, "The Grape Debate," p. 41.

political activity, however, and even considered opening an interdenominational church lobby in Washington, D.C., although this might cost it its tax exemption. How might such high-level decisions, such as endorsing the boycott, affect the general membership of the Protestant churches?

> This may suggest growing indifference toward NCC even on the part of its constituency. Financial support from denominations is as hard to get as ever. The council has asked its thirty-four member denominations for $300,000 for a summer "Crisis in the Nation" priority program. Fifteen—among them the one to which the program's coordination belongs—gave nothing. The NCC's 1969 budget is being trimmed, another hint that the organization may be experiencing crisis fatigue.[8]

Fresno's Council of Churches had to make budget cutbacks as a result of its strike support, as did the NCC. It seemed that the organized church was facing its own crisis—the crisis of responsibility—and that the grape strike and boycott were only making the crisis more immediate and severe.

THE STRIKE AND THE PARTICIPATION BY THE CLERGY

Once the strike began, some clergymen did get actively involved—even to the extent of being arrested in some of the incidents of violence in the early months. For example, the Reverend David Havens of the Migrant Ministry was arrested for disturbing the peace just for reading Jack London's "Definition of a Strikebreaker."

> After God had finished the rattlesnake, the toad, and the vampire, He had some awful substance left with which He made a strikebreaker. A strikebreaker is a two-legged animal with a corkscrew soul, a waterlogged brain, and a combination backbone made of jelly and glue. When a strikebreaker comes down the street, men turn their backs and angels weep in Heaven and the devil shuts the gates of Hell to keep him out. . . .[9]

Chavez and two Catholic priests were arrested for flying over a grower's fields and dropping leaflets (the charge was violation of the grower's air space). About the same time forty-four pickets, including nine ministers, were arrested in New York. And one of the organizers of the first boycott against Schenley was the Reverend James Drake.

[8] *Ibid.*
[9] Dunne, *Delano, the Story of the California Grape Strike*, pp. 13–14.

Churchmen in other parts of the country faced the issue, and militant ministers and laymen began to join the strike lines. The churchmen involved in the strike became a secret weapon: Violence was diminished since most people "don't want to beat up a minister."[10]

Then a group from the National Catholic Rural Life Conference, headed by Father James Vizzard, moved into Delano to study the problem. They came under orders from the diocesan level to avoid public involvement in the strike. Father Vizzard stated the group's objectives:

> (1) to establish a better understanding of the facts of the situation of the conflict between the growers and the grape strikers, and (2) to meet with the leaders of the strike, the representatives of the growers, a group of clergymen of all faiths and listen to their ideas and feelings, after which the group will make its own conclusions and make statements and/or recommendations.[11]

At the end of the conference, the group issued a statement supporting the workers. They were promptly denounced by Bishop A. J. Willinger of the Monterey-Fresno diocese, who accused them of disobeying orders. An *Ave Maria* editorial stated that national problems could not be dealt with on a local level and that it was, therefore, up to the church itself to take a stand. This trip was the first of many made by church groups to the Delano area to see for themselves what was happening. The visits and participation of outside ministers were bitterly criticized by the local clergy, who said that "clergy should confine themselves to 'spiritual areas.' "[12] The growers referred to the visitors as "outside agitators."

When in March 1966 Chavez organized his march to Sacramento to dramatize the strike and the boycott in the hope of getting some tangible results by the pressure of publicity, the religious orientation was again evident. The marchers carried two banners—one the banner of the Thunderbird, symbol of the NFWA; the other, the banner of Our Lady of Guadalupe, religious patroness of Mexico. The marchers frequently stopped for open-air rallies at which prayers were offered. And included in the march were many clergymen. The archbishop of San Francisco, Joseph T. McGucken, sent Father Thomas Fry to represent him. Catholic groups were finally becoming actively involved in the movement. In addition to the National Catholic Rural Life Conference, two more Catholic groups gave the strikers support—the Bishops Committee on Migratory Labor and

[10] "Massive Awakening of Religious Community to Responsibility," *The New York Times*, February 20, 1966, p. 11.

[11] National Catholic Rural Life Conference, *Report*, Washington, D.C., December 10, 1965, p. 1.

[12] "Grapes of Wrath," *Time*, December 10, 1965, p. 96.

the Bishops Committee on the Spanish-Speaking. Before the march they had dared give only vocal support, but now they contributed funds and sent representatives to walk with the workers.

After the capitulation of Schenley and the end of the march came the merger of AWOC and NFWA into UFWOC and the controversy over the DiGiorgio election in the summer of 1966. At this point the growers began to criticize the Catholic Church for using unfair pressure tactics on them to recognize UFWOC. They accused Catholic priests of trying to talk the Teamsters into cooperating with UFWOC. Bishops of the San Francisco diocese wrote to Napa Valley suppliers, hoping to get them to recognize a union without a vote of the vineyard workers. Growers contended that the bishops engaging in these pressure tactics had no idea of what was going on in Delano and, therefore, had no right to criticize the growers. The bishop of Sacramento shortly thereafter reprimanded a Father Eugene Lucas for actively supporting union activities, and Bishop Alden Bell ordered him to refrain from picketing. Members of the Diocesan Assembly of Sacramento then held a pray-in in defense of the reprimanded priest and sent the bishop a petition asking for his reconsideration. The Catholic Church was caught: What position should it take vis-à-vis the growers and the workers?

Pope Paul VI had warned all bishops not to take a direct and active role in reforming the social and economic order. And the attitude of the hierarchy in most churches in the United States had severely limited the effectiveness of the churches in working in and on social problems. For example, most of the clergymen who went to Delano did not support Bishop Willinger of the Fresno diocese, as he opposed the formation of the union. He was later replaced by a younger man, Bishop Timothy Manning, who consistently but not unconditionally supported the union. Bishop Manning appointed a full-time worker for the migrant workers and the growers. The appointee, a Franciscan named Mark Day, succeeded with the workers but not with the growers because of his open support of the union.

When in October UFWOC began the strike and boycott against Giumarra, the Reverend James Drake of the United Church of Christ and the Migrant Ministry was in charge of organizing the nationwide boycott. When Giumarra countered the boycott by persuading other growers to let him market grapes under their labels, ministers began working in the packing sheds to observe which labels were being used.

In the early part of 1968, Chavez, still not satisfied with the results of the boycott and fearful of possible violence as the strike/boycott dragged on and on, decided to make a public fast. He ended the twenty-five-day fast in March at an open-air mass which was attended by Catholic Senator

Robert Kennedy and a large number of the clergy, again demonstrating publicly church support of the movement.

Role of the Church—Conflicting Views

The role of the churches and the clergy varied throughout the long strike. It was often difficult to distinguish the role and difficult to generalize about it because each established church and even the individual clergy within it had different conceptions of what the church ought or ought not to be or do. A Catholic clergyman, Father James Vizzard, said:

> But the Church institutions do not exist for their own sake. Nor does the Church itself exist solely for the comfortable, affluent, and powerful who use or support those institutions. In other words, I'm saying that I believe we . . . have to put it on the line now—or at least, that my convictions dictate that I have to.[13]

(This statement was made in connection with the problem of financial support versus support for the workers felt particularly by the local clergy in Delano.) At one point, Cesar Chavez tried to explain the movement and the position of the farm workers to an old priest of Spanish descent after a wedding one day; the witness to the conversation, Father James Conway, stated that this priest could not understand what Chavez was talking about: He simply did not comprehend the notions of "union," "workers' rights," "civil rights," and so forth. On the other side, the Reverend Francis Geddes said, "The Church cannot remain silent," and the Reverend Wayne Hartmire of the California Migrant Ministry said, "The Churchmen should lead the way."[14] (The Reverend Francis Geddes was later arrested and jailed with thirty others in October 1965; he also took part in the Selma March.)

Should the church role have been that of mediator between grower and worker, that of medium of communication between the two groups? Or should it have been that of protector of the weak, in this case the workers? Should the church have been active, passive, or deliberately neutral? Did the church have the right to impose moral standards and values—that is, tell the growers they were wrong and must allow a union? The church

[13] *National Catholic Rural Life Conference*, Washington, D.C., December 10, 1965, pp. 3, 5.

[14] Alice Ogle, "Revolution in the Vineyards," *America*, 113 (December 11, 1965), 747–748.

hierarchy, especially the Roman Catholic hierarchy, had on particular
occasions demonstrated support for the workers, or opposition, but there
had been no clear-cut sign of the formulation and implementation of a real
policy concerning the church and the social issues of the day.

Church Activities—Results

Outside of the Delano area, the churches in general had been more
cooperative: they had given rooms for meetings; clergymen had participated in every picket line that had been set up; the official paper of the
bishop of Saint Paul had recommended that everyone boycott grapes.
Catholic bishops from all over the country, including those in the San
Francisco area, were continually putting pressure on the growers to allow
elections among their workers to determine if they wanted a union. At
least one priest believed that Chavez's "religiosity is too ostentatious not to
be contrived."[15] He believed that Chavez was using the church and that
the church let itself be used, a common notion expressed by many.

The disapproval of the growers, influential laymen, and parishioners
notwithstanding, church support had been one of the primary forces
behind Chavez, although the rationale for such support had been different
for different denominations and clergy. For example, in May 1969, Archbishop Joseph T. McGucken, declaring Catholic Church support for the
grape boycott, stated: "If the priests weren't with the strikers, the Communists would be. The only thing that keeps the extreme radicals out is
our priests being there."[16] However, this statement drew a sharp rebuke
from Giumarra, one of the most militant growers, who accused the archbishop of "acting in a most negative way, exacerbating a social ill."[17]

The National Conference of Catholic Bishops played a key role in the
resolution of the grape dispute. At its semi-annual meeting in November
1968, the conference endorsed the right of the grape pickers to organize,
but, at the request of two California bishops, the conference struck out
endorsement of the boycott. At their next meeting in April 1969, the
bishops sent telegrams to congressional leaders urging farm labor legislation. After the conference's November 1969 meeting, a committee of five
bishops began investigating farm labor problems in detail. The group,
headed by Bishop Joseph F. Donnelly of Hartford, Connecticut, was

---

[15] Bergon, Frank, Norris, and Murray, *Delano* (*Another Crisis in the Catholic
Church*) (Washington, D.C.: Ruddell Publishing Company, 1968), p. 19.

[16] "A Grower's Rebuke for Archbishop," *San Francisco Chronicle*, May 15, 1969,
p. 5.

[17] *Ibid.*

impressed by arguments from both sides, and decided that collective bargaining was the only way to resolve the dispute. In March 1970, after five months of study, the committee, which included Archbishop Timothy Manning of Los Angeles and Bishop Hugh Donohoe of Fresno first sat down with Chavez and a group of growers.[18]

The conference's 260 United States Catholic bishops represented the nation's 32 million Catholics, and this lent weight to the bishop's efforts at convincing the growers of Chavez's sincerity and religious convictions. The bishops remained neutral during the talks.[19] Indeed, Monsignor Roger Mahoney, secretary of the bishops' committee, said, "Our participation in the negotiations has usually been at the invitation of growers, not the union. So many people think the church has tried to push Chavez down on these companies—it's not the case."[20]

The success of the bishops efforts, considering the bitterness behind the dispute, was spectacular and somewhat unexpected. As Bishop Donnelly said, "To tell the truth, we didn't expect it would happen this year." The bishop said that his committee would continue its efforts in other farm labor negotiations.[21]

---

[18] Dick Meister, "A Break in Grape Strike—2 Growers OK Contracts," *San Francisco Chronicle*, April 2, 1970, p. 3; "Grape Boycott: Round 2," *New Republic*, April 25, 1970, pp. 10–11; "Big Grape Growers Sign with Union," *San Francisco Chronicle*, May 22, 1970, p. 3; Edward B. Fiske, "Catholic Bishops Worried by Priests Who Wed," *New York Times*, November 14, 1968, p. 22; Edward B. Fiske, "U.S. Bishops Back Priest's Celibacy," *New York Times*, April 18, 1969, p. 40.

[19] "A harvest nears for Cesar Chavez," *Business Week*, June 27, 1970, pp. 62–63; Steven V. Roberts, "First Grapes with Union Label Shipped to Market from Coast," *New York Times*, May 31, 1970, p. 56; "One Grower Who Saw the Inevitable," *San Francisco Chronicle*, July 8, 1970, p. 9.

[20] Henry Elliot Weinstein, "With the Grape Pacts Signed, Cesar Chavez Looks to Other Crops," *Wall Street Journal*, July 31, 1970, p. 1.

[21] "Chavez Plans a March," *San Francisco Chronicle*, July 31, 1970, p. 4.

IV

———◆———

THE CHANGING NATURE
OF
GOVERNMENT
AND
BUSINESS
RELATIONSHIPS

A.
INDIRECT/DIRECT USE OF THE PRESIDENT'S EXECUTIVE AUTHORITY

—◆—

The Steel Price Controversy

*Kennedy-Johnson and the Discretionary
Use of Presidential Power*

Sometime ago I asked each American to consider what he would do for his country, and I asked steel companies. In the last twenty-four hours we had their answer.

My father always told me that all businessmen were sons of bitches, but I never believed it until now.

—PRESIDENT JOHN F. KENNEDY

The steel controversy was the result of a power struggle in which—either by accident or design—U.S. Steel openly challenged the office of the Presidency, and the President chose to meet that challenge with the full powers of the office of the Presidency—but . . . he paid a tremendous price for his "victory."

—ROY HOOPES
in *The Steel Crisis*

The steel industry has been involved for years in crises and confrontations both with its unions and with the United States government. President Truman even "nationalized" it temporarily (but the Supreme Court ruled the action unconstitutional). Indirect attempts to keep down steel prices, called "jawboning," have been tried successively by Presidents Eisenhower, Kennedy, and Johnson. Nixon, although an active participant in Eisenhower's attempts to keep steel prices stable, opposed this policy in his election campaigns and by mid-1970 had refrained from interfering in price raisings by steel and other industries in the face of unabating inflation, rising unemployment, and the nosediving stock market.

The primary focus of this study is the social and political environment in the United States as it affects vital industrial enterprises—the concepts of

355

free market, competitive economy, and freedom of private enterprise not-withstanding—and the obligation of the government to protect the public interest as it sees it. What happens when the delicate balance between government and business spheres of activity is upset by changes in eco-nomic circumstances or by the outlook, beliefs, and actions of men who control these institutions? The ensuing struggle and the outcome are never confined to the immediate issues but have a lasting effect on all social institutions. The steel price controversy provides us with a classic example. Brewing since the Eisenhower days, it exploded with tremendous impact on the national horizon when, despite President Kennedy's urging, the U.S. Steel Corporation defied him and announced an across-the-board price increase on April 10, 1962. As one observer pointed out, the issues surrounding the price of steel were not of economics, but of power.[1] The complicated and controversial economics of steel pricing cannot be treated here exhaustively. Treatment of economic issues is limited to providing an understanding of some of the motivations of the parties involved in the controversy and the use or misuse of statistics to support various view-points.[2]

BACKGROUND: THE EISENHOWER LEGACY

In June 1959 the United Steelworkers Union called for a strike against the steel industry, and in the same month the Eisenhower administration, acting through Vice-President Richard M. Nixon and Secretary of Labor James P. Mitchell, began participating in the negotiations between indus-try and union. To both parties in the negotiations, who had been preparing for the talks for nine months, the government intervention came as a surprise. The government, calling for an agreement that would not necessi-tate a price increase in steel, said any wage increases should be justified on the basis of increased worker productivity alone. The contract not only did

---

[1] Roy Hoopes, *The Steel Crisis* (New York: The John Day Company, 1963), p. 243.

[2] Some sources concerned with the economics of steel prices are Charles L. Schultze, "Study Paper No. 1, Recent Inflation in the United States," for the Joint Economic Committee's "Study of Employment, Growth, and Price Levels," United States Con-gress, September 1959; "Employment, Growth, and Price Levels: Report of the Joint Economic Committee," Congress of the United States, January 26, 1960; "Administered Prices: A Compendium on Public Policy," Subcommittee on Antitrust and Monopoly of the Committee on the Judiciary, U.S. Senate, 88th Cong., 1st sess., March 11, 1963; G. J. McManus, "Has Steel Turned Profit Corner?" *The Iron Age*, November 7, 1968, pp. 57–58; Robert R. Miller, "Price Stability, Market Control, and Imports in the Steel Industry," *Journal of Marketing*, April 1968, pp. 16–20; Gertrude Shirk, "The 5.94-Year Cycle in Steel Production," *Cycles*, May 1968, pp. 54–60; Richard S. Thorn, "The Trouble with Steel," *Challenge*, July–August, 1967, pp. 8–13.

not prevent a price increase but the increase was rather long lasting. The contract, to extend until mid-1962, called for periodic wage increases—the final one being in October 1961.

By July 1961 both industry and union were planning ahead for the 1962 talks. According to *Business Week*, "the industry is uncomfortably aware that its every move will be under the close scrutiny of the Administration." In fact, these feelings began when John F. Kennedy was elected to the presidency the previous November, for "both his position as a senator and his labor policies as a presidential candidate left no doubts about a quick end of any hands-off policy in disputes." The steel industry, always opposed to third-party intrusion in management-union relations, considered it potentially as dangerous to a continuing competitive free market society as compulsory arbitration. The steel industry became even more uneasy in July 1961 when Kennedy's advisory committee on labor-management relations began a study of "free and responsible collective bargaining and industrial peace."[3]

STEEL PRICES AND THE LIBERAL DEMOCRATS

Inflation was a key concern of the 1961 Congress. The Democratic majority, determined to control it, was sure of sympathetic understanding in the New Frontier activism of the Kennedy administration. Therefore, when the steel industry publications speculated about a price increase of four to five dollars per ton to compensate for the union pay raise, there was a flurry of debate and activity in the Senate. The debate was significant because some saw it as an attempt by the liberal Democratic congressional majority to prevent a price hike by threatening the industry with government regulation.[4]

On August 22, 1961, Senator Frank E. Moss (D-Utah) contended that between 1947 and 1958, 40 percent of the rise in the wholesale price index stemmed from steel prices being pushed up faster and further than the average of all other commodity prices. He felt that steel's importance in the United States price structure could scarcely be overestimated as it was not only a truly basic commodity, upon which most of our industrial capability depended, but its price had an enormous psychological effect on the price-setting process in other industries and was traditionally a bellwether of the economy. Through pyramiding, a $6 per ton rise in the price

---

[3] "Steel Has Eye on Washington," *Business Week*, July 22, 1961, pp. 102–3.

[4] For documentation of senators' statements, see the *Congressional Record* for the 87th Cong., 1st sess., 1961, August 22, pp. 16679–88, 16694–708, 16710–14; August 29, pp. 17324–25; September 7, pp. 18519–64.

of steel in 1958 raised the cost of a tractor using only half a ton of steel as much as $97!

Senator Albert Gore (D-Tenn.), by far the most vociferous Senate opponent of steel's pricing policies, charged that the steel industry administered prices—prices set without regard to economic laws of supply and demand. He cited a study by the Joint Economic Committee of the Congress[5] which "proved beyond reasonable doubt that administered prices played the key role in the inflation of recent years." According to Gore, the industry had "established something of a ritual when the time for administered price increase is upon them." Months before any increase, steel executives used their trade publications "as a medium of communications in their mock sparring" to see which company was to be the price leader and "how far it is safe to push up the price." All this was done, not by "collusive understanding," but almost by habit. "It almost reminds one of the mating season dances of the Gooney birds," said Gore.

Gore charged that there was a plan afoot for the steel companies, acting as always in concert, to raise the price of steel by an appreciable amount some time in the fall of 1961. He further contended that "market forces will not bring about, nor will they justify, this increase," since the industry was earning a "good rate of return on low levels of production." The senator concluded that public welfare demands prevented a price rise and "the real question is how to prevent such a rise within the framework of our free enterprise system." This prevention would have to be the government's job and Gore indicated several ways it could act:

1. The president of the United States should use his great legal and moral powers in which he would be backed by the majority of the Congress. Should the steel industry show any recalcitrance, he should not hesitate to pursue many options open to him including "bringing to bear the vast weight of public opinion."
2. The Federal Trade Commission could move to police the steel industry according to the mandate laid down for it by Congress.
3. The Department of Justice, Antitrust Division, could investigate the steel industry in light of administered prices.

Gore made one of the more controversial statements of the debate when he said that large steel companies should possibly be divided into smaller units to restore true competition and free enterprise to the steel industry. And, if all else failed, steel prices could be brought under utility-type regulations. Few would favor this, but it might be necessary. The public and the government must not be victimized by either big business or big labor, or both.

Senators Gale W. McGee (D-Wyo.) and Paul H. Douglas (D-Ill.) also

[5] John F. Kennedy, while still a senator, was a member of this committee in 1959.

warned the steel industry against price increases, citing their adverse effect on the United States balance of payments, and suggested that higher revenues would accrue if prices were reduced instead of increased.

Senator Estes Kefauver (D-Tenn.), chairman of the Subcommittee on Antitrust and Monopoly which investigated the steel industry after the 1959 strike, also felt that the steel price rise was unjustified. He noted that between 1947 and 1959, according to the Bureau of Labor Statistics, average hourly earnings in the steel industry rose 113 percent while man-hour productivity increased only 43 percent. Thus the unit labor cost grew, but by only 70 percent, while steel prices jumped 109.7 percent.

Kefauver added that there was no basis for the industry's frequent claim that an increase in employment costs was accompanied by increases in nonemployment costs, since the industry had failed to show any such nonemployment cost increases. Moreover, the price of one steelmaking material, purchased scrap, had declined sharply since 1956. Kefauver noted that steel industry defenders often erroneously attributed uniform price increases in the industry to uniform increases in wage costs (all steel companies dealt with the same union).

> . . . the fallacy in this argument is that while it may explain the uniformity of the increases, it does not explain the identity of price levels after the increases. Even if the wage increases were the same for each company, the costs bases to which they were applied were not, and are not, uniform.

Kefauver contended that a price hike in the face of unused capacity was "a violation of the consent order entered into in 1951 by the steel industry under Section 5 of the Federal Trade Commission Act," under which the industry was "ordered to cease and desist from entering into any 'planned common course of action, understanding or agreement' to adopt, establish, fix, or maintain prices."[6]

Kefauver began his argument by noting that when one steel company lowered its prices, competing companies also lowered theirs. However, illogically, the same rationale was used for price increases: prices were *raised*, to meet competition! Why, Kefauver asked, did firms with equal or greater efficiency invariably feel it necessary to go along with U.S. Steel's increases? And why, in view of the relationship between operating rate, as a

[6] In 1948, the Federal Trade Commission issued a complaint against virtually all members of the steel industry, charging that there had been a conspiracy to fix prices in violation of section 5 of the Federal Trade Commission Act. It was a major antitrust case. There were 1,237 exhibits and 5,458 pages of testimony. Finally, on June 15, 1951, the steel companies voluntarily entered into a consent decree which they themselves had proposed to the commission.

percentage of capacity, and return on investment, did no major steel producer adopt a *smaller* price increase than the leader's?

> By simply not participating in a general price advance, any major
> steel producer would in a very short time secure a sufficient volume of
> orders to significantly raise its operating rate and thus its profit rate.
> Yet in the recession year of 1958, when all of the leading firms were
> operating below 60 percent of capacity, none availed themselves of
> this opportunity.

A final economic point presented by Senators Albert Gore and Hubert
H. Humphrey (D-Minn.) was the impact any steel price increase might
have on the industry's talks with the United Steelworkers Union. They
contended that "by refraining from raising prices of steel in October, the
steel companies would improve their bargaining position when wage
negotiations are again undertaken in 1962. . . . If steel prices rise in
October it would be naive of the steel companies to believe that the
advance in profit margins which results will last much longer than the end
of the next series of labor-management negotiations in mid-1962."

THE REPUBLICAN REPLY

The widespread and generally negative press reaction to the Democratic
attack on the steel industry was variously used by the Republican senators
to support their arguments. The press comments were divided into three
main areas: The attack on the steel industry was also an attack on the free
enterprise system, the attack was well planned, and the tactics used were
those of intimidation and fear and were unworthy of the representatives of
the people in a democratic society. The following comments were perhaps
typical of those expressed by the news media in general.

A *New York Times* editorial attacked Gore's "threats" to break up the
steel industry:

> The private enterprise system operates on the assumption that
> prices should be set in the marketplace, and reflect the force of
> competition among buyers and sellers. The Senate floor is not the
> marketplace. . . . Competition is probably a much more real force
> in the American economy than Senator Gore believes. . . .
> In the case of steel, for example, there is not only the elementary
> competition of different producers and sellers, but also the competi-
> tion to steel from other metals and plastics, and the significant
> competition given domestic steel by imports of foreign steel.[7]

---

[7] "Price Fixing in Congress," editorial, *The New York Times*, August 24, 1961.

Senator Gore replied that steel price increases involved the public interest—they activated the price/wage spiral—and unless big industry and big
labor used self-restraint, government would have to intervene to safeguard
the public interest.[8]

The August 31 issue of *Iron Age*, a steel industry trade publication, said
of the Democrats who led the attack on steel that the timing of "this well-
planned attack" had a definite purpose. It added up like this:

> Congress will be adjourned soon for the fall recess; therefore, scare
> the steel companies out of increasing prices during the time Congress
> is unable to act.
>
> Although this type of moral suasion is not direct control, it can
> have the same effect. The importance of the group attack can not be
> over-emphasized. This group represents the Senate majority, the
> Administration, and the forces of trustbusting, small business, the
> consumer, and labor. Like a single voice, they agreed the nation's
> steel companies could not justify price increases this fall.[9]

On September 7, 1961, the Republican minority in the Senate responded to the Democratic attacks on a possible steel price increase. Their
rebuttal questioned the Democrats' use of intimidation tactics and the
accuracy and appropriateness of their statistics and logic.

On the first point Senator Everett Dirksen (R-Ill.) said:

> This appears, so far as I know, to be the first attempt at psycho-
> logical price control by using threats, and by using persuasion, as
> weapons and as appeals to a kind of fear instinct. . . . One has no
> business trying, through the powers of government and through
> threats, to tell the producers what the price shall be unless they have
> had an opportunity to present their case, because that is an ex parte
> action, if I have ever seen one.

Republican senators criticized the Democrats' economic reasoning.
Senator Barry Goldwater gave the most complete and detailed answer to
the attacks on the steel industry by counterattacking the Democrats'
strategy, their analysis of inflation's causes, their contention that competition did not exist in the industry, their statistics, and their analysis of the
balance-of-payments problem.

STRATEGY. Of the Democrats' strategy, Goldwater said that by attacking
the industry before it had made any price increases the Democrats were

[8] "Gore Defends Steel Debate—Senator Opposes Price Increase as Spur to Inflation,"
Letters to the Editor section, *The New York Times*, August 27, 1961.

[9] R. W. Crosby, "Senators Launch Attack against 'Phantom' Steel Price Hikes," *The
Iron Age*, August 31, 1961, pp. 55–57.

"laying the groundwork for controls," and they should "explain why they have not [also] taken vigorous anti-inflation action on unnecessary government spending, or have not exerted equal pressure on current wage demands which, in the past, have proved to be the most contributory factor behind 'cost-push' inflation."

CAUSES OF INFLATION. Inflation, said Goldwater, must be attributed to three broad influences "far beyond the confines of a single company or industry" such as steel: government deficit spending; cost-push inflation; and "better business conditions," or "the reemployment of production resources which have been idle for the past year and a half."

When government blamed the wrong sources for inflation, it put the steel industry "in an economic-political dilemma." Economics prevented raising prices during bad market periods (although costs continued to rise), but in good periods the government tried to prevent a price-cost adjustment.

COMPETITION IN THE STEEL INDUSTRY

Goldwater contended that there *was* competition in the steel industry, that many large steel buyers frequently divided their orders, playing one steel company against another, and cited specific voluntary price cuts.

> The Senators are really saying that free enterprise—the competitive marketplace—is not the proper place to set prices. They are also saying that American business is not public-interest minded, but is avaricious to the point where it must be broken into little pieces or completely regulated by a political body.
> This, by any other name is socialism.

STATISTICS. Goldwater attacked the Democratic senators' use of statistics. The base years for their statistics, the senator said, were designed to favor their argument and were "nontypical."

As an example of what changing the base year could do for statistics, Senator Wallace F. Bennett (R-Utah) later noted that if 1940 were used as a base year, employment costs from 1940 to 1960 increased 322 percent and output per man-hour increased 40 percent. "This represents an inflationary gap of 282 percentage points. Prices were bound to increase under such pressures. And this they did, to the extent of 174 percent."

Iron Age criticized using 1947 as a base year as a "setup to prove one point alone—what the White House wanted to prove." During the Depression steel prices were "among the lowest in the century" due to a "blood-letting spate of price cutting" from 1932 to 1939. The industry was thus caught with its prices so low during the wartime price freeze that it "was in danger of financial chaos." The fast pace of wartime production resulted in an industry "hard up for money to expand its capacity, to repair its plants and equipment."[10] Steel began to raise its prices after the war, not to gouge the consumer but rather, in the words of *Business Week*, to "recover profitability and generate heavy retained earnings to help finance massive plant rehabilitation and expansion." Thus began a price spiral lasting until 1955. In 1958, however, U.S. Steel, feeling that it "might be pricing its product too high," refused to lead in any price increase after the labor settlement and "forced its competitors to take the initiative. . . . Thus began the price stability of the past 37 months."[11]

In addition, Goldwater said the Bureau of Labor Statistics' indexes were misleading as they were made up of one size and quality for each of the common forms of steel products and "tend to overstate the actual prices prevailing on the market." They did not reflect changes in freight absorption, in product quality, or in extras added by a steel company. In fact, if all factors were included, an excellent case could be made that steel prices had actually dropped in the face of rising costs.

BALANCE OF PAYMENTS. Goldwater accused the Democratic senators of implying that the country's balance-of-payments problems were due solely to the excess of steel imports over exports when in fact the trend was paralleled by almost all of American industry. The American steel industry could not compete because employment costs had risen faster than the productivity level, but to compete and produce, industry needed the best of equipment, and that came only from private investment. Therefore, the profit incentive must be kept alive if the United States steel industry was to be competitive.

Finally Goldwater argued that "if the steel companies charged too much, they must have made too much money. Yet, every investment yardstick shows just the opposite." Securities and Exchange Commission figures demonstrated that steel was less profitable than many other industries, and in spite of all the power its antagonists ascribed to it, it had not been able to increase its profitability to the level of other industries.

If it has that kind of power—and ended up with that kind of result—it is the most public spirited private enterprise in the history of this country. Certainly no amount of public control and regulation could do as well.

[10] Tom Campbell, "Steel Men Hot under the Collar at President's Price Attack," *The Iron Age*, September 14, 1961, pp. 143–44.

[11] "Steel Price Increase Hopes Are Dashed," *Business Week*, September 16, 1961, p. 25.

THE PRESIDENT ACTS

On September 6, 1961, the day before the Republican rebuttal in the Senate, President Kennedy sent telegrams to the chief executive officers of the twelve[12] largest steel companies, saying: "I am taking this means of communicating to you, and to the chief executive officers of 11 other steel companies, my concern for stability of steel prices. . . ."

Using 1947 as the base period he contended that between 1947 and 1958 steel prices rose by 120 percent—during the same period industrial prices as a whole rose by 39 percent, and employment costs in the steel industry rose by 85 percent—providing much of the inflationary impetus in the American economy and adversely affecting steel exports and United States balance of payments. He went on to say that although since 1958 the general price level and steel prices had stabilized, this was accomplished at the cost of persistent unemployment and underutilized productive capacity including that of the steel industry whose utilization rate during the preceding three years had averaged 65 percent. In consequence,

> many persons have come to the conclusion that the United States can achieve price stability only by maintaining a substantial margin of unemployment and excess capacity and by accepting a slow rate of economic growth. This is a counsel of despair which we cannot accept.
>
> For the last three years, we have not had to face the test of price behavior in a high-employment economy. This is the test which now lies ahead.
>
> The amount of the increase in employment cost per man-hour [on October 1] will be difficult to measure in advance with precision. But it appears almost certain to be outweighed by the advance in productivity resulting from a combination of two factors—the steady long-term growth of output per man-hour, and the increasing rate of operations foreseen for the steel industry in the months ahead.
>
> The Council of Economic Advisors has supplied me with estimates of steel industry profits after October 1, . . . and the steel industry, in short, can look forward to good profits without an increase in prices.
>
> The owners of the iron and steel companies have fared well in recent years.

[12] Armco Steel Corporation, Bethlehem Steel Corporation, Colorado Fuel & Iron Corporation, Inland Steel Company, Jones & Laughlin Steel Corporation, Kaiser Steel Corporation, McLouth Steel Corporation, National Steel Corporation, Republic Steel Corporation, United States Steel Corporation, Wheeling Steel Corporation, and Youngstown Sheet & Tube Company.

A steel price increase in the months ahead could shatter the price stability which the country has now enjoyed for some time. In a letter to me on the impact of steel prices on defense costs, Secretary of Defense McNamara states: "A steel price increase of the order of $4 to $5 a ton, once its effects fanned out through the economy, would probably raise the military procurement costs by $500 million per year or more. . . ."

In emphasizing the vital importance of steel prices to the strength of our economy, I do not wish to minimize the urgency of preventing inflationary movements in steel wages. I recognize, too, that the steel industry, by absorbing increases in employment costs since 1958, has demonstrated a will to halt the price-wage spiral in steel. If the industry were now to forego a price increase, it would enter collective bargaining negotiations next spring with a record of three and one-half years of price stability. The moral position of the steel industry next spring—and its claim to the support of public opinion—will be strengthened by the exercise of price restraint now.

I have written you at length because I believe that price stability in steel is essential if we are to maintain the economic vitality necessary to face confidently the trials and crises of our perilous world. Our economy has flourished in freedom; let us now demonstrate again that the responsible exercise of economic freedom serves the national welfare.

I am sure that the owners and managers of our nation's major steel companies share my conviction that the clear call of national interest must be heeded.

Sincerely,
JOHN F. KENNEDY

RESPONSE TO THE PRESIDENT'S LETTER

According to *Iron Age*,[13] Kennedy's letter stunned the industry. The steel executives thought that by refraining from a price rise for three years, despite employment cost boosts, they were already acting in the national interest and being competitive with foreign steel and domestic substitute materials.

Business Week[14] said the response to the letter was "immediate anger and long-term alarm." The steel industry scorned Kennedy's reasoning, resented his motivation, and the list of United States presidents it did not trust now read: Harry Truman, Dwight Eisenhower, John Kennedy. Compounding the resentment was the widespread belief that Kennedy

[13] Campbell, "Steel Men Hot under the Collar," pp. 143–44.
[14] *Business Week*, September 16, 1961, p. 25.

would not act against any excessive wage demands by the United Steel-workers. Where only selective price boosts were the most any "realist" could have expected from the industry, now even that was extremely unlikely. Where would the industry with such a rapidly advancing technology get the $1 billion a year needed to replace obsolete plants and implement new efficiencies?

The recipients of the president's letter—who were generally critical of the steel industry's being singled out while other causes of inflation were ignored—were largely noncommittal in regard to steel prices. The most publicized reply came from Roger Blough, chairman of U.S. Steel.

> I am certain, Mr. President, that your concern regarding inflation is shared by every thinking American who has experienced its serious effects during the past 20 years. . . . First, let me assure you that if you seek the causes of inflation in the United States, present or future, you will not find them in the levels of steel prices or steel profits.

Blough then used 1940 as a base year and noted that although steel prices had risen 174 percent since that time, employment costs had risen 322 percent. Wage-earner costs had increased and "far exceeded any productivity gains that could be achieved," despite new investment. Blough continued:

> So far as profits are concerned, your advisers have chosen to measure them in terms of the return on reported net worth; and again I am afraid that this does more to confuse than to clarify the issue in the light of the eroding effects of inflation on investments in steel-making facilities over the past 20 years. If we compare the 50-cent profit dollars of today to the 100-cent dollars that were invested in our business 20 years ago, the resulting profit ratio can hardly be said to have any validity. . . .

> The most useful measurement of the profit trend in a single industry, over an inflationary period, is, of course, profit as a percentage of sales. On this basis . . . profits in the steel industry have only once in the past 20 years equaled the 8% level at which they stood in 1940, and have averaged only 6½% in the past five years. . . . [Moreover] averages can be dangerously misleading. Some companies will earn more than the average, while some may be suffering losses which they cannot sustain indefinitely. So it was in 1960 that among the 30 largest steel companies the profit rate as a percentage of sales ranged from a plus 9.3% to a loss of 5.2%.

> Whatever figures your advisers may elect to use, however, the simple fact is that the profit left in any company, after it pays all costs, is all that there is out of which to make up for the serious

inadequacy in depreciation to repay borrowings, to pay dividends and to provide for added equipment. If the profit is not good enough to do these things, they cannot and will not be done; and that would not be in the national interest.

So reviewing the whole picture, I cannot quite see how steel profits could be responsible for inflation—especially when their portion of the sales dollar over the last 20 years has never exceeded 8 cents and is lower than that today.

As for the admittedly hazardous task which your economic advisers have undertaken in forecasting steel industry profits at varying rates of operation . . . it might reasonably appear to some—as frankly, it does to me—that they seem to be assuming the role of informal price-setters for steel—psychological or otherwise. But if for steel, what then for automobiles, or rubber, or machinery or electric products, or food, or paper, or chemicals—or a thousand other products? Do we thus head into unworkable, stifling peacetime controls of prices? Do we do this when the causes of inflation—in a highly competitive economy with ample industrial capacity such as ours—are clearly associated with the fiscal, monetary, labor and other policies of Government?

Blough noted that steel prices were at a level "slightly lower" than two years previously and that competitive factors such as foreign steel and domestic substitute materials provided effective competition for steel. He argued that no company, industry, or for that matter, country could disregard the inexorable pressure of the market if it wanted to maintain its position in a competitive world. Furthermore, he contended that as far as inflation was concerned the price of steel was a symptom and not the major cause of the problem.

THE ADMINISTRATION AND THE STEEL TALKS[15]

That steel prices were not raised in October was attributed to economic forces and not to the president's letter. Kennedy's letter was not the final involvement of the government in the industry's affairs, however, for—although the United Steelworkers' contract was to expire on July 1, 1962—in November 1961, Labor Secretary Arthur Goldberg pointed out that the administration was willing to use its good offices to achieve an early settle-

[15] Documentation for this section appears in Hoopes, *The Steel Crisis*, especially pp. 45–52, which is a complete, almost moment-by-moment account of the administration's activities in regard to steel from Fall 1961 to Fall 1962. A shorter book of the same nature is Grant McConnell's *Steel and the Presidency*, 1962 (New York: Norton, 1963).

ment not only to prevent steel users from stockpiling but also to achieve a modest contract and thus prevent another wage-price spiral.

In January several union and industry officials met at the White House to discuss with the president the importance of an early settlement. Goldberg later contacted both union and industry and they began negotiating in early February—the first time since World War II that the two parties had met so early in the year. By discussing the new contract at this time, the union was setting aside its strongest weapon—the threat of a strike at the last minute if its demands were not met. The union also limited its demands to a seventeen-cents-per-hour job security package, forgoing a wage increase. The four industry representatives to the talks said that while the demands "cannot be considered moderate in any sense," they were more moderate than previously and were appropriate considering the problems the country faced.

Apparently, after pressuring the industry, the administration was now pressuring the union (even on national television). Goldberg said that large-scale labor-management conflicts were intolerable because of the Soviet threat and the competition from the European Common Market. (George Meany, head of the AFL-CIO, was reported to have exploded with anger at Goldberg's statements and said that he was "infringing on the rights of a free people and a free society.")

During the talks, in an intereview in *U.S. News and World Report*, Blough said that steel employment costs had risen 12 percent in three years:

> And you're asking me how long can that continue to increase and how long it can be borne without some kind of remedy. I would give you the answer that it's not reasonable to think of it as continuing. In other words, even now there should be a remedy. If any additional cost occurs, the necessity for the remedy becomes even greater.

Renewed negotiations fell flat on March 2, industry saying the benefit package cost was too high. Secretary Goldberg then talked to Roger Blough, who said that the union proposal was inflationary but agreed to resume talks if the union would lower its proposals. Upon Goldberg's intervention, David J. McDonald, president of the United Steelworkers Union, agreed to lower the demands.

Toward the end of March, agreement was reached for a contract which would add ten to eleven cents an hour in a job security package. The contract, signed on April 6, was to be effective at least until April 1963. President Kennedy said the settlement was "obviously noninflationary and should provide a solid base for continued price stability."

Even the business community praised the contract. Roy Hoopes said:

Of course, the steel industry had given no commitment that it would hold the price line, but many people, including most businessmen, assumed that labor's restraint would be followed by no increase in the steel prices for at least six months to a year. Obviously the White House assumed this, and the settlement was considered not only a major victory for the Administration, but a long stride toward a historic transformation in labor-management relations.

THE SHATTERED MASTERPIECE[16]

With the strike threat averted most executives were optimistic about the near future. On April 9, 1962, the *Wall Street Journal* reported that most producers of steel doubted there would be a general rise in steel prices in 1962 (14). However on Friday, April 6, U.S. Steel's operations policy committee—the company's top ten executives—unanimously decided to raise base steel prices about 3.5 percent. On the following Tuesday the Executive Committee of the Board of Directors approved the decision. The Public Relations Department prepared a press release announcing the "catch-up" price as "adjustment."

The reason given for the price increase was the profit squeeze facing the company. The company had spent $1.2 billion for modernization and replacement of plant and equipment since 1958 of which the two sources of money for this investment—depreciation and reinvested profit—contributed only two-thirds. The rest of the money had to be borrowed and "must be repaid out of profits that have not yet been earned and will not be earned for some years to come." The release concluded that the new resources that would be generated by the price increase would improve the company's products and would be "vital not alone to the company and its employees, but to our international balance of payments, the value of our dollar, and to the strength and security of the nation as well" (293).

When the board meeting broke up at 3:00 P.M., Roger Blough phoned for an appointment with Kennedy and after flying to Washington was admitted to see the president at 5:45 P.M. on his as yet unannounced business (220). With a minimum of amenities, Blough handed Kennedy the company press release which was at that moment being sent to newspapers in Pittsburgh and New York, explaining that it was a matter of courtesy to inform the president personally. Kennedy is reported to have said, "I think you have made a terrible mistake." Forthwith he summoned Labor Secretary Arthur Goldberg who raced to the White House and

---

16 All statements in the ensuing discussion not otherwise specifically documented can be found in Hoopes, *The Steel Crisis* (page references shown).

angrily lectured Blough on the effect of the company's decision on the administration's economic policy, in which U.S. Steel also had an important stake, and the effect of the decision on Goldberg's, indeed the whole administration's, credibility in its pleas to unions to restrain their wage demands.

Bough quietly defended U.S. Steel's price increase and left the president's office in less than an hour. Neither Goldberg nor the president asked him to rescind the increase.

As soon as Blough left, Kennedy was reported to have "exploded" with anger and called together high level administration officials and the Council of Economic Advisers. During the meeting the president found that only a "gentlemen's agreement" and never a firm price commitment had been made during the negotiations. Indeed, a request for such a pledge might have violated antitrust laws. As the meeting progressed, the president called his brother, Attorney General Robert F. Kennedy, who later released the announcement that "because of past price behavior in the steel industry, the Department of Justice will take an immediate and close look at the current situation and any future developments." The president also called Senator Kefauver who agreed to issue a statement of "dismay" at U.S. Steel's action and to say that "I have ordered the staff of [my] subcommittee to begin an immediate inquiry into the matter" (22–26). Thus ended the opening moves of the war to hold steel prices. The *Wall Street Journal* said of the day's events, "Wage-price stability in steel was intended as the graven image of a total program of stability; the Kennedy sculptors unveiled it as a finished masterpiece—and then suddenly it was shattered" (53).

REACTION TO THE PRICE HIKE

At the very least, U.S. Steel's timing was extremely poor and clearly embarrassed the White House for, as expected, the United Steel workers were later to say that they would have upped their demands if they had known prices would be raised. The business community was surprised at the move since the early settlement meant that steel users had not stockpiled and that demand was expected to be low until fall. Even so, any price increases were expected to be selective—not across the board—and to occur *after* the union security package took effect on July 1.

The company's lack of understanding of the "gentlemen's agreement" angered administration officials because it had entered into labor-management negotiations to keep the price of steel down. The *St. Louis Dispatch* was skeptical of U.S. Steel's motivations and said that "it looks very much as if the steel masters used the President and his Secretary of Labor, who happens to have been the steelworker's own agent in the 1960 settlement, for the purpose of beating down wage demands prior to a price decision they had in mind all along" (108).

The administration knew about Roger Blough's statement concerning the industry's poor profit situation but attributed it merely to the game of collective bargaining where each side attempts to justify its position. Regardless of Blough's actual reasons it appeared to the White House as either of two things: (1) a challenge to the administration on the broad issue of government intervention in labor-management disputes, or (2) a personal affront to Democratic President John F. Kennedy designed to demonstrate that American industry could be as tough as the much publicized toughness of the New Frontiersmen.

The president accepted the challenge. Rumors soon circulated in Washington that both the Justice Department and the FTC would be conducting antitrust investigations, that the Treasury Department would abandon plans to relax tax depreciation rules, and that the IRS was checking up on U.S. Steel's stock option plan.

In the Congress the Democrats attacked U.S. Steel's action and Speaker John McCormack called it "shocking, arrogant, irresponsible." Most Republicans were cautiously silent as the price hike had taken them by surprise. Senator Gore prepared legislation that would begin government regulation of the steel industry and would establish a cooling-off period before the new prices would be allowed to go into effect.

THE FIRST DAY OF BATTLE

On Wednesday morning, April 11, the president met with members of his administration at a regular pre-press-conference breakfast which was devoted entirely to what to do about steel. The decision was to concentrate on persuading a select group of the large steel companies to hold the price line. Industry sources friendly to the administration had told the White House that if companies producing 16 percent of the industry's output were to hold the line, they would soon capture 25 percent of the market. In a market as competitive as steel, this action would force the other companies to lower their prices. Everyone in the administration who knew anyone in the business world—especially in the steel industry—was urged to telephone him to explain the president's point of view. These calls were "an organized, strategic, integral part of the Administration's campaign." In none of the calls was there an attempt to coax or to threaten—the approach was to explain the government's position, nothing more. The callers discovered that important segments of the business community were far more opposed to the increase than they had been willing to admit publicly.

Inland Steel was deemed to be the key company in the dispute because of its close ties with the government through its board chairman, Joseph L. Block, and because it was probably the most profitable of the large steel companies. But Block was vacationing in Japan at the time.

The purpose of the calls was to get the industry to delay price increases long enough for the administration to launch a counterattack that would make other companies hesitate before raising their prices. The administration learned that if Inland or Armco Steel were to raise prices they would wait at least one or two days, but Bethlehem Steel did not wait. By noon Wednesday Bethlehem announced a raise of six dollars a ton, although less than a day before—at its annual meeting and before U.S. Steel raised its prices—its president had told reporters that Bethlehem would *not* increase prices.

According to *Business Week,* after Bethlehem's announcement, "it looked like a race against time for other producers to get themselves on record before Kennedy's press conference at 3:30 P.M. Most of them made it."[17] These were Republic, Wheeling, Youngstown, and Jones & Laughlin —half of the twelve largest companies had announced higher prices. The president felt that the steel company actions had blatantly and openly challenged the antitrust laws in the noon to 3:30 P.M. rush. Of the six large companies that had not yet raised prices, five had not reached a decision. The combined volume of these five was 14 percent of the market—close to the 16 percent the administration thought necessary to hold the price line.

That afternoon as Kennedy rode to the State Department where he usually held his weekly press conferences, he put the finishing touches on his statement.

> Good afternoon, I have several announcements to make.
> The simultaneous and identical actions of United States Steel and other leading steel corporations increasing steel prices by some six dollars a ton constitute a wholly unjustifiable and irresponsible defiance of the public interest.
> In this serious hour in our nation's history when we are confronted with grave crises in Berlin and Southeast Asia, when we are devoting our energies to economic recovery and stability, when we are asking reservists to leave their homes and families . . . to risk their lives— and four were killed in the last two days in Vietnam—and asking union members to hold down their wage requests . . . the American

17 "The Storm Over Steel," *Business Week,* April 14, 1962, pp. 31–33.

people will find it hard, as I do, to accept a situation in which a tiny handful of steel executives whose pursuit of private power and profit exceeds their sense of public responsibility, can show such utter contempt for the interest of one hundred and eighty-five million Americans. . . .

In short, at a time when they could be exploring how more efficiency and better prices could be obtained, reducing prices in this industry in recognition of lower costs, their unusually good labor contract, their foreign competition and their increase in production and profits which are coming this year, a few gigantic corporations have decided to increase prices in ruthless disregard of their public responsibility.

Kennedy then praised the steel workers' union for abiding by its responsibilities; announced that the FTC would conduct an "informal inquiry" into the possibility that its 1951 consent order with the steel industry had been violated; hinted that the Department of Defense might shift its contracts for steel to price-line holding companies; and mentioned that proposed tax benefits to the steel industry through liberalized depreciation schedules were being reviewed (77–86).

In response to the president's accusation that U.S. Steel had not acted in the public interest, Roger Blough declared: "I feel that a lack of proper cost-price relationship is one of the most damaging things to the public interest." Blough announced that he would be giving his own news conference the next afternoon, Thursday, April 12.

THE SECOND DAY, APRIL 12

The Justice Department, considering a possible antitrust suit against various members of the steel industry, was much interested in the reported Tuesday afternoon statement by Bethlehem's President Martin that his company would not raise prices. But when U.S. Steel raised its prices, Bethlehem was the first to follow suit. There were antitrust implications here—U.S. Steel, because of its immense size, might exercise undue influence over other steel producers—so at 6:00 P.M. Wednesday, Attorney General Kennedy ordered his department to proceed with all possible speed in gathering necessary information. Apparently the FBI overreacted to this order, and between 3:00 A.M. and 4:00 A.M. Thursday phoned several reporters who had been present at Martin's press conference and announced their intention to come calling immediately.

On Thursday morning, Kennedy asked every cabinet member to hold press conferences in the next few days to outline the effect the price increase would have on each department and on every citizen of the land. The Justice Department, instead of the FTC, was given the principal responsibility for investigating the steel industry. The investigation was to include possible price collusion and the extent to which U.S. Steel had monopoly powers dangerous to the national interest.

Also on Thursday two more steel companies, one in the top twelve, announced price increases. On Wall Street the stock market dropped to a new low for 1962, with steel leading the retreat. On Thursday morning Blough himself called Treasury Secretary Douglas Dillon for his assessment of the situation. At the same time FBI agents showed up at eight steel companies with subpoenas requesting information and a look at their files—all but two of these (Inland and Armco) had already raised their prices. Talk from the Pentagon was that exceptions to the Buy America Act might allow the Pentagon to increase its purchases of foreign steel. Secretary Luther H. Hodges gave a noon speech denouncing price fixing and other unethical business tactics (109–10).

THURSDAY AFTERNOON—BLOUGH'S PRESS CONFERENCE

On Thursday afternoon Blough held his news conference:

> . . . We have no wish to add to acrimony or to misunderstanding. We do not question the sincerity of anyone who disagrees with the action we have taken. Neither do we believe that anyone can properly assume that we are less deeply concerned with the welfare, the strength, and the vitality of this nation than are those who have criticized our action. . . .
>
> The President said, when questioned regarding any understanding not to increase prices, "We did not ask either side to give us any assurances, because there is a very proper limitation to the power of the Government in this free economy." Both aspects of this statement are quite right [118–120]. . . .
>
> Our problem in this country is not the problem with respect to prices; our problem is with respect to costs. If you can take care of the costs in this country, you will have no problem taking care of the prices. The prices will take care of themselves [133].

Blough also denied that U.S. Steel was in any way defying the president by its decision, which it had a right to make, and, on the White House role in labor negotiations said, "I have no criticism. I do believe that when the air clears a little bit, I think we will all realize that this type of, shall I say—assistance?—has some limitations."

Blough denied having an understanding with other companies about prices. That prices were raised in a Democratic administration but had been kept level during a Republican one was not significant: "You can readily see that I do not know anything about politics!" One reporter asked if the increase "coming as it did right on the heels of the labor pact—was timed to check expanded government influence in collective bargaining; in other words, that you acted politically as well as economically." Again Blough denied any political motivation. He did mention, though, that if other companies did not raise their prices, U.S. Steel would be obliged to reconsider. The administration interpreted this to mean that victory was possible and that U.S. Steel was seeking an escape route.

All in all, industry sources felt that Blough did not present the best possible case.

THE TURNING POINT

At seven o'clock Thursday evening Attorney General Kennedy announced that he had authorized the Grand Jury to investigate the steel price increases and to find out if U.S. Steel "so dominated the industry that it controls prices and should be broken up." At about the same time Walter Reuther, head of the United Auto Workers Union, proposed that a price board be created to hold hearings on important prices such as steel before they could be increased. Later in the evening Tyson (chairman of the Finance Committee of U.S. Steel's board of directors) and several other U.S. Steel executives met in New York. According to Hoopes, "If there was any single turning point in the steel crisis, it probably came at this meeting." Previously the executives had thought all the uproar political in nature and probably short-lived but were now "convinced that the Administration men meant business." The executives had noticed that Inland had not gone along with the increase, and if it did not soon, Bethlehem would rescind its price and others would naturally follow (145).

THE THIRD DAY

Early in the morning of Friday the thirteenth, Kennedy talked to Roger Blough who suggested that communications should be maintained. Seeing this as a hopeful sign, Kennedy then moved to restrain members of his administration and to preserve a mood of conciliation. Also on Friday morning, Inland's late-Thursday decision not to raise prices was made public. The statement by Joseph Block was that although "profits are not adequate, we do not feel that an advance in steel prices at this time would be in the national interest." Attention now turned to Armco Steel, which had led off the price increase in 1958 when U.S. Steel refused and had a reputation for unpredictability. The real maverick of the industry, Kaiser Steel, had also not yet raised its prices.

Meanwhile rumors circulated that Roger Blough would resign; Inland's stock prices rose; other steel stocks fell; Colorado Fuel and Iron intimated that any price increase would be selective; Youngstown and Reynolds Metals implied that they would wait and see before acting on price levels.

At 10:00 A.M. Defense Secretary Robert S. McNamara stated that "where possible, procurement of steel for defense production will be shifted to those companies which have not increased prices," but he put an end to speculation that the department might increase its purchases of foreign steel because of the resulting unemployment that it might cause in this country.

All during the battle between steel and the administration, public opinion was firmly behind the president as was shown by a number of newspaper polls and by telegrams received by the White House. According to Roy Hoopes, "the majority of the nation's most influential newspapers [were] critical of the steel companies' action, [and] the business community [was] only lukewarm in its support of the steel industry. . . ."

THE FINAL BATTLE

The direct result of Blough's telephone conversation with Kennedy on Friday morning was a meeting the same afternoon of Clifford and Goldberg, and Blough, Tyson, and Worthington (president of U.S. Steel). According to reports, Clifford (a Washington attorney who was friendly to the Kennedy administration) explained that many continuing investigations of steel would be very uncomfortable, especially since Kennedy would be in office for a number of years and doing business in Washington might be difficult. Clifford and Goldberg also explored ways U.S. Steel could roll back its prices and still save face. During the meeting the various members were kept informed of events as they occurred outside: one in particular came at 3:25 P.M. announcing that Bethlehem had rescinded its price increase in order to remain competitive. This was the final blow to the company, and before the meeting was over, Blough and his fellow executives told Clifford and Goldberg that they too would later be announcing a rollback (164).

Within a few hours, in the words of *Time* magazine, there was a "precipitous rush to surrender" as the other steel producers rolled back their prices. The reason given for the rollbacks was "to remain competitive" in spite of poor profit conditions.

GRANT AT APPOMATTOX

Naturally the administration's plans for further attacks on the steel industry and proposed legislation were canceled or filed away and, for once, the administration was not crowing about its victory. As *Business Week* aptly said, "The President went out of his way to assure there will be no public recriminations now that the mistake has been retracted. Like Grant at Appomattox, he is letting the vanquished forces keep their horses and sidearms."

The relationship between the White House and U.S. Steel returned to normal, and Roger Blough agreed to stay on the president's business advisory committee. On other fronts, although the Grand Jury probe would continue, it was obvious that the administration would not press too hard for any indictments. (However, a New York Grand Jury did indict U.S. Steel, Bethlehem, Erie Forge and Steel, and Midvale-Heppenstall on price fixing charges from an investigation begun in March 1961.) The activities of the Justice Department and the FTC were effectively curtailed, and the House investigation of the steel industry was called off, but Kefauver's Senate subcommittee investigation did proceed as scheduled.

THE KENNEDY ANTIBUSINESS CRUSADE

Most of the steel companies held their annual meetings soon after the "price fiasco." All those that had originally raised prices and then backed down maintained that they were forced to do so because the competition did not follow. One element of agreement among all steel spokesmen was that the need for a price increase had not passed—even Joseph Block agreed on this point and said Inland had refused to raise its prices only as a concession to the national interest. One steel executive said, "No company or industry may now raise prices without harboring the fear, and justifiably so, that the Administration may decide to employ the crushing weapons so recently displayed." Despite the industry's unanimous cry for more profits, every company's profit picture for the first quarter of 1961 showed a substantial improvement over the recession-affected first quarter of 1961 (224–25).

Despite its campaign of conciliation, the administration persisted in its economic policies and announced that it might act to prevent a price hike in the aluminum industry. There then began to emerge a "growing hostil-ity" by the business community toward Kennedy, and a stock market crash in the summer of 1962 was attributed by many businessmen to the "Kennedy crowd." According to Roy Hoopes, "By late June and early July, the 'hate Kennedy' mood in the business community had almost reached a state of hysteria" and even rated a cover story in *Newsweek*. Even the Kennedy jokes became bitter and personal.

The animosity collapsed, however, by mid-autumn, perhaps because the administration's attempts at dialogue eventually got through or because a number of business leaders (including Blough and Block) helped to restore the peace. During the summer the Congress passed an administra-tion-backed investment tax credit law and the Treasury Department announced revised tax depreciation schedules.

KENNEDY'S LAST YEAR WITH STEEL

A year passed without steel's making any price increases, but in April 1963 Wheeling Steel Corporation, with less than 2 percent of the United States market, announced a selective price increase of $4.50–$10.00 per ton on six items. "It was as though an electric shock had hit the President and his aides. . . ."[18]

The President's formal reply to the hike was a surprise:

> I realize that price and wage controls in this one industry, while all others are unrestrained, would be unfair and inconsistent with our free competitive market . . . and that selective price adjustments up or down—as prompted by changes in supply and demand as opposed to across-the-board increases—are not incompatible within a frame-work of general stability and steel-price stability and are characteristic of any healthy economy.
>
> In a free society both management and labor are free to do volun-tarily what we are unwilling to enforce by law—and I urge the steel industry and the steel union to avoid any action which would lead to a general across-the-board increase.[19]

Actually, throughout 1963 the government allowed increases on 75 per-cent of the industry's product mix—all without protest.[20]

---

[18] "Can Price Rise Help Steel?" *U.S. News and World Report*, April 22, 1963, pp. 35–37.

[19] *Ibid.*, p. 37.

[20] "Inflation Hassle," *The Wall Street Journal*, October 4, 1967, p. 16.

LYNDON B. JOHNSON'S LESS-VISIBLE POWER

After President Johnson took office, government-industry crises took longer to reach the confrontation stage. During 1967 the administration did not really flex its muscles (saying it did not need to), but in 1968 it acted vigorously to roll back a price boost. The Johnson administration's actions were less visible than Kennedy's but its victory was also less clear-cut. The government criticized Bethlehem Steel's small ($5.00 a ton) increase in structural steel and piling prices on New Year's Day 1966. U.S. Steel, on the other hand, deliberated about a week before raising prices on the products $2.75 a ton and drew praise from Washington. Bethlehem thereupon trimmed back its announced increase. However, the industry's later increases in large volume steel and strip received "only a mild comment of displeasure," and the government "only privately urged stainless steel makers to eschew any price boosts" in the fall, although prices were raised anyway.[21]

The government said nothing publicly about price increases until late August 1967 when Republic Steel hiked its prices 1.8 percent on carbon and alloy steel bars and the administration finally began to move to head off another increase.[22]

1967: THE BIGGEST BINGE IN FOUR YEARS

In response to Republic's boost, Gardner Ackley, chairman of the Council of Economic Advisers, called on the rest of the industry not to follow suit, but U.S. Steel, Bethlehem, Armco, Inland, Jones & Laughlin, and Kaiser raised prices anyway.

Thirteen top industry executives met with Johnson and Ackley on September 13 (at a meeting scheduled before the price rise) and told of the need for increased prices. Ackley later said that discussion of specific price actions would be a violation of antitrust law, and Secretary of Commerce Alexander B. Trowbridge said that no pledge was requested or made.

The *Wall Street Journal*, analyzing the significance of steel's move, said that the steel industry had just treated itself to the biggest price-raising

---

[21] *Ibid.*

[22] "What's News—Business and Finance," *The Wall Street Journal*, September 1, 1967, p. 1.

binge in four years and that the government had even encouraged steel makers by allowing the previous increases.

> The increases so far this year covered 42% of the industry's volume. By contrast, once it became clear that the mills wouldn't back down on sheet and strip in August 1966, Johnson Cabinet members began to describe the increases as covering "only a small fraction" of industry sales and as being "within bounds." Yet those products account for almost 40% of the steel mill sales. . . . The Government may have encouraged more steel price increases but the decision to cover so many products was made by the mills themselves. Their enthusiasm is bound to broaden, at least to some extent, the inflationary movement in the economy.[23]

The *Journal* then went on to criticize the administration's fiscal attempts to control the inflation [tax surcharge and investment tax credit] as being too late or too little.

The *Journal's* predictions were right—a sizable increase in steel orders occurred late in the year. In the first week of December, U.S. Steel raised its base price for cold rolled sheet, the prime steel product by volume, five dollars a ton.

Ackley's response to U.S. Steel's move was to urge the other companies to "consider carefully" the "interests of the industry and the nation" before following suit.

THE PRESIDENT'S RESPONSE: VERBAL POWER

President Johnson's simple response to the increase was that "we have exercised such rights as we had" to keep prices on cold rolled sheet steel down, that Mr. Ackley had expressed the strongly felt views of the administration, and that wage and price controls might be required in the future to avoid inflationary increases.[24]

Clearly Johnson's style toward steel price hikes differed markedly from Kennedy's. A *Wall Street Journal* editorial complimented Ackley for not blaming inflation on steel and also for criticizing the auto union settlement. The editorial pointed out that the administration's pressure on the industry seemed to have been "largely verbal—so far, anyway," and noted the

---

[23] "Inflation Hassle," *The Wall Street Journal*, October 4, 1967, p. 16.

[24] After the industry put through a $3-a-ton increase on hot and cold rolled sheet in August 1966—the previous rise on the product—auto prices rose by $5 to $100. *The Wall Street Journal*, December 4, 1967, p. 3.

contrast with actions Kennedy took, saying, "At least this time they didn't try to hang Roger Blough from the nearest lamppost."[25]

WEDNESDAY, JULY 31, 1968: TIME OF "DIRE CONSEQUENCES"

In May 1968, according to the *Wall Street Journal*, U.S. Steel began to cut prices in areas subject to foreign competition and attempted to keep these "reductions quiet, hoping to prevent them from leading to any general break in steel prices." Big Steel's actions broke with industry precedent which said that importers, backed up with lower labor costs, could easily win a price war, and indeed the price cut occurred as American industry was stocking up for a possible steel strike on August 1.

No strike occurred, however, and on July 30 labor won a rather hefty settlement—one union estimate was that it represented a 6.1 percent increase in employment costs to the industry, the largest since the 7.5 percent increase in 1958.

Less than a day after eleven companies signed the contract several increased their prices, led by U.S. Steel which announced a limited hike on can-making steel. An hour later, Bethlehem brought on yet another crisis by raising its prices *across the board* by nearly 5 percent, citing the extra labor costs of the new contract. If the rest of the industry followed Bethlehem's general price increase, it would be the first since 1958.

Later that day (July 31, 1968) Armco Steel announced it too would soon make across-the-board increases, and Republic Steel announced a 4.5 percent increase on its principal mill products. Republic said its "substantial" labor cost increases and "other unreimbursed costs will be recovered only partially by the price increases announced."

Business Week said:

> All during the ballyhoo over passage of the tax increase, Administration officials felt they were making progress on selling the country on the dangers of inflation. Says one Administrator economist: "We were beginning to turn the corner, and were getting back to price stability." . . . And that explains the "jawboning" strategy emanating from Washington the past few days.[26]

At a hastily called press conference the president labeled Bethlehem's hike as "unreasonable" and said it "just shouldn't be permitted to stand." Johnson added that he was "very hopeful that other steel companies

[25] "The High Price of Inflating," *The Wall Street Journal*, December 12, 1967, p. 16.

[26] "Calling the Shots on Steel Prices," *Business Week*, August 10, 1968, pp. 26–30.

wouldn't join the parade" and he had singled out Bethlehem because its increases were "across the board," and he said that he was not opposed to "selective increases that individual companies have made gradually." He noted that if the industry did not follow Bethlehem's lead, "competitive factors would, as they have in the past, bring about a readjustment," but if followed "it will have dire consequences for our nation." Furthermore, Bethlehem did not need a price increase since it had increased its first half earnings by 41 percent over the previous year. According to the *Wall Street Journal*, when it announced its price increases, "Bethlehem also announced second quarter earnings of $49.7 million . . . up 47% from $33.8 million . . . a year before on a 29% sales rise to $869.5 million from $675.5 million." Also, "second quarter profit increases of other major steelmakers, buoyed by strike-hedge buying ranged from 36 percent to U.S. Steel's 79 percent." Though conceding the labor settlement terms were "high," Johnson felt that increased prices "far exceed" these costs.

A government economist later explained the administration's position that although it was not justified, a 2 percent price increase would cover the industry's increased labor costs. The question was, the economist said, whether the steel *users* should be absorbing all of the cost increases or whether steel should absorb some of them—especially at a time when the United States was "trying to turn the corner" toward stable prices.

Bethlehem's Chairman Edmund F. Martin responded to the president saying, "our announcement this morning speaks for itself. In our opinion our price increase is absolutely necessary, and we don't intend to withdraw it." The general feeling was that if other producers were to follow Bethlehem's lead, the increases would stick—as they had before even in times of decreased demand.

THURSDAY: NO FBI AGENTS THIS TIME

On Thursday, August 1, the administration continued its quick response to the steel price increases: the chairman of the president's Council of Economic Advisers sent telegrams to twelve steel companies that had not raised their prices asking that they consult him before doing so, and the president wrote to both the Speaker of the House of Representatives and the Senate Majority Leader repeating his warning of the "dire" consequences that would result if Republic's and Bethlehem's increases were followed by the rest of the industry. The president said, "The Congress, which has acted in the national interest to help stem inflation by passing the recent tax bill, should be informed of the inflationary threat that the actions of a few pose for us all." The letters, however, did not make any specific requests for congressional action.[27]

At this juncture the administration felt that U.S. Steel was the key factor in preventing across-the-board hikes from spreading throughout the industry, although later in the day both Inland and Pittsburgh announced general increases of nearly 5 percent, matching Bethlehem's move the day before. By evening the flurry of activity reached its peak, for "all within a matter of minutes" U.S. Steel again raised its prices, the government acted to buy steel only from firms not going along with the price hike, and the president called for a meeting with twenty congressional leaders. The U.S. Steel price boost, the second in two days, increased prices an average of more than 5 percent on items that, industry wide, accounted for 14 percent of all shipments. The company said that further increases on other products would be made soon.

Clark Clifford once again entered the battle of steel prices on the government's side—now as secretary of defense. Clifford ordered the military services to buy their steel only from those companies that had not increased their prices and said that in the future "there must be positive assurance that steel products are acquired only from those firms which offer the most advantageous terms." The orders were also to apply to defense contractors and subcontractors. (Department purchases of military goods using steel totaled approximately $600 million per year—about 3.7 percent of the nation's steel production.) In addition it was reported that the Transportation Department was considering similar action in regard to its steel purchases for highway construction.

Since industry requested and Congress considered import quotas, one high government official thought the price boosts were "incredible" and said, "It seems the American consumer is the one who needs protection" from the steel industry.

FRIDAY: THE MAVERICK MOVES

On Friday night, August 2, Kaiser Steel raised its prices on carbon-steel plates, structural shapes, and tin-mill products, saying it would make further increases on other products soon. According to the *Wall Street Journal*:

> Industry sources saw significance in Kaiser Steel's move, because they said, the company is particularly vulnerable to pressure from

[27] "Government, Steel Industry Escalate War over Prices; U.S. Steel Posts Second Rise, Says More Are Likely," *The Wall Street Journal*, August 2, 1968, p. 3.

Washington [since its] defense-related production is estimated at 20 percent to 25 percent of its total volume. Moreover, they said, a price increase, if it holds, would clear the way for even further inroads by foreign steel into the West Coast market, in which Kaiser Steel is the major factor.[28]

OVER THE WEEKEND: "DOUBTFUL TACTICS"

Other companies raised their prices over the weekend and said the increase might mean employee layoffs because of declining demand. The president applied his order to buy steel "at the lowest possible price" to all government agencies. Their combined civilian requirements for steel totaled $700 million per year.

The *Wall Street Journal* said that the government's punishment of "those nasty firms for spurring inflation" was "surely pretty stupid; if anyone deserves punishment for spurring inflation it's the government. . . . Washington, after all, is spending the taxpayer's money with considerable abandon. Last week's fanfare surely suggests that the only time the government shops carefully, looking for bargains and low prices, is when it wants to chastise someone for something or other."[29] A government official said that the government was considering increasing its purchases of foreign steel, although the *Wall Street Journal* said that using foreign steel was a "doubtful tactic" as "long standing requirements" prohibited purchasing foreign goods unless the price differential was "overwhelming."

Also over the weekend Senator Philip A. Hart, chairman of the Senate Antitrust Committee, wrote to the chairman of the FTC, Paul Dixon, asking for an investigation "in light of the [steel] industry's pricing practices."

MONDAY: SEEMING CONTRADICTIONS

On Monday morning the FTC commissioners decided to gather information on Senator Hart's request before going ahead with an investigation. Dixon said that any investigation would be concerned with whether or not the steel price boost was "cost justified" and that no investigation would be

---

[28] "More Steelmakers Boost Prices: Several Concerns Schedule Layoffs," August 5, 1968, p. 3.

[29] "What's Going On Here?" *The Wall Street Journal*, editorial, August 5, 1968, p. 12.

needed if a price rollback occurred and the commission action was taken solely at the request of Senator Hart.

Congressman Joe L. Evins, chairman of the House Small Business Committee, ordered a staff investigation preliminary to a "full inquiry" on steel price hikes and their effect on small businesses which would "square up to the dangers posed by the greedy actions of the steel industry."

Meanwhile the Department of Transportation, the General Services Administration, and HUD (Housing and Urban Development) took steps to insure that steel orders—direct and indirect through contractors—went to lower-priced steel. Secretary of Commerce C. R. Smith said that even existing contracts should be reviewed and amended wherever possible to obtain steel at the lowest possible price.

On Monday it was clear that the administration was still hoping to force a partial rollback through competitive pressures by keeping U.S. Steel and others who had announced selective increases from extending them across the board. Republic Steel promised not to increase prices on steel used to make items for the Vietnam War; Armco said its hike would not apply on two of the three items it sold to the department; Bethlehem said its increases did not include certain military items. However, Pittsburgh Steel stood firm on its hike, and Inland Steel said nothing—but its Defense Department shipments were less than 2 percent of its total sales.

Defense officials were "exultant" at the steel companies' promises, but the companies said they had been planning to exempt defense items all along. Indeed these defense "rollbacks" were thought by some to be symbolic victories showing weakness in the industry's position, but they also raised the question: Why weren't government *civilian* steel prices also lowered?

Tuesday was uneventful in the battle of steel prices. As long as U.S. Steel held firm, the government could expect Bethlehem eventually to roll back its prices, for the Pentagon did 80 percent of its steel business with U.S. Steel, Bethlehem, Pittsburgh, and Republic.

WEDNESDAY: THE BOOST'S BROKEN BACK

On Wednesday, August 7, U.S. Steel raised some of its prices 2.5 percent on the average—not much above the 2 percent government guidepost—and thus "broke the back" of the Bethlehem-led 5 percent general increase. "Within minutes" Bethlehem and others (Inland, Armco, Youngstown Sheet and Tube, Pittsburgh, Jones & Laughlin) compared their prices to U.S. Steel's levels and rescinded increases on prices U.S. Steel "had omitted from its boosts." The actual increased prices would average 4 percent to 6 percent but would "cover only about 63 percent of the industry's products, and exclude such big volume items as tubular and wire products and galvanized sheet, which are minor items in U.S. Steel's product line. . . ." Some companies, on the other hand, also made price *increases* to bring their prices in line with U.S. Steel. U.S. Steel said that there would be other price adjustments from time to time over the following twelve months.

White House Press Secretary George Christian said the president welcomed the move by U.S. Steel, and Arthur M. Okun, chairman of the president's Council of Economic Advisers, found the developments "gratifying" and, "taking account of all recent developments in steel prices and costs, the nation has a right to expect renewed price stability in this basic product in the months ahead." The White House said that it expected no more U.S. Steel price hikes during the year and that price rises and productivity gains in the auto and appliance industries should temper temptations to raise these prices because of increased steel costs.[30]

"No One Now Will Ever Know"

A *Wall Street Journal* editorial said the administration's claim to victory in the war over steel prices was "strange" under the circumstances and expressed regret at its price-holding actions.

> In our supposedly free economy companies naturally try to set prices high enough to cover their costs and provide them with a reasonable profit. That, essentially, is what the steel companies did in the wake of the costly contract settlement with the United Steelworkers.
>
> [The Government's] extra-legal price control naturally distorts the workings of competition. With imports sizable and with steel users working off inventories built up in fear of a strike, it's more than possible that the original price increases would not have held for very long even if the Government had not said a word.
>
> Unfortunately, no one now will ever know.[31]

But the editor lamented too soon for reports in October were that "a price war has broken out in the domestic steel industry," as some high-volume products had their prices slashed as much as 20 percent. According to the *Wall Street Journal:*

[30] "U.S. Steel Increases Prices 2.5%, Spurs Partial Rollback," *The Wall Street Journal*, August 8, 1968, p. 3.

[31] "A Peculiar Price Victory," *The Wall Street Journal*, August 9, 1968, p. 6.

The price cutting has taken much of the significance from President Johnson's success two months ago. . . . But current selling prices, in many cases, are considerably below even the pre-August list prices.[32]

Also in October, according to *Business Week:*

U.S. Steel initiated a 4% price increase on various types of steel pipe. Bethlehem refused to support all the boosts, holding firm on two categories. This forced Big Steel to retreat—but only partly. It deferred the effective date of the increases from November 1, 1968 to February 1, 1969.[33]

One novel twist to the price war was that most mills were denying the price cuts, which went only to large-volume customers, while insisting that everyone else was cutting prices! In November the whole industry was jolted when Bethlehem "cut its price of hot rolled sheet—the industry's second largest tonnage product—by 22 percent. . . . Bethlehem stressed that it acted to meet domestic competition. Steel executives translate this into retaliation against covert price cutting by U.S. Steel."[34] The rest of the industry soon fell into line with Bethlehem's cuts. According to *Business Week*, "Steel executives couldn't recall a more drastic price cut since the rampant competition of the early 1930s, nor could they recall a more direct challenge to the industry's leader, U.S. Steel Corp." Indeed, said the magazine, the industry's "administered price structure may be disappearing. Competition from foreign steel as well as other materials such as concrete, aluminum, and plastic has put the industry in a different posture. No longer is the materials business a seller's market, and steel may finally be adjusting to this."[35] Indeed, "Price cutting has pushed the industry's traditionally stable pricing structure close to chaos."[36]

---

[32] "Makers Quietly Cutting Prices as Much as 20% in Bid to Unload Surplus," *The Wall Street Journal*, October 7, 1968, p. 1.

[33] "Steel Industry Hit by Major Price Cut," *Business Week*, November 4, 1968, p. 35.

[34] *Ibid.*

[35] "Revolution in Steel Pricing?," *Business Week*, December 14, 1968.

[36] "Pittsburgh Expects to Be Happier," *Business Week*, December 14, 1968, p. 40.

B.
GOVERNMENT AND BUSINESS AS PARTNERS

The Supersonic Transport (SST)

A Case Study in Government-Industry Cooperation and the Determination of National Priorities

You're darn right. It's a patriotic program.

—WILLIAM MAGRUDER
Director of SST Development with the Nixon administration

The federal government is guaranteeing everything. . . . Would not a businessman fight for this kind of opportunity? . . . What would he have to lose? . . . And the taxpayer is the pigeon, the fall guy—as Texas Guinan or P. T. Barnum would put it, the sucker.

—SENATOR WILLIAM PROXMIRE

On June 5, 1963, President John F. Kennedy announced to a startled world his decision to commit the United States and its government to develop and build a supersonic plane. This was clearly in response to the British-French joint effort in building a supersonic plane—the Concorde. The declaration was appropriately made in a speech on graduation day at the United States Air Force Academy in Colorado Springs, Colorado. Among other things, the president said:

As a testament to our strong faith in the future of airpower, and the manned airplane, I'm announcing today that the United States will commit itself to an important new program in civilian aviation. Civilian aviation, long both the beneficiary and the benefactor of military aviation, is of necessity equally dynamic.

388

Neither the economics nor the politics of international air competition permit us to stand still in this area. Today the challenging new frontier in commercial aviation and in military aviation is a frontier already crossed by the military—supersonic transport.

[After reviewing the recommendations of the leading members of this Administration] it is my judgment that this government should immediately commence a new program in partnership with private industry to develop at the earliest practical date the prototype of a commercially successful supersonic transport superior to that being built in any other country in the world. . . .

An open preliminary design competition will be initiated immediately among American airframe and powerplant manufacturers with a more detailed phase to follow. *If these initial phases do not produce an aircraft capable of transporting people and goods safely, swiftly, and at prices the traveler can afford and the airlines find profitable, we shall not go further* [emphasis supplied].

. . . Spurred by competition from across the Atlantic and by the productivity of our own companies, the Federal Government must pledge funds to supplement the risk capital to be contributed by private companies. It must then rely heavily on the flexibility and ingenuity of private enterprise to make the detailed decisions and to introduce successfully this new jet age transport into world-wide service. . . . This commitment, I believe, is essential to a strong and forward-looking nation. . . .[1]

President Kennedy's statement came one day after Juan Trippe, president of Pan American World Airways, announced that the airline was taking options for six Anglo-French SST Concordes. Pan Am's action was clearly a competitive move and followed those of BOAC and Air France, both of which had earlier ordered eight Concordes each. Kennedy's decision to move on SST was not a spontaneous response to Pan Am's action but was the outcome of long deliberations and study of the social, economic, and political impact of SST on the United States position in aviation industry both at home and abroad.

The idea of a civilian SST has been around since the early fifties, but there were serious doubts about its economic and technical feasibility. In 1956, the National Advisory Committee for Aeronautics, which has since been transformed into the National Aeronautics and Space Administration (NASA), launched a research program to explore the possibility of developing an engine capable of flying airplanes at speeds of near Mach 3.[2] This was a prelude to the B-70 bomber program, the contract for which was awarded to North American Aviation Corporation in February 1958.

[1] *The New York Times*, June 6, 1963, p. 25.
[2] *National Aeronautics*, June 1966, p. 24.

Quite a bit of research work had already gone into the various aspects of the program, and the nation's aircraft industry hoped to rely heavily on the technology developed in the B-70 program for later exploitation in a civilian version of SST. However, by the end of 1959—and after spending more than $330 million—the B-70 program was on the verge of being scrapped, along with the hopes of aircraft manufacturers. In the interest of economy, the Eisenhower administration had decided to terminate the program when Dr. George Kistiakowsky, the president's scientific adviser, predicted that intercontinental ballistic missiles would make the development of manned bombers needless.

There were strong supporters of the SST program who advocated the development of the B-70 for both its military use and its benefits to the civilian SST program. These included Senator Lyndon B. Johnson, chairman of the Preparedness Investigating Subcommittee of the Senate's powerful Committee on Armed Services, Air Force Chief of Staff Thomas White, Senator A. S. (Mike) Monroney, and General Elmwood R. (Pete) Quesada, President Eisenhower's appointee to run the new Federal Aviation Administration (FAA).

During the summer of 1960, Quesada put together a high-level committee composed of the members of FAA, NASA, and the Department of Defense (DOD) to develop strategies for commencing the SST program. However, in October 1960, an FAA sponsored SST feasibility study conducted by United Research of Cambridge, Massachusetts, predicted that United States plane makers would not enter into an SST race with Britain, France, and the Soviet Union without the intervention and support of the United States government. This prediction was based on the high development costs (estimated at over $1 billion), the high risk and uncertainty of the economic feasibility, and the prospect of getting government subsidies (which seemed highly probable because the government publicly advocated the program).[3]

As Quesada saw it, the United States could not afford to lose face or market dominance by letting the Russians or the Anglo-French win the SST race. In November 1960, shortly before his resignation due to change in the administration, Quesada recommended to President Eisenhower an initial FY-61 funding of $17.5 million. However, the Bureau of the Budget reduced this figure to $5 million. At the same time he awarded the first SST engine-design research contracts to General Electric and Pratt & Whitney.[4] President-elect Kennedy's appointee to succeed Quesada as the

[3] *United States Supersonic Transport Program Summary*, Federal Aviation Agency, Washington, D.C., July 1965, p. 1.
[4] *Ibid.*

chief of FAA was Najeeb Halaby who recommended that Congress spend $12 million a year for SST studies. Despite President Kennedy's support, the Senate only narrowly defeated amendments to the administration's appropriation bills which would have eliminated the SST studies.

In March 1961, President Kennedy asked Halaby to develop a program of national priorities to give the nation the "safest, most efficient and most economical national aviation system attainable."[5]

The Halaby report, titled "Project Horizon," was submitted to President Kennedy on September 5, 1961. It painted a picture of a fast-growing and changing world in glorious terms and described the role of air travel in it. "Faster, bigger aircraft have shrunk the globe to the point where the capitals of the world are almost as accessible to an American as the county seat of a few decades ago. . . ."[6] Recommending government participation in the SST program, the report said: "Government funds should be utilized through the research, design, development, prototype and probably production stages. Every effort must be made to recoup the Government's financial investment through some type of royalty system to be paid by the operators."[7]

In November 1961, the Supersonic Transport Advisory Group (STAG) was created by Halaby to advise the SST steering group. STAG developed technical guidelines for the SST, visited various aircraft plants, advised members of Congress, and shortly before its dissolution recommended to the president that he publicly announce the development and production of commercial SST as a national policy objective.[8]

In 1962, President Kennedy established a cabinet-level committee headed by Vice-President Johnson to report on all aspects of the SST program. The committee included the heads of the Atomic Energy Commission (AEC), Bureau of the Budget (BOB), Civil Aeronautics Board (CAB), Council of Economic Advisors (CEA), FAA, Department of Labor (DOL), NASA, Office of Science and Technology, Department of State (DOS), and Treasury Department. The report of the committee strongly recommended a go-ahead on the SST program and formed the basis of Kennedy's June 5, 1963, announcement.

---

[5] *Supplementary Report to the Supersonic Transport Steering Group*, FAA, May 14, 1963, p. 8.

[6] *Report of the Task Force on National Aviation Goals—Project Horizon*, FAA, September 1961.

[7] *Ibid.*

[8] *US/SST Program Summary*, FAA, July 1965, p. 4.

THE POTENTIAL THREAT OF BRITISH-FRENCH AND RUSSIAN SSTs

Since the early fifties both British and French aircraft and engine manufacturers had been working separately on a commercial SST for the world markets, the British to develop a long-range and the French a medium- and short-range version. However, the tremendous financial costs and the fear of American and Russian domination brought the British and French governments together. On November 29, 1962, the two countries agreed to establish a consortium of British and French interests (Concorde) to develop an SST jointly. The Anglo-French SST, called the Concorde, was to have a top speed of Mach 2.2 (1450 m.p.h.), thus staying within the present state of the technology. The Concorde is heavily dependent on the financial subsidies provided by the French and British governments.

The goal of the program was to get the Concorde into airline service by 1971, thus giving it a three to four year time lead over the United States SST. Despite various doubts as to its economic feasibility, several airlines ordered Concordes. BOAC and Air France were first, with orders of eight each, and by 1967 orders for seventy-four Concordes worth $1 billion had been placed. The market projections were for two hundred to three hundred Concordes by 1980 with most of the sales coming in the early years.

The original plans called for a "dual purpose" SST with long- and short-range versions to meet the differing primary needs of BOAC and Air France respectively. The British share of the costs was estimated at £50 million. As can be expected with any technical project of the Concorde's size and complexity, the program ran into serious technical problems which resulted in increased costs and time delays. Furthermore, BOAC, fearing that the contemplated long-range version would not adequately meet its requirements, insisted on a still longer range for the aircraft, thus causing a major redesign effort and escalating the costs to £140 million for England alone.

The rising costs of the program, the unfavorable balance of payments, and other domestic problems caused England to review her commitment to the Concorde when the Labour Government came into power in the fall of 1964. Fearing a jettisoning of the program, BOAC reserved a position for six US/SSTs. Air France immediately followed suit. However, by January 1965, when the British Government discovered that the agreement with the French was irrevocable, estimates for the British share of the cost had gone to £165 million.[9] The cost estimates for the Concorde kept rising, and in November 1966 it was estimated that the program would cost $1.4 billion—up from the original estimate of $400 million—and that eventual costs might go as high as $2.4 billion![10]

The first Concorde 001 (the French version) was test flown on March 2 1969. Concorde 002 (the British version) was flown a few weeks later. Neither was flown at supersonic speeds, for the requisite more-powerful engines were not slated to be completed until late 1970 or early 1971. A model of the Russian SST TU-144 was first shown to the West at the Paris Air Show in 1955 and was test flown in Russia on December 31, 1968.[11] The Soviet plane was designed to operate at 1550 m.p.h. carrying more than 90 passengers (Concorde's estimates were 126 passengers for short-to-medium range and 112 for distances of four thousand miles). TU-144 was expected to cost about $20 million, or the same as Concorde. Most aviation officials in the West, however, believed that TU-144 would not offer much competition because in the past Soviet planes had proved uneconomical.[12]

PROGRESS OF THE US/SST—THE KENNEDY-JOHNSON ERA

On June 14, 1963, following his Air Force Academy announcement, President Kennedy sent a message to Congress in which he flatly stated that "in no event will the Government investment be permitted to exceed $750 million [and] the Government does not intend to pay any production, purchase or operating subsidies to manufacturers or airlines."[13] The development costs of the program were estimated as approximately $1 billion over the next six years, of which the manufacturers were expected to pay a portion of the government's development costs through royalties.[14]

The government proposed to pay 75 percent of the development costs with the manufacturers paying the balance. This three-to-one formula prevailed in the early phases of the design but was raised to nine to one when the manufacturers balked at paying 25 percent because of increasing technological difficulties and rising costs.

President Kennedy's request for a $60 million appropriation to fund the

---

[9] *Los Angeles Times*, January 20, 1965.

[10] "Race for a Superjet—Can U.S. Catch Up?" *U.S. News and World Report*, March 17, 1969, pp. 38–39.

[11] *Ibid.*

[12] *Ibid.*

[13] *Congressional Record*, July 9, 1963, pp. 12283–84.

[14] *Ibid.*

government's share of SST design ran into some sharp congressional criticism. One of the program's critics, Senator Fulbright, remarked:

> This Congress has been asked to demonstrate that a "democratic, free enterprise system" in the President's words, can compete with Britain and France. . . . I had always thought that the outstanding virtue of our free enterprise system was that it was free and that it rested on the enterprise of individuals. Thus, I fail to see how a Government subsidy of three-quarters of a billion dollars to the airplane builders is going to represent a triumphant vindication of free enterprise.[15]

On another front, Stanford Research Institute (SRI), in a study of the SST program conducted for the FAA, concluded that there was "no economic justification for an SST program."[16] Despite criticism, both in Congress and in some well-informed public quarters, the House voted $60 million for the program in the fiscal year 1964 as requested by the president.

In January 1964, three airframe and three engine companies submitted initial design proposals. The proposals were evaluated independently both by the government and by a panel of ten airlines. The government's evaluation found that none of the airframe designs met range-payload, economic requirements. In May, the president directed the FAA to award contracts for further design to two airframe companies (Boeing and Lockheed) and two engine companies (General Electric and Pratt & Whitney, a division of United Aircraft), which ranked best in the evaluation. The president also asked the Department of Commerce to conduct economic studies and the National Academy of Sciences to continue its supervision of the sonic boom studies. The selected airframe designs: (1) Boeing proposed a swing-wing (which would fold back during supersonic flight) and would carry 150 passengers at Mach 2.7 for four thousand miles; and (2) Lockheed proposed a double delta wing design and would carry 218 passengers at Mach 3.0 for four thousand miles. In November, the airframe and engine competitors submitted their revised designs. After more than six months of review by various technical committees and the President's Advisory Committee on Supersonic Transport (established in March 1964 under the chairmanship of Secretary of Defense Robert McNamara), President Johnson, in July 1965, announced an eighteen-month design program running to the end of 1966. He also requested that Congress appropriate $140 million for the program for the fiscal year 1966.

---

[15] *Congressional Record*, June 26, 1963, pp. 11706–7.

[16] *Final Report: An Economic Analysis of the Supersonic Transport*, SRI Project No. ISU–4266, p. 1.

Criticism in Congress became more severe and the public arguments both for and against the program more vocal. President Johnson's request for $140 million to get the eighteen-month Phase II of the program finished in only eleven months raised eyebrows in Congress. Was this only a "speed-up," or was it an indirect way of committing the government to the program? To secure congressional approval, and also to put the program in more favorable hands, the administration did two things: Considerable pressure was brought to bear upon various senators and congressmen to vote for the appropriation, and the president nominated, and the Senate approved, General Seth J. McKee as FAA administrator to replace Najeeb Halaby who was retiring. To do this, the FAA act which specified that the FAA administrator must be a civilian had to be amended. This was done at a time when the FAA was already top-heavy with military personnel with ninety-four retired and active officers holding down key jobs.[17]

Between July and December 1966, the SST prototype designs of Boeing, Lockheed, General Electric, and Pratt & Whitney were submitted and evaluated. In October 1966, Congress appropriated another $140 million for the fiscal year 1967. On December 31, 1966, the FAA announced that Boeing and General Electric had been selected to construct the SST airframe and engine respectively. Thus, after a government commitment of $311 million and expenditure of $244 million, in addition to $70 million spent by the plane manufacturers, the program was finally on the go. In the process, it had been reviewed by three presidential committees, the National Academy of Sciences, seven congressional committees, and thirteen federal agencies and departments.[18] It had also been analyzed and pronounced ill-advised and uneconomical by SRI, the Rand Corporation, and a host of other profit and nonprofit consulting organizations.

Construction contracts were signed on May 1, 1967, at which time Congress was also requested to appropriate $198 million for the fiscal year 1968 to help finance the prototype construction phase of the program. It was, however, still not clear how the $4.5 billion program would eventually be paid for.

President Johnson and the other supporters of the program notwithstanding, the SST program kept encountering new technological problems.

In the fall of 1968, after a year and a half and millions of dollars had gone into the swing-wing design, Boeing announced that its design would have to be scrapped. The corporation said it had found that the swing-wing, and especially its pivots, had made their 2707 (FAA-Boeing contract-designated name for Boeing's SST) too fat by twenty-five tons. Thus, the

[17] *Los Angeles Times*, July 12, 1965.
[18] *Newsweek*, August 29, 1966, p. 48.

design would have to be rejected in favor of a fixed-wing after all. Unfortunately, Boeing's design was now even less well along than Lockheed's had
been a year and a half earlier, *before the contract had even been awarded!*
Had Lockheed's more realistic fixed-wing design been awarded the contract, it is safe to say that much time and money would have been saved.
This, however, is only one of the unforeseen technical problems which have
constantly blocked progress on the SST and threatened it with ultimate
failure. As early as 1965, some of the airline executives had expressed
doubts on the desirability of depending on the construction of one prototype based essentially on a paper design. In a report, R. W. Rummel,
TWA's vice-president for planning and research, had recommended the
construction of two prototypes, one each based on Boeing's and Lockheed's SST designs. This approach, in his view, could save a minimum of
$480 million in the long run.[19]

THE NIXON ERA

When Richard Nixon was elected president in November 1968, the
future of the program once again became clouded as both friends and foes
hoped for a fresher and, from their point of view, more favorable consideration from the new administration. The Nixon administration obliged
both groups. Soon after his inauguration, President Nixon, on February 19,
1969, announced yet another ad hoc committee to review the Supersonic
Transport Program and to "investigate the national interest questions
associated with the pending SST decision."[20] The presidential guidance
was that the "SST must be safe for the passenger, profitable for the
manufacturers and airlines, and superior to any other aircraft."[21] The Ad
Hoc Committee, chaired by Undersecretary of Transportation James M.
Beggs, included high-ranking representatives from the Departments of
Commerce, Defense, Justice, HEW, State, and Treasury, the Council of
Economic Advisors (CEA), NASA, and Dr. Lee A. DuBridge, the
National Science Advisor. The committee held hearings and heard expert
testimony during February and March 1969. As it turned out, the report of
the committee was highly critical of the SST program. Consequently, the
Department of Transportation, which had consistently advocated continu-
ance of the SST program, kept the report secret until October 31, 1969,

---

[19] L. Stewart Rolls, David G. Koenig, and Fred J. Drinkwater III, "Flight Investigation of the Aerodynamic Properties of an Ogee Wing," NASA Technical Note
D–3071, December 1965, p. 1.

[20] *Congressional Record*, October 31, 1969, H10432.

[21] *Congressional Record*, November 17, 1969, H10950.

when it was released at the request of Congressman Henry S. Reuss (D-Wis.).[22]

REPORT OF THE AD HOC COMMITTEE

The committee created four panels to examine the impact of the SST program in four specific areas: balance of payments and international relations, economics, environmental and sociological impact, and technological fallout. A summary of their findings follows.[23]

BALANCE OF PAYMENTS AND INTERNATIONAL RELATIONS

The SST's balance-of-payments effect (BOP) was analyzed in terms of its overall impact on the United States BOP. This included both import and export of aircraft (the Commerce Department wanted to consider only the aircraft account), and increase in international air travel and its distribution between United States and foreign carriers (the Treasury and State departments wanted to include all aspects of BOP). The panel observed that on aircraft sales alone the United States BOP was likely to improve by between $11 billion and $18 billion (depending on competition from a commercially viable Anglo-French Concorde) from introduction in 1978 through 1990. The committee then analyzed the effect of SST on air travel expenditure. The current United States deficit in this category was estimated at $1.6 billion and "even in the absence of any commercial supersonic aircraft, it is expected to increase in absolute amount . . . totalling around $70 billion for the period 1970 through 1990." After taking the impact of SST and even revising their estimates of deficit downward, the committee concluded that "an adverse impact of speed-induced supersonic travel on the U.S. travel account [was likely to be] considerably greater than the estimated beneficial impact of supersonic aircraft sales on the U.S. aircraft account."

In terms of foreign relations impact the committee observed that the United Kingdom and France would frown at hasty action on the SST as designed to scuttle the Concorde. Similarly, strict noise standards could bar the Concorde from major United States airports. The committee recommended that both the United Kingdom and France be kept advised of

---

[22] "Reuss Bill Would Ban Commercial Supersonic Flights in U.S.," Press Release from the Office of Congressman Henry S. Reuss (D-Wis.), November 11, 1969, p. 2.

[23] *Congressional Record*, October 31, 1969.

"U.S. noise developments to ensure their full understanding if not acceptance of the U.S. position on noise."

ECONOMICS

The Economics Subcommittee expressed deep concern on the grave uncertainty associated with all economic aspects of the program: development and production costs, financing costs, and employment potential. The subcommittee observed that "almost every economic aspect of the program reflects unverifiable matters of judgment with great variance in the opinion of experts. Probably the single most uncertain aspect of the whole program relates to the uncertainty as to whether an SST can be built in the given time that will meet the specifications of being efficient, safe, and economical."[24]

The subcommittee did not put much faith in the assurances given by the manufacturers, FAA, and other interested government agencies and private business interests in view of similar assurances given to earlier investigating committees and also past experience with plane developments. It noted that even where commercial plane development, such as the Boeing 707, was based on well-established technology of military planes, "production costs have often been more than three times what they were predicted to be." The SST represented a jump of unprecedented magnitude in new technology, and even if all technical problems were solved, there was little doubt that costs would escalate considerably.

Demand for the SST was another uncertain area. Assuming that consumers value their time at one and one-half times their hourly earnings, the FAA projected that 500 SSTs would be sold. However, the Institute of Defense Analysis (IDA) model for forecasting demand, which estimates that passengers value their time as equal to their hourly earnings, reduced sales estimates to 350.

Similarly, in a 1967 Columbia Ph.D. study, Ruben Granau "concluded on the basis of a very detailed statistical study of air travel time from New York City to other points that businessmen value their time in air travel at 0.4 times their average hourly family income and that pleasure travellers valued their time in aircraft travel at zero."

The FAA in its base case assumed that supersonic transport would have a 25 percent passenger fare premium over subsonic planes. The FAA estimated that 1978 SST fares would equal 1965 subsonic fares and that subsonic fares would decline 25 percent in real terms between 1965 and

[24] *Ibid.*

1978, thus producing the rate differential. However, subsonic fares declined 18 percent between 1965 and 1968, so—if we accept the IDA and FAA estimates of 1.8 percent per year fare decline—the relative difference between supersonic and subsonic fares would increase to 36 percent, thus reducing SST sales estimates to 200.

These highly speculative estimates are based on an untenable assumption—that American SSTs and British-French Concordes will not compete in the same markets. However, Concorde will be introduced five years before SST and may secure a considerable foothold in the market, and SST, despite its lower operating costs, may not be able to lower fares and obtain a greater market share. The subcommittee noted that:

> International fares are set by unanimous agreement of IATA in which each airline has a vote. With many airlines having the Concorde and with two airlines being intimately connected with its production—BOAC and Air France—it seems unlikely that the SST will force supersonic fares below those that are economical for the Concorde and drive the Concorde out of the market—the FAA assumption. The Concorde will be sold for about half the price and will have the seating capacity of an SST. Thus, two Concordes can be secured for each SST giving airlines an additional flexibility in scheduling. If fares are kept high enough to protect the Concorde so that both types of supersonic planes operate in the same markets at the same price, then they may split the market which will reduce SST sales from 500 to 250.

In terms of rate of return on investment to the United States government, the subcommittee observed that:

> It should be noted that by the terms of the FAA–Boeing contract, Boeing establishes the price of the plane. Given the demand model specified, Boeing . . . could make more money at a price of $40 million than at a price of $37 million. In fact, Boeing could maximize its profits if it charged about $48 million. Such a price would reduce sales of planes to something under 350. This would in turn reduce government royalties to the point that the government barely got its money back.

The return on investment (ROI) for the airlines was based on a load factor of 58 percent which is unrealistically high when compared with the industry average of 52.6 percent in 1968 or 55 percent achieved during 1962–68.[25] Assuming the more realistic 55 percent load factor, it is esti-

---

[25] The load factor for domestic airlines in the U.S. was reduced to 50 percent in 1969. *The New York Times,* January 11, 1970, Sec. 12, p. 17.

mated that airlines would earn a ROI of 25.2 percent before taxes. In view
of the recent declines in ROI after taxes (8.9 percent in 1966, 7.7 percent
in 1967, and an estimated 6 percent in 1968), it is likely that the airline
industry may already be overcapitalized and therefore declining ratios
would make the problem of financing the purchase of SSTs quite difficult.

The subcommittee also questioned FAA's estimates of additional direct
and indirect employment of more than one hundred thousand workers.
First, an unknown proportion of this number was to result from relative
declines in other parts of the aerospace industry. Second, this employment
would be concentrated in highly skilled and semiskilled managerial and
professional occupations which are in short supply and in periods of full
employment may prove inflationary. "The net employment increase from
SST would likely be negligible and . . . the project would have practically
no employment benefits for the disadvantaged hard-core unemployed with
low skill levels."

After considering all the evidence, the subcommittee recommended that

no funds for prototype construction be included in the 1970 budget.
The funds still available under the old design contract, and possibly
some additional funds for research, should be used to clarify the
characteristics of the SST. . . . We would also suggest that any
further research on this plane be done under the responsibility of an
agency other than FAA. While we do not wish to suggest that the
role of FAA in the development of the aircraft has been improper in
any way, we are concerned about possible conflicts of interest in the
future.

ENVIRONMENTAL AND SOCIOLOGICAL IMPACT

The subcommittee considered four areas of environmental and sociological impact of SST to be its main concern. These were sonic boom, airport
noise, hazards to passengers and crew, and effects of water vapor in the
stratosphere. On all these counts it was concluded that major problems
remained to be solved and "should be the subject of further intensive
research before proceeding with prototype construction."

TECHNOLOGICAL FALLOUT

The subcommittee considering the effects of technological fallout from
the SST program concluded that:

The SST program will advance many areas of technology and will
result in technological fallout both to the aircraft industry in general

and to other industrial and military applications. The magnitude of this effect is very difficult to assess, but it appears to be small. Nevertheless, there are a number of areas which can be identified as having a high probability of potential benefit, such as: flight control systems, structures, materials, aircraft engines, aerodynamics.

While technological fallout will inevitably result from a complex, high technology program such as the SST development, the value of this benefit appears to be limited. We believe technological fallout to be of relatively minor importance in this program and therefore should not be considered either wholly or in part as a basis for justifying the program. In the SST program, fallout or technological advances should be considered as a bonus or additional benefit from a program which must depend upon other reasons for its continuation.

Following the deliberations of the Ad Hoc Committee and its subcommittees, Chairman James Beggs prepared a draft report purportedly summarizing the views of the members of the committee. This draft report was later to be submitted to the secretary of transportation and President Nixon. The draft was highly biased in favor of the SST program; it completely ignored or sharply toned down the criticism leveled at the SST program by various panels and greatly exaggerated the positive findings. Understandably the reaction of the committee members was sharp and bitter. Here are some examples:

1. The draft report, transmitted with your memorandum of March 18, has just been received. In my opinion the summary does not convey the sense of the Environmental and Sociological Panel report, and does not adequately reflect the concerns of the members of this panel.

    On the contrary, the editorial comments, interpretations and implied conclusions in the draft summary tend to convey the impression that the panel considered the environmental factors to be of small moment. Quite to the contrary these must be recognized as being of significant concern and emphasized at every step leading to a final decision in this matter.

    CHARLES C. JOHNSON, JR.
    Assistant Surgeon
    General Administrator

2. I believe that your draft report attaches more significance to technology fallout from the program than does the actual report of that subcommittee.

    RUSSELL E. TRAIN
    Under Secretary of the
    Interior

3. My reaction to the draft report at this time is negative.

    First, it is my understanding that "The objective of the Committee is to assess the impact of the SST on the national interest." The draft report fails to make this assessment. It neither reflects a Committee consensus concerning the net effects of proceeding with the SST, nor does it provide a basis for such a conclusion for Committee consideration. Instead, it merely reviews and summarizes some of the material presented by the subcommittee.

Second, the draft report presents a possibly misleading summary of the subcommittee reports. These raised numerous problems which bring into serious question the wisdom of proceeding with the SST; these problems are understated in the draft report.

ARNOLD R. WEBER
Assistant Secretary
of Manpower

4. I have carefully reviewed the Draft Report of the SST Ad Hoc Review Committee and have found that it does not adequately reflect the views of the working panels and of the members of the Committee. It contains primarily the most favorable material, interspersed with editorial comments, and thus distorts the implications and tenor of the reports. Unfortunately, you have not given us time enough to rewrite this draft. The report as it stands cannot be accepted as an accurate representation of either our views or those of other members. . . .

   If the committee is not to be allowed to make joint recommendations to Secretary Volpe, I want to make clear our views. While the risks both economically and technically are great, the potential benefits are uncertain. With budget needs so great, I cannot see how this program can be justified at the present time and would recommend that no new funds be devoted to the project for at least FY 1970. This would mean that about $70 million would be available after April 15 [1969] for research on noise suppression, environmental effects, and market studies.

HENDRIK S. HOUTHAKKER
Council of Economic
Advisors

5. There are no overriding foreign policy grounds either for pushing ahead with the SST project now, or for delaying it, or for dropping it altogether. One specific aspect of this position is our view that it would not be proper to base the decision to go ahead with the project on any generalized concept of enhancement of U.S. prestige, or the like.

U. ALEXIS JOHNSON
Under Secretary
for Political Affairs

AIRLINES' REPORT ON SST

The FAA also sought the views of nine major American airlines concerning the SST program. All these airlines were holding positions on the reservation list for the SSTs. While all of them were agreed that a prototype of SST should be built, they were at best less than enthusiastic about the current design, timing of delivery, and sharing of development. None indicated any increase in its reservation positions and most of them wanted the government to bear the major financial burden. Here are some examples of the early 1969 comments:

AIRLINE 1

The recent SST review along with an assessment of the environment in which we are currently operating has led us to take a different posture than has been the case to date. The factors influencing this change are:

First, the operating economics of the presently proposed SST indicate that a substantial fare premium undoubtedly will be required to match the economic performance of the present generation of subsonic jets.

Second, there appears to be serious doubt that the proposed. SST can meet existing or proposed airport noise criteria.

Third, the SST undoubtedly will be limited to overwater operation because of the sonic boom problem.

Fourth, the final cost per airplane will undoubtedly fall in the $40–50 million area representing an enormous risk per single vehicle.

Fifth, important and costly improvements are immediately required to bring both our airways and airports up to a capacity compatible with the current and future traffic demand.

There are other factors which weigh against unqualified commitment to the SST development schedule, but the above are the most important ones in my view. In light of the somewhat negative aspects bearing upon the SST program as of now and our existing capital commitments, I would be unwilling to recommend to Board of Directors the venturing of any additional risk capital. . . .

If our government's assessment of this program indicates that the United States must retain its dominant position in the aircraft manufacturing industry for national reasons, then it is my opinion that the development cost risks must be assumed by the government. Finally, if our country must make a choice between appropriations for improvements of our airways-airport systems or furthering the development of the SST, then there is no question that airways-airports must be the choice.

In summation, the provision of completely adequate airways and airports in this country must take precedence over any other consideration if the vigor of our economy is to be maintained. If there are funds available after the above need is satisfied, then these funds should go toward the orderly development of an SST at whatever rate of progress is possible.

I hope that the above may be helpful to Secretary Volpe in arriving at a sound decision on the future of the program.

AIRLINE 2

It is obvious that there are still some serious problems in the areas of community noise and economics. It also appears certain that the operation of the SST will be restricted to subsonic speeds over inhabited areas because of sonic boom. This will limit utilization and place an arbitrary ceiling on the total market for supersonic aircraft, increasing the unit cost.

AIRLINE 3

The 5-abreast 234 passenger prototype airplane design currently proposed by Boeing and validated by the FAA is not an airplane that embraces sufficient weight or space payload to be economically viable at other than substantially increased fare levels over those which we know today. The unknown changes in our economy between now and the planned availability of a production SST in 1978 or 1979 make the economic factors in this regard even more difficult to assess.

AIRLINE 4

We continue to be concerned about many of the technical aspects of the program, including weight and balance, flutter and dynamics, engine inlet design, and airport and community noise. Experience has indicated that solutions to problems of this type invariably add complexity and weight to an aircraft. Since the design payload-range characteristics already appear marginal, we question whether an economically viable airplane can be produced until these solutions are accurately defined.

AIRLINE 5

Present indications are that the SST program will not produce a vehicle as economically viable for airline use as formerly was believed to be the case. Nevertheless, in view of the efforts of other nations in the SST field . . . we remain convinced that national interest considerations, relating to the balance of payments and the competitive position of our aeronautics manufacturing industry, would be served by development and production of U.S. SSTs at an early date.[26]

The differences between Chairman Beggs's draft summary report and those of the individual members were so strong that a meeting of the full committee was called and, when reconciliation proved impossible, it was decided that the entire record of the proceedings should be sent to the president for his consideration.

Despite the highly critical and unfavorable findings of his own committee, on September 23, 1969, President Nixon announced that he would ask Congress for a $96 million appropriation for the fiscal year ending June 30, 1970, for the "start of construction of two prototype SST aircraft."[27] Mr. Nixon said the decision was "based on need to keep the U.S. as world leader in air transport and to shorten flying times"[28] between the United States and the rest of the world. "Transportation Secretary and other department officials said *the SST won't be permitted to fly over the U.S. mainland because of the sonic booms.*"[29] [Emphasis supplied.] There were also indications that the project would be removed from FAA jurisdiction and be placed directly under Secretary Volpe. The government, which had already spent $600 million, estimated that its cost burden for the development phase would be $1.29 billion out of a total estimate of $1.51 billion, the remainder to come from the manufacturers and the airlines. It might be noted here that in 1963 when the SST project was launched President Kennedy said: "In no event will the government investment be permitted to exceed $750 million."[30]

On November 13, 1969, the House Appropriations Committee approved the Nixon administration request for $96 million funding for the SST program in the fiscal year 1970. A motion by Congressman Yates (D-Ill.) to delete the SST appropriation from the Transport Department budget was defeated by twenty-six to thirteen vote.[31]

During the debate on the House floor it further appeared that the Department of Transportation (DOT) had tried to keep from Congress the highly unfavorable views of Lt. Gen. Elmwood L. Quesada, the former

[26] *Congressional Record*, October 31, 1969, H10444–45.

[27] "SST Faces Hard Fight in Congress but Chances of Funding Seem Good," *The Wall Street Journal*, September 24, 1969, p. 3.

[28] *Ibid.*

[29] *Ibid.*

[30] *Congressional Record*, July 9, 1963, pp. 12283–84.

[31] "House Panel Approves $96 Million SST Sum for This Fiscal Year," *The Wall Street Journal*, November 14, 1969, p. 21.

head of FAA (1958–61) and currently a director of American Airlines. Congressman Henry S. Reuss (D-Wis.) reported to the House that he had tried to obtain a copy of General Quesada's testimony from DOT before the SST Ad Hoc Review Committee in March 1969. According to Reuss, "DOT at first told me that no transcript of the General's testimony even existed, but finally, after repeated requests, they were able to produce one copy. It had been found in a safe in the office of the Under Secretary of Transportation."[32]

In his testimony, General Quesada stated that the SST program as originally conceived was never intended to develop an entirely new technology but to adapt commercially the know-how that was being developed for the B-70 program. As it turned out, the B-70 program was later canceled, thus bringing about a significant change in the circumstances which must cause us to re-evaluate the program priorities for the SST.

> It was never anticipated that the Federal Government would be the major sponsor of a supersonic transport. It was anticipated that a major sponsor of the supersonic transport would be economic demand and when economically feasible a supersonic transport program would proceed, hopefully helped by the government.[33]

(We might recall here that Boeing 707 was more than two years behind British turboprop Electra in coming into the market. Electra was a combination prop-jet while Boeing was a pure jet. Despite its delay in entering the market, Boeing was successful in capturing the world markets for its plane because of a superior product and lower operating costs.

In terms of world competition, Quesada stated that our competition with the Anglo-French Concorde or the Russian TU-144 must be on the basis of the product quality and economic feasibility alone. Finally, he urged a more judicious use of the country's scarce economic resources while continuing the SST program on a more orderly basis.

> There are limited funds that this country or any other country has; and they seem to be more limited all the time. And I would urge those of you who are struggling with this problem to bear in mind, as I am sure you do, that there are many other sources of demand that are reasonable and justified and this can very well be pitted against them, hopefully not eliminated. It would be a great tragedy if this program were ever eliminated.[34]

[32] *Congressional Record*, November 17, 1969, H10947.
[33] *Ibid.*, H10948.
[34] *Ibid.*, H10948.

BOEING'S REPRESENTATION TO THE AD HOC COMMITTEE

The Boeing Company also submitted its views[35] to the Ad Hoc Committee, supporting the continuation of the SST program and the government participation in it. It has also since then continuously defended its position in the news media and before various public and private bodies. A summary of Boeing's position follows.

1. Traffic forecasts by various independent analysts indicate that revenue passenger miles in the free world will increase at least sixfold between 1968 and 1990, and $125 billion of new aircraft will be needed to carry this traffic.

2. Supersonic transports will constitute a significant part of this $125 billion market. A comprehensive analysis of operating costs, competing equipment, and appropriateness to various routes show that even without flying over populated areas to avoid sonic boom effects, the SST market will total $25 billion by 1990.

3. SSTs will be built whether we like it or not. Because of our technical capacity, the United States is now in a position to obtain $20 billion of this $25 billion market through the sale of an estimated 500 SSTs, 270 of them to foreign airlines.

4. In terms of balance of payments, the SST program (aircraft account) would bring in an additional $11.9 billion between 1975 and 1990. Conversely, if a timely US/SST is not introduced, the negative effect on aircraft account in the balance of payments could reach $16 billion by 1990.

   To counteract the argument of balance of payments deficits in travel account, Boeing argued that "if so inclined, U.S. tourists will travel overseas in Concordes (or even TU-144s) to spend their money. Actually, the foreign tourist coming *to* the U.S. also spends money, and the number of foreign visitors coming to the U.S. has been increasing in recent years."[36]

5. On a direct business venture basis, the government will be paid royalties on the sale of production airplanes in an amount returning the original investment ($1.2 billion) by approximately the three hundredth plane and producing in excess of investment by the five hundredth delivery. In addition, it will bring in an additional $5.4 billion to the federal government and $1.3 billion to

[35] *The SST Program and Related National Benefits* [*The Boeing Report*], The Boeing Company, Seattle, Washington, February 12, 1969.

[36] Communication to the author by the Boeing Company, November 12, 1969.

various state and local governments through corporate and personal income taxes of program participants and secondary employment through the "multiplier" effect.[37]

6. The production phase will yield prospective employment of approximately five hundred thousand highly skilled, high-wage persons at peak production. It will also provide secondary employment of over one hundred thousand in trade and professions including substantial numbers in semiskilled and unskilled categories.

7. There are impressive technological effects of the program for the nation which alone could justify the development of the prototypes. The benefits will, furthermore, not be confined to the transport industry but will be spread in all phases of industry through the development of new materials, manufacturing techniques, and electronics equipment.

8. The program will relieve congestion both at the airports and in the air by providing speedier movement at higher altitudes not presently used and quicker turnaround.

The company argued against the need for additional expenditure for airport modifications because of SSTs by stating that the SST was designed for operations from existing international airports. No modifications to runways will be necessary. By the time it enters commercial service in 1978, airports and loading docks will have been developed to take care of the 747 and the other large capacity subsonic jets. The SST will use these same facilities.[38]

[37] *Development of a National Asset—The American SST*, The Boeing Company, Seattle, Washington, October 1969, p. 9.

[38] Communication to the author by the Boeing Company, November 12, 1969.

C.
CORPORATIONS AND UNITED STATES FOREIGN POLICY CONFLICTS

Coca-Cola and the Middle East Crisis

[It is] very disturbing indeed and very mischievous—when private groups or businesses or individuals take it on themselves, by act or omission, to alter or dictate or defeat official policies of the United States Government. This amateur policy making—or policy breaking—can be accomplished by almost any group or organization endowed with the conviction that it knows more about some aspect of foreign policy than anybody else and with the will to intimidate officials or other organizations that are not very hard to intimidate. It has been done by business interests seeking a competitive advantage, by organized labor, and by those sterling patriots whose self-designed task it is to keep the rest of us in line, loyal and true to the red, white, and blue . . .

—SENATOR J. WILLIAM FULBRIGHT

In late 1964 the management of the Coca-Cola Company was faced with a crucial policy decision concerning its overseas business—whether to grant a bottling franchise in Israel to its then distributor, the Tempo Bottling Company of Israel, thereby antagonizing its Arab customers who were, in effect, at war with Israel.[1]

In 1951, three years after the modern State of Israel was founded (May 14, 1948), the Arab nations set up an economic boycott against certain companies doing business with the Israelis.[2] In most instances the Arabs

---

[1] Irving Spiegal, "Coca-Cola Refuses Israelis a Franchise," *The New York Times*, April 8, 1966, p. 1.

[2] *MSU Business Topics*, Spring 1968, p. 74.

409

had not objected to ordinary trade with Israel but had enforced the ban when capital goods or military equipment was involved.[3]

Had Coca-Cola accepted Tempo's application for the bottling franchise, the Israeli company would have built its own bottling plant and purchased syrup but not the finished product from Coca-Cola.

In January 1965, the company decided that the potential demand for Coca-Cola in Israel did not justify a bottling plant at that time and therefore refused the franchise. Several important considerations were responsible for the company's decision.

The principal reason was profits: The potential Israeli market for Coke—some 2.5 million Israelis—was dwarfed by the 104.7 million Arab population in the Arab League countries.[4] The Arabs had been among Coke's heaviest consumers from the time the soft drink had been introduced in the Middle East during World War II. Even tiny Kuwait had a per capita consumption of 175 bottles a year—nearly double the average United States rate. The hot desert climate and the Arab taboo against alcoholic spirits combined to make Coke a widely consumed beverage in the Middle East.[5]

In contrast, early governments of Israel, to minimize their exchange problems, had yielded to local citrus fruit lobbyists and had abrogated Abraham Feinberg's contract to bottle Coke in 1949. Coca-Cola knew that American companies such as Zenith Radio Corporation and Ford Motor Company had been barred from doing business in Arab countries because they sold their products in Israel. Therefore, it seemed that Coca-Cola might be able to operate either in the Arab countries or in Israel, but not in both.[6] If business firms have an obligation to their customers as well as to their stockholders, then Coca-Cola certainly owed such an obligation to the Arabs who had long been devoted to its products.

Moreover, in view of the competitive conditions, the danger of losing the lucrative Arab market appeared very real. The Arab countries could shut down the twenty-nine franchised Coca-Cola bottling plants because they could easily substitute Pepsi-Cola for Coca-Cola. Psychologists have tested panels of regular cola drinkers and have concluded that people could not differentiate between colas by taste alone.[7] Pepsi competed with Coke

[3] "Business in Mideast Walks on Shifting Sands," *Business Week*, July 2, 1966, pp. 26, 28.

[4] Luman H. Long, ed., *The World Almanac and Book of Facts, 1967*, New York, Newspaper Enterprise Association, 1966, p. 630.

[5] "Bottled Up," *Newsweek*, April 18, 1966, p. 78. See also Thomas Buckley, "Coca-Cola Grants Israeli Franchise," *The New York Times*, April 16, 1966, p. 1.

[6] *Business Week*, July 2, 1966, pp. 26, 28.

[7] James A. Myers and William H. Reynolds, *Consumer Behavior and Marketing Management* (Boston: Houghton-Mifflin Company, 1967), Chap. 2.

in the Arab market and would most probably capitalize on Coke's fall from Arab-leader favor.

A second consideration in refusing the franchise to Tempo was the company's dissatisfaction with its Israeli distributor. In 1963, Coke filed suit in a Tel Aviv court against Tempo for infringing upon the Coca-Cola trademark. Coca-Cola was also unhappy with Tempo because it bottled other soft drinks. By custom, Coca-Cola franchises are granted in perpetuity as long as the bottlers uphold rigid quantity standards specified by the company. Although many Coca-Cola bottlers also manufacture and sell other soft drinks, the company's tradition of granting franchises of indefinite duration made it necessary for them to choose only those companies with whom they could get along.[8] Obviously, Tempo's past record did not meet this criterion.

REPERCUSSIONS OF COCA-COLA'S REFUSAL TO GRANT FRANCHISE TO TEMPO BOTTLING COMPANY OF ISRAEL

Tempo was not satisfied with Coca-Cola's contention of insufficient market in Israel. They averred that Coca-Cola's management had set arbitrary and unusually high quotas for Tempo, which were impossible to meet. They charged that the main reason for the refusal of the franchise was to support the Arab boycott and asked the Anti-Defamation League of the B'nai B'rith to undertake an investigation.[9] If Coca-Cola was indeed supporting the boycott, it would be violating United States government foreign policy.[10]

In April 1966, after a fifteen-month investigation, the Anti-Defamation League released a report stating that Israel was one of the few countries in the free world without a Coca-Cola bottling plant. The reason for this, the report alleged, was that the Coca-Cola Export Corporation was cooperating with the Arab League boycott. The report cited the three major prerequisites Coca-Cola had for granting a bottling plant franchise: a $1 million minimum investment, a "viable market," and "practically exclusive manufacture of Coke." Tempo, which had $2.2 million in sales in 1965, had supposedly met the first two requirements and had agreed to the third.[11] The Anti-Defamation League stated that the Israeli market was potentially more profitable than that of the Arab franchise. Therefore,

---

[8] E. J. Kahn, Jr., "Profiles," *The New Yorker*, February 14, 1959, pp. 37–40ff.

[9] "Israel: Capping the Crisis," *Time*, April 22, 1966, p. 75.

[10] Spiegal, "Coca-Cola Refuses Israelis a Franchise," p. 1.

[11] *Newsweek*, April 18, 1966.

"The deducible facts seem strongly to indicate that, while submitting to the Arab boycott, Coca-Cola has assiduously attempted to camouflage its submission as a pure nonpolitical, economic decision."[12]

The aftermath of the report was sheer confusion. James A. Farley (former United States postmaster general), chairman of the Coca-Cola Export Corporation, vigorously denied the charge of honoring "any boycott." He said that detailed surveys of economic and market conditions evidenced a low success potential in the Israeli market but indicated that "all decisions of this kind are constantly under assessment and reassessment." Farley also said that the Tempo Company "had been found guilty in a Tel Aviv court of infringing the Coca-Cola trademark and bottle design in the marketing of its own product, Tempo Cola."[13] Denying that the company had yielded to the threat of an Arab boycott, Robert L. Gunnels, Coca-Cola export vice-president, said that an Israeli bottling plant would not be "mutually profitable" to Tempo and Coca-Cola and added that a similar decision had been made regarding bottling franchises in Jordan and Syria.

Some of the information advanced by Coca-Cola was unknown to the Anti-Defamation League. Arnold Foster, who prepared the report, said that the league was unaware of Coca-Cola's granting Abraham Feinberg's earlier application for a franchise and also of Tempo's infringement on the Coke trademark. He said that these facts had not been mentioned when the league contacted Coca-Cola in regard to the franchise denial to Tempo.[14]

The managing director of Tempo, in turn, objected to Coca-Cola's statements, saying that Tempo had not been found guilty by the court as the case had been settled out of court and that the shape of the Tempo Cola bottle was not at issue. According to the *New York Times*, court records bore out the Tempo statement.[15]

Coca-Cola's basic position was that if it was to operate profitably at home and abroad it must cater to everybody. A year before the Anti-Defamation League report, Coca-Cola President J. Paul Austin had received a human relations award from the American Jewish Association. The company had a record of being a goodwill ambassador for the United States. In 1949, as a result of left-wing agitation, an anti-Coke bill had become law in France. This aroused anti-France feelings in the United States, leading to several proposals of boycotts of French products. How-

[12] Spiegal, "Coca-Cola Refuses Israelis a Franchise," p. 1.

[13] Buckley, "Coca-Cola Grants Israeli Franchise," p. 1.

[14] "Coca-Cola Unit ·Denies Charge It Is Supporting Arab Boycott of Israel," *The Wall Street Journal*, April 13, 1966, p. 11.

[15] Buckley, "Coca-Cola Grants Israeli Franchise," p. 1.

ever, the company refused to exploit the anti-France feelings; and James Farley succeeded, through persuasion and diplomatic negotiations, in getting France to repeal the law.[16] The company had also begun operations in Bulgaria in response to the United States government's policy of "building bridges to the East."[17]

Coca-Cola, of course, was aware that Congress had gone on record opposing foreign initiated boycotts in the Williams-Javits law of 1965[18] and pointed out that its decision was solely based on economic grounds and that it was not violating the statute or the intent of Congress.

The Anti-Defamation League had, since its founding, become a powerful force in the use of reason and moral suasion to eradicate prejudice against Jews. Despite Coca-Cola's arguments and the league's admission of ignorance of some of the facts, the company stood to lose the patronage of some 5.6 million Jewish people in America—since a rumor had spread that Coca-Cola was anti-Jewish. (It should be noted, however, that the 104.7 million Arab population dwarfs the 13.3 million worldwide Jewish population; so, from the standpoint of income, the Arabs appear to be more desirable friends than the Israelis.)[19]

Mount Sinai Hospital in New York stopped taking delivery of Coca-Cola for its cafeteria. A New York theater chain and Coney Island's Nathan's Famous Hot Dog Emporium threatened to follow suit, and the New York City Human Rights Commission called for an investigation of Coca-Cola. Within a week of the league's charges, and despite Coca-Cola's denial of them, the company again issued a bottling franchise for Israel to Abraham Feinberg, now a New York banker, president of the Israel Development Corporation, and a promoter of Bonds for Israel. The Anti-Defamation League said that Coca-Cola's decision "will show other American corporations the sham that the Arab boycott really is."[20]

Actually, Feinberg had contacted Coca-Cola about his "renewed interest" a week before the league's charges were made public. Feinberg commented that he would not have accepted any franchise "if I believed Coca-Cola bows to Arab boycott threats."[21]

Now it remained to be seen what the Arabs would do. Israeli officials predictably reported that the boycott's influence had declined in recent years since the Arab governments had not invariably backed up their threats. The Israeli Consulate General stated there were more than two

[16] Kahn, Jr., "Profiles," pp. 37–40ff.

[17] "Thaw that Refreshes," *Time*, December 3, 1965, p. 98.

[18] Spiegal, "Coca-Cola Refuses Israelis a Franchise," p. 1.

[19] Long, *World Almanac*, pp. 332, 594–670.

[20] "Israel: Capping the Crisis," *Time*, p. 75.

[21] Buckley, "Coca-Cola Grants Israeli Franchise," p. 1.

hundred American companies doing business with both Israel and the Arab League nations. *Business Week* reported that although the rich nations—Saudi Arabia, Kuwait, Libya—were the strictest enforcers of the boycott, Egypt often "winks at boycotts" (Nasser was a heavy Coke drinker), and Tunisia, Algeria, and Morocco "ignore the boycott more than they observe it."[22] Despite these reassurances, however, the possibility of large sale losses was real.

The reprisals from the Arab countries were not long in coming. In July 1966, the Central Office for the Boycott of Israel of the Arab League asked the company about its plans for setting up bottling plants in Israel and warned Coca-Cola that it faced a ban on its product and that the bottling plants would be closed within three months if the Israeli plant was approved. In November the thirteen-country Arab League Boycott Conference met in Kuwait.[23] The Boycott Bureau told the conference it had received unsatisfactory replies from Coca-Cola.

The conference then passed a resolution to stop the production and sale of Coca-Cola within Arab League countries. Enforcement of the ban, however, was left to the discretion of the individual countries.[24] The Boycott Bureau established a nine-month time limit to allow Arab bottling plants to use up Coke concentrates in stock.

The company made some belated efforts to placate Arab opinion. One month before the Arab League meeting, the company ran an advertisement in a Cairo newspaper showing the important economic and social role played by Coca-Cola in the Arab countries. However, a month was apparently not enough time for the advertisement to have any effect. In December 1966, Baghdad Radio announced that Iraq had begun its ban on Coca-Cola. The company said that it had received no official notification from Iraq but that in the three months since the ban had been announced by the Arab League the boycott "has not manifested itself in production sales."[25]

In September 1967, nine months after Arab League representatives had met to approve the boycott, the Boycott Bureau announced that the ban was effective. Despite the ban and the Arabs' increased hatred of Israel after the six-day war, Coke was not deterred and a Coca-Cola bottling plant opened for business in Tel Aviv in February 1968.

[22] *Business Week*, July 2, 1966, pp. 22, 26.

[23] Composed of the United Arab Republic, Iraq, Jordan, Lebanon, Saudi Arabia, Syria, Morocco, Yemen, Algeria, Kuwait, Libya, Sudan, and Tunisia.

[24] Thomas F. Brady, "Arabs Vote to Bar Ford, Coca-Cola," *The New York Times*, November 21, 1966, p. 1. See also *Business Week*, November 26, 1966.

[25] "Iraq Plans to Boycott Three U.S. Companies," *The Wall Street Journal*, December 20, 1966, p. 11.

D.
POLITICS
AND
BUSINESS

"La Huelga o La Causa" (C)

California Farm Workers' Strike:
The Politics of It All

Your representative owes you, not his industry alone, but his judgment, and he betrays instead of serving you if he sacrifices it to your opinion.

—EDMUND BURKE

Cesar Chavez's leadership of the UFWOC transformed what would normally have been considered a mere labor dispute into something of a crusade which affected not only the parties involved but the nation at large and even evoked sympathy for farm workers in foreign countries. However, as various segments of society responded to this transformation, a number of problems were created. Because of the union's concern for the poor, its nonviolent techniques, and its appearance of a righteous underdog fighting a ruthless economic monster, the strike and the boycott had strong moral overtones. It thus appealed to many of the clergy and the liberal elements in the country. But the grower (read farmer) was not considered an "exploiter" in American folklore and had traditionally been protected as a relatively defenseless and economically vulnerable member of society.

Efforts in Congress to enact legislation to protect farm workers reflected this underlying attitude which was further reinforced by the presence of a powerful farm lobby.

Politics and the Boycott

The boycott succeeded in becoming a national issue, and by the 1968 elections it had forced politicians of both major parties to take sides. However, before the election year, and even before the boycott itself, the strike had won the backing of the man who was to become the cause's most noted political supporter, Senator Robert F. Kennedy. Kennedy had been a member of Harrison A. Williams's Senate Subcommittee on Migratory Labor and had accompanied Williams to Delano for the hearings in March 1966. At the hearings Kennedy was immediately recognized as a friend of the farm workers by the way he demolished the arguments of the growers and their supporters by asking very simple questions. Kennedy's technique was demonstrated in the following exchange with Kern County Sheriff Roy Galyen pertaining to the incident in which pickets threatened by nonsympathetic workers were arrested instead of the threateners.

Kennedy: "What did you charge them with?"

Galyen: "Violation of—unlawful assembly."

Kennedy: "I think that's most interesting. Who told you that they were going to riot?"

Galyen: "The men that they were talking to right out in the field said, 'If you don't get them out of here, we're going to cut their hearts out.' So rather than let them get cut, we removed the cause."

Kennedy: "This is the most interesting concept, I think. How can you arrest somebody if they haven't violated the law?"

Galyen: "They're ready to violate the law."

Kennedy: "Can I suggest that the sheriff read the Constitution of the United States?"[1]

During the 1968 political campaigns the Democrats generally supported the boycott, and the Republicans, except New York Senator Jacob Javits, generally opposed it. Presidential contender Senator Eugene McCarthy

---

[1] John G. Dunne, *Delano, the Story of the California Grape Strike* (New York: Farrar, Straus, and Giroux, Inc., 1967), pp. 28–29.

came out early in favor of UFWOC, urging support of its efforts by "all those who are concerned with human dignity and determined to lift poverty from our land." Hubert Humphrey later told UFWOC that "as more people know that the boycott is almost your only effective organizing device, more and more will support it." One of the ironies of the campaign was that long after Humphrey had made the statement his vice-presidential candidate, Senator Edmund S. Muskie, astounded a group of California reporters by saying that he had never heard of the boycott.

Senator George McGovern's first street-corner appearance after announcing his presidential aspirations in August was on a picket line in front of a Greenwich Village supermarket in New York City where he and a group of Mexican-Americans were protesting the store's grape sales. When he joined the line he was not immediately recognized, despite the Secret Service men and reporters accompanying him. When the crowd finally recognized him, he said, "I am here in support of the boycott, I am here in support of Cesar Chavez, I want to make it clear right now that I am not here to ask for support; for in history, Cesar's cause right now may be much greater than mine." According to a reporter, "the pickets, hungry for new support in their strike, cheered and clapped."[2]

After Robert Kennedy's assassination, the farm union did not make public its preference for a presidential candidate until late October, after both party conventions, when it voted to support Hubert Humphrey.

On the Republican side, according to a *New York Times* reporter, "Mr. Nixon was silent until after the national party conventions. Then he spoke out against the boycott and at a California campaign rally gleefully popped grapes into his mouth."

Nixon called the boycott a "form of illegal economic pressure." "At the root of the migratory workers' problems," he declared, "is not the farmer but an economy that is forcing the farmer to the wall. That is why I oppose the grape boycott."[3] However, he later acknowledged the poverty, housing, and education problems of the migratory worker and promised economic incentives to farmers to raise wages, co-op housing for workers, and arrangements for the growers to work together to increase earning opportunities for the migrants. According to a *New York Times* reporter, however, "Mr. Nixon was careful not to promise too much." The candidate said, "I have no instant answer, and I don't want to give you the impression I have, but we're going to find the answers."[4]

[2] John Herbers, "Kennedy Role as the Candidate of Poor Is Sought by McGovern," *The New York Times*, August 14, 1968, p. 26.

[3] Gene Logsdon, "The Wrath of Grapes," *Farm Journal*, February 1965, pp. 33–35.

[4] Robert B. Semple, Jr., "Nixon Gives Hint of Summit Move," *The New York Times*, September 19, 1968, p. 1.

Early in the campaign Nixon pulled a boner equal to Muskie's. Nixon, a lawyer, suggested that the grape workers take their grievances to the National Labor Relations Board, not realizing that the NLRB did not cover farm laborers.

Maryland Governor Spiro Agnew, the successful Republican vice-presidential candidate, felt that the boycott was an "unfair tactic" and also felt that both sides should be "sitting across the bargaining table from each other and trying to solve that thing in the traditional American fashion."[5]

When Republican Spiro Agnew left the governorship of Maryland for the vice-presidency in January 1969, Lieutenant Governor Marvin Mandell, a Democrat, succeeded him. The following May, Mandell became the first governor to support UFWOC activities. Mandell wrote to Chavez wishing "success in your long fight for proper living and working conditions for the people employed in the grape industry."[6]

Chavez's strategy put the plight of the grape picker before the country and presented a cause and a way for people to participate in the cause by simply not eating grapes. UFWOC benefited from both pro and con as well as from political publicity, and Chavez's public appearances with liberal politicians probably helped them win votes among their liberal constituency. For instance, in August 1968 Mayor Carl B. Stokes of Cleveland lent his office for the signing of an agreement between UFWOC, represented by Chavez, and the Cleveland Food Industry Committee and the Cleveland Federation of Labor. The agreement promised that local supermarkets would post signs in their stores urging support for the strike and boycott of California grapes. During the New York City mayoralty campaign of 1969, Chavez met with John Lindsay in his office to thank him for his requests, first made in July 1968, that the city stop buying grapes for its schools, hospitals, and other institutions. Chavez said that the city's position had influenced others. According to *Time* magazine, "Edward and Ethel Kennedy, following the late Robert Kennedy's example, have embraced Cesar Chavez as a brother . . . UFWOC support is one of the few issues that find Chicago Mayor Richard Daley, iconoclastic writer Gloria Steinem, and liberal Senators Jacob Javits and George McGovern in total agreement. Ralph Abernathy lends black help to what is becoming the Brown Power movement."[7] The Hawaiian State Legislature, in April 1969, adopted a resolution supporting the boycott and urged all public agencies in the state to refrain from buying grapes until California's

[5] Ben A. Franklin, "Agnew Lectures Skyscraper Workmen Heckling Him in Toledo," *The New York Times,* October 1, 1968, p. 30.

[6] "Aid to Grape Boycott," *San Francisco Chronicle,* May 23, 1969, p. 9.

[7] "The Little Strike That Grew to La Causa," *Time,* July 4, 1969, pp. 16–21.

vineyard owners had granted their workers the union bargaining rights they were seeking through the boycott. A majority of California state assembly-men eventually supported a proposal to grant union bargaining rights to farm workers against the opposition of Governor Ronald Reagan and most of the senators.

Politicians were usually invited to UFWOC demonstrations—indeed during the last leg of the march to Calexico in May 1969, Senators Edward Kennedy (Massachusetts), Ralph Yarborough (Texas), and Walter Mon-dale (Minnesota) showed up along with Congressmen James G. O'Hara (Michigan) and John V. Tunney (California).

The farm workers union generated support from at least sixteen of California's Democratic state legislators (who held almost half the seats in the legislature), including George Mosconi, Willie Brown, and John Burdow.

Obviously, more people in high places opposed the union's efforts or more favorable legislation would have been passed. Some of this opposition came from Democrats, for instance Hugh M. Burns, the California state senate's Democratic leader who thought the boycott illegal. The union's most noteworthy political enemy, however, was California Governor Ronald Reagan. In a telegram to President Nixon, Reagan—representing precisely to the letter the growers' position—stated:

> I believe that applying the principle of the National Labor Rela-tions Act is unwise. Such factors as crop perishability and weather require an approach that will achieve a balance of union and farmer bargaining power so necessary to reach a fair decision and avoid loss of food and fiber, in the public interest.[8]

The governor called the strike and boycotts "immoral" and "attempted blackmail." He said UFWOC activities were not designed to improve the life of grape pickers but were rather "an attempt to compel employers to force farmworkers to join the United Farm Workers against their wishes." Reagan proudly declared that federal statistics showed that wages paid to California farm workers were higher than those of any other state in the nation and well above New York and Michigan where the boycott was successful.[9]

In 1967, the governor authorized the use of convict labor to harvest

[8] Ronald B. Taylor, "The Boycott and the NLRA," *The Nation*, May 12, 1969, p. 501.

[9] Federal statistics do show California farm wages to be the highest in the country, but these statistics do not include Hawaii which has a higher farm wage rate than California largely due to the efforts of a farm labor union. See "Can They Pull Off a Nationwide Boycott?," *Nation's Business*, October 1968, p. 46.

grapes in San Bernardino in the guise of "rehabilitation." The AFL-CIO brought suit against the governor, stating that this merely provided cheap labor at a time when there were large numbers of unemployed local workers. However, it was not until early 1969 that a San Francisco superior court declared the governor's action to be unconstitutional.

One thorn in the governor's side had been the activities in various Office of Economic Opportunity projects. In June 1969, Reagan found yet another reason to attack an OEO project—a federally financed OEO agency in Southern Alameda County sponsored a newspaper which in turn supported the grape strike. An aide to the governor said, "we are just not going to tolerate the use of public funds for any labor organizing and political activity."[10] Five months later, however, the State Board of Agriculture decided to conduct an antiboycott publicity campaign, although privately financed, and the governor said he was "delighted."

Allan Grant, president of the board, had initiated the proposal to try to win citizen support for Senator Murphy's legislation—to outlaw union-organized consumer boycotts of farm produce—and the board agreed.[11] Also some efforts were to be aimed at countering union publicity about the poor living conditions of California farm workers and pesticide poisoning. Grant maintained that "violence to the truth has blackened the name of California agriculture and the producers who have made it our No. 1 agricultural state" and suggested that magazine writers be brought to the vineyards to see the other side of the dispute instead of accepting UFWOC claims at face value. "They have not had the truth and this board could very well make the knowledge available to them. . . . I would hope we could get subsequent articles in those magazines, if they are as ethical as I hope they are."

Grant also said that the "failing" boycott "has cost some growers a great deal and all growers a considerable amount." Reagan agreed with Grant's statements saying, "I've always been one to believe that the truth will out, and the truth is coming out."[12]

State Assemblyman John Burton of San Francisco, a boycott supporter, quickly called the State Board's proposals an "outrageous conflict of interest"—he felt that a state agency should not take sides in a labor

[10] Dick Meister, "Reagan vs. Poverty Group over Grape Boycott Stand," *San Francisco Chronicle*, June 30, 1969, p. 6.

[11] All twelve members of the board are Reagan appointees, and ten are growers or food processors. Grant, also president of the California Farm Bureau Federation, regent of the University of California, and head of the California Grape and Fruit League, was already sponsoring one publicity campaign against the boycott through his position with the Farm Bureau Federation. See Dick Meister, "A State Board vs. The Grape Boycott," *San Francisco Chronicle*, December 18, 1969, p. 1.

[12] *Ibid.*

dispute and solicit funds to support one side of such a dispute and violate its "official neutrality." Burton said the action was "another indication that Reagan represents the rich against the poor, and is using the government as an instrument to keep the poor oppressed."[13]

Reagan himself had come out in favor of California Republican Senator Murphy's bill in July 1969, calling it "equitable Federal legislation . . . a responsible solution to protect the American consumer, the farm workers and growers alike . . ." Reagan pointed to the slow-moving negotiations between UFWOC and the ten growers from the Coachella Valley and said it "demonstrates in dramatic fashion the needs of American agriculture for congressional action."[14]

USE OF CELEBRITIES

Chavez borrowed heavily from the tactics of political campaigns and adapted them for UFWOC use to generate national boycott publicity. He garnered support from people already in the news who, in turn, directed more publicity toward "la causa." Three items from the society pages of the *New York Times* demonstrated Chavez's genius. Under the title "Two Different Parties Were 'The Place to Be,'" a society writer described a benefit party ($25 a person) given by George Plimpton in April 1969 for the grape pickers. The reception included "tieless grape pickers, Norman Mailer and his political entourage, a hefty slice of new filmmakers, the Alan Jay Lerners, Rip Torn and Geraldine Page. . . ." Champagne from vintners having UFWOC contracts was served.[15]

A photograph in the society pages of the same newspaper in December 1968 showed Senator George S. McGovern with two socialites. The caption said that they met "in Senator's suite at the Hilton to discuss program for benefit on Wednesday at Carnegie Hall for California grape workers. Alan King, and Peter, Paul and Mary are among those who will perform at the event."[16]

In June 1969, UFWOC held a combination rally and elaborate buffet for wealthy Southampton Long Island resort people, giving them a chance to meet some blue-jeaned union grape pickers. The sponsors included Mrs.

---

[13] "Burton Blasts State Board's Grape Plan," *San Francisco Chronicle*, December 19, 1969, p. 12.

[14] "Reagan Supports Murphy Farm Bill," *San Francisco Chronicle*, July 18, 1969, p. 4.

[15] Robert McG. Thomas, Jr., "Two Different Parties Were the 'Place to Be,'" *The New York Times*, April 19, 1969, p. 23.

[16] Photo captioned "Aiding Vineyard Workers," *The New York Times*, December 1, 1968, p. 99.

Robert F. Kennedy, Mrs. Giancarlo Uzielli (the former Anne Ford), and Senator Fred Harris of Oklahoma. W. Averell Harriman sent a pledge.

Time magazine noted:

> To enter the public consciousness, a labor conflict must ordinarily threaten the supply of essential goods and services, like steel or transportation. Politicians and the public take notice only when there is great impact on the economy, when spectacular bloodshed occurs or when well-recognized issues are at stake. The grape strike seems to meet none of these criteria.[17]

How then had Chavez managed to involve so much of the nation in the issue of *la huelga?* Steven Roberts, a *New York Times* reporter, explained that:

> The boycott has become a major liberal cause—and one of the few that most factions can agree on. . . . In a time of confusion Mr. Chavez and his union appear to present a clear moral issue. "They're entitled to a living wage and decent housing as much as anyone," said one suburban matron on the picket line.
>
> Moreover, the union espouses non-violence and welcomes the help of everyone. Thus La Causa, as the movement is known, is particularly attractive at a time when white liberals often feel rejected by black leaders and uneasy at the talk of violence. . . .
>
> In New York, an alliance with the Black Panthers was quietly dropped when several stores selling grapes were mysteriously fire bombed.[18]

UFWOC AND OTHER ORGANIZATIONS

UFWOC received help from other unions, most notably from its parent federation, the AFL-CIO, and also from the United Auto Workers. Although the UAW had broken away from AFL-CIO in July 1968, both unions continued their support; and Walter Reuther, president of UAW, promised he would assign a number of UAW organizers to help with the boycott efforts. The parent federation said that it had spent $2 million on organizing farm workers in the period 1959–1969, $550,000 of which went to UFWOC between 1965 and 1969. The auto workers union said it had

[17] "The Little Strike That Grew to La Causa," *Time*, July 4, 1969, p. 16.

[18] Steven V. Roberts, "Chavez Tours Nation to Revive Grape Boycott," *The New York Times*, November 12, 1969, p. 39.

given $80,000 to UFWOC since 1965, $50,000 of which went into UFWOC's new $80,000 headquarters building in Delano dedicated in September 1969.[19]

The United Farm Workers Organizing Committee received support from the National Maritime Union and the New York Newspaper Guild's representative assembly. In October 1969, more than one thousand workers from twelve or more different unions picketed New York City Defense Department offices to protest its "strikebreaking" grape purchases. The demonstrators included such union notables as Harry Van Arsdale, president of the Central Labor Council, and Albert Shanker, president of the United Federation of Teachers.

The New York Civil Liberties Union backed the boycott, whereas other organizations, such as the National Education Association, backed UFWOC's *strike* but would not support the *boycott* of California grapes. The boycott had been strongly opposed by the John Birch Society, the National Right-to-Work Committee, and the American Farm Bureau Federation.

INTERNATIONAL REVERBERATIONS OF THE BOYCOTT

During 1968, UFWOC engaged in boycott activity in thirty-five cities in the United States and Canada. However, during 1969, the boycotts spread to two hundred American cities and spilled over to other countries such as Norway and Japan. In May 1969, Dominion Stores, Ltd., Canada's largest retail grocery chain, announced that it would no longer purchase California table grapes. Prior to this announcement, the Canadian Labor Congress pledged to refuse to patronize table grapes. Canada, which purchased about $20 million worth each year, provided the largest export market for grapes. Norway, which imported 2.7 million pounds of California grapes in 1968, had a full boycott against them by August 1969. The Transport Workers' Union and Fresh Fruit Importers agreed that grapes that were not already loaded on board ships be kept out of Norway and sent a telegram to Los Angeles which caused 90 percent of the grapes headed for Norway to be left on the docks. In January, the Transport Workers' Union in Sweden announced a blockade of grapes in that country. In London, the Executive Council of Transport and General Union, which had one and one-half million members, refused to handle grapes at the London docks

---

[19] The building includes medical clinic, credit union, and newspaper and administrative offices. See "Churches Back Grape Boycott," *San Francisco Chronicle*, September 4, 1969, p. 6.

and pressured Safeway, which had a twenty-five store chain in London, to stop stocking table grapes from California.

UFWOC AND THE PENTAGON

In the midst of the negotiations the union disclosed plans to seek an injunction against the federal government for its increasing purchases of California grapes saying that the government was illegally taking sides in a labor dispute and trying to make up for growers' lost sales. The Department of Defense (DOD) purchased 11 million pounds of grapes in fiscal 1969—up from 6.9 million in fiscal 1968. Two and one-half million pounds of the 1969 purchases went to Vietnam—eight times the amount in any previous year. (Table 1)

A Department of Defense spokesman said that it "does not purchase grapes merely because they have been made more available and less expensive due to the effects of the boycott . . . In the interests of objective and systematic management, menu planners (often working a year to 18 months in advance) should not be required to consider whether a labor dispute exists when making these decisions."[20] A Defense Department deputy later told a Senate subcommittee that more grapes were being purchased because prices were lower, which of course was due to the boycott. Meal planners overseas were encouraged to take advantage of low prices especially when substitutes such as oranges were in short supply.

TABLE 1

DEPARTMENT OF DEFENSE GRAPE PURCHASES

	Fiscal 1966	Fiscal 1967	Fiscal 1968	Fiscal 1969
Defense Purchases				
millions of pounds	7.5	8.3	6.9	11.0
cost in millions of dollars	1.04	1.25	1.32	1.98
Shipments for Vietnam		.648	.555	2.5[a]

[a] In a later release the Department of Defense said that a total of 4.1 million pounds of grapes would be shipped to Vietnam by the end of 1969.

Source: Roy Reed, "Pentagon Faces a Suit on Grapes," The New York Times, June 27, 1969, p. 17.

[20] Dick Meister, "Legal Attack on U.S. Grape Buying," San Francisco Chronicle, June 27, 1969, p. 2.

Additionally, improved preserving methods had facilitated the shipping of grapes, making them more popular with meal planners. Finally, grapes had a "high troop acceptability."[21] Indeed, the military bought eight pounds of grapes in fiscal 1969 for every American in Vietnam.

Immediately after the subcommittee hearing, Alan Cranston requested Defense Secretary Melvin Laird, who had previously directed the department, "to show 'a social consciousness in evaluating the domestic impact of all its actions,' "[22] to consider cutting back the department's grape purchases to the preboycott level. On August 13, 1969, Chavez petitioned the Washington, D.C., Federal District Court for an injunction against the Defense Department. "The petition says the department's increased purchases violate federal regulations, 'requiring them to be neutral in labor disputes and to refrain from taking a position on the merits of any dispute.' "[23] A department spokesman had previously stated that the department maintained its neutrality by not taking the labor dispute into account but further added that "the department will continue buying grapes as long as the growers can supply them."[24] If Chavez's court action was successful, the department would not be allowed to increase its grape purchases above the preboycott 1967 level.

Chavez called the Pentagon's action "a blatant case of Government sources subsidizing scab grapes," and a union official added, "Here is the government killing one of the union's chief sources of battle, the boycott. It may not be their intention to have their finger in it, but they have their finger in it"[25] The UFWOC attorney, however, thought there was malice in the department's actions, saying that it consistently bought its grapes from growers under the most pressure from the unions.[26] An AFL-CIO farm labor organizer expressed his bitterness:

> It ill behooves the United States government to, on the one hand, pay lip service to the concept of collective bargaining which embraces striking and consumer boycotting—and then to play the role of a massive scab and strikebreaker by upping its consumption of grapes.
>
> I think they are buying them simply because the people who want to sell them—the producers, the associations, the business associa-

[21] "Grape Boycott Fails to Slow Pentagon Purchases," *The New York Times*, June 24, 1969, p. 1.

[22] Dick Meister, "Pentagon and Grape Growers," *San Francisco Chronicle*, July 21, 1969, p. 13.

[23] "Grape Suit against Pentagon," *San Francisco Chronicle*, August 14, 1969, p. 8.

[24] Meister, "Pentagon and Grape Growers," p. 13.

[25] Meister, "Legal Attack on U.S. Grape Buying," p. 2.

[26] *Ibid.*

tion, the industrial power structure—have a great deal to say about what the policies of the Defense Department are.[27]

A Pentagon "fact sheet" stated that the military purchases represented less than one percent of the nation's table grape production.[28] Several months after this statistic appeared Chavez was quoted as having said that the strike would end immediately if the Pentagon were to stop its purchases. The union leader said table grape sales were down 30 percent from the 1965 levels, and these 30 percent were going into fruit cocktails, raisins, and increased military purchases.[29]

LEGISLATIVE ACTION

When New Deal programs were being developed in the late 1930s, Congress realized that, for new plans to succeed, voluntary participation of those involved would be imperative. Therefore, Congress adapted programs to the various needs of influential participants. For this reason agricultural labor was excluded from all federal protection. The National Labor Relations Act, the industrial bill, was responsive to the demands and influence of the organized labor movement whose support was mandatory. The act, as passed, specifically excluded agricultural laborers from its provisions. The Agricultural Adjustment Act, the New Deal's response to the agricultural problems, recognized the farmers and growers as the crucial element of support. Therefore, the principal objective of the act was to raise agriculture's purchasing power by restoring price levels, thereby restoring a balanced economy for the agricultural segment. Farm labor provisions were also excluded in this act. The agricultural interests were violently opposed to unions and collective bargaining. Also at this time, the existing union organizations were ineffective and were not affiliated with the organized labor movement.

In 1939, there were hearings before Congress on bills to amend the NLRA so that it would include agricultural workers. Agricultural interests argued against the inclusion of agricultural labor, employing two specific contentions.

Promoting an idyllic image of agricultural labor relations, somewhat inappropriate and even ridiculous in view of the number and extent of the labor problems occurring in agriculture during the

[27] "Pentagon Called Massive Scab," *San Francisco Examiner*, July 3, 1969, p. 2.

[28] Roy Reed, "Pentagon Faces a Suit on Grapes," *The New York Times*, June 27, 1969, p. 17.

[29] "Pentagon Accused by Chavez for Rise in Grape Purchase," *The New York Times*, September 29, 1969, p. 96.

thirties, it was first claimed that there was no need for the NLRA in agriculture at all. Second, it was argued that regulation under the NLRA, besides disrupting the allegedly peaceful relationships, would also impose impossible financial burdens on farmers.[30]

These arguments were still being used . . . Allan Grant, president of the California Farm Bureau Federation, member of the National Right-to-Work Committee, University of California regent, and the major spokesman for agribusiness interests "likes to boast that his workers come to the back door of his 2,000-acre ranch in Visalia to talk problems over with him. He told a church audience he would feel he had failed in his Christian Duty if they told him they wanted a union."[31] Thirty years later, in 1969, the issue of federal protection of farm workers was once again before Congress and the same arguments were being voiced.

Harvest Time in the Congress?

The presidential campaign of 1968 forced many politicians to take sides on the UFWOC strike and Chavez gained support from the ranks of the uncommitted, but when Richard Nixon, who opposed the boycott, was elected there was fear that the White House might prevent farm labor action. Yet in February 1969, Mr. Nixon asked the secretaries of agriculture and labor to conduct a study of whether or not farm laborers should be covered by the Taft-Hartley Act. Such inclusion would give farm workers legal protection in their organizing and provide federal machinery for conducting elections and settling grievances. However, a proposed amendment to the act threatened to make boycotts illegal.

Although no farm labor legislation was passed in 1969, the farm workers' plight became an issue of congressional and administration concern. Some seventy-nine liberal congressmen quickly supported various farm labor bills, and more conservative legislators, such as California's Senator George Murphy, also introduced legislation.

The bills differed on several counts, one being the size of the farms to be covered (as a function of yearly sales or annual hours of labor hired). The most controversial differences were in the weapons to be granted agricultural unions. Although strikes were germane to unionization, and farms and vineyards were particularly vulnerable at harvesttime, the grape growers wanted to prohibit harvesttime strikes while UFWOC insisted that it was the *only* time a strike could be effective.

[30] Austin P. Morris, "Agricultural Labor and National Labor Legislation," *California Law Review*, 1966, p. 1968.

[31] Hal and Anne Draper, *The Dirt on California: Agribusiness and the University*, Independent Socialist Clubs of America, 1968, p. 11.

In May 1969, Secretary of Labor George P. Shultz presented the administration's proposals to the Senate Labor Subcommittee. Shultz favored collective bargaining rights for farm workers employed on large farm units (those with more than five hundred man days of labor during their peak quarter of the previous year), which constituted 2 percent of the nation's farms hiring outside help. He also felt that farm workers should be treated somewhat differently in other respects. Farm unions under the administration's plan would be recognized as bargaining agents when so approved by the workers on a farm, but organizing and grievance disputes would be settled by a three-member Farm Relations Board which would, said Shultz, "not be bound by 34 years of industrial precedent established under the NLRB (National Labor Relations Board)." The secretary also presented a "method to assure continuity of work at critical periods such as harvesttime." That is, if harvesttime strikes or grower lockouts were imminent, a ten-day notice of intention would have to be given to the other side. Either side could then invoke a thirty-day no-strike or no-lockout period by agreeing to the "binding recommendations" of outside arbitrators. After the thirty-day period, the arbitrator's recommendations would be binding only if both sides had agreed to accept the recommendations before the delay. (Whether the *delay* would be binding or not was not clear. That the arbitrator's decision was binding was clear.) Of course at the beginning the grower could shun the federal settlement machinery and risk a strike. The grape growers who had previously opposed any form of labor legislation generally favored the administration's proposals as written into Senator Murphy's bill.

Needless to say, UFWOC vehemently opposed this proposed legislation which, if passed, would apply to 45 percent of all farm employees in the nation—a force of approximately four hundred thousand. This bill would effectively strip the union of its two main weapons—the rights to boycott and to strike at harvesttime. By the time the thirty-day period would be over, the union laborers would have already harvested the drop. The bill would also ban organizational picketing. Shultz stated that the administration decided upon the separate Farm Labor Relations Board because "there are unique characteristics about the agricultural setting."[32] Ted Barr, president of the California Grape and Tree Fruit League, praised the proposed legislation, stating that "Murphy's bill . . . is designed to protect the consumers' right to the free flow of food from the farm to the supermarket."[33] It must be noted here, however, that the canners, packers, and transportation workers were all equally able to prevent the "flow of food" from farm to supermarket.

[32] "The Wrath of Grapes," *Time*, May 16, 1969, p. 24.

[33] Dick Meister, "Grape Pickets in Financial District," *San Francisco Chronicle*, July 11, 1969, p. 3.

Since the beginning of the strike in 1965, UFWOC had repeatedly proclaimed that the union's primary goal was to attain coverage for agricultural labor under the NLRA. However, on April 9, 1969, Chavez announced in a press conference that UFWOC could not accept coverage under the NLRA as that act was then written. The reason for this drastic shift in position was that the current amendments to the NLRA, the Taft-Hartley Act of 1947 and the Landrum-Griffin Act of 1959, would severely weaken UFWOC. In fact, coverage under the act would weaken the union almost as much as Nixon's proposed Farm Labor Relations Board would weaken it. The Taft-Hartley Act defines the secondary boycott as an unfair labor practice and requires that a sixty-day notification of desire to alter contract be made before a strike can legally be called. The act also allows states to prohibit the union shop. Under this provision, over one-third of the states have enacted "right-to-work" laws that forbid union membership as a condition of continued employment. The Landrum-Griffin Act has a provision that tightens the restriction on secondary boycotts and the act also authorizes injunctions against organizational and recognition picketing. Chavez also called for federal protection against nonresident green carders who were used by growers during a strike. At the Newman Hall Farm Labor Legislation Workshop on July 12, 1969, Austin P. Morris S.J., an assistant professor of law at the University of San Francisco and an authority on farm labor legislation, stated that UFWOC would now rather be covered by no legislation than be covered by the NLRA.

There were two bills before Congress that favored farm workers and UFWOC. H.R. 9954 was introduced in the House on April 3, 1969, by fifty-seven representatives, mostly from urban areas. The bill, proposing to extend coverage of the NLRA to farm workers, was amended. S.8 was introduced by Senator Harrison Williams, Jr., before the Ninetieth Congress in 1968. Harrison was then chairman of the Subcommittee on Migratory Labor, and the bill was sponsored by most of the members of that committee. The original purpose of the bill was to bring the corporate farm and its employers under the collective bargaining provisions of the NLRA. The bill would apply only to farms that provided interstate shipments worth more than fifty thousand dollars a year. This would cover only 3 percent of farms in the United States. However, these 3 percent employed more than 30 percent of the farm labor. S.8 later came before the Ninety-first Congress with amendments.

It was these amendments that were of the utmost importance to UFWOC for only with them did the union desire to be covered by the NLRA. The first amendment called for an exemption for a twelve-year period from the provisions of the Taft-Hartley and of the Landrum-Griffin Acts. The Taft-Hartley Act was passed twelve years after the Wagner Act (NLRA), during which time the unions were able to grow in membership and in strength. UFWOC felt that it should be given this same period in which to grow and develop strength. The second amendment would exempt agricultural workers from section 14(b) of the Taft-Hartley Act, which allows state "right-to-work" laws in industries involved in interstate commerce. California did not have the "right-to-work" laws, but other states where UFWOC is active, notably Arizona and Texas, did have them. Previous UFWOC contracts, such as with Schenley and DiGiorgio, provided for union shops. The third amendment would define as an unfair labor practice the employment of anyone during a strike or lockout who had not actually established permanent residence in the United States. This was an attempt to prevent the use of green carders, of which there were four hundred thousand, in strikebreaking activities. Senator Edward Kennedy introduced a bill that would require the Labor Department to certify every six months each commuter alien, showing that each individual was depressing neither the wages nor the working conditions of American farm laborers. The bill required the revocation of the visa of any individual engaging in strikebreaking. The State Department refused to intervene in the commuter program stating that "it would deprive many Mexican nationals of their earning power, reduce trade along the frontier and perhaps cause the Mexican Government to retaliate . . ."[34]

Support for S.8 came from the National Farmers Union and the National Farmers Organizations, both organizations of small farmers. In a statement released on June 18, 1969, the legislative representative of the National Farmers Organization announced NFO support for S.8 and its desire for NLRA coverage for farm workers. The spokesman also announced that the membership opposed the use of the secondary boycott although it did not oppose a union shop. Perhaps one of the major factors explaining the support of S.8 by these small farmer organizations was that because of the fifty-thousand-dollar interstate commerce restriction most, if not all, of the memberships would not be affected by the legislation. UFWOC, however, wanted to see the exemption of the small growers removed.

Senator Murphy, a member of the subcommittee that proposed S.8, voiced a strong opposition to the bill. He submitted an individual report at the end of the subcommittee hearings wherein he used most of those arguments advanced by the growers against the bill. However, he made one additional point which should be mentioned. In discussing the federal minimum wage for farm laborers, which went into effect in 1966 and provided for a minimum of $1.30 per hour in 1969, he stated that these minimum rates have caused "widespread unemployment" of farm workers because employers cannot pay this wage. In an astonishing statement, Senator Murphy said:

[34] Homer Bigart, "Unions Deplore Influx of Mexican Laborers along the Border," *The New York Times*, May 4, 1969, p. 78.